PATTERN IN CORPORATE EVOLUTION

PATTERN IN CORPORATE EVOLUTION

NEIL M. KAY

OXFORD UNIVERSITY PRESS
1997

Oxford University Press, Great Clarendon Street, Oxford OX2 6DP

Oxford New York

Athens Auckland Bangkok Bogota Bombay
Buenos Aires Calcutta Cape Town Dar es Salaam
Delhi Florence Hong Kong Istanbul Karachi
Kuala Lumpur Madras Madrid Melbourne
Mexico City Nairobi Paris Singapore
Taipei Tokyo Toronto

and associated companies in
Berlin Ibadan

Oxford is a trade mark of Oxford University Press

Published in the United States
by Oxford University Press Inc., New York

British Library Cataloguing in Publication Data
Data available

Library of Congress Cataloging in Publication Data
Data available
ISBN 0–19–829047–0

1 3 5 7 9 10 8 6 4 2

Typeset by Hope Services (Abingdon) Ltd.
Printed in Great Britain
on acid-free paper by
Bookcraft (Bath) Ltd., Midsomer Norton, Somerset

For Lorna Ahlquist

PREFACE

If it is possible to identify something without which a book would not have been written, then it is only fair to start by acknowledging the fact. In the case of the present work there are two such somethings. The first is the work of O. E. Williamson especially as represented by *Markets and Hierarchies* (1975) and *The Economic Institutions of Capitalism* (1985) and commonly described as transaction cost economics. Such acknowledgement may appear strange given that much of the book argues a position contrary to Williamson, but Williamson must take immense credit for effectively creating and elaborating a research agenda whose outline had been sketched many years before by Coase. Before Williamson's work, there was only passing acknowledgement of the possibility that the firm had any more significance for resource allocation than as a device for responding to, or making, prices. Williamson's contributions revolutionized microeconomics and stimulated a whole generation of researchers to explore the firm as an economic institution in its own right. The differences between the present work and Williamson's follow from pursuing Williamson's agenda and using his concepts and techniques. It was the series of difficulties and puzzles encountered in trying to apply transaction cost economics in a variety of contexts that encouraged the development of the approach represented by the present work.

The second something without which the present work would not have been written was the development of computer graphics. Many of the lines of argument followed through here were started off in my work during the 1980s. However, it was difficult to develop them in many cases beyond a particular point. In the 1980s it really required special (and expensive) graphics skills to record the systems and relationships which in many cases were central to the analysis. Even commissioning graphic artists' help was disappointing and frustrating since it frequently proved impossible to communicate accurately the ideas behind a figure using pen, ink, and words. As a consequence, my research began to drift into areas where such problems were non-existent or of minor importance. This was unfortunate since if there is a single theme to which my work might make some contribution it is in analysing complex systems such as firms in terms of their constituent linkages.

In part these problems were exacerbated by working in a discipline where constructing maps of complex interactions was an alien concept. It is not a problem which colleagues working in, say, chemistry or architecture, are likely to encounter. In those disciplines, graphical representation of relationships and linkages between different parts of the system is natural, obvious and habitual, and they have developed their own graphical techniques for dealing with these issues. On the other hand, mainstream economics remains firmly an aggregative framework in which higher level entities are generally the aggregation of lower level entities. In this perspective, there is no need to infer (let alone construct) linkages between different parts of the system at a particular point in time, since the only relationships that matter are causal ones taking place over time in the form of price changes. As long as relationships can be expressed in such a fashion, then there is no more need to construct pictures of economic phenomena than there is to show a picture of a ball of gas in thermodynamics. However, if these basic elements begin to combine together and form complex interlinked systems, graphics begins to perform an invaluable function as it does in chemistry research and teaching. Indeed, it is difficult to see how chemical ideas could be communicated simply in many cases without such graphical representation. This extends to the analysis of the present work. One test of whether or not it makes a contribution is to ask how such (or similar) analysis could be performed *without* using the various graphical representations of patterns that are developed in the course of the book.

It was a chance remark (and subsequent demonstration) by a colleague, Doug Wynn, in another department at Strathclyde University (the Scottish Local Authority Management Centre) that belatedly sparked off the realization that computer graphics could be an invaluable tool for my purposes. This led to my developing the graphics reproduced here using Aldus FreeHand (latterly Macromedia FreeHand). In retrospect, many of the diagrams may look disappointingly simple, and readers may wonder why such a tool should be regarded as so invaluable. However, what the package allowed me to do was to experiment with a whole range of ideas and with maps of varying degrees of complexity. This tool did influence and improve the final analysis considerably in many cases. The diagrams that actually found their way into the book are only the tip of a very large iceberg, though in this case it is probably just as well that the rest of the iceberg remains hidden.

Having said something about where the book came from, it might seem reasonable at this point to give some idea as to what the book is about. This is a bad point for such reflection. Ideally, prefaces should reflect the verve, elan and enthusiasm which the author brought to the project. Instead they are written by tired, jaded, hollow-eyed men and women, obsessed with spell checks, style consistency and word counts. The vision may be holistic, but the end is reductionist. Then they are expected to rise above this and provide a grand overview. Despite these barriers, I think it is possible to give a simple summary. This book is about why firms exist, what determines their boundaries, and why they may adopt different forms of internal organization. This is essentially the agenda as developed by Williamson. A basic starting point here is that in order to understand the nature of the firm, problems must be analysed from the point of view of the firm. This may seem trite, but in fact it is a quite different perspective from transaction cost economics which analyses the firm from the perspective of the assets it deals with. Chapter 3 provides a comparison of these two perspectives from the point of view of the vertical integration problem, and it is argued that the approach developed here provides a more satisfactory basis for analysing vertical integration than does the transaction cost approach.

The rest of the book is concerned with analysing the firm as an administered collection of resources making decisions in an uncertain world characterized by limited cognitive abilities and significant technological change. Writers with a major influence on the ideas developed in this context include Loasby, Nelson, March, Penrose, Richardson, Schumpeter, Simon, and Winter. The firm is generally seen here as linked through competencies shared between some or all of its constituent businesses. These links or linkages define the nature of the firm, identify potential sources of potential economies, and may also trace lines of vulnerability to external attack on the firm's chosen strategy. Graphing the linkages involved in different contexts helps make explicit the kinds of issues that may be involved, and the approach is applied to patterns of behaviour involved in diversification, multinational enterprise, joint venture and other cooperative agreements, alliances and networks. It also serves as a basis for comparing alternative solutions to the problem of which organizational form the firm should adopt. While the different issues are analysed in their own right, there are a few simple principles of organization running though the book that provide a unifying theme for the book as a whole.

I am extremely grateful to the friends and colleagues who gave of their time to read samples of the material, especially Trevor Buck, Norman Clarke, Peter Earl, Felix Fitzroy, Geoff Henderson, James Love, Alf Molina, Christos Pitelis, Phillip Raines, John Scouller, Grahame Thompson and Steve Thompson, as well as to three anonymous reviewers who read the synopsis and some draft chapters at an early stage. Thanks also are due to the students taking the M.Sc. in Business Economics in my Department, 1994–95 and 1995–96. The framework in the book was frequently used in the various classes to which I contributed on this course. These two cohorts appeared to find the approach useful as a basis for delivering and discussing ideas, and they made a number of helpful contributions and suggestions in the various discussions. Joyce Russell also provided the essential task of converting the final manuscript into a form that could be accepted by the publisher. On the publisher's side, the editor David Musson has been a source of useful advice and criticism, and I also benefited from the help of Leonie Hayler on the production side and Donald Strachan on the marketing side. I am particularly grateful to Kim Allen who made a superb job of copy-editing the text despite the various impediments left in the way.

This book was begun just before my daughter Katerina had celebrated her second birthday. It was completed twenty months later, just before my son Kieran's first birthday. Normal people might grant undue credit to the author for this feat in the circumstances, but parents will immediately guess where the true credit lies. There could only be one person to whom this book could be dedicated, and I do so to my wife Lorna Ahlquist with love and gratitude. Katerina and Kieran frequently devoted much of their waking hours to finding ways to help me, endeavours which were greatly appreciated once I learnt to hit the 'save' button first. One thing that helps alleviate the creeping guilt which accompanies a project like this is the knowledge that there will be an ending. At the same time, the family seemed to have coped very well over the past few months, and I hope that my return in a more intrusive and less detached form will not come as too much of a disappointment or shock.

Neil M. Kay

Email address: n.m.kay@strath.ac.uk

CONTENTS

xiv   *Contents*

FIGURES

1. Introduction

What is this book about and how does it approach its chosen topics? It is essentially a book about links and how they may form patterns of resource allocation involving the firm. A link is composed of a bundle of resources shared between different elements in the economic system. Patterns refer to some consistency or balance in the way the links are joined together. The approach here is economics based and builds on concepts of scarce resources, opportunity cost, rationality (albeit of the bounded kind), and efficiency (albeit constrained by history).

In this first paragraph we have already encountered two standard problems, not in economics, but in cognitive psychology; ambiguity and mental set.[1] First, language is ambiguous, with the same word often having very different meanings in different contexts. For example, to some French economists, 'regulation' means something like fine tuning, while to English-speaking economists it is more likely to suggest direct control and manipulation of critical variables. Anyone prepared to tell the French they are wrong should first pause and note that 'regulator' is used to refer to a device which adjusts and balances the flow of steam in a steam locomotive. Also, in many of the so-called economies in transition, 'economist' has traditionally had a much more generous interpretation than in the West, typically encompassing specialisms such as accountancy, financial analysis and administrative sciences. Anyone wishing to tell the Albanians they were wrong should also be prepared to explain how Western style economists are more concerned with the allocation of scarce resources than are these other professions.

Secondly, 'mental set' refers to the tendency to transfer to new situations the techniques and solutions that have been learnt in the past. It can be a barrier to problem solving and indeed can lead to sub-optimal outcomes where it impedes the adoption of better solutions. For example, the introduction to various editions of Samuelson's *Economics*[2] has drawn on an illustration drawn from Gestalt psychology to make the point that different observers with different frames of reference may perceive the same set of facts differently. Samuelson (1976, p. 11) used the example to point out that if the problem of depression unemployment is looked at through pre-Keynesian and then through Keynesian spectacles, they would lead to very different interpretations of the nature of the problem and the power of government to solve it.[3] The old (and now rather tired) joke about the physicist, the chemist, and the economist on a desert island trying to open a can of beans is a joke about mental set.[4] However, old jokes and tired clichés have a habit of achieving their status by containing at least a few grains of truth.

The combination of mental set and ambiguity can be destructive.[5] In the area of the firm, Machlup (1967) showed how the concept of 'the firm' was ambiguous, and indeed pointed out how the standard 'theory of the firm' was really about markets, not firms in the common sense of the word. He suggested there could be as many as twenty-one different conceptions of what was meant by the firm (though he only got round to naming ten). Since each conception could imply an alternative context, and mental set, it would not be surprising if we encountered many conflicting and inconsistent theories of 'the firm' as Machlup suggests. In turn, there may appear be nothing unusual about our first paragraph considered in conventional economic terms. Economists already talk about 'patterns' of resource allocation and the economic 'system', and would be unlikely to blink at the description of the price mechanism 'linking' the various components of the economy. However, when an economist looks at a firm he or she tends to see a series of contractual relations, while an organizational theorist is likely to see other devices for coordinating resource allocation within the firm.

The key to understanding the contribution that the particular perspective developed here can make lies first in analysing how relations are typically expressed in neoclassical theory, the standard or received basic economics approach. In neoclassical theory there is a close connection between aggregation, causality and methodological individualism.[6] In the price 'system', relationships and interdependencies are typically expressed causally, as when an event in time period $t+1$ is influenced by an event in time period t. For example, a rise in the price of labour may push up product prices, a price ceiling may make goods more difficult to obtain, while a duopolist dropping price may stimulate its rival to respond in kind. Relationships between products also tend to be defined in causal terms; if an increase in the price of good A leads to increased demand for good B then they are substitutes, if it leads to decreased demand they are complements. Expressing relationships in this fashion has the direct benefit of enabling a description of higher level behaviour to be reduced to the behaviour of its constituent elements. Since causal relations take place over time, if we were to freeze an economy at a point in time, these relationships would disappear. We would be left with a series of individual elements whose characteristics *at this point in time* could be treated as separable and independent. Economies, or lower level entities such as industries and firms, can then be treated as simple aggregates of lower level elements.

The neoclassical price 'system' is like a set of traffic signals. It provides guides to movement, or stimuli to action. Just as with a set of traffic signals, the relationships can only be observed over time. Take a single snapshot of city centre traffic at a point in time and the effect of traffic signals is obscured; take a series of snapshots over time, and the tendency of cars to stop after a red signal and to go after a green can be observed, or at least inferred. In economics this process of comparing snapshots is called comparative statics. Restricting interest to causal relations may permit us[7] to treat higher level entities as simple aggregates by looking at a single snapshot, whether we are interested in industry output, GNP, or the number of cars in a city centre at peak period.

However, relationships that take place over time are not the only ones that can be observed in the physical world. For example, chemical models may represent atoms bonding together to form molecules, such as the combination of sodium and chlorine through an ionic bond to form sodium chloride, or common salt. If we could take a series of snapshots of such a molecule, we might observe that there was no apparent change in it from one time period to the next. A chemist who concluded that this implied the absence of any relationships between the constituent atoms would be unlikely to have a bright future in his or her chosen profession. Their fate would be sealed if they further analysed the characteristics of sodium chloride as the simple aggregation of the characteristics of its constituent atoms, sodium (a grey metal) and chlorine (a poisonous green gas).

There is nothing mystical about ionic bonds, but they do make it impractical to treat molecules as the simple aggregation of constituent atoms. However, once their existence is recognized, it becomes possible to talk of other features of molecules such as their structure or organization. The existence of *relations between elements at a point in time* is something which is fundamental to many disciplines; for example kinship relations in anthropology, anatomical structures in physiology, building designs in architecture. The crucial test is whether or not a snapshot shows up links or bonds between elements. Examples of such snapshots would be a family tree in anthropology, a skeleton in a medical laboratory, an architect's blueprint. It is clearly possible for each of these entities to be treated as aggregates for certain purposes and when we ask certain questions—for example we may want to know the number of members of a family, the weight of a skeleton, or the numbers of rooms in a house. However, if we wanted to ask questions concerning the relations between the parts that we tend to associate with normal anthropological, anatomical and architectural analysis, aggregation would generally misrepresent and obscure the nature of the systems in the respective cases. The existence of relations at a point in time is usually implied in terms like map, organization, structure, pattern, design, template, arrangement, group, team, blueprint, network, and cluster. Recognition of snapshot linkages between elements is a normal, indeed pervasive, feature of the natural and social sciences. It is only in isolated areas (such as neoclassical economics and its intellectual touchstone, thermodynamics) that such linkages are ignored to the extent that higher levels can be commonly treated as aggregates of lower level elements. The idea of linkages existing between elements in the system at a point in time constitutes the basic foundation on which this book is constructed.

So the approach is based on linkages and the overall objective of the book is to contribute to questions relating to the nature and the existence of firms. Because of this objective, frequent reference is made to transaction cost economics throughout the book. This is unavoidable since transaction cost economics claims to provide the foundations that help and will help economists to analyse exactly the same agenda that we have set ourselves, from the existence of firms, through the shaping of their boundaries, to the relationship between strategy and internal organization. Analysing the questions as to why firms exist and why their boundaries are set and organized in a particular way without reference to transaction cost economics would be a bit like studying warfare without reference to Clausewitz or politics without reference to Machiavelli. It may be done, but the first question reviewers may ask is why are these seminal works neglected. Consequently, a great deal of time and resources is devoted to analysing the transaction cost perspective in different contexts. It is no exaggeration to say that this present book could not have been written without the landmark contributions of Coase and Williamson in transaction cost economics. If it is true that alternative explanations for the existence, boundaries and organization of firms are provided at various parts of the book, it is equally true that the explanations could not have been developed without the prior existence of the respective transaction cost economics explanations. Indeed evidence for this is scattered throughout the book in the form of various puzzles which it is felt are left over by transaction cost economics.

The analysis here typically suppresses business level or product-market considerations. Just as most approaches in industrial organization ignore links between product-markets, so the approach here generally neglects business-specific characteristics. One convention frequently adopted in the book is to assume that the various businesses operated by the firm are identical in terms of scale and profitability characteristics, though we recognize differences between businesses in this respect in Chapter 6 when we analyse actual firms. The purpose of this is to simplify the analysis and focus on the implications of linkages in the construction of the firm. This does not mean that business level considerations are unlikely to be important in practice, any more than conventional treatments of the firm as the aggregation of its various product-markets mean that linkages are likely to be unimportant in practice. However, it does allow us to focus on questions relating to the boundaries of the firm, just as conventional economics tends to focus on business level questions such as pricing and output levels. A complete analysis of the firm would integrate both corporate and business level characteristics, one set of approaches to the latter being provided by conventional treatments in industrial organization.

Holmstrom and Tirole (1989) argue that there are two main questions that a theory of the firm must attend to; first the question of why firms exist, and secondly the question of what determines the boundaries of the firm. This sets the transaction cost agenda, and the agenda to be pursued here, but in addition to the 'why' and 'what' aspects of the nature of the firm, we would tack two 'how' questions on to this agenda; how do firms survive in the face of the forces of creative destruction described by Schumpeter (1954) and how do firms organize resources to pursue the strategy represented by the boundaries of the firm?

Before we turn to these questions, Chapter 2 considers the context in which the subsequent approach has been developed. It argues that alternative theories of the firm have typically been characterized by a hub and spoke relationship to the traditional or neoclassical theory of the firm. The agenda of neoclassical theory can be broadly summarized as being concerned with questions relating to *optimal product-market price* in various contexts. Attempts to modify the neoclassical base of the theory of firm have usually begun by modifying one or other of the components of this agenda. Thus, Simon (1955) tackled the question of the optimality assumption in neoclassical theory, the basis of Penrose's (1959) definition of the firm was resources and not products, Coase (1937) opened up the neoclassical black box to show the firm as a hierarchy and not just a market-making device, while Schumpeter (1954) shifted the focus from price competition to technological competition. Each of these approaches took as their starting point one of the four components of the neoclassical agenda, and each has an influence on the approach developed here.

In Chapter 3, the nature of vertical integration is explored. We start by pointing out that transaction cost economics creates some puzzles as far as the boundaries of the firm are concerned. For example, a transaction cost explanation as to whether or not the boundaries of the firm should encompass production of a particular good would focus on the economics of the make-or-buy decision; are the costs of organizing production of the good in-house less than the transaction costs of obtaining it in the market-place? This may provide an answer to the question of the lowest cost location for producing the good, but it does not provide an answer to the question as to whether the good should be produced. If the *value* of the good fluctuates, so also may the decision as to whether the boundaries of the firm should include it, irrespective of the relative costs of alternative modes of organizing its production. It is also argued that transaction cost explanations for the existence of firms mistakenly focus on alternative uses of assets when the more appropriate focus is the relation of assets to other resources in the firm. The analysis in this chapter also analyses hierarchy in terms of comparative advantage when making certain kinds of decisions. It is suggested that the fundamental reasons for the existence of firms are to be found in the nature, degree of interdependence, and timing of decisions.

While transaction cost economics starts with markets and then moves into the firm[8] we start from the Penrosian perspective of the firm seen as a managerially controlled collection of resources, and then analyse the logic of how the boundaries of the firm may be varied. In Chapter 4, the logic of corporate specialization is examined first, and then reasons for diversification are explored. The chapter develops the role of linkages in defining the nature of corporate strategies and examines the double-edged nature of links as possible sources of vulnerability to external threats as well as potential sources of internal economies. In Chapter 5 we start by tying some threads together and relating the perspective developed here to the spoke theories of Chapter 2. The notion of linkage is built on to introduce the possibility of systematic patterns in the evolution of corporate strategy. The chapter then draws upon the framework that has been developed to set out a range of specific issues which it is felt a theory of the firm should be able to deal with and which constitute the subject matter of the rest of the book.[9]

The next five chapters are concerned with further questions relating to the boundaries of the firm. In Chapter 6 we map the corporate strategy of five major corporations and look at how they have tackled the question of surviving in their respective environments. This exercise performs a number of functions. First, it is intended to explore whether the idea of mapping strategy discussed in Chapters 5 and 6 is feasible and practical. The results are extremely encouraging in this respect, with the mapping of linkages helping to provide a graphic representation of the results of expert industry and financial analysis in the respective cases. Secondly, it is intended to see whether the mapping of strategies is useful. As far as this is concerned, the mapping of linkages helps analysis go beyond conventional interpretations and emphasizes the potentially double-edged nature of links in that they may provide both internal economies and vulnerability to external threats. The result of the mapping exercise is a systematic basis for analysing the past development and potential development of strategies. Thirdly, it helps provide foundations for the more abstract analysis of subsequent chapters. In this respect it helps provide a bridge between the framework developed in earlier chapters, and the various issues analysed later.

Chapters 7 and 8 are concerned with substantive issues in boundary-setting, corporate diversification and multinational enterprise respectively. Both chapters start with the premise that firms prefer to exploit richly linked options compared to more weakly linked options, *ceteris paribus*. The respective chapters then explore circumstances which are likely to lead to alternative patterns in diversification and multinational expansion. Chapter 7 explores the idea that the diversification of the firm proceeds according to certain design rules or principles, particularly in relation to the establishment of consistency or balance within the pattern of links exploited by the firm. It turns out that the framework helps account for a number of features of firm diversification, including (contrary to popular belief) the surprisingly persistent nature of conglomerate strategies. Chapter 8 starts off by establishing the thinness of linkages exploited by the multinational option and builds on this base to account for circumstances in which the multinational enterprise is likely to develop. The extension of the framework into this area again helps to account for a variety of empirical evidence, some of which again runs against the conventional wisdom.

Chapters 9 and 10 are both concerned with the evolution of cooperative agreements between firms. Chapter 9, in particular, looks at the evolution of joint ventures between individual businesses. Chapter 10 deepens the analysis of cooperative behaviour and examines the evolution of alliances between firms and networks characterized by club-like behaviour and comprising a number of cooperating firms. Many analyses of joint ventures in industrial organization and strategic management start by analysing the joint venture in isolation, and then explore possible advantages of joint ventures in relation to do-nothing alternatives. However, this leads to certain puzzles. First, why not merge the businesses and achieve the same objectives without the well documented problems of running a joint venture? Secondly, if joint venture, alliance, and networks are such good things, why is it only in recent years that they appear to have become so popular? Were firms passing up efficiency enhancing opportunities in the old days, or has there been some qualitative shift in circumstances that has encouraged firms to switch to such modes of operating? The two chapters explore such issues by showing how the evolution of joint venture, alliances and networks can only be properly analysed by setting these arrangements in the context of the pattern of linkages that have evolved at firm level. Both chapters analyse how different types of cooperative arrangements may be triggered at different stages in the evolution of firms and sectors. As with the analysis of diversification and multinational enterprise, the results help account for an array of empirical evidence in the respective chapters.

The next two chapters, 11 and 12, are concerned with our second 'how' question, in particular how do firms organize to pursue alternative strategies as represented by the boundaries of the firm. Again, our starting point is the analysis of linkages. Chapter 11 looks at how hierarchy first helps to cluster linkages in nested layers to facilitate decision-making, and Chapter 12 looks at how strategy and hierarchy may be related. A basic theme is that organizational design generally involves trade-offs; individuals and groups usually have to interact with a variety of other individuals and groups within the firm, and any hierarchical arrangement designed to facilitate one type of interaction is likely to finish up impeding others. The pattern of linkages that hold in practice can influence the nature and severity of potential trade-offs, and the varieties of organizational designs that the modern corporation has developed can all be analysed as attempts to handle this trade-off as efficiently as possible. The two chapters show how mapping patterns of linkages can help trace the extent to which alternative organizational solutions provide coherent solutions to the trade-off problem.

Finally, we conclude with a summary chapter that also explores possibilities for future research. In the chapters that follow we limit our conclusions to a single paragraph at the end. This was felt to be a useful disciplinary device to ensure focus on the major points of the chapter. Hopefully the result is not too terse and truncated. Also, plain English is used as far as possible and jargon is only used when it is felt it does help to simplify the analysis.

NOTES

1. These topics are covered in most basic texts in this area. For those interested, Matlin (1994) provides a basic introduction to the discipline and the literature.
2. See, for example, Samuelson (1976) and latterly the editions co-authored with Nordhaus (e.g. 1985). Samuelson drew upon Hanson (1961) for his Gestalt example.
3. In fact, the arrival in the 1970s of stagflation (conjunction of inflation and unemployment) has stimulated the design of further perspectives, such as the rational-expectations revolution.
4. After the others have failed in their attempts, the economist announces he has the solution; 'first, assume we have a tin opener . . .'. Those prone to quibbling might say this is really a joke about methodology.
5. For example, I have participated in seminars with French- and English-speaking lawyers in which communication was impeded because they were using 'regulation' in a very different way. There is also evidence that at least in some cases of economies in transition, authorities asked for Western 'economists' to help in the transition process in the belief that this would include financial and administrative specialisms.
6. 'Methodological individualism . . . asserts that explanations of social, political, or economic phenomena can only be regarded as adequate if they run in terms of the beliefs, attitudes, and decisions of individuals' (Blaug, 1992, p. 44).
7. This is not a sufficient condition for entities to be treated as aggregates; other conditions may be necessary, such as being able to classify elements as belonging to the same category.
8. 'In the beginning there were markets' (Williamson, 1975, p. 21). Williamson suggests that analysis is symmetric and leads to essentially the same broad set of outcomes if the alternative starting point of central planning is adopted. However, we suggest here that this is not the case if a Penrosian perspective is adopted.
9. With the exception of reasons for firm existence and specialization, which has been dealt with in earlier chapters.

2.   The Agenda

Where do we start to analyse the nature and existence of the firm? The obvious starting point is *neoclassical theory*, the mainstream economics approach which has proved a robust and enduring foundation for analysis of prices and markets. The neoclassical agenda in microeconomics can be largely reduced to a simple question relating to *optimal product-market price*; does price (P) equal marginal cost (MC)? A variety of issues follow from the answer to this question, ranging from the efficiency of perfect competition, to the implications of various deviations from $P = MC$, such as monopoly distortions, externalities and public goods. Indeed, until relatively recently modifications in the theory of the firm tended to focus on modifications in the assumptions surrounding market structure and conduct, rather than more radical alterations in the components of the neoclassical agenda itself (e.g. Chamberlin, 1933; Robinson, 1933).

Neoclassical theory has a highly limited and simplistic view of human behaviour and decision-making, and is reductionist in tending to treat higher level entities (e.g. firms, industries, economies) as simple aggregates of lower level entities (e.g. products, consumers).[1] However, these features can represent strengths rather than weaknesses of the theory. *Ceteris paribus*, a simple theory is always to be preferred to a more complex alternative, and this also extends to the description of higher level entities. If an aggregative approach can perform as well in explaining behaviour as one which adds further elements and complications at higher levels, then there is no question but that the simpler alternative should be preferred. There are whole swathes of economic behaviour in which neoclassical theory passes this test, particularly situations involving short-run pricing behaviour in standardized commodity-type markets. Anyone who doubts this should attempt to help MBA students understand the behaviour of markets as reported in the 'Commodities and Agriculture' section of *The Financial Times* without drawing on neoclassical theory. It is no doubt possible to make sense of problems involving such concepts and issues as elasticity, quotas, price ceilings and floors, rationing, regulation, cartels, price discrimination and externality without invoking neoclassical theory, but there is usually no compelling need to do so.

As long as neoclassical theory continues to offer simple and adequate explanations of economic behaviour, there is little point in generating more complex alternatives. It is in the areas beyond short-run pricing in commodity-type markets that neoclassical theory begins to encounter

difficulties. One of the first objections to the market bias in neoclassical economics' view of resource allocation was provided by Coase (1937): 'in the
real world, we find there are many areas where the (allocation of factors by
the price mechanism) does not apply. If a workman moves from department
Y to department X, he does not go because of a change of relative prices,
but because he is ordered to do so' (p. 387). Other approaches focused on
other limitations of neoclassical theory: Schumpeter (1954) argued that 'it
is not (price competition) that counts, but the competition from the new
commodity, the new technology, the new source of supply, the new type of
organization' (p. 84). Additionally, Simon (1955) criticized the optimizing
perspective of neoclassical theory given the existence of conditions of
bounded rationality on the part of decision makers in complex or uncertain
situations, while Penrose (1959) saw the firm not as a collection of product-
markets as in neoclassical theory, but as a collection of resources (pp. 24–6).

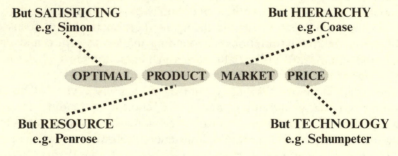

Fig. 2.1. The neoclassical agenda and some alternatives

It could be said that there is a tendency for new approaches to follow a
hub and spoke pattern in relation to neoclassical theory as in Fig. 2.1. The
neoclassical agenda represented by *optimal product-market price* has four
basic components; *optimal* decision making, the *product* as basic building
block, the *market* mode of organization, and *price* as decision variable.
Thus, Coase was primarily concerned with firms as alternatives to markets,
and less with the form or focus of decision making. Schumpeter's contribution was mainly concerned with the focus and form of the competitive
process (though he also expressed reservations about the assumption of
profit maximization), and he still tended to deal in conventional product-
market structures such as competition, monopoly and oligopoly. Simon
(1955) introduced satisfactory or acceptable standards as an alternative to
optimizing behaviour, but tended to retain the focus of product-market
price, as in his examples of decision making behaviour in the housing market. Penrose changed the focus of analysis from products to resources, but
still saw her analysis as consistent with neoclassical conceptions of long-run
profit maximization, (1959, p. 29). Each of these seminal contributions

removed an item or items from the neoclassical agenda; equally impor-
tantly, each retained other items from that same agenda in their reformula-
tion of the economic problem.

Therefore, spoke theories tend to deal with selected modifications to the
neoclassical agenda, and this can lead to other elements of the neoclassical
agenda appearing as default features on spokes, as in the cases discussed
above. The hub and spoke relation of alternative theories to neoclassical
theory encourages, and indeed can facilitate, comparison of the performance of spoke theories with that of the neoclassical hub. In some
approaches this can lead to allegations that the spoke is little different from
the neoclassical hub, as in Posner's (1993) critique of transaction cost economics. In other cases, more extensive efforts have been made to fashion an
alternative approach out of different spokes, for example Nelson and
Winter (1982). Nelson and Winter draw heavily on Simon and Schumpeter
to develop boundedly rational models of technological change, and they
also acknowledge the prior work of Penrose in helping to shape their view
of the firm as composed of organizational capabilities. If there is an area
which is relatively underdeveloped in terms of the alternative agendas discussed above, it is probably organizational structure or hierarchy.

A composite or unified spoke perspective on the firm would picture it as
an organized collection of resources making imperfect non-price decisions.
However, it should be said that there is no automatic merit in putting all
the elements of the spoke theories together in one integrated approach. For
some purposes there may be no justification in drawing upon any of them.
In other cases, the neglect of certain spoke perspectives may reflect the level
of the analysis or the types of problems being looked at. The important
issue is that the hub and spoke relation of neoclassical theory to its alternatives does help to reinforce the traditional dominance of neoclassical
theory, and permit it to continue to restrict heavily the agenda for economic
theorizing and research. With these points in mind, we can turn to the main
business of this chapter which is to review briefly some of the important
contributions in each of the four spokes, and to consider their possible relevance for the analysis that follows.

2.1. Spoke 1: Bounded Rationality

Spoke 1 theories emphasize the importance of bounded rationality in
decision-making. Bounded rationality refers to limits of human intellectual
capacities in comparison to the complexities and demands of the problems
facing individuals and organizations (March and Simon, 1958, p. 169). In
such circumstances, optimizing behaviour is typically replaced by satisficing
behaviour, or the search for a satisfactory outcome; 'an alternative is
optimal if: (1) there exists a set of criteria that permits all alternatives to be

compared, and (2) the alternative in question is preferred, by these criteria, to all other alternatives. An alternative is *satisfactory* if: (1) there exists a set of criteria that describes minimally satisfactory alternatives, and (2) the alternative in question meets or exceeds all these criteria.' (p. 141). March and Simon (1958, p. 147) gave the example of searching a haystack to find the sharpest needle in it (optimizing), and searching the haystack to find a needle sharp enough to sew with (satisficing).

March and Simon also suggested (p. 169) that rational behaviour in such circumstances calls for simplified models that contribute to workable solutions without capturing all the complexities of the situation. They suggested that these simplifications tended to have consistent features such as: (a) optimizing is replaced by satisficing, (b) sequential rather than simultaneous search for solutions, (c) repertories of action programmes serve as choice alternatives in recurrent situations, (d) specific action programmes are appropriate to a specific sets of circumstances, (e) action programmes are only loosely coupled to each other (p. 169). The implications of satisficing behaviour has been pursued in a number of studies (e.g. Simon, 1955; Cyert and March, 1963; Nelson and Winter, 1982). Also, Nelson and Winter's (1982) concept of organizational routines ('regular and predictable behavioral patterns of firms', p. 14) may be interpreted as deepening and broadening exploration of the notion of action programmes in an explicitly economic context.

Few, if any, economists would disagree with the contention that individuals may not optimize in certain circumstances. Anybody who has searched for a meal in a strange town late at night is likely to have found that their choice was characterized by satisficing rather than optimizing criteria. The real question is whether or not non-optimal decision-making represents a sufficiently important phenomenon to make it worthwhile to modify or abandon neoclassical models in particular circumstances.[2] March and Simon (1958, pp. 140–1) argue that optimizing behaviour is very much the exception rather than the rule, but even granting this point is not sufficient to shake the foundations of the neoclassical citadel. Day (1967) pointed out that in certain circumstances involving stable but unknown parameters, decision-makers may use satisficing criteria to converge on the optimizing solution. Indeed, it is possible to go further and accept that satisficing represents the general case, while still denying that this requires revision of the neoclassical agenda. For example, buying and selling decisions for many individual human and electronic traders could probably be best characterized by satisficing models, with specific 'sell' and 'buy' decisions triggered by significant discrepancies with respect to certain standards (e.g. deviations from a particular trend line; differences with respect to comparable investment opportunities). However, it is generally not clear how satisficing models reflecting individual history and experience could improve on the analysis of commodity markets provided by simple aggregative neoclassical models. Cyert and March's (1963) description of pricing behaviour by a retail department store was extremely successful in predicting price changes, but this was a case of an oligopolistic operator requiring a great deal of institutional detail to model the decisions. When it comes to traditional neo-classical questions such as the short-term price elasticity of demand for crude oil, neoclassical approaches still appear to be simpler to construct, and they continue to give answers which economists appear to find useful. Cyert and March chose to fight neoclassical theory on its own ground (price behaviour). While this facilitated comparability of behavioural and neoclassical predictions, granting the choice of question to the incumbent theory conceded to it a strong home advantage that probably limited the breaches that behavioural theory could make in neoclassical defences.

Of course, pricing behaviour is not the only issue which may involve questions of resource allocation, as Nelson and Winter's later analysis (1982) of technological change helped to demonstrate. Also, March has continued to work with associates in developing models of organizational decision-making in conditions of bounded rationality. The 'garbage can' model (Cohen, March, and Olsen, 1972; March and Olsen, 1976*b*) is one significant development. In the garbage can model, organizations are viewed as collections of situations, problems, solutions, and participants (who are expected to put problems and solutions together in a decision). While garbage can decisions can have a structure and order, bounded rationality considerations means that outcomes may be sub-optimal. Chance events can affect the conjunction of problems with solutions, which in turn can influence choice. One interesting possibility is that garbage can reasoning may usefully complement the work of evolutionary theorists[3] in that it provides a perspective on decision-making level considerations that may generate path dependent outcomes involving organizations.

The areas in which models explicitly recognizing bounded rationality are likely to be of most relevance are areas involving pervasive uncertainty. Uncertainty in this context refers to true or unmeasurable uncertainty. This is not the type of uncertainty which can be reduced to a probabilistic risk estimate. Not only might decision-makers have little basis on which to assess the likelihood of future possible states of the world occurring, there is likely to be a lack of knowledge as to what these future states of the world might be. Any activities involving non-trivial innovative content are likely to be marked by severe problems of bounded rationality, and indeed most of the strategic issues we shall be concerned with in the book are characterized by decision-makers having to deal with novel situations in which the past represents only a limited guide to future action. It follows that bounded rationality will be a live issue in much of the analysis that follows.

There is a natural affinity between spoke 1 and spoke 2 theories in that decisions deplete resources such as managerial time (March and Olsen,

1976*a*). It is therefore appropriate to view the next spoke as complementary to these spoke 1 approaches.

2.2. Spoke 2: Resources

Penrose (1959) defined the firm as 'a collection of productive resources the disposal of which between different uses and over time is determined by administrative decision' (p. 24). These could be physical resources (plant, equipment, land and natural resources, raw materials, semi-finished goods, waste products, by-products, and unsold stocks) or human resources (unskilled and skilled labour, clerical, administrative, financial, legal, technical, and managerial staff). In turn, 'resources consist of a bundle of potential services and can, for the most part, be defined independently of their use' (Penrose, 1959, p. 25).

At first sight Penrose's definition of the firm appears reasonable, uncontroversial, indeed even obvious. However, it is difficult to overstate how different a picture of the firm this provided compared to neoclassical theory. In neoclassical theory, resources were embodied as factors of production, and in turn these factors only had meaning in so far as alternative uses for them could be specified. In turn, the traditional neoclassical theory of the firm was a theory of market behaviour and part of the broader neoclassical theory of value, not a theory designed to explain the behaviour of firms considered as administrative units (Loasby, 1976). There was no irony or contradiction in the idea that in the theory of the firm, the firm was not a firm (Penrose 1959, p. 13); the neoclassical 'firm' was a black box which costlessly made optimal decisions in response to price signals in the market place. Penrose's apparently innocuous argument that resources might be defined independently of their use was in fact the critical first step that allowed the firm to be studied as an institution of economic importance in its own right.[4] Resources still generated services in Penrose's approach; however, here resources dictated opportunities rather than opportunities dictating resources as in neoclassical theory.

In recent years a number of resource-based approaches have been developed in economics[5] (e.g. Nelson and Winter, 1982; Lippman and Rumelt, 1982; Porter, 1985, 1987, 1990; Rumelt, 1986: Teece, 1980, 1982; Kay, 1982), while the concept of 'resource' itself has been subject to a variety of interpretations in economics and strategic management, such as firm-specific competencies (Pavitt, 1992), core competencies, (Prahalad and Hamel, 1990), capabilities (Richardson, 1972; Chandler, 1990; Langlois and Robertson, 1995), and even simply resources (Ansoff, 1968; Collis, 1996; Kay 1979). Like Collis (1996) we prefer to make a cautious start with the more general and neutral term 'resource'; for one thing it is simpler, since notions of distinctive competence immediately involve demand side as well as supply side considerations. More problematically, notions such as distinctive competencies suggest we can sift through the chaff of ordinary resources until we get to the essence of what makes a firm unique. Such an exercise may obscure the nature of the firm, and the reasons for its existence and survival. Suppose, for example, we have in a locality a number of ice cream makers, a number of drivers, and a number of vans. In isolation each of these resources may be fairly common and not worth much in commercial terms. Even two of these three elements together may not excite the attention of potential investors; but find a way to put the three elements together, and there may be the basis for an ice cream business.

The search for distinctive competencies or unique assets in the strategic management literature is typically associated with analysis of firms like 3M, Xerox, Canon, and Apple, and it is a perspective that finds comfort in the transaction cost emphasis (discussed below) on the role of specialized assets in determining the boundaries of firms. However, it would be more persuasive if the same exercise could be conducted for, say, Mobil, Shell, Exxon, and Texaco. Clearly the oil majors are different from each other; equally clearly, a high degree of commercial competence is a prerequisite for survival in the fiercely competitive oil market. Less clear is the identity of a critical and distinctive competence that is essential to Mobil's ability to compete against Shell, or which gives Exxon a competitive advantage relative to Texaco. In this context, it is worth noting Coase's (1937) insight that efficiency may reflect not just the characteristics of resources, but how and where they are organized. In the case of the oil majors, the integration of various stages in the oil business within the firm has involved substitution of potential markets for intermediate products with firm-specific planning and control procedures. The resulting vertical integration has given each of these firms a degree of control over their supplies and outlets and helped to provide some insulation from the vagaries of market forces. Even if the resources and the internal control systems adopted by the respective firms were sufficiently similar to the extent that the firms appeared as virtual clones of each other, these gains should still be realizable. It is one thing to argue that the viability of these firms reflects a particular combination of resources in the respective cases; it is less convincing to suggest that viability in general may be attributable to firm-specific distinctive competencies, or unique and inimitable assets.

This may hold even in cases where firms appear to be characterized by particular distinctive competencies. When Boeing was trying to get into the guided missile market in the late 1950s, it was extremely successful in winning the role of prime contractor for large missiles despite the fact that the critical technology was widely acknowledged as being in the possession of the electronics companies—Boeing's technological expertise lay in the duller and less critical areas of body assembly. The reason that Boeing did so well in competition against the electronics companies was its experience and expertise in contracting to government. Take away its marketing expertise and it would have lost its edge over the electronics companies. Take away its technological expertise and it would have had no credibility as a potential prime contractor. Put them together, and the complementarities generated competitive advantage in the market place. Taken one at a time, it is not necessary that individual competencies are 'distinctive' relative to those of rivals for the firm to compete effectively in markets, and indeed what makes a firm strong or weak at any one point in time may not be well understood, even within the firms themselves (Nelson, 1991, p. 62). Firms may be distinctive (Nelson, 1991) and display competence in order to survive (Alchian, 1950), but it is a fallacy to conclude that this means that firms must display a distinctive competence in order to survive.

If an audit was taken of the resources that constitute individual firms in practice, it would typically throw up a mixture of the exotic and the humdrum, ranging from the highly specialized to the standardized, from scientists and strategic planners to test tubes and typewriters. However, when individual assets are actually analysed in isolation they can often appear remarkably mundane and prosaic rather than distinctive, as in the case of the MS-DOS operating system which was basically bought off the shelf by Microsoft from a small firm for a few dollars; the rest, as they say, being history. If we try to whittle the picture of the firm down to some particular feature which provides it with its 'distinctive' or 'core' competence, then we may be left with a very small rump—as, indeed, Prahalad and Hamel (1990, p. 82) appear to argue when they talk of reducing the highly diversified 3M corporation to a few shared core competencies.[6] It is entirely conceivable that such an exercise conducted on some conglomerates would leave us with no discernable rump at all, and by implication no reasons for their existence. It therefore seems preferable to hold on to the Penrosian notion of the firm as 'essentially a pool of resources the utilisation of which is organised in an administrative framework' (Penrose, 1959, p. 149). We develop our analysis later on the notion that it is the relationships between resources that may help us analyse the nature of the firm, and that there are two basic relationships based on resource complementarity (e.g. Boeing putting together technology and marketing resources in the guided missile business) and resource similarity (e.g. Boeing obtaining synergies or economies of scope in sharing technology between its civil and military businesses).

A particular issue we shall be concerned with later is differences in the functional characteristics of resources (whether technological, marketing, etc.). Other important distinctions which cross functional boundaries include the distinction between tangible and intangible resources (broadly corresponding to Penrose's distinction between physical or material resources and human or knowledge-based resources (1959, pp. 76–8)). In turn, a common distinction is between knowledge which is codifiable, articulable, or transmissible (Penrose, 1959, p. 53; Arrow, 1969; Winter, 1987), and knowledge based on experience (Penrose, 1959, p. 78), now generally described as tacit knowledge or know-how, following Polanyi (1958, 1967).[7] Nelson and Winter's (1982) concept of routines reflects concern with the varied forms in which know-how can be embodied, ranging from tightly specified rules and procedures (such as order handling) to higher order conventions and principles (such as advertising expenditure as a percentage of sales (p. 15)). In Nelson and Winter's evolutionary theory, routines play the role that genes play in biological evolutionary theory (p. 14). The firms themselves evolve over time and industries bear the stamp of path dependency 'with the condition of the industry in each period bearing the seeds of its condition in the following period' (p. 19).

Particular mention should also be made in this context of the work of Michael Porter. Porter's work has also mistakenly been regarded by many economists as basically an adaptation of the traditional industrial organization framework into the area of strategic management. That may well be an appropriate description of his first major work (1980), but Porter (1985) very much reflects a resource based perspective of competitive advantage, while more recently (Porter, 1990, 1991) his work has been concerned with long-run processes and the development of firms, sectors, and economies. One of the most interesting lines of argument in Porter (1990) implies that the sources of long-term competitive advantage may be the reverse of those traditionally associated with short-term competitive advantage in some cases. Thus, a relative factor disadvantage (e.g. Japan, and scarce indigenous natural resources) may stimulate actions that lead to competitive advantage (e.g. fuel efficient technology); a firm that actively seeks an extremely competitive environment may find that this sharpens its long-term competitive edge compared to a firm that seeks the comfort of less rivalrous arenas; choosing to enter markets with the highest or most restrictive standards may be expensive in the short run, but may hone and generalize ability to compete in the long run; and so on. In trying to unravel the sources of competitive advantage, Porter's argument often turns the logic of short-run neoclassical theory on its head. A provisional result of this very interesting research programme is to demonstrate that evolutionary processes, in relation to the strategies of corporations, can behave according to very different competitive principles compared to those represented in neoclassical accounts; an implication which is unlikely to surprise a student of evolutionary economics, but which is powerfully demonstrated and illustrated in the various cases and examples analysed by Porter.[8]

2.3. Spoke 3: Hierarchy

In Chapter 1 we warned of the ambiguous nature of words, and nowhere will we find this better illustrated than in the territory that is most associated with the analysis of hierarchies; institutional economics. Institutional economists can be separated into 'old' and 'new' categories; these are similar to the extent that the former can be broadly defined as descriptivist, anti-formalist, holist, behaviourist, collectivist, and fairly interventionist, while the latter can be broadly defined as more formalist, individualist, reductionist, rationalist, and generally anti-interventionist (Rutherford, 1994, p. 4). As if this is not a guarantor of sufficient variety, both 'old' and 'new' camps can be subdivided into disparate tribes that appear to encompass just about any approach in economics that cannot be crammed into the receding interstices represented by traditional neoclassical theory (Rutherford, 1994, pp. 1–4). None the less, it is possible as Rutherford suggests to identify some central or general themes in both old and new institutional economics, as well as some fairly definitive authorities in the respective spheres. We shall make our first approach to the notion of hierarchy by way of both these routes.

The *old institutional economics* is associated with a variety of writers, but if one could be identified as the leading figure of the approach, it is probably Thorstein Veblen (see Veblen, 1925). Rutherford (1994) and Samuels (1995) provide good overviews of this area. The difficulties with the 'old' institutionalism can be summarized in perhaps just one question; what patterns of behaviour could it not explain? It is in fact very difficult to provide a meaningful answer to this question given 'old' institutionalist methodology. 'Old' institutionalists employ case studies heavily, and Blaug points out that 'none of them will have any truck with concepts of equilibrium, rational behaviour, instantaneous adjustments, and perfect knowledge, and they all prefer the idea of group behaviour under the influence of custom or habit' (Blaug, 1992, pp. 109–10). As Blaug points out (1992, p. 110), this makes it all too easy to verify and makes it virtually impossible to falsify. Consequently, a provisional answer to our question must be that there is just about no pattern of behaviour that institutionalism could not describe. The danger that 'old' institutionalists run is that an approach that accommodates everything may be accused of explaining nothing. This is certainly the conclusion that Coase (1984, p. 230) comes to, and Posner (1993, p. 74) endorses. On the other hand, the rich and detailed institutionalist analyses often anticipated or complemented later theoretical and empirical work. For example, Rutherford (1994, p. 109) points out that Veblen's work noted the separation of ownership and control in the corporation that was later to be documented more systematically by Berle and Means (1932). Also, the work of Galbraith (1952, 1967) sits comfortably alongside more formal managerial theories of the firm (such as those of Baumol, 1959; Marris, 1964; Williamson, 1964) as well as Schumpeter's analysis of the corporation as an instrument of technological change. While Rutherford (1994, p. 40) also (justifiably) endorses the criticism of both Veblen and Galbraith that their methodological approach is prone to *ex post* rationalizations, the 'old' institutionalist approach still adds colour, detail, and insights to the analysis of the firm.

The *new institutionalist economics* has been associated with a variety of writers, most notably perhaps Oliver Williamson (e.g. 1975, 1985 and 1993*a*) and Douglass North (e.g. 1990). Langlois (1986*b*), Williamson (1993*a*), Eggertsson (1990) and, again, Rutherford (1994) provide good overviews of this area. The new institutionalist approach tends to reflect the hub and spoke perspective of Fig. 2.1, with a great deal of emphasis being given to alternative institutional arrangements for allocating resources, though still reflecting neoclassical influences in many other respects, such as its static nature (Langlois and Robertson, 1995, p. 25). Indeed, Posner (1993) has recently gone so far as to suggest that, save for its concern with institutions (p. 75), there is little to distinguish new institutionalist economics from traditional neoclassical theory. This is certainly going too far,[9] but there are strong neoclassical influences at work in new institutional economics. Interestingly, the only new word in Williamson's vocabulary that Posner finds useful—opportunism, or self interest seeking with guile—actually found its best expression in the earlier work of the 'old' institutionalist Veblen:

Freedom from scruple, from sympathy, honesty and regard for life, may, within fairly wide limits, be said to further the success of the individual in the pecuniary culture. The highly successful men of all times have commonly been of this type; except those whose success has not been scored in terms of either wealth or power. It is only within narrow limits, and then only in a Pickwickian sense, that honesty is the best policy   (Veblen, 1925, p. 223).

Williamson then adds Simon's interpretation of bounded rationality and the concept of asset specificity (assets specialized by use or users) to the notion of opportunism to set out his three prerequisites for the appearance of interesting transactional problems (Williamson, 1985, pp. 31–2). Opportunism and bounded rationality tend to be interpreted in Williamson's approach as general features of the human condition, leaving asset specificity as 'the principal factor that is responsible for transaction cost differences among transactions' (Riordan and Williamson, 1985, p. 367). In Williamson's analysis, the absence of asset specificity generally describes a world in which 'discrete market contracting is efficacious' (1985, p. 31), while the existence of asset specificity can lead to markets failing to organize transactions effectively, and the internalization of the transaction within corporate boundaries (1985, pp. 30–2). If assets are specialized by use or user (say a machine customized for a particular customer), then the supplier has nowhere to turn to if the present transaction breaks down. If a supplier has built a customized machine to supply specialized components to an assembler, this opens up the possibility for the assembler to indulge in opportunistic recontracting; for example by demanding that the component be supplied at a much lower price. The assembler is secure in the knowledge that the supplier is locked into the present relationship and has no escape route. Consequently, market transactions may break down in the case of transactions characterized by asset specificity. Rational suppliers would avoid circumstances which would leave them open to opportunistic re-contracting, which means that the assembler may have to build their own customized machines to supply themselves with their own specialized components. At the other extreme, the world of non-specific assets is the neoclassical world of standardized commodities in which market alternatives can be quickly and easily found if the present trading relationship turns out to be unsatisfactory. Therefore, asset specificity becomes a key condition which helps determine whether or not a firm performs a particular economic activity itself or contracts for it in the market place. The transaction cost perspective then naturally leads to an analysis of the boundaries of the firm in terms of its degree of vertical integration. Thus hierarchy (the firm) may replace contract and market exchange alternatives, and we have in principle a third spoke along which to modify the neoclassical agenda: alternative modes of organization to market exchange.

The transaction cost approach to the boundaries of the firm has stimulated a number of empirical studies of the role of asset specificity in vertical integration.[10] We shall argue in the next chapter that this is too narrow a foundation on which to base a theory of the nature and the boundaries of the firm. Williamson does provide a theory of the conglomerate (1975, pp. 155–75, 1985, pp. 286–90), and we shall look at this explanation in Chapter 4.

An important recent development running parallel to the transaction cost literature is the literature on incomplete contracts (Grossman and Hart, 1986; Hart, 1988, 1995). This literature starts with the arguments of Coase, Williamson, and Klein *et al.* (1978) regarding the existence of transaction costs and the consequence that parties to a relationship may not be able to write a comprehensive contract that anticipates all the events that may occur and the appropriate actions in each case. Instead they will write a contract that is incomplete in the sense that all relevant events and actions are not included. A consequence of this incompleteness is that in the face of unfolding events parties may wish to act differently from the ways specified in the contract and may wish to revise its terms, and indeed may disagree about what the contract really means. Incompleteness of contract leads to a theory of ownership in this approach, which is in turn linked to the notion of residual rights of control, or rights to the use of the asset after specified uses of the asset have been satisfied. Residual rights of control provide a mechanism whereby the gaps in the contract can be filled in as time goes by. Alternative distributions of residual rights of control in particular assets may have efficiency implications, which in turn may have implications for the setting of the boundaries of the firm (Hart, 1988, 1995, p. 92).

Early work in this area has tended to follow transaction cost economics in emphasizing the role of asset specificity (Grossman and Hart, 1986; Hart, 1995, pp. 29–92). However, the primary emphasis here is on property rights and it may be less wedded to the notion of asset specificity than those working from the transaction cost perspective. The orientation still tends to be in terms of whether the firm or the market should coordinate the use of assets (in this case from the perspective of property rights). It is still essentially focused on the characteristics of individual assets, making it difficult to relate it to the Penrosian perspective of the firm as a bundle of resources. We shall also look at some other implications of this literature in Chapter 3.

Douglass North is another writer whose work has been associated with the new institutional economics, and his work also tends to echo neoclassical theory in some important respects. North comments:

Perfect measurement and enforcement are implicitly assumed in what we call efficient factor and product markets, but their existence entails a complex set of institutions that encourage factor mobility, the acquisition of skills, uninterrupted production, rapid and low-cost transmission of information, and the invention and innovation of new technologies. Realizing all these conditions is a tall order never completely filled because . . . the actual institutional framework is in fact usually a mixed bag of institutions that promote such productivity-raising activities and institutions that provide barriers to entry, encourage monopolistic restrictions, and impede the low-cost flow of information   (North, 1990, p. 64)

The arguments here appear plausible, especially since they are presented as critical of neoclassical theory, and there is certainly little that a reasonable person could disagree with in the latter part of the quote. The problem lies in the identification by North of a notional 'complex set of institutions' that could somehow eliminate coordination or transaction costs of measurement and enforcement. Suppose, for example, an individual has developed a new and better mousetrap, and they are considering licensing it to a corporation that has the marketing resources necessary to convert the idea into commercial reality. They work out that they could either (1) incur substantial costs of monitoring and enforcing the license agreement, (2) economize on monitoring and enforcement costs and open themselves up to opportunistic behaviour on the part of the corporation,[11] (3) give up. It turns out that the second option would remove the incentives to cooperate with the corporation, which means they either incur substantial costs of measuring and enforcing the exchange agreement, or they give up. The idea that there is a 'complex set of institutions' (presumably available on a free good basis) that could somehow avoid these costs is a fiction, but one that follows naturally from North's interpretation of the study of institutions as complementary to neoclassical theory (1990, p. 5). Neoclassical theory remains in the background in this perspective as a tantalizing ideal; achieving its optimal outcomes remains a 'tall order' that is continually frustrated by the tendency of individuals to develop institutions, which North defines as 'the constraints that human beings impose on themselves' (1990, p. 5).

The problems inherent in such a perspective were previously exposed in 1969 by Demsetz in a critique of Arrow (1962). Demsetz contrasted the 'Nirvana' approach with what he described as the comparative institution approach in which the relevant choice is between alternative real world institutional arrangements. The Nirvana approach tended to commit three fallacies: the 'grass is always greener' fallacy, in which it was sufficient to perceive a discrepancy between the ideal and the real for the perceived discrepancy to be presumed solvable; the fallacy of the 'free lunch' in which it is implicitly assumed that moves towards optimality can be achieved costlessly; and the 'people could be different' fallacy in which ideal outcomes are assumed in which problems such as moral hazard are implicitly assumed to be absent. The Nirvana approach is inherent in North's interpretation of institutions as constraints, as when he talks of the importance of institutions in terms of 'self-imposed rules of behaviour in constraining maximising behaviour' (North, 1990, p. 43). This suggest an obvious question; why not find ways of removing the constraints (inefficient institutions) and move towards optimality? The economics of Nirvana still lurks in the background of North's work; if neoclassical theory is the study of maximizing behaviour and institutional theory is the study of constraints on such behaviour, then it is certainly reasonable for North to assert that neoclassical theory and the study of institutions are complementary.[12] This may make the study of institutions more acceptable to mainstream economists, but the price to be paid here is vulnerability to Demsetz's three fallacies.

In a comparative institutional approach as defined by Demsetz, institutions do not just 'define and limit the choices of individuals' (North, 1990, p. 4), they *expand* as well as limit choice. It all depends what one is comparing. If Nirvana still lurks, then it may be legitimate to define institutions as simply representing constraints. On the other hand, if someone is trying to develop a better mousetrap in a world of boundedly rational individuals (some of whom may have non-altruistic motives), then the important question is what is feasible, not what is optimal in the neoclassical sense of the word. The world of comparative institutions is a world of *relative* efficiency, not absolute efficiency. Institutions enable as well as constrain.

2.4. Spoke 4: Technological Change

The fourth and last spoke is the role of technological change in the growth and development of firms, industries and economies. The foundations for modern work in this area were laid by Schumpeter (1942), and his arguments have informed and guided much subsequent theoretical and empirical research on corporate and economic development. Schumpeter argued that it was not price competition that really mattered in the development of economies, but competition from new ways of doing things, which could encompass new ways of organizing as well as technological change (1954, p. 84). Schumpeter saw the modern large industrial corporation as providing a favourable environment for the generation of technological change, though there is some ambiguity as to whether he believed scale or monopoly power played the dominant role in stimulating innovative activity (Tirole, 1988, p. 390). What is clear is that in focusing on very long-run processes, Schumpeter exposed the limitations of the traditional perfect competition model in providing a basis for positive and normative analysis of industrial behaviour in modern economies.

Compared to the other three spokes, this approach had one major advantage in attracting the interest of those in the traditional structure-conduct-performance area (the applied wing of neoclassical theory in industrial organization); these economists already worked with independent variables implied by the Schumpeterian paradigm such as 'scale' and 'concentration'. Simply replace 'price' with some measure of innovative activity (such as patent counts), and the same techniques that had been used to investigate price could be easily redeployed on innovative activity. Unfortunately, the price that had to be paid here for such easy acceptance into the conventional wisdom was that much of Schumpeter's emphasis on dynamic evolutionary processes was lost in translation into a framework designed for other purposes. Beyond the applied industrial organization field, Schumpeter's work has had a major impact on economists employing a variety of perspectives.[13] However, two contemporary approaches have made serious claims to be the heirs of Schumpeter: the game theoretic literature on innovation races (e.g. see Tirole, 1988), and evolutionary theory as in Nelson and Winter (1982). We shall look at both below and consider some implications for analysis of corporate strategy.

If there is now a dominant paradigm in the study of industrial organization (IO), it is game theory. It is not widely recognized that a new form of competition called 'technological competition' (Dasgupta, 1986) has either been discovered or invented by the game theorists. Although game theoreticians such as Dasgupta (1986, pp. 139–42) and Tirole (1988, pp. 389–421) acknowledge their debt to Schumpeter, and generally see themselves as following in that tradition, they are actually talking about quite different competitive forces from those postulated by Schumpeter. The radical nature of the game theoretic contribution is obscured by a crucial missing preposition; the forces of creative destruction associated with Schumpeterian competition involves competition *from* a new technology, while technological competition in the game theoretic sense is typically competition *for* a new technology. There is now a considerable literature in game-theoretic formulations of technological competition and a number of excellent surveys exist (e.g. Dasgupta, 1986; Tirole, 1988, chapter 10; Beath *et al.*, 1994), but a common representation involves a race between rivals to innovate first. However, rather like the Sherlock Holmes mystery of the dog that did nothing in the night, studies and literature surveys of the innovative process have not been characterized by widespread observations of such technological competition[14] (that is not to say that game theorists do not refer to empirical evidence; some do, but we shall turn to that issue below). Whilst technological innovation is only one form of creative endeavour leading to intellectual property, the assumption that rivals race to be first appears to be largely peculiar to this area. However, if there is one lesson that resource-based perspective provides, it is that firms differ in their capabilities and perceptions (Nelson, 1991). In such circumstances, there is absolutely no reason to believe that at any one time they will be perceiving, and searching for, the same sets of opportunities as their rivals.

In fact, the game theoretic assumption that the opportunity determines the allocation of resources reflects its hub parentage; it would be more consistent with Schumpeter's treatment of technological change to acknowledge (as do spoke 2 theories) that the nature and quality of resources within the firm may influence the opportunities that can be generated. Further, in this literature there is typically an explicit or implicit assumption of transparency of rival decisions to some degree at least. But most corporate R&D (research and development) projects are conducted as part of a diversified stable of projects within the R&D departments of large firms; even if the firm releases information about its global R&D budget, it can usually vary strategy involving the nature, funding and timing of specific projects without informing competitors. The existence of internal capital markets and internal labour markets (and non-disclosure agreements signed by employees) also help to insulate the larger firm from leakages of strategically sensitive information which it wishes to withhold from the outside world. The deliberate release of R&D information to the outside world is likely to be restricted to special cases, such as situations where suppliers, users or consumers have to be informed or consulted before introduction, or occasions when information is systematically leaked to rivals for co-operative or collusive purposes.

Thus, when Scherer (1992) develops an R&D rivalry model in which one firm has established a lead in the R&D race, and talks in terms of 'when Firm 1 awakes to the challenge, it commences a crash course to recoup . . . recognising the competition, Firm 2 accelerates . . . seeing that it cannot be the first mover, Firm 1 reacts submissively' (p. 33), it invites a simple question: how? More specifically, how can firms awake to, recognize, see, or react to their rival's decisions at the R&D stage when it is generally in the interests of rivals to make their R&D project decisions as opaque as possible? The characteristics of R&D projects discussed above means that such concealment is generally feasible as well as desirable, and so firms can generally be presumed to be blind to rivals' R&D decisions up to the point of commercial introduction, whether these relate to the nature, the budget, or the timing of the respective projects. Consequently, the existence of R&D races implicitly necessitates other *ad hoc* assumptions involving irrational or inefficient behaviour on the part of firms, such as accidental, negligent or criminal leakages of information by firms or employees to rival firms. Explicit acknowledgement of the fact that rational and efficient firm behaviour implies R&D blindness has implications for a considerable proportion of the literature that has now been developed by game theorists in this area. At the very least, arguments in support of any specific R&D rivalry model should make explicit what irrational, incompetent, and/or inefficient behaviour is being implicitly assumed by the model builder.

There is a escape clause which many theorists would employ at this point, and it is important to specify what it is and pin it down. It is Friedman's (1953) methodological paper, in which he argues that the realism of assumptions is largely irrelevant to the status of a theory[15] and that what really matters is the ability to predict behaviour. The first part of this argument at least has been taken to heart by many game theorists. However, analysis of how three blind mice[16] run is likely to be improved if we assume they are optically disadvantaged.[17] Correspondingly, if we wished to examine the behaviour of blind organizations,[18] an approach that recognizes such perceptual impairment is likely to have more mileage in it than one that does not. The problem is that Friedman's thesis has been taken as providing a *carte blanche* by many modern theorists to proceed as if it does not matter if assumptions directly contradict reality.[19]

However, if functions and causal mechanisms are not properly identified, theories may be regarded as incomplete and unsatisfactory on scientific grounds; if a statistical association is shown between the incidence of cancer and the proximity of electro-magnetic fields, the proper scientific response is not to conclude that such fields cause cancer, but to ask *how* such fields could cause cancer.[20] The role of causality in scientific theorizing encourages consideration of 'but how . . .' type questions, as in; 'but how could electro-magnetic fields cause cancer?' Asking 'but how' type questions can help expose structural weaknesses in economic theories—as can be seen if we ask naïve but crucial questions such as: 'but how can Scherer's R&D performing firms see competitors' R&D project decisions?' In turn, a proper scientific answer provides a 'because' explanation, not an 'as if' explanation. As Blaug (1992) points out, such theorizing of type supported by Friedman 'makes predictions without being able to explain why the predictions work: the moment the predictions fail, the theory has to be discarded in toto because it lacks an underlying structure of assumptions, an *explanans* that can be adjusted and improved to make better predictions for the future. It is for this reason that scientists usually do worry when the assumptions of their theories are blatantly unrealistic' (p. 99).

As Kreps (1990) points out, 'game theorists are very clever individuals, and given almost any form of behaviour, they can build models that "explain" the behaviour as the result of an equilibrium in a sufficiently complex elaboration of the game originally written down' (p. 104).[21] Rasmussen (1989) describes this as 'no-fat modelling' in game theory, in which a stylized fact is first observed and then a set of premises are developed that imply behaviour resembling the stylized fact. However, the malleability of game theory in these respects is a weakness rather than a strength, and its weaknesses relate directly to the conduct of empirical research. Cohen and Levin (1989) have commented that: 'One neglected issue in the empirical literature is the role of strategic interaction, which has been the major preoccupation of theorists concerned with R&D investment and technical change. Curiously, this activity was given greater attention in the 1960's and 1970's than in recent years' (p. 1096). In fact, this dearth of empirical evidence is not at all curious when game theory is compared with the Schumpeterian theory it has effectively replaced (or assimilated according to some game theorists) in the IO field. Schumpeterianism was a 'good' theory in that it was possible to identify a range of behaviour patterns with which it was *not* consistent, as well as a range of behaviour patterns with which it *was* consistent. The ability to discriminate between the two sets of behaviours provided signposts for applied work, and stimulated a considerable body of empirical research.[22] The theory of technological competition does not provide a basis for such discrimination, and so there are no signposts to stimulate and direct empirical research. There is no surprise in the withering away of empirical research into strategic interaction at the same time that the theory dedicated to the study of strategic interaction has achieved dominance. Since it does not matter what the facts are, game theory does not so much stimulate empirical research as eliminate the need for it.

At the same time, it is to the credit of researchers such as Dasgupta and Scherer that they look at empirical behaviour to examine their contention that innovative behaviour can be modelled by assuming firms indulge in games at the R&D stage. Ironically however, the evidence they produce tends to be consistent with R&D blindness; if other firms' actions do affect a firm's R&D activity, it tends not to be actions at the R&D stage. For example, Dasgupta (1986) reports that 'imitative behaviour is a pervasive phenomenon. Mansfield, Schwartz and Wagner (1981) have reported that 60% of the innovations in a sample of 48 industries studied by them were imitated within four years' (p. 145). This is true, but Mansfield, Schwartz, and Wagner also comment in the same study 'in the bulk of the cases, the new product could have been imitated in two years or less, even if the imitator carried out the project at the most leisurely pace. In practically all of the cases, it could be imitated in three years or less. Thus four years was plenty of time for an imitator to enter' (1981, p. 914, footnote). In other words, the evidence suggests that the decision to imitate was taken *after* rival innovation, not while the rival was still at the R&D stage. In this study at least, imitative R&D followed rival R&D and subsequent innovation, it did not parallel track it as in a race to be first. Similarly, Scherer (1992) looked at a number of case studies of innovative activity in different sectors, as well as how US firms' innovative activity responded to import competition in various markets. Again, firms' innovative activity tended to be influenced by observable events in the outside world, whether it was rival product introduction, changes in government policy, or intensified import competition. There is virtually no evidence found of firms responding to rivals' decisions at the R&D stage.[23]

Scherer regards the lack of such evidence as a data problem; for example 'data permitting an analysis of how US firms responded to changes in rivals' R&D are not available. We therefore measure the vigour of foreign competition by changes over time in . . . measures of import penetration into US markets' (1992, p. 146). However, if firms could not observe rivals' R&D in the first place, it was not surprising that Scherer could not find data recording responses to rivals' R&D. Scherer's reliance on supposedly inferior data that was observable to him (and consequently to rivals) actually provides a much sounder basis for analysis. He concludes 'company reactions (to import competition) tended to be more aggressive, the greater a company's domestic sales were, the more concentrated were the US markets in which the company operated, and the more diversified the company's domestic operations were. The first two patterns almost certainly reflect predictions from the pure theory of inter-firm R&D rivalry' (Scherer, 1992, p. 175). In fact, these empirical findings are consistent with R&D blindness rather than R&D rivalry, and can be reconciled with the ability of firms with deep pockets to respond to *revealed* competitive threats by rivals. If there is a thesis which postulates aggression out of deep pockets, it is the Schumpeterian thesis. Scherer produces an excellent, detailed and skilled empirical analysis of innovative activity in industry, but it does not serve to reinforce faith in game theoretic R&D rivalry modelling as he claims. His book can instead be read and interpreted as providing valuable evidence that tends to be consistent with old fashioned Schumpeterianism.

If there is a single approach which could really be said to be in the Schumpeterian tradition, it is probably Nelson and Winter's (1982). Indeed, as noted above, they go beyond Schumpeter and explicitly build on the earlier work of Penrose, Simon, and Cyert and March to incorporate what we describe above as spoke 1 and spoke 2 type perspectives in their theory. As Nelson and Winter argue, 'an essential aspect of real Schumpeterian competition is that firms do not know *ex ante* whether it pays to try to be an innovator or an imitator, or what levels of R&D expenditures might be appropriate. Indeed, the answer to this question for any single firm depends on the choices made by other firms, and reality does not contain any provisions for firms to test out their policies before adopting them' (1982, p. 286). Instead of tying the firm's R&D decisions to the R&D decisions of rivals, Nelson and Winter (1982, pp. 248–62) base their description of such decisions on evidence drawn from actual observation of the process. The R&D decision-maker has a search strategy which obeys certain rules and reflects certain influences, such as the nature of the resources possessed by the firm, and perceived opportunities for developing present technology further. The determination of the overall R&D budget in the firm usually follows a simple rule of thumb, such as maintaining expenditure as a constant proportion of sales. Nelson and Winter also report that studies suggest that firms allocate effort within the overall budget either by screening for projects that would deliver high pay-offs if successful,[24] or by technologically interesting possibilities. Evidence suggests that the first strategy tends to be more consistently commercially successful, while the second tends to be high risk, but high pay-off when successful. These are very different resource allocation rules from the ones inferred by the game theoretic literature.

Nelson and Winter's firm is a firm with a history, it has bundles of resources inherited from previous time periods, and it has sub-optimal rules which have been developed though experience. Whilst these decision rules may be inferior to the corresponding set of 'optimal' decision rules, if these could somehow be identified, they are generally superior to starting each time period with a blank slate. This advantage may be all that the firm can reasonably expect to work with in a world of bounded rationality. The breadth and depth of Nelson and Winter's analysis encompasses a considerable range of material drawn from the resource-based perspectives, the organizational decision literature, and of course the Schumpeterian paradigm. Interestingly, Nelson (1991) has more recently suggested that if there is an area which was underdeveloped in the 1982 work with Winter, it was consideration of the work of Alfred Chandler, and by implication hierarchy and spoke 3 perspectives. What the 1982 work does provide is clear guideposts signalling directions that economic analysis of technological change and the firm should take, and we shall pursue some implications of these guidelines later in this work.

2.5. Conclusions

The nature and behaviour of the firm considered as a device for allocating resources has been the subject of considerable interest for some years now, and a variety of alternative perspectives have been developed. Each approach has tended to begin from a hub-and-spoke relationship to the dominant paradigm in economics, neoclassical theory. The neoclassical hub revolves around the question of optimal product-market price. Each of these four components of the neoclassical hub has been subject to modification. One route has been to question the reasonableness of the optimality assumption and this spoke has pursued how decisions may be made in a world of imperfect information and limited cognitive abilities. Another route has been to replace the product as a basic building block in economics with the notion of resource, and this spoke explores how the firm can be characterized as an enduring entity, changing and adapting over time. A third route challenges the market mode as the sole basis for resource allocation and notionally opens up the idea of the firm as a hierarchically organized substitute for market exchange in certain circumstances. Finally, the Schumpeterian paradigm represents a distinctive spoke in its own right, and replaces price with technological change as the critical decision-making variable. Each of these approaches has made significant contributions to the analysis of the firm as a device for allocating resources, and the composite picture that emerges is of the firm as a hierarchically organized collection of resources making imperfect decisions in which technological change is typically the critical strategic variable. This composite picture of the firm is very different from the neoclassical agenda in which the firm is simply a black box responding automatically and optimally to changes in prices and costs. However, it is a frame of reference which will prove extremely useful in the succeeding chapters.

NOTES

1. See Milgrom and Roberts (1992, pp. 56–71) and Hart (1995, pp. 15–17) for good summaries of neoclassical theory in the context of the theory of the firm.
2. See Loasby (1976) and Langlois (1986c, pp. 225–30) for discussion for the implications of bounded rationality for decision-making.
3. See Arthur (1989) and David (1985, 1992) below.
4. It could be argued that Coase (1937) first put forward arguments for the existence of the firm. This is true and we discuss the transaction cost literature inspired by Coase further below. However, while Coase emphasized the role of the firm as a device for economizing on transaction costs of market exchange (where transactions were organized), Penrose focused more directly on the nature and composition of the firm (what was doing the organizing).
5. See Mahoney and Pandian (1992) and Peteraf (1993) for surveys of the contribution of resource-based approaches from the perspective of the strategic management literature.
6. Winter (1988, p. 177) similarly emphasizes 'the complex interdependence of sub-problems' that contributes to the 'performance of the system as a whole' and which in turn determines competitive advantage. He also notes with respect to capabilities that 'the fragment stored by each individual member is not fully meaningful or effective except in the context provided by the fragments stored by other members' (Winter, 1982, p. 76). This helps to illustrate the potential dangers and illusions inherent in perspectives suggesting that the firms may be reducible to a 'core' competence.

7. See Winter (1987, pp. 170–3), Dasgupta and David (1994, pp. 493–5), and Metcalfe (1995, pp. 34–5) for analysis of the differences between tacit and codifiable knowledge and discussion of some implications.

8. This is not to say that Porter's analysis and conclusions can always be accepted uncritically. His analysis suffers to some extent from the desire to make strong policy recommendations on the basis of a framework which is still in its early stages. For example, Porter (1990) argues at various points that competitive advantage is favourably influenced by well developed home demand, and rich and extensive clustering of related industries in a domestic context, while conglomerate strategies and a strongly interventionist government are likely to impede the development of national firms and industries. Korea has weak home demand, weak or non-existent industrial clusters, a tradition of strong governmental interference in industry, and its major corporations tend to have adopted conglomerate strategies. Porter warns that unless Korea mends its ways its growth will suffer as a consequence. This may well be true, but if it is, it still leaves the puzzle of why Korea has turned out to be one of the success stories of the late twentieth century while apparently doing all the wrong things.

9. See the responses by Williamson (1993*b*) and Coase (1993) in the same issue.

10. For example, in the automobile industry (Monteverde and Teece, 1982: Walker and Weber, 1984), electronic components (Anderson and Schmittlein, 1984), aerospace (Masten, 1984), coal (Joskow, 1985, 1987), aluminium (Stuckey, 1983: Hennart, 1988*b*), tin (Hennart, 1988*b*), naval shipbuilding (Masten *et al.*, 1991), samples of industries (Caves and Bradburd, 1988; John and Weitz, 1988) and the division of a manufacturing corporation (Walker and Poppo, 1991). See also Williamson (1985, pp. 103–30 and Joskow, (1988), for reviews of some of the early empirical evidence in this area.

11. It may be that (1) and (2) are opposite ends of a dimension, and that other outcomes can be generated by trading off security against opportunism in exchange for reduced monitoring and enforcement costs.

12. Nirvana may appear fainter and more distant in Williamson's approach, but it still appears as in the M-form hypothesis which states that 'the M-form favors goal pursuit and least-cost behaviour more nearly associated with the neoclassical hypothesis than does the U-form alternative' (1975, p. 150)

13. See Cantner and Hanusch (1994) for a summary of some of these fields of influence.

14. For example, my doctoral research (Kay, 1979) which surveyed a large number of studies in this area.

15. Friedman was more careful than many who have taken up this theme since he generally asserted that unrealistic assumptions are 'largely' irrelevant for assessing the validity of a theory (Blaug, 1992, p. 97). The qualifying adjective has often been lost in many subsequent translations of Friedman's argument.

16. Three blind mice/ see how they run/ They all ran after the farmer's wife/who cut off their tails with a carving knife/ did you ever see such a thing in your life/ as three blind mice? *anon.*

17. For one thing, it was probably an enabling factor in the mutilation of these unfortunate rodents by the farmer's wife.

18. At the same time, it should be recognized that organizational blindness in this context is selective. Organizations may more readily 'see' other types of

decisions made by rivals, such as those involving advertising campaigns, and physical investment or pricing decisions. Consequently, it may be possible to apply game theory to more visible situations, and the comments above may not be seen as being directly relevant to them.

19. In one of the most celebrated and quoted passages in economics, Friedman suggests the hypothesis that leaves are positioned around a tree 'as if' each deliberately sought to maximize the amount of sunshine it receives given the position of its neighbours. Friedman argues that despite the apparent falsity of the assumptions of the hypothesis, it has great plausibility because of the conformity of its implications with empirical evidence; for example, leaves are generally denser in sunlight than shade. Unfortunately, while this constructed hypothesis may give apparently accurate predictions in some cases, equally there are many other cases where it does not. Leaves may aid photosynthesis, and in that role it may well be the case that leaf arrangements approximate to those predicted by Friedman's constructed hypothesis; alternatively, they may be designed to capture insects (venus flytrap), store food (onion bulbs), capture and store water (agave), act as twining tendrils (vicia), or provide thorny protection (some cacti). In such cases, Friedman's constructed hypothesis will almost certainly give inaccurate predictions as to likely leaf arrangements. The solution to this problem is to identify functions and causal mechanisms.

20. In recent years public concern has grown in many countries with respect to possible health hazards from electro-magnetic fields associated with high-voltage power lines. Despite an apparent statistical connection being established in some studies between these fields and the incidence of certain cancers, controversy surrounded the findings since no proven mechanism had been found through which such cancers could be caused by electro-magnetic fields. However, in January 1996 researchers from the University of Bristol published findings in the *International Journal of Radiation Biology* which demonstrated that radon gas could be attracted to the source of an electro-magnetic field. Since radon gas occurs naturally and has been implicated as a carcinogenic substance in other studies, the study was widely regarded as providing for the first time a plausible causal mechanism running from the existence of electro-magnetic fields to the incidence of cancer. Despite the fact that the study contained absolutely no additional statistical evidence concerning the possible relationship between electro-magnetic fields and cancer, it was widely hailed as a scientific breakthrough. By identifying a possible causal mechanism, it helped provide a theoretical explanation for the statistical findings, and by suggesting refutable hypotheses the new study also provided foundations and directions for further scientific testing and experimentation.

21. Rumelt (1990) recently argued that if a bank manager was to stand in the street and set his trousers on fire, some game theorist would explain this as rational, and Postrel (1991) obligingly responded with a model of bank manager behaviour which had a subgame perfect Bayesian Nash equilibrium involving public immolation of the appropriate male apparel.

22. Kamien and Schwartz's (1982) survey possibly documents the high water mark of this research activity.

23. Two cases (digital switches and fibre optic cables) do seem to suggest that firms were responding to rivals' R&D decisions. In both cases, AT&T's Bell

Laboratories was involved, and it is conceivable that the open, science based culture of this institution could have created the conditions for a race. However, this would be more properly labelled science competition rather than technological competition.

24. Usually these projects also have cost or feasibility criteria applied to them before they are given approval (Nelson and Winter, 1982, p. 255).

3. Vertical Integration

We shall start with a puzzle. If we can answer it, then we hope it should enable us to say something about the nature and boundaries of the firm. According to Williamson, 'asset specificity refers to durable investments that are undertaken in support of particular transactions, the opportunity cost of which investments is much lower in best alternative uses or by alternative users should the original transaction be prematurely terminated' (Williamson, 1985, p. 55). Williamson argues that intermediate product-markets in which asset specificity combines with conditions of bounded rationality and opportunism are likely to be characterized by transaction costs. For example, if an asset has no alternative use, then the supplier of services using this asset is effectively locked into its relationship with the user. The user could then use its privileged position to opportunistically renegotiate the contract and force the supplier to provide services on even more advantageous terms to it. Such situations are characterized by substantial transaction costs and it may be difficult or impossible to create and maintain such arrangements. In such circumstances, these costs may be eliminated or reduced by the direct monitoring and control apparatus provided by internalizing markets within the firm. Consequently, exchanges characterized by asset specificity are likely to be carried out within the firm, while the market remains the appropriate (indeed efficient) mechanism for conducting transactions involving standardized assets (Williamson, 1985, pp. 78–9). He also notes that, 'transaction cost economics . . . maintains that the most important dimension for describing transactions is the condition of asset specificity' (p. 30) and 'the importance of asset specificity to transaction cost economics is difficult to exaggerate . . . the absence of asset specificity (would) vitiate much of transaction cost economics' (p. 56).

So our puzzle is, why do firms tend to contract out their advertising campaigns to an external agency, while generally preferring to do their own R&D? If there is an asset which could be said to be specialized by use and user, it is an advertising campaign, while the public good characteristics of R&D suggest that it is by definition a highly non-specific asset; indeed, the various issues associated with imitation, diffusion, and appropriability of innovative activity all start from an explicit or implicit recognition of the non-specificity of R&D in terms of its effects.

This should be an unsettling puzzle for transaction cost economists in view of its stated objectives; the approach aims to examine 'the comparative costs of planning, adapting and monitoring task completion under alternative governance structures' (Williamson, 1985, p. 2). This is an agenda that runs well beyond questions relating to the nature and the boundaries of the firm, but it does subsume such issues as part of its remit. Yet when the empirical analyses of the nature and the boundaries of the firm are actually subjected to audit, (Shelanski and Klein, 1995) it turns out that this question in transaction cost economics largely reduces to vertical relations with little mention of diversification, and even the analysis of vertical integration is itself largely restricted to within the production department and reduced to the economics of the make-or-buy decision for components. It is true that there have been other extensions (such as studies of forward integration from production into selling and distribution) and it is of course early days for such a new research programme, but the restricted scope of the explanations so far do appear rather disappointing. It is difficult to dissent from the opinion of Demsetz (1988) who argues that asset specificity is a 'frail reed upon which to build a theory of the firm. It is silent in regard to the survivability of firm-like organization in the absence of asset specificity, and it is directed primarily at explaining the vertical depth of firms rather than the existence of firms or other parts of their internal organization' (p. 153).

Our purpose in this chapter is to analyse the ability of transaction cost economics to deal with the particular problem in which it has specialized, vertical integration, and suggest alternative explanations if necessary. Williamson has claimed (1985, pp. 123–8) that in terms of its ability to explain the vertical integration decision, transaction cost economics has beaten all-comers (including theories built around domination, market power, technology, life cycle, pecuniary economies, and strategic behaviour). Certainly, as long as we concentrate on the production department, asset specificity does appear to give good indications as to whether or not the firm itself is likely to conduct the activity or contract it out to a supplier. For example, Monteverde and Teece (1982) found that Ford and General Motors tended to produce their own specially made components such as bumpers, radiators, shock absorbers, and steering gear, but were more likely to contract to outside suppliers for such standardized items as paint, steel, oil, and antifreeze. The economics of the make-or-buy decision has now become one of the most intensively studied topics in the modern theory of the firm (Holmstrom and Milgrom, 1994). But if transaction cost economics is to be represented as a general theory of vertical integration, it must explain integration and non-integration in other functions such as R&D and advertising as well as in the more limited scope of the production function. The problem is that when we leave the production department (and the make-or-buy decision for components), our puzzle suggest that things appear to be far less straightforward.

In the case of advertising, it could be argued that advertising is not a 'durable investment' as described by Williamson above, but this is not really persuasive: advertising can outlive particular components, processes and versions of products and indeed Nerlove and Arrow (1962) interpreted advertising as contributing to a stock of goodwill. Another possible reason why advertising agencies exist could be that there are economies of scale in the particular activities they are concerned with, leading to concentration in the hands of a few external firms. However, there is little evidence for the existence of economies of scale in this industry. Some firms such as Motorola and Bloomingdales actually do conduct their advertising in-house, with the general advantages of in-house agencies being reported as cost savings and speed of response to the firm's needs (Bovee and Arens, 1982, pp. 106–10). If significant economies of scale existed, such firms should find their in-house activities costly compared to externally sourced alternatives. Also, the existence of economies of scale should be picked up indirectly in terms of improved performance by firms that merge. However, Simon *et al.* (1996) found that advertising agency merger was associated with a worsening of merged firms' performance relative to non-merging controls. In fact, there were about 8,000 advertising agencies in the United States in 1982 employing only 82,000 employees. The mean size of about ten employees is typically lower than for other professions (Bovee and Arens, 1982, p. 116). While the top ten US agencies controlled 28 per cent of the volume of business in 1982 (Bovee and Arens, 1982, p. 116), it seems that the big and successful advertising firms are big because they are successful (Bovee and Arens, 1982, pp. 137–8), not successful because they are big. Thus, economies of scale do not appear to provide a credible explanation as to why contracting out advertising is so widespread.

As far as the non-specificity of R&D is concerned, this was noted in the particular context of industrial research by Penrose; 'a firm's opportunities are necessarily widened when it develops a specialized knowledge of a technology which is *not* in itself *very specific* to any particular kind of product, for example, knowledge of different types of engineering or industrial chemistry' (1959, p. 115, italics added). The non-specificity can be taken beyond the boundaries of the firm, for example in the form of appropriability problems; Teece (1987*a*) points out that tight appropriability (with ironclad protection of intellectual property rights) is the exception rather than the rule in industry (pp. 193–7), and indeed once innovations are out in the market place, many patents can be circumvented at modest cost (pp. 188–9). Thus, rated in terms of measures of asset specificity (whether in terms of specialization by use *or* user), the typical advertising campaign will rank extremely high on the scale, and the typical R&D project will certainly rank much lower. Which brings us back to our puzzle. Why do advertising agencies and corporate R&D labs exist, and indeed why do these institutions appear to represent the normal mechanisms through which the large modern corporation conducts its activities in the respective areas?

Before we tackle this question in section 3.3 below, we analyse the foundations of transaction cost economics in section 3.1. We then look at vertical integration in the oil industry in section 3.2, and long-term contracts as a substitute for vertical integration in section 3.4. A comparison of decision-making characteristics in markets and hierarchies is carried out in section 3.5.

3.1. The Question of the Nature of the Firm

The question as to why firms should exist was raised by Coase as follows:

As D. H. Robertson points out we find 'islands of conscious power in this ocean of unconscious co-operation like lumps of butter coagulating in a pail of buttermilk'.[1] But in view of the fact that it is usually argued that co-ordination will be done by the price mechanism, why is such organisation necessary? Why are there these 'islands of conscious power?' Outside the firm, price movements direct production, which is co-ordinated through a series of exchange transactions on the market. Within the firm, these market transactions are eliminated and in place of the complicated market structure with exchange transactions is substituted the entrepreneur-coordinator who directs production (Coase, 1937, p. 388).

The question that Coase poses is clearly set out; 'Our task is to discover why a firm emerges at all in a specialised market economy' (1937, p. 390). Coase concludes that there may be costs attached to market exchange (transaction costs) and firm organization may be substituted for market exchange if the costs of using the market to co-ordinate certain tasks exceed the costs of organizing them within a firm: 'the operation of a market costs something and by forming an organisation and allowing some authority (an "entrepreneur") to direct the resources, certain marketing costs are saved' (1937, p. 392). It is this signpost that has guided and instructed much subsequent research into the complementary issues of the possible sources of marketing (transaction) costs and organizational devices to overcome or reduce these costs. Once researchers were alerted to the possible existence of transaction costs, it quickly became almost a routine matter to identify them or infer them for a wide range of non-standardized transactions. The problems and costs of search, bargaining, and policing market agreements have been recognized to be exacerbated by the intrusion of moral hazard and opportunism in many circumstances. Much recent research has concentrated on identifying ways in which internal organization may be a lower cost solution in situations characterized by transaction costs.

Williamson's summary of his 'general approach to economic organization' embodies the perspective that these approaches to the nature of the firm have tended to follow: '(1) Markets and firms are alternative instruments for completing a related set of transactions; (2) whether a set of transactions ought to be executed across markets or within a firm depends on the relative efficiency of each mode' (1975, p. 8).[2] Thus, the question as to why firms exist is answered in terms of the lower cost of internal organization compared to market exchange in certain circumstances. This is entirely consistent with Coase's earlier analysis. The problem with such approaches to the nature of the firm is the focus on means and processes to the general exclusion of serious consideration of differences in purpose and function.

In this context, Grossman and Hart (1986, pp. 692–3) make the point that whilst the Coase/Williamson transaction cost perspective[3] shows that the cost of contracting between separately owned firms may be high, they do not elaborate on the benefits of organizing the transaction within the firm. Dietrich (1991, 1994) pushes this further and argues that transaction cost economics ignores the possibility that alternative forms of governance can affect revenues from various activities as well as costs. He points out that revenues from activities may be affected by issues such as differences in reputational effects and quality control between firms and markets. If these are ignored then transaction cost economics does not provide an adequate basis for comparing alternative forms of economic organization. Dietrich argues that transaction cost economics is 'only half a theory' (1994, p. 37) because possible benefits from resource allocation are ignored, and that benefits must be incorporated in transaction cost analysis if it is to provide a basis for a comparative analysis of economic organization.

Dietrich's arguments are correct and make a valuable contribution, but it could be argued that considerations of value have even deeper implications for transaction cost economics. Transaction cost economics not only generally neglects the possibility that demand side considerations are affected by mode of organization, it neglects value considerations generally. This can be demonstrated by considering Williamson's argument above that the question of whether a given set of transactions should be executed within the firm or across markets depends on the relative efficiency of the respective modes. This perspective is consistent with Coase's original argument concerning the limits to the size of the firm: 'a firm will tend to expand until the costs of organising an extra transaction within the firm become equal to the costs of carrying out the same transaction by means of an exchange on the open market or the costs of organising in another firm' (1937, p. 395). Building on this, Williamson (1985) develops a trade-off model of the comparative costs of corporate governance and market exchange in the case of vertical integration and concludes 'the fundamental limitation to firm size thus must turn on the comparative cost disabilities of internal organization where asset specificity is insubstantial' (pp. 131–2).

This fails to give an explanation for the limits to firm expansion and we can demonstrate this with a simple mental experiment. Suppose a diversified firm produces product A and that asset B is used in the fabrication of product A. Asset B has no other uses except in this context. Product A is extremely successful in the market place, but transaction costs involved in negotiating the use of asset B between our firm and the supplier mean that our firm decides to make asset B itself instead of buying it from its supplier, and the boundaries of the firm expand accordingly. So far we are merely following the logic of Williamson's interpretation of transaction cost economics as inspired by Coase's argument that the boundaries of the firm are determined by the relative costs of alternative forms of economic organization. But consider what happens if demand for product A suddenly disappears, say because of product obsolescence? Common sense and economic logic would tell us that the firm would cease production of product A and scrap asset B, with the boundaries of the firm receding accordingly. Yet there is no reason why organizational and transaction costs should be affected by changes in the derived demand for asset B, and so no mechanism by which such alteration of the boundaries of the firm can take place in transaction cost economics.

The problem is that if the costs of organizing a task within the firm are assessed as being lower than the costs of coordinating the task through a system of market contracts, then transaction cost economics would predict that the task would be internalized within the firm, and the firm would consequently expand in size. However, if the present value of the proposed task turns out to be negative once the stream of future revenues are compared to future costs for all forms of economic organization, it would be both inefficient and irrational to expand the firm and undertake the new task. Yet since transaction cost economics concerns itself with means to the neglect of what the firm is trying to achieve, that is exactly the kind of prediction that would be drawn from such analysis. Conversely, it is difficult to see how Coase's description of the limits to firms' expansion helps explain how firms actually expand their boundaries. In the 1980s, the boundaries of firms like Apple and Microsoft did not change because the relative cost of firm versus market organization suddenly shifted, but rather because they developed new opportunities that had value in the market place. Differential costs of governance may help explain why specific tasks are located in one organizational mode rather than another, but this is not the same thing as explaining why firms exist in the first place or why the boundaries of individual firms are set where they are. The neglect of value considerations in transaction cost economics means that its assessment of comparative cost is not the same as opportunity cost, and therefore it provides no basis for judging the comparative merits of alternative expansion *strategies*.

Transaction cost economics has a missing 'off switch': as long as costs of the market exceed the costs of firm organization, we have a signal for continued corporate expansion irrespective of value considerations. Indeed, the converse holds: as long as costs of market organization are less than costs of corporate organization, transaction cost economics would predict the expansion of markets. The relevant question regarding firm expansion in transaction cost economics is not *whether* a task should be organized, but *where* it should be organized. The Coasian explanation of corporate boundaries as being determined by the equating of marginal costs to alternative forms of organization must be wrong if we are not to find ourselves in an irrational world where it is sufficient to articulate a task to guarantee it will be worth organizing, the question then reducing to where it should be organized. Indeed, the economics of the make-or-buy decision highlights the narrow scope of the transaction cost perspective in that the decision on whether or not to internalize the making of the incremental component is only possible *once the firm has decided to make the product in the first place.* But what determines why the firm has decided to include this product within its boundaries in the first place? Asset specificity does not appear to give meaningful answers to this question, because it is not a question it is designed to deal with. However if transaction cost economics cannot explain why the boundaries of the firm include the product as well as its components, it appears as a rather weak and incomplete explanation, even in this restricted context.

Does an implicit assumption that transaction cost economics is only concerned with economically viable tasks save the analysis? Not really, because variation in non-cost task characteristics can still affect the nature and boundaries of various forms of economic organization, but there is no mechanism by which such considerations can be introduced into the means-dominated transaction cost agenda; it is, after all, termed the transaction *cost* approach, not the transaction value approach. Nor is this problem solved by a blanket assumption that the viability of projects has already been settled before choice of mode of organization is attended to. This is simply not possible since viability or value will depend on the costs of conducting tasks, and the fundamental thesis of transaction cost analysis itself is that this will in turn depend on choice of mode of task organization. The viability issue is inextricably bound up in the choice of mode of organizing tasks and cannot be treated implicitly as an issue which has somehow been settled *ex ante* the question of choice of form of economic organization.

The answers generated by transaction cost economics are means-oriented, and if the *questions* it concerned itself with were similarly restricted and narrowly defined, then it is less likely that such problems would arise. Unfortunately, the means oriented transaction cost approach is also presented as dealing with fundamental questions of why firms exist at all, and as we have seen it is in this context that particular difficulties become apparent. In the next section we shall explore these implications further.

3.2. Vertical Integration in the Petroleum Industry

It may be instructive to consider how transaction cost explanations can deal with the industry that is often cited as the archetypical case of vertical integration, the petroleum industry. The major firms in this industry tend to be active at all stages, from exploration and extraction of crude oil right through to distribution of the final product to the consumer, and ever since quantitative measures of vertical integration have been applied to various industrial sectors, petroleum has tended to stand out as an example of extreme vertical integration (e.g. Gort, 1962).[4] The petroleum industry would therefore appear an obvious area to try out asset specificity explanations for vertical integration.

However, Williamson does discuss vertical integration in petroleum in discussing the evidence on vertical integration (1985, pp. 102–30), but in the particular context of integration within the *refining* stage (pp. 105–6). For this particular stage, Williamson argues that considerations of human, physical, and site asset specificity tend to encourage vertical integration of refining operations. He suggests that these questions are rarely attended to because analysts commonly believe that the 'interesting questions of integration involve assessments of backward vertical integration into crude oil supply or forward integration into distribution of final product' (p. 106). However, while it is certainly the case that vertical integration within refineries has been typically neglected in favour of questions which analysts have regarded as more 'interesting', this does not necessarily make the more commonly raised questions less interesting or less in need of answering.

Klein *et al.* (1978) go further than Williamson in applying the specialized assets explanation to the petroleum industry. Like Williamson, they argue that specialized assets may lead to common ownership of different stages of the production process. They give the example of several oil wells located along a pipeline that leads to a cluster of independently owned refineries with no alternative crude supply at comparable cost. Klein *et al.* conclude that neither the well owners (producers) nor the refinery owners would wish to tolerate a situation in which the local monopoly of an independently owned pipeline could hold them hostage once they have entered into irreversible commitments of oilfield development or oil refinery control. Nor would the problem be resolved if either the producers or the refiners owned the pipeline, since the threat of monopoly (or monopsony) control would still hang over the excluded group. They conclude that in such circumstances, we would expect to find common ownership extending throughout all three stages, and they go on to cite evidence that this does in fact tend to be the case, with a common solution being joint ownership of the pipeline by producers and refiners, with shares in the pipeline company corresponding roughly to shares in the oil to be transported.

Pipelines and refineries are areas in which asset specificity arguments for vertical integration are most obviously applicable, if they are applicable at all. Clearly, construction or creation of relatively immobile assets within a refinery or around a pipeline does create potential hostages that may be vulnerable to opportunistic actions in the absence of unified governance. Yet internal refinery operations and pipeline transportation reflect only part of the process by which oil is converted and transported to the final consumer. At some point or points on its journey from reservoir to consumer, oil will tend to be shifted by sea, road, or rail, and *as soon as that happens the transaction cost (asset specificity) justification for vertical integration disappears.* Williamson and Klein *et al.* explicitly acknowledge that this holds for physically mobile assets such as trucks or ships; since they can be easily redeployed and accessed, asset specificity will typically be non-existent or negligible, and therefore market transactions can normally deal with users' needs for such transportation equipment effectively. However, what holds for transportation equipment holds equally for the commodities that they transport. Once standardized oil products are on the open seas or the open roads (or possibly even on an open rail network), the transaction cost explanation for vertical integration no longer applies, except in some special circumstances such as limited or closed local markets.

It should also be noted that pipelines are only economic in special circumstances. They tend to be uncompetitive compared to road or rail transport where smaller amounts are being distributed, and they are typically more costly than sea routing where the option exists to deploy tankers. Thus, the $9 billion Trans Alaska Pipeline (by some accounts the most expensive engineering project in history at time of construction) was only built after it was decided that the alternative of building and maintaining an oil terminal in the Arctic Ocean with year-round access was not a commercially viable solution in this instance. Pipelines usually only come into consideration when large volumes are to be regularly and predictably transported over distances considerably shorter than the tanker route, or in some cases where tanker access is otherwise problematic or impossible (Watkins, 1977, pp. 179–80). Thus, even if transaction cost considerations can provide explanations for vertical integration or co-ownership solutions over the limited and special domains of refineries or assets linked by pipelines, such explanations do not carry over into those stages and circumstances where standardized intermediate inputs are highly mobile and easily redeployable between transactors.

The question, 'why is the petroleum industry populated by large vertically integrated firms?' is one for which transaction cost economics has no convincing answer. There are typically stages and cases where the asset specificity condition is clearly breached, yet vertical integration is practised extensively. One way forward may be to reformulate the question. Suppose we were to rephrase the vertical integration question and focus it at the level of individual majors, for example 'why is Shell vertically integrated?' It is not difficult to find credible and convincing answers to this question for all the majors by simply considering the alternatives; if Shell were to divest its retail outlets and oil wells it would be vulnerable to the vagaries and whims of the market place in terms of finding supplies and outlets for its refining activities. This could be an expensive or even dangerous strategy in view of the thinness of the market for crude oil and the locking up of many retail outlets by its vertically integrated competitors. Fear of foreclosure, or simply concerns regarding reliable and predictable throughput, are rational and persuasive explanations for vertical integration in this context. Clearly these firms could withstand the removal of individual oil wells, or individual petrol stations. They are not likely to be highly dependent on individual assets considered one at a time. It is instead the collection of resources at each stage that constitute a significant commitment, and whose removal would signal major problems for the firms.

However, while this provides a rationale for maintaining vertical integration on the part of individual oil majors, it does not explain how the industry itself *developed* such patterns. The question, 'what triggered vertical integration in the first place?' also has to be addressed. In this context, a plausible counterfactual situation could be conceived in which the global oil industry was vertically disintegrated, with crude oil entirely transacted in the open market, and extractors, refiners and retailers specializing in the respective stages reflecting their core competencies. The existence of orderly and flexible markets for standardized intermediate oil products would remove the obvious transaction cost economics justifications for vertical integration. Indeed, such conditions would make it difficult or impossible to explain any subsequent vertical integration by firms as a consequence of transaction costs.

Seen from such a perspective, vertical integration in oil only begins to make sense when viewed in a historical context. The possible development of smoothly functioning competitive markets in oil markets has faced major impediments since its earliest days, with various drives towards monopoly, monopsony, and cartelization disrupting or threatening to disrupt the ability of stage-specialized firms to compete on equal terms with more dominant powers. A pivotal force helping shape the early development of the industry was John D. Rockefeller's Standard Oil Company in which moves towards monopoly control through horizontal and vertical integration were pursued aggressively through a variety of legal (and some illegal) means. In the late nineteenth century, Standard Oil's pursuit of economies of scale and dominance at the refining stage were augmented by the pursuit of vertical control through vertical integration in production, refining, and marketing (Chandler, 1990, pp. 73–4). For firms that did not wish to accept a subservient role to Standard in such circumstances, the typical defensive response was also to integrate vertically, and it is interesting to note that through such processes the American oil industry had been transformed from monopoly to oligopoly characterized by a high degree of vertical integration before the anti-trust decision to dissolve Standard Oil in 1911 (Chandler, 1990, p. 96).

Clearly the processes of growth and development in the oil industry are far more complex than this partial sketch allows us to illustrate, but it is sufficient to demonstrate that analysis of vertical integration in the oil industry may have to be couched in historical terms. The oil majors typically vertically integrated for strategic reasons, to ensure their survival or to enable them to achieve or maintain parity with their peers. They maintain vertical integration today for broadly similar reasons.

3.3. Specificity and Replaceability

We are now in a position to return to the puzzle with which we started the chapter, and we shall approach it by considering an example in which asset specificity is a central phenomenon. Until fairly recently, the seas around Scotland were criss-crossed with numerous ships owned by various companies transporting cargo and passengers to various parts of the Highlands and Islands. In many cases the sea was the only viable route through which contact could be maintained. However, improvements in road communications and a declining population has contributed to a decline in the sea transportation of goods and people. Over considerable areas of the Highlands and Islands the sea transport option now has local natural monopoly characteristics, which has typically led to the licensing of a single operator. Such an operator needs a variety of assets including ships, (which they typically own), access to a well qualified and experienced pool of potential crew members, and harbour facilities. Now, suppose we have a region in which a single ferry company is the only regular operator of shipping services, and it needs to crew its boats and secure harbour facilities. The ferry company faces minimal problems in finding a highly qualified pool of seamen to draw from. The decline in both domestic shipping and the UK merchant navy over past decades has tended to create an excess supply of locally based seamen. It is not unknown for even experienced captains, returning from overseas service, to have to take jobs at reduced rank in this particular region of Scotland.[5] At the same time, suppose a recent report commissioned by the local authority has suggested that the harbour facility currently used by the ferry company in this region (and owned by the authority) could also be used by yachts and fishermen. The company might find that the local authority overseeing the use of the harbour facilities sees more commercial potential in running the facility as a marina or a fishing port. The ferry company faces the threat of losing access to this facility and being sidelined to a grossly inferior one down the coast with the threat of considerable loss of business.

There are some simple but important points that this example brings out. First, the seamen in this region are characterized by a high degree of asset specificity. There is only one use (seamanship) and one user (the ferry company) for their services. Secondly, the harbour facility is characterized by an extremely low degree of asset specificity. It turns out that there are multiple uses to which the harbour may be put, and multiple potential users of the facility. The difficulty for a transaction cost interpretation of this state of affairs is that asset specificity absolutely does not create a problem for the ferry company in the case of the labour market, since it is easy to get replacement seamen if the need arises, while low asset specificity creates considerable transactional problems in the case of the harbour facility, since the discovery of alternative uses for the asset poses a direct threat to the viability of the ferry company's business in this region. If there is a transactional relation in which the ferry company has a strong incentive to fashion safeguards (such as long-term contracts or even vertical integration), it is with respect to the asset characterized by asset non-specificity, the harbour facility. This is the opposite to that predicted by transaction cost economics. How do we resolve these apparent inconsistencies?

The answer is that we can do so very simply. As in the case of the vertical integrated oil majors discussed in the last section, it is not the lack of alternative opportunities for the asset in question (asset specificity) which creates problems for the firm, but the lack of equivalent or similar substitute assets should the present ones no longer be available. It does not matter as far as the running of the ferry company is concerned whether or not anything else can be done with the particular assets it deals with. It *does* matter if it cannot easily replace these assets if they are no longer available. The key issue is replaceability of assets, not specificity of assets, and the two have no necessary relation to each other. It may seem obvious to state this, but it is not the view from the asset that is important as far as the boundaries of the firm is concerned. What is important is the view from the firm.

We can now make a fresh attempt to deal with the puzzle we started the chapter with. Asset specificity seems to work quite well as an explanation of whether the production department will produce a component in-house or contract it to an outside supplier. However, it appears to perform very badly as an explanation when we move out of production and look at how other functions are performed. So why should highly specific advertising typically be contracted out, while R&D (which is normally much less specific to use and user) tends to be performed in-house? The key to understanding this apparently perverse behaviour involves a switch of perspective. The transaction cost perspective is with respect to *market* opportunities for the asset; asset specificity refers to the opportunity cost of assets *outside* the firm; However, this does not necessarily tell us anything at all about how the assets relate to other assets *within* the firm, and the ease with which they could be replaced if this proves necessary. It is this latter (resource-based) perspective which is more appropriate for dealing with questions as to whether a particular resource should lie inside or outside the boundaries of the firm. In this respect, the important question is not degree of *specificity* (with respect to market opportunities), but ease of *replaceability* (from external market sources). In some contexts (such as production) these two questions lead to very similar answers, while in others (such as R&D and advertising) the transaction cost and resource-based answers as to where the asset should be located can be very different indeed. It should also be noted that questions of appropriability of assets are subsidiary to questions of their replaceability. If assets can be easily replaced then appropriability ceases to be an area of potential concern for the firm.

For example, Canon has identifiable competencies in precision mechanics, fine optics and microelectronics (Prahalad and Hamel, 1990). To the extent that these skills lend themselves to diversification opportunities and appropriability problems, they will rate very low when assessed in terms of degree of asset specificity, though tacitness, secrecy, and patents may mitigate appropriability problems for Canon. However, the existence of these opportunities *outside* the particular use or user tell us nothing directly about the contribution that these competencies make *inside* the firm itself. Indeed the only hint that non-specificity provides in this context is that Prahalad and Hamel describe such competencies as the glue binding together the businesses of the firm and the engine for new business development. Such low specificity in this context is liable to strengthen rather than weaken the desire of rational management to bring these competencies within the boundaries of the firm. The issue that firms like Canon have to consider is not the value of their assets to someone else, but how important is the contribution of these assets to the firm, and how difficult would it be to replace them should the need arise. If the answer to the last two questions is 'very', the firm is more likely to organize control over the assets within the firm.

Loasby (1967) anticipates these issues by pointing out that one of the advantages of planning is that it helps to articulate interdependencies with other parts of the organization, and these points can be interpreted more widely as providing a justification for hierarchy over market alternatives. Bearing in mind the points we made in Chapter 2, this does not automatically imply the existence of 'unique' or 'distinctive' assets. It may be particular characteristics and complementarities associated with a combination of assets that are distinctive and difficult to replace as far as the firm is concerned.

We must now return to the role of R&D in our first puzzle. The credentials of R&D in terms of non-specificity were first set out at the start of this chapter following Teece (1987a). Teece goes on to argue that the decision as to whether to internalize a particular asset involved in the innovative process reflects whether or not that asset is critical to the success of the venture, with 'critical resources' being the ones most likely to be internalized (1987a, pp. 201–7). By implication, if an asset is difficult or impossible to replace, it may be regarded as a 'critical asset' in this context. But note that this is a very different question from asset specificity; asset specificity focuses on alternative opportunities for the resource *into* the market place. Replaceability focuses on substitution possibilities for the resource *from* the market place. For example, when Pisano (1990, p. 158) talks of 'transaction-specific' investments made by some firms that do negotiate R&D contracts in the biotechnology industry, he is really talking about replaceability; 'whether such investments are transaction-specific and allow the R&D supplier to bargain opportunistically depends on the sponsor's options for transferring the project to an alternative supplier'.[6] If a firm has expended a lot of resources in-house in helping an R&D engineer get to the leading edge in fuel efficient technologies, then interest from competitors in poaching this expert may confirm the non-specificity of his or her skills, while at the same time the firm may find it difficult or impossible to replace his or her particular skills and experience in the R&D team. Non-specificity of the resource with respect to exit opportunities may co-exist with non-availability of close substitutes in the market for the firm left stranded.

Mowery (1983) points out that 'as firms grow in size and structural complexity, the more complex, riskier research project, with severe requirements for interaction and information exchange among various corporate functions, should form the core of their in-house research activities;[7] the acquisition of (in-house research) knowledge is a dynamic, cumulative learning process, which relies upon the preservation of continuity in research projects and personnel for its effectiveness' (p. 355). Thus, Teece, Pisano and Mowery all emphasize that it is the relationship between R&D and other resources that is crucial to the internalization decision. If there are a number of potential substitute suppliers of the research (Pisano, 1990, pp. 171 and 174) or if the R&D project involves generic research or detachable and separable aspects of a firm's operations (Mowery, 1983, p. 355), then the firm becomes more likely to offer a contract to a separate firm to supply the research. Where R&D is more liable to be internalized is in the areas of research which are highly integrated with the other activities of the firm, and which are not easily replaceable from outside sources.

We also have to account for the observation that external contracting is the norm in the advertising business, with advertising agencies supplying highly firm-specific and product-specific services to client firms. Why do firms not undertake the service themselves, given the apparent absence of economies of scale and the apparent transaction-cost hazards of such transaction-specific activities? A partial answer is that the threat of opportunistic recontracting by the agency may effectively be zero in this context. Suppose a contract is nearing product launch and the agency did try to renegotiate its fee by 'holding-up' the client and threatening delay, reasoning in the process that its client now has no freedom to manoeuvre and can therefore be held to ransom? If one of the 'greatest sins' in the advertising agency business is to miss a deadline (Bovee and Arens, 1982, p. 127), it would be interesting to see where opportunistic recontracting would rate in the industry's list of most heinous crimes, were an agency ever adventurous enough to try it out. Most advertising agencies get their clients through word of mouth (Bovee and Arens, 1982, p. 138). It is to be presumed that it would be even easier to lose clients through the same mechanism, especially if there are other agencies willing and able to step into the transgressor's shoes. The price of opportunistic recontracting would be guaranteed loss of one client to begin with, with other clients also liable to reconsider their position with such an agency. It is unlikely to be a serious issue in this industry and there is no evidence that it is. Incidentally this has interesting implications for the relevance of the supposed 'hold-up' problem, especially in view of Coase's and Demsetz's stated opinion that they do not believe that asset specificity necessarily leads to problems that cannot be handled by market contracts (Coase, 1988*b*, pp. 42–3: Demsetz, 1988, p. 153).

Other dangers that have been associated with in-house advertising agencies include the stifling of creativity and the reduction of variety and flexibility arising from making advertising an in-house activity (Bovee and Arens, 1982, p. 110). These arguments certainly do have a plausible ring to them, but it is interesting to note that essentially similar arguments have been made in the past concerning the dangers of institutionalizing R&D within the firm. Indeed, there has been considerable interest in recent years in techniques developed by companies to counteract the dangers of bureaucratization and to stimulate innovative activity within the firm.[8] The problem is not that the 'dangers of institutionalisation' argument does not have weight considered in isolation, rather the problem is that it does not take us very far in explaining why R&D is typically carried out internally but advertising is typically undertaken by an outside contractor.

In fact, the question of potential replaceability provides a good explanation as to why advertising is so often carried on by outside agents. If opportunistic recontracting is not a problem, the issue of replaceability during a contract is unlikely to be a serious issue for the client except in unusual cases;[9] instead, the question of replaceability is more likely to be contingent on client evaluation of agency performance, and may reflect client dissatisfaction, and/or positive reports on alternative agencies. In view of the importance agencies place on seeking new business and their general availability and openness in this regard (Bovee and Arens, 1982, p. 128), agency availability does not appear to be regarded as a major issue in this industry. Also, successive campaigns (even for the same product) are frequently episodic and differentiated from each other, an enabling factor in terms of potential detachability and substitutability of agencies seen from the perspective of clients. To put it in perspective, if an agency did not seek to renew its contract with the firm, this is likely to be regarded as a less serious issue than if the corporate R&D team resigned *en masse*.

Thus, a firm's R&D may be both an integral aspect of its operations, and something that could considerably benefit its competitors if they could get their hands on it. On the other hand, a firm's advertising may be completely product-specific, but the firm may regard its relationship with its agency as contingent on adequate performance. There is no conflict in R&D activity being a non-specific public good *and* highly integrated with the other activities or routines of the firm, while advertising agency work tends to be highly product-specific *and* potentially detachable and replaceable. A transaction cost perspective would focus on the first condition in the respective cases (degree of asset specificity) while a resource-based perspective would focus on the second (ease of detachability and replaceability). The first perspective would lead us to expect that advertising would be more likely than R&D to be conducted in-house, while the second perspective would lead us to expect the reverse.

But this still leaves the results of tests of asset specificity in the context of the production process to be explained. The solution here is that in this context, low asset specificity actually *does* coincide with high replaceability, and vice versa. From the point of view of the firm, it may be easy to find replacement supplies of standardized components like paint. Again, seen from the point of view of the firm, it may be less easy to obtain replacement supplies of specially made components like shock absorbers. The transaction cost perspective would suggest that the component associated with a higher degree of asset specificity (shock absorbers) would be more likely to be internalized. The resource-based perspective would suggest that the asset potentially associated with greater problems of replaceability would be more likely to be internalized (again, shock absorbers). As long as asset specificity and ease of replaceability are inversely related to each other (as they tend to be in the case of components and the economics of the make-or-buy decision), then transaction cost economics and the resource-based perspective tend to make similar predictions. However, moving out of production and into other functions appears to sever the inverse relationship between specificity and replaceability, and we find ourselves faced with cases in which resources can be rated low in terms of both specificity and replaceability (R&D) and cases in which they can be rated high in terms of both criteria (advertising). In such cases the transaction cost explanation is clearly seen to be faulty.

Lastly, we can also clarify important relational differences between the notion of dependence and replaceability. The idea that the firm may be dependent on particular resources is a theme that has been picked up in the organizational (Pfeffer and Salancik, 1978, 46–54) and economics literatures (Alchian and Woodward, 1987, p. 114). However, it is actually very difficult to identify resources used by an organization that it is not in turn dependent on.[10] For example, most organizations would find it very difficult to function effectively without copious and regular supplies of paper, but that is not an issue that usually appears on the corporate agenda. If a supplier fails to perform satisfactorily, most corporations are in a position to turn to alternative suppliers easily and effectively. The important issue is not how dependent firms are on particular assets, but how easily a firm could replace the services provided by particular assets or combinations of assets if these were no longer available to the firm. The notion of problems of replaceability (and associated search and investment costs) is implied in Alchian and Woodward's discussion (1987, p. 114) of problems caused by the departure of a resource that is 'depended upon'.

3.4. Long-term Contracts and Vertical Integration

One more puzzle: why do long-term contracts between record labels and artists exist in the music industry? The obvious reason is that a label may make substantial investments in developing and promoting acts such as singer/songwriters in order to try to create a commercial success. In some respects these investments may resemble R&D investments in the pharmaceutical industry, since there can be a high degree of uncertainty as to which investments will turn out to be commercial successes and which will be flops. However, if the act eventually turns out to be valuable to the record label, it is likely to be viewed as a potentially valuable property by other labels also: 'after a songwriter becomes established he has an incentive to take advantage of any initial investment made by a publishing firm and shift to another publisher' (Klein, 1980, p. 361). Since record label executives will want to protect their earlier investments and internalize as much of the benefits as possible, the industry has been characterized by restrictive long-term contracts between label and artists, as well as by frequent attempts by artists to 'escape' (often through legal redress) from what may be represented in court as draconian restrictions on their personal and artistic freedom.[11] Klein (1980) cites a case of an ten-year exclusive service agreement between a songwriter and a music publisher which was only made void by the English courts on the basis of a doctrine of inequality of bargaining power.[12] In such an industry, low specificity (and substantial opportunity costs in terms of commercial opportunities for the group or artist *in the market place*) goes hand in hand with low replaceability (and the lack of ease with which the group or artist can be replaced *in the firm*). Again, this is the reverse of the typical case involving tangible assets (and the economics of the make-or-buy decision) in which low specificity tends to signal high replaceability.

However, transaction cost economics interprets long-term contracts as arising from essentially the same reasons as vertical integration, and tending to be turned to when vertical integration is not possible: 'transaction cost economics further predicts that if, for regulatory or other reasons, prohibitions or penalties against vertical integration for these transactions are posed, then long-term contracts will be devised in which bilateral (private ordering) safeguards are carefully crafted' (Williamson, 1985, p. 106). Williamson sets the discussion here in the context of transactions within a refinery involving a high degree of asset specificity (e.g. site specificity of storage tanks and asphalt units; site and human asset specificity of the quality control laboratories), but the argument follows from general transaction cost reasoning in cases involving asset specificity. Certainly, vertical integration in the sense of complete ownership of assets is not possible in the case of recording artists—the abolition of slavery constituting an obvious regulatory barrier—and consequently conventional contracts generally follow legalistic rather than Faustian traditions. But transaction cost economics does not explain the attempts of record labels to devise schemes to lock their 'properties' into enduring long-term contracts in cases where the problem is that these assets are demonstrably *not* specialized to a particular user. The explanation that labels try to lock up assets precisely because they might be tempted to walk out of the door is not the kind of answer provided by transaction cost economics.

Williamson's interpretation of long-term contracts as arising from the same asset specificity roots as vertical integration draws on a study by Joskow (1985) of vertical integration and long-term contracts involving coal-burning electricity generating plants. Joskow concentrates particularly on the case of mine-mouth plants which he suggests are 'characterized by at least three of the four types of asset specificity identified by Williamson: (a) site specificity—the plant and mine are deliberately located next to one another to minimize costs; (b) physical asset specificity—the plant is designed to burn the particular types of coal in the adjacent reserves; and (c) dedicated assets—the mine would not be built but for the promise of supplies from the adjacent plant, and the plant would not be built but for the availability of coal from the adjacent mine' (1985, p. 47). Joskow does indeed find that such relationships tend to be characterized by either vertical integration or long-term contracts.

The problem here is that only the mining investments could be characterized as involving asset specificity in the transaction cost sense; bear in mind that the definition of asset specificity is that the value of the asset is much lower 'in best alternative uses or (to) alternative users should the original transaction be prematurely terminated' (Williamson, 1985, p. 55). While there may be implications for the use or users to which the output of the plant (as opposed to the mine) may be oriented following the location decision, this is *not* why plant owners wish to forge long-term contracts in fear of possible termination of the supply arrangement; the reason is again the replaceability issue, in this case in terms of comparable supplies or suppliers of fuel.

Williamson (1985, p. 62) suggests that the effects of the supplier making specialized investments are often symmetrical 'in that the buyer cannot turn to alternative sources of supply and obtain the item on favorable terms, since the cost of supply from unspecialised capital is presumably great'. It may indeed be the case that such reciprocal dependence is involved in the supplier making specialized investments, and something like this certainly seems to be at work in the economics of the make-or-buy decision. However, the influences that decide supplier dependence on the user are different from those that decide user dependence on the supplier, and it is extremely easy to draw up plausible scenarios based on the proximity of alternative mines and/or coal-burning plants that may tilt the balance of dependency one way or another. Indeed, the message of our analysis of component purchase, R&D, advertising, and music contracts is that vulnerability may be mutual in some cases but unilateral in others. In the cases of the record label and power station, the respective managements have strong incentives to insist on long-term contracts, irrespective of the asset specificity condition on the supply side—which indeed may be low in the case of the pop group and high in the case of the dedicated coal mine. A perspective designed to analyse dependence simply from the perspective of asset specificity is too narrow and biased a perspective to explain how firms organize the governance of resources. Instead, concerns with potential replaceability do help to explain why firms wish to fashion long-term contracts in both the music and the energy industries.

3.5. The Nature of Decisions in Markets and Hierarchies

The replaceability issue helps us to make some progress in explaining the boundaries of the firm. However, there is a further issue that we need to consider and which will be important in subsequent discussion; how are decisions concerning resource allocation made? It is possible to see quite different devices by which firms coordinate resources depending on one's perspective, experience, and intellectual and ideological outlook. As Putterman (1986, pp. 5–6) points out, for some theorists in this area the firm is seen as a hierarchical entity distinct from the markets' price system, whilst for others it is a nexus of contracts not readily distinguishable from the market environment. The former perspective is generally regarded as more sympathetic to Coase's original interpretation, but Coase (1988*a*) has recently argued that he always acknowledged the role that contract has to play in the internal operations of the firm.

The range of potential interpretations can be observed by comparing Mintzberg's (1979) analysis with that of Jensen and Meckling (1986). Economists like Jensen and Meckling are concerned with 'the division of labour into various tasks to be performed and the coordination of these tasks to accomplish the activity. The structure of an organisation can be defined simply as the sum total of the ways in which it divides its labour into different tasks and then achieves coordination among them'. However this quote is not Jensen and Meckling setting out their research agenda, but Mintzberg (p. 3). Yet the *mechanisms* by which organizations coordinate tasks in Mintzberg's analysis bears no resemblance to those identified by Jensen and Meckling. In Mintzberg, 'five coordinating mechanisms seem to explain the fundamental ways in which organisations coordinate their work: mutual adjustment,[13] direct supervision, standardisation of work processes, standardisation of work outputs, and standardisation of worker skills' (1979, p. 4). However, for Jensen and Meckling, 'contractual relations are the essence of the firm' (p. 215), while the firm 'serves as a focus for a complex process in which the conflicting objectives of individuals (some of which may "represent" other organisations) are brought into equilibrium within a framework of contractual relations. In this sense the "behaviour" of the firm is like the behaviour of a market' (1986, pp. 216–17).

Thus, Mintzberg and Jensen and Meckling appear to share the same research agenda (how is resource allocation coordinated within the firm?), yet there appear to be incompatible answers as to how such coordination takes place. For Jensen and Meckling, the 'essence' of coordination in a firm is found in contractual relations, while for Mintzberg the 'fundamental ways' in which coordination takes place involve the non-contractual mechanisms of authority, communication, and/or standardization. It is clear from their subsequent discussion that there is a strong overlap in terms of the types of organizations they are describing,[14] which raises such interesting questions as how such divergent and apparently incompatible interpretations can be sustained.

Nor does the literature on incomplete contracts[15] help much in terms of clarifying how resources are coordinated within the firm. This literature recognizes the information costs of search, negotiation, and policing involved in making market transactions in many cases, as well as the role of the firm in helping to overcome or reduce such costs. It could be argued that an incomplete contract may tell us why the player is playing in the stadium, but that does not tell us much about how he is going to perform his work now he has arrived there. To see the firm as a contractual hierarchy as in Williamson's analysis, or characterized by incomplete contracts as in Jensen and Mecklings' case is really to beg the question.

The problem of how resources may be coordinated within the firm may be clarified a bit further with reference to Coase's original analysis which set out this research agenda: 'in the real world, we find that there are many areas where the (allocation of factors by the price mechanism) does not apply. If a workman moves from department Y to department X, he does not go because of a change in relative prices, but because he is ordered to do so.' However, Coase's strong statement is not necessarily supported by observation of real world processes. Whilst a workman may move between departments because he is ordered to do so (the exercise of authority), he may decide to do so himself because it may assist in carrying out a task that has been delegated to him (e.g. to obtain a tool or advice and help). Also, if the department is distant (e.g. abroad), his move may be subject to discussion, negotiation, and joint agreement with his superiors. Further, and contrary to Coase's categorical statement, departmental moves can and do take place within the firm because of a change in relative prices; another subsidiary of the firm may internally advertise a position with a higher wage than that presently enjoyed by the workman, and he may apply for, and receive, an internal move.

Thus, such internal shifts of resources may be effected by instruments that include (1) imposed decisions, (2) autonomous decisions, (3) joint or negotiated decisions, or (4) internal market decisions. Specifying one set of instruments as being *the* definitive mechanisms through which the firm coordinates resources would appear to be inappropriate and even misleading. Such explicit recognition of the considerable diversity of coordinating mechanisms that the firm may invoke would appear to present real difficulties for an orderly analysis of the nature of the firm. If anything can, and does, go in this context, how are we to identify distinguishing characteristics of the firm as an institution? The solution is implied by our earlier discussion. These coordinating devices are all means for effecting and implementing decisions. The key to understanding the nature of the firm lies in exploring the ends to which it is oriented. This requires us to investigate the nature of the decisions which the firm is designed for, rather than just focusing research on the devices for putting decisions into practice and policing them.

This exercise can be considerably simplified if some basic features of markets and hierarchies in terms of their relationship to decision-making is concerned are pointed out. A market exchange agreement can be taken to represent an agreement that reflects decisions taken by the respective parties about how resources should be allocated. For example, a contract to ship ten tons of ore at a specified price reflects the seller's past decision to sell at that price and the corresponding decision of the buyer to buy at that price. However, if we look at a hierarchy (say any organizational chart of a large firm) the implications for decision-making are quite different. What an organizational structure does is put into place capabilities for *future* decision-making. A manager holds his or her position in the firm in order to participate in decision-making in the future. While they may have got there on the basis of past decisions, they exist in the hierarchy solely to make future decisions. Effectively, hierarchy is a device for procrastination. Market agreements and their supporting contracts are the embodiment of past decisions, while hierarchy enables future decisions.

If we define hierarchies in contractual terms and the firm as a series of internal markets, the possibility that markets and hierarchy may have different comparative advantages in relation to qualitatively different types of decision is obscured. For example, hierarchy is particularly suited for cases in which strategic decisions involving the coordination of resources remain to be made in the future, or over a period of time. By 'strategic' in this context is meant decisions involving the nature and characteristics of what the end result of coordination is to be, what is to be coordinated, how the coordination is to be effected, and so on. Hierarchy facilitates continuity of association of potentially interrelated resources within the umbrella of organization in the face of uncertainty without the need to specify precisely what the nature of future coordination will be. On the other hand, markets are particularly suited for situations in which only operational decisions involving the coordination of resources remain to be made, strategic issues having been largely or entirely resolved. By 'operational' is meant decisions involving standardized and routine variables such as quantity, price, grade, delivery time, etc.

Strategic options and decisions that reflect resource interdependencies in the *future* may require commitments to be made in the *present*. Unless the R&D scientist is employed today, he or she will not be given access to the firm's R&D labs to help contribute towards developing the products of tomorrow. The issues surrounding strategic decisions to be made involving cases in which the scientist has been an element (e.g. a proposed new drug) may usually become clearer over time, but unless he or she has been employed at earlier stages his or her contribution would not have been made in the first place. The firm reflects the fact that strategic decisions may have to be deferred, or be streamed over time, but that commitments still have to be made now to enable these future decisions to be made at all. The firm is a device that facilitates the connection of these future decisions to present commitments. Thus, the R&D scientist may contribute to future innovation in exchange for present benefits, while the firm may be in an improved position with respect to future strategic decisions as a consequence of these past commitments. It is misleading to talk of activities such as R&D being internalized by the modern corporation, since that implies the firm is simply carrying out activities that would otherwise be carried out by the market but at a higher cost. The organized corporate R&D laboratories that Schumpeter (1942) saw as being the mark of the modern corporation were not developed to reduce R&D costs. They were developed to create possibilities and outcomes that market co-ordination would not have achieved in the first place.

The idea of connectedness over time of the firm's strategic decisions and commitments is the basis of Loasby's 1967 article on long range formal planning. The advantages of long range planning cited by Loasby include the explication of the future implications of present decisions, the present implications of future events, and the securing of commitments to future action as a basis for monitoring performance. Although Loasby's article is intended as a critique of long range planning it can also be read more broadly as unintendedly providing a justification for the existence of hierarchy. Remove hierarchy as a device for maintaining the association of its constituent resources and you remove the institution that facilitates connection between present actions and future outcomes.

By way of contrast, contractual arrangements tend to be intolerant of situations in which future strategic options and decisions require present commitments. Such arrangements typically involve real commitment of resources in the present (e.g. R&D scientist time in exchange for salary and lab access) on the expectation of unspecified or incompletely specified gains in the future (e.g. new ideas from the scientist, possibly continuity and security of employment from the employer). Whilst the possibility of opportunistic behaviour may certainly create problems in dealing with such problems through contractual means, the fundamental problem here is that contract typically contains no systematic provisions for making decisions in the future. Presumably arbitration could be agreed if parties recognize the possibility of future conflicts in the light of unfolding events, but this would be an administered solution, an *ad hoc* hierarchy in effect. Rather than rely on *ad hoc* situations, stable hierarchies provide an orderly foundation for the making of future decisions. The comparative advantage of markets remains in areas in which the gains from the association of parties can be well specified, such as exchanges in agriculture and commodity markets in which what is on offer can typically be measured, scaled, or allocated to standard grades.

This leads us to one last point which we shall pick up again in later chapters. As our example of the redeployment of the workman within the firm suggests, questions relating to the siting of the boundaries of the firm and questions relating to the need for hierarchy are not necessarily the same thing. For example, questions of replaceability may lead to oil companies vertically integrating, but the coordination of resources between some stages may be effected by transfer pricing. On the other hand, two oil companies may agree to jointly explore the prospects for developing a new oil field. Since there is considerable uncertainty as to what the real potential of the field is, they may set up a co-owned (and co-administered) subsidiary as a joint venture and provide the 'child' with appropriate decision-making capacity to help it cope with unfolding events. The first represents the construction of a market within a firm, the second represents the construction of a hierarchy between firms. Whilst we may normally expect to see inter-firm relations expressed in market terms, and intra-firm relations expressed in hierarchical terms, these examples help to emphasize that questions as to what determines the boundaries of the firm are not necessarily the same as questions as to what determines the adoption of hierarchy.

3.6. Conclusions

Resources do not stick to the firm because they have nowhere else to go as in transaction cost economics; they stick to the firm because they are glued to it. The answer to the riddle of why firms vertically integrate is not to be found in the opportunities for resources in the market place; it is to be found in the role of that resource in the activities of the firm. Asset specificity does not explain why firms vertically integrate. Instead, issues associated with asset replaceability (including appropriability) provide a better guide as to why firms prefer to vertically integrate in certain circumstances and not in others. The resource-based explanation appears to offer a simple and satisfactory explanation that accounts for important decisions in all three contexts: production, R&D, and advertising. We conclude that the questions of vertical integration and long-term contracts do not revolve around questions of degree of asset specificity (with respect to market alternatives) but are more closely connected instead to issues of resource replaceability (with respect to the role of the resource in the firm). It was also argued that hierarchy is essentially a device for deferring decisions; whilst contract tends to embody past decision-making, hierarchy facilitates future decision-making. Finally we note that, while replaceability issues may improve on the asset specificity explanations for vertical integration, we still need to explain how and why individual firms operate in particular areas of economic activity. For this we need to build up a resource or competence-based picture of the firm, and this will be our task in most of the remaining chapters.

NOTES

1. D. H. Robertson (1930) p. 85.
2. Williamson lists two other characteristics of his approach relating to the human and environmental characteristics that contribute to transaction costs.
3. Grossman and Hart also include Klein *et al.* (1978) in this description of the transaction cost perspective.
4. See Scherer and Ross (1990, pp. 94–6) for an analysis of some problems attached to the empirical measurement of degrees of vertical integration in practice.
5. Of course, eventually this pool of experienced seamen will dwindle as they age and retire from the labour market. However, all it would take to maintain a significant pool of seamen in the (small) domestic market would be for it to be replenished by seamen wishing to return to a domestic base from overseas service (say for family reasons).
6. We shall look at possible reasons for the evolution of cooperative agreements in industries such as biotechnology (especially those involving R&D) in Chapters 10 and 11.
7. Mowery also talks about the 'specificity' of acquired technical knowledge, but since this arises from jointness in production and technical knowledge activities (p. 355), it appears that what he is talking about in terms of specificity should be interpreted in terms of potential difficulties of replacing these assets should the need arise.

8. See, for example, Miller and Dess (1996, pp. 261–4) for various corporate solutions to this problem.
9. Events which may stimulate considerations of replaceability might include the deaths or departure of key personnel; however, these could be issues even if the advertising was carried on in-house.
10. Thus, Pfeffer and Salancik (1978, pp. 46–7) suggest there are two important dimensions to how important a resource is to an organization, the magnitude of the exchanges involved and the criticality of the resource. Criticality is defined in terms of the 'ability of the organization to continue functioning in the absence of the resource or in the absence of the market for the output' (p. 46). This would certainly seem to imply that paper would be a critical resource for most organizations. The reason that this is not usually an issue from the point of view of corporate governance is that disruption in paper supplies can typically be handled by turning to alternative sources; the important point is that paper used by the firm may be a critical resource, but it is also highly replaceable if particular supplies dry up. This is implicitly recognized by Pfeffer and Salancik when they acknowledge that even for 'important' resources there is no problem for the organization as long as supplies are stable and ample (1978, p. 47).
11. The recent well publicized dispute between the singer George Michael and Sony is a case in point.
12. Interestingly, Klein (1980) also prefaces his discussion of cases (which includes the songwriter example) by acknowledging Williamson's contribution and referring to the problem of 'hold up' that exists when 'a firm invests in an asset with a low-salvage value and a quasi-rent stream highly dependent on some other asset' (1980, p. 357). Clearly, neither of these conditions hold here with respect to the asset in question. The problem for the firm is that the value of the asset is *not* dependent on the firm that made the earlier investment.
13. Mutual adjustment is defined by Mintzberg as 'the coordination of work by the simple process of informal communication' (1979, p. 3).
14. Thus, Jensen and Meckling make it clear they believe their analysis is potentially applicable to corporations, non-profit organizations (such as universities), mutual organizations, cooperatives, some clubs and some government agencies (1986, p. 215). The topics and examples covered by Mintzberg indicate that his analysis is intended to have fairly similar range and coverage.
15. See Hart and Holmstrom (1987) for a survey of this literature.

4. Links and Patterns

As we noted in the previous chapter, transaction cost analysis of the determinants of the boundaries of the firm has tended to become synonymous
with the economics of the make-or-buy decision in the empirical literature.
However, there are difficulties with this interpretation. It is first worth noting that it tends to identify vertical relations as the focus for questions concerning the boundaries of the firm. In practice, questions of corporate scale
and growth tend to be more strongly marked by diversification rather than
by vertical integration. Indeed, Scherer and Ross (1990, p. 96) conclude that
patterns of vertical integration have changed little in American industry
over the course of this century; if the boundaries of the firm did mostly
revolve around questions of vertical integration, then it would suggest that
nothing much has happened here for a very long time.[1] However, transaction cost economics does provide a theory of diversification, at least for the
special case of the conglomerate. We shall begin our investigation of the
diversification decision by looking at this explanation[2] in section 4.1. In section 4.2 we shall look at simple diversification using a resource-based perspective, and then derive a logic for specialization in section 4.3 and for
diversification in section 4.4. The question of firm survival is explored in section 4.5, which leads to a discussion of selection processes in economics in
section 4.6, and then selection processes and the firm in section 4.7. While
the early sections (4.2 to 4.4) analyse diversification partly as a response to
environmental pressures, the later sections (4.5 to 4.7) consider how diversification may actively transform the nature of the environmental selection
processes facing the firm at corporate level.

4.1. The Conglomerate and Limited Comparators

Conglomerates are firms which have diversified into a variety of unrelated
areas. As Williamson (1975, p. 155) points out they have often been thought
of as a 'puzzle' by analysts. Attempts to explain the conglomerate as devices
for spreading risk tend to founder on the point that shareholders can spread
risk cheaply and more easily by spreading their investments in a number of
companies. However, Williamson (1975, ch. 9 and 1985, pp. 286–90) does
argue that an efficiency defence for the conglomerate can be found if it is
regarded as a logical consequence of the development of the multi-divisional
or M-form organizational structure. In the M-form structure, divisions are

usually organized around products (sometimes processes or regions). The separation of products into separate divisions allows them to be assessed as profit centres, while senior management are primarily concerned with strategic decisions, including takeover, divestment, and the allocation of resources between divisions. In short, the M-form is set up to act as an internal capital market, and it is the coincidence of conglomerate strategy and M-form structure which Williamson argues can lead to efficiency gains.

We can look at Williamson's arguments in this context with the help of Fig. 4.1. Assume we start with 16 individual and separately owned businesses in four sectors. For simplicity, we assume that the businesses can be treated as identical in terms of scale, growth, and profitability considerations. A conglomerate strategy could be formed by acquiring a firm from each sector, as indicated in Fig. 4.1. and making each of them a division within a four-business conglomerate. Williamson suggests that the combined effects of divisionalization and internalization of the capital market can have several efficiency advantages. Compared to the starting point at which the individual businesses had to obtain resources from the external capital market, the internal capital market of the conglomerate has access to more abundant and better quality information, it can fine tune resource allocation more sensitively, and the costs of senior management intervention are relatively low. It can also serve as an effective device for take-over, with small specialized acquisitions becoming divisions within the expanded internal capital market of the conglomerate. For these reasons, organizing the four businesses as divisions within the conglomerate can be more efficient than leaving them to the cruder and less sensitive external capital market.

There is nothing wrong with these arguments as they stand, and indeed they have validity as well considered reasons as to why internal organization may be more efficient than external market alternatives in certain cases. However, they are entirely concerned with choice of *mode* of organization, in this case hierarchy within the firm versus external market alternatives. The problem is that this does not explain why the *strategy* of conglomerateness is preferred to specialization by the corporation. In fact, the advantages of internalization of markets and divisionalization exploited by the conglomerate can also be exploited by specialized firms. There is nothing to stop specialized firms forming an internal capital market around the multidivisional form (M-form) favoured by conglomerates, and specialized strategies may have additional bonuses (Kay, 1992*a*).

Suppose we were to form an electronics company around the four businesses in the electronics row in Fig. 4.1. The new electronics company could form an M-form structure with the original firms as divisions, and extract the same internal capital market advantages as the conglomerate. In fact, many large electronics companies such as Hewlett-Packard have indeed adopted M-form structures. However, the specialized firm potentially has

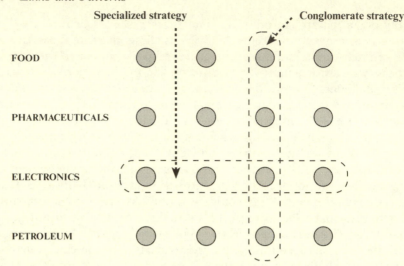

Fig. 4.1. Specialized versus conglomerate strategies

additional efficiency advantages over the conglomerate. For example, the results of R&D may be made available to other divisions within the firm without fear of appropriability problems, an advantage which may be more difficult or impossible for a grouping of separate firms to arrange. In general, strategically important information may be more freely shared within a firm than between firms. What might be an external benefit from the point of view of the donor when technological or marketing know-how is shared between two separate firms, becomes internalized within the firm when it is shared between two divisions of the same firm. Such internalization of externalities should lead to an improvement in overall resource allocation, an advantage generally denied to the conglomerate because of the unrelated nature of its various markets and technologies. In short, anything the conglomerate can do, the specialized electronics firm can do, and more; but if this logic works for the electronics firm versus the conglomerate, it also works if we were to form three more specialized firms out of the four firms in food, the four in pharmaceuticals, and the four in petroleum respectively. There is no room left for the conglomerate strategy once its efficiency attributes are compared to those of more specialized strategies.

The transaction cost explanation of the conglomerate strategy fails because it is an explanation of a mode rather than a strategy. Once the range of comparators is widened to include alternative strategies as well as the external capital market, it ceases to provide a satisfactory explanation of the reasons for the existence of the conglomerate strategy. This is an example of what we shall call the problem of limited comparators, which in the context of the corporation, usually involves a strategy or mode of organization being justified in terms of being more efficient when compared to do-nothing or market exchange alternatives. The problem of limited comparators follows from not opening up the analysis far enough to include all relevant opportunities, which in this case includes specialization and related diversification opportunities. We shall come up against the problem in a number of contexts in this book. It is a particular feature of the literatures on diversification, multinationalism, joint ventures, and strategic alliances.

Could explanations of diversification in transaction cost economics be extended to include related diversification? This is difficult or impossible to achieve given the current orientation of transaction cost economics. Since Williamson insists that asset specificity (specialization of assets by use or user) plays an essential role in the replacement of market transactions with hierarchical alternatives (1985, pp. 31–2), his approach is congenitally unable to recognize related diversification by firms since this involves internalization of assets which are by definition *non*-specific to a particular application. For these reasons, transaction cost economics has largely concerned itself with the special cases of vertical integration and the conglomerate while neglecting the more general case of internalization through related diversification.

4.2. Simple Diversification

In Chapter 3 we looked at the question of vertical integration in terms of ease of replaceability of assets seen from the perspective of the firm. Replaceability represents one form of relationship between resources, and in this chapter we shall analyse the firms diversification problem by looking at other possible resource relationships. We shall approach the problem of diversification by considering the hypothetical example of a firm considering alternative expansion strategies as in Fig. 4.2. The firm presently is a single product firm. It makes and sells disposable pens and is considering acquiring other disposable products.[3] On the technological side, its resources are appropriate to the development and production of cheap, fluid-filled, plastic and light metal containers. On the selling side, its resources are appropriate to the marketing and distribution of disposable products characterized by numerous geographically fragmented retail outlets, and point-of-sale marketing. The firm is pursuing diversification strategies that can exploit its technological and marketing bases, and the two options which the firm is considering involve acquiring a perfume firm (Fig. 4.2b) or a cigarette lighter firm (Fig. 4.2c) respectively. Both are disposable products, with the perfume and lighter fluid containers produced using plastic and light metal. The products are also marketed in much the same way as the disposable pen product, and they are distributed to similar outlets.

Figure 4.2a illustrates the type of economies or synergies that the firm hopes to exploit from commonalities in resources between the two product

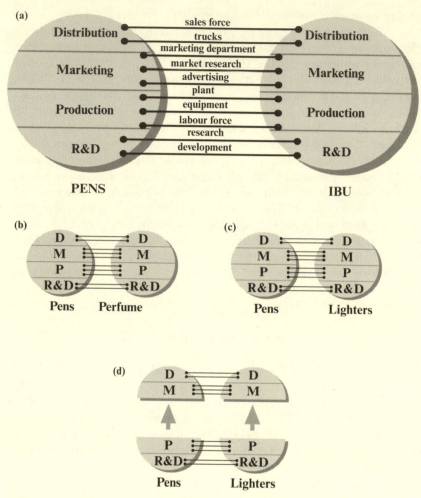

Fig. 4.2. Linkages from diversification and vertical integration

lines. These are illustrated by *links or linkages* in the form of shared resources between the Pens unit and the other IBU (or Individual Business Unit) in the respective cases, whether perfume or lighters. On the technological side, there would be some commonalities in the firms R&D strengths in designing cheap fluid-filled plastic and metal products, while these technological similarities may also give scope for sharing plant, equipment, tools, and labour force skills. On the marketing side, similarities in the selling characteristics of the respective products may give scope for sharing the skills of the marketing and market research staff, while the sharing of outlets will allow sharing of the resources servicing these outlets, such as sales forces, and various aspects of the physical distribution system such as trucks. Clearly the overlap between resources will be only partial in the respective cases, and the particular pattern of linkage will depend on the case in point; whilst pens, lighters and perfume may exploit some resource sharing, they will each have need for IBU-specific resources to the extent that there is a differentiation of marketing, distribution, production, and R&D characteristics between the respective businesses. We assume here that both diversification opportunities offer comparable opportunities in terms of the economies or synergies that might be generated in the respective cases. As far as the sources of synergies or economies of scope from resource linkages are concerned, these are exactly the same as the sources of economies of scale and may be obtained by, for example, making fuller use of indivisible assets or by facilitating the exploitation of specialization and division of labour.

After considering the options, the firm decides to acquire the lighter firm. (Figure 4.2c.) The market for cheap perfume products is unclear, but the firm is convinced that even if perfume did turn out to be a worthwhile avenue to explore in the future, it wishes to concentrate its attention on the lighters diversification option first. There are a number of issues relevant to the setting of firm boundaries which this diversification example may help to illustrate:

1. *Firm growth is a historical process*

First, the firm options are partly determined by existing resources, and secondly, the ability to pursue options are constrained by available managerial and financial resources (Penrose, 1959). Even if both diversification options were attractive, the firm may not have the internal resources to pursue both simultaneously and they may have to be dealt with sequentially. Current strategies build up over time and reflect the accumulation of decisions made in the past. In the example here, these points are evident in a very primitive sense, but the path dependent nature of corporate strategies is something that will be a central feature of the discussion in later chapters.

2. *Bundling of transactions performed by resources*

In Coase's original article (1937, p. 391) he pointed out that by internalizing resource coordination within the firm, 'a factor of production (or the owner thereof) does not have to make a series of contracts with the factors with which he is co-operating within the firm, as would be necessary, of course, if this co-operation were a direct result of the working of the price mechanism. For this series of contracts is substituted one'. In the example above, there will be many individual factors associated with individual links;

for example, within 'labour force' there are likely to be many workers. Each resource may perform a variety of tasks as a consequence of its association with the firm; a different contract does not have to be written for each task, instead there is a bundling of transactions associated with each particular resource.

3. *Bundling of resources within the firm*

The firm either acquires the lighters firm, or it does not. Whilst there may be options for selective disposal of assets (especially where there are economies from duplication of resources), the acquisition of the lighter firm involves a discrete bundle of resources. Here internalization involves not the incremental transaction, nor even the incremental resource, but instead bundles of complementary resources. The reason is that resources can perform two roles, a *complementary role* in which they are bundled with other resources to produce a particular product (vertical integration), and a *synergistic role* in which the resource is spread across product markets to provide economies (related diversification). For example, in the case above, the acquisition of the lighter firm means that some trucks may be shared by both products providing economies or synergies in distribution, while these same resources combine with complementary marketing and technological resources to make and sell the respective products. These resources are Janus-faced, playing crucial roles both within businesses and across them. Even if there were only limited synergies from resource sharing across the two businesses, resource complementarities within each business means that the pen firm cannot pick and choose which resources to acquire, but instead will have to acquire the bundle of complementary resources involved in lighter production.

4. *Internalization focuses coordination*

Resources may be bundled together when internalized, but there is no guarantee that this process of bundled internalization will ensure that the best possible matches are made at the level of individual links. For example, there may be three disposable lighter firms that the pen manufacturer could potentially combine with. Lighter firm A might have the strongest overlaps with the pen firm in terms of distribution; plant and equipment associated with lighter firm B may be the most compatible with the pen firms production process; while lighter firm C's R&D team might be most closely duplicate the capabilities of the pen R&D team. If we were to go deeper than the level of linkages by identifying the best matches in terms of synergistic potential at the level of particular resources, it could signal that the pen firm should be sharing resources with a large variety of firms. However, when the pen firm internalizes the bundle of resources associated with the lighter firm, it sacrifices resource sharing with many potential collaborators in favour of coordinating synergies with one. The benefits of keeping together the complementary bundle of resources associated with the lighter business within the hierarchical solution outweigh the flexibility of resource matching associated with the market mechanism.

5. *The role of value*

The decision by the pen firm to extend corporate boundaries is influenced by value considerations. Both lighter and perfume diversification opportunities are expected to generate similar levels of economies in our example, but the former option is preferred because it has a higher expected value. Indeed, the disposable perfume market may be so unattractive considered in value terms that our firm may have no interest in pursuing this option even after the lighter and pen value chains have been integrated as far as possible. The comparative merits of modes of conducting transactions (e.g. markets versus hierarchy) as outlined in transaction cost economics is only one part of the internalization agenda. It is essential to consider *whether* it is worthwhile to pursue a strategy, as well as *how* to pursue it.

6. *Non-specificity of internalized assets*

Here hierarchy replaces market alternatives to internalize the coordination of *non*-specific assets within the firm. This is contrary to Williamson's explanation for the evolution of hierarchy which sees asset specificity as integral to the internalization process. If the assets in the two firms were indeed committed to specialized uses in the respective businesses, there would be no potential for generating synergies through merger.

7. *The role of vertical integration*

The example can also be used to demonstrate the difference between diversification and vertical integration. In Fig. 4.2c the pen firm has diversified and it is also vertically integrated. In Fig. 4.2d the firm has been broken up into two vertically separated divisions, an upstream division concentrating on technological (R&D and production) aspects of the disposable products, and a downstream division concentrating on the marketing and distribution of these products. Both the upstream and the downstream division continue to exploit resource linkages across the respective businesses. The arrows in Fig. 4.2d indicate the movement of intermediate products between upstream and downstream businesses. Thus, whilst the exploitation of synergies as in our diversification example involves the *sharing* of assets, vertical integration involves the *transfer* of assets, in this case in the form of an intermediate product. This might seem a simple convention for operationalizing the role of assets in the expansion of firm boundaries, but using it suggests that real world strategies may involve both vertical and horizontal elements. For example, as we shall see in Chapter 6, Thorn EMI in 1995 was vertically integrated in both the production and retailing of music. However, it could be argued that the ability to monitor music trends at the distribution end of the value chain generated know-how that could be shared with the production side of Thorn EMI. Thus, the integration of production and retailing operations in this case may exhibit both vertical (movement of product) and synergistic (sharing of knowledge) relations. Whether or not the firm in Fig. 4.2d would vertically integrate in this fashion is likely to reflect the considerations we looked at in Chapter 3.

8. *Links are a double-edged sword*

In Fig. 4.2c the links can generate internal economies or synergies. They can also expose the firm's businesses to common threats from the environment. If each link can represent a shared capability that helps generate competitive advantage in the present, environmental changes may convert them into shared weaknesses in the future. For example, if a competitor develops a superior technology for producing disposable products, the firm's technological lead in both pens and lighters may be threatened. If another firm develops a more efficient production process for manufacturing disposable products, the firm may find both of its products undercut in terms of price. If major customers (e.g. supermarkets) decide to go for own labelled products, dependence on particular shared distribution channels may hit both businesses. If customers tire of disposable products, then the shared marketing characteristics of both products may turn out to be a joint weakness. The link is a double-edged sword; the price of internal economies it may help generate is potential vulnerability to external threat (Kay, 1982). In later chapters we shall develop some implications of this issue, beginning with the analysis of corporate strategies in Chapter 6, and we also discuss this further below.

4.3. The Logic of Specialization

So why might firms want to specialize? We have already touched on this problem in Chapter 1, but we shall take it further here. It should be noted that firm specialization is not an issue that is well dealt with by either Coase or Williamson, since the paradigm case of corporate boundaries (vertical integration) by definition involves specialized firms. It is determinants of the degree of vertical integration that is the major focus of attention in that framework, not degree of specialization. However, this raises a question that is difficult to answer within the terms of the transaction cost framework: why do firms tend to specialize in the first place? Specialization is assumed rather than explained in this approach. Similarly, the diversification of large firms discussed by Williamson in his analysis of the development of the M-form corporation (1975, pp. 132–54; 1985, pp. 279–81) is described rather than explained. For an approach that sets out to explain the boundaries of the firm, this would appear to be a potentially serious deficiency. Figure 4.3 provides a basis for analysing this problem.

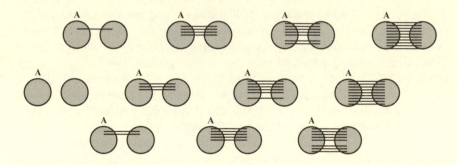

Fig. 4.3. Alternative strategies

Figure 4.3 shows eleven alternative strategies involving pairs of businesses. The same business (A) is involved in each situation with different possible partner businesses in the respective cases. Taken in isolation, each business has similar scale, profit, and growth characteristics, the only relevant difference between the eleven strategies being the degree of linkage. The pairs are typically linked through common resources that may generate synergy, though the extent of linkage varies. Each link represents a category of resource that may generate synergies as in Fig. 4.2; advertising, market research, marketing department, trucks, sales force, plant, equipment, labour force, and research and development. Each of the synergies are expected to be associated with some innovative content over time, so some form of hierarchy will be required to coordinate synergy (as we discussed in Chapter 3). In principle, the installation of hierarchy could be accomplished at the level of the firm through full scale merger, or at the level of linkages by setting up some cooperative arrangement between firms that makes provision for decision-making adjustments in the future. As we discussed at the end of Chapter 3, a hierarchical form that could make such provision would be a joint venture between the separate firms at the level of the respective linkages, for example in R&D, marketing, distribution, and so on.

However, one thing about the internalization or merger process that is important in this context is that opportunities tend to come in discrete packages. This was discussed under points 3 and 4 above, but it warrants further discussion. It could be that our firm knows that one of its potential matches is good at technology, one at production, one at marketing, and so on. Why not 'pick and mix' linkages from the different matches, taking the best from each one? The problem is that none of these potential linkages exist in isolation, instead each of these potential matches have already thrown corporate boundaries around the respective businesses in order to exploit and coordinate complementary assets. If our firm fixes cooperative arrangements such as joint venture at the level of each linkage to exploit potential synergies with, say, ten different matches, we shall have ten different firms each with their separate hierarchies, and ten separate hierarchical solutions at the level of linkages to coordinate. This clearly creates considerable potential for conflict and confusion. By way of contrast, if the firm merges with a single partner that offers possibilities for connecting along all ten linkages, a single unified hierarchy may be created in lieu of the Tower of Babel that multiple joint ventures would have created. It may well be the case that the linkages associated with the bundle that this particular match brings to the merger may be weaker taken one at a time compared to the best available in each linkage category from the strongest match. However, the savings in organizational costs are likely to more than dominate the opportunity cost of exploiting the set of best possible linkage matches taken from a variety of sources.

As we shall see in Chapter 9, there are circumstances which may stimulate the adoption of cooperative agreements such as joint venture between firms, but for the moment we wish to focus on the question of the boundaries of the firm rather than hierarchical alternatives in general. So, for the purposes of comparing strategies, we shall make the reasonable assumption that our firm is only considering merger as a means of imposing hierarchical solutions on the problem of linkage coordination. Given these restrictions, our firm's choice appears to remarkably simple; if you are going to expand, exploit as many linkages as possible. If unbundling resources within businesses is not possible because of resource complementarities, and if your discrete bundle of resources then has to merge with another discrete bundle of resources, make sure that the bundle you pick generates as much synergy as possible with your present bundle. Why merge with an opportunity that may generate weak linkages if one which offers potentially stronger linkages is available? The economies obtained from the richer linkages represent bonuses which can generate extra resources for management. As long as needs are not satiated, it is rational for management to prefer to have more resources rather than less, irrespective of the uses to which they wish to apply these resources. These considerations suggest that management would pursue as richly linked a match as possible, which would mean that the firm in Fig. 4.3 would try to pick a match as far to the right of Fig. 4.3 as possible. Thus, the firm's problem is not to decide the economics of internalizing the 'incremental transaction' (Williamson, 1975, pp. 118–26) as in transaction cost economics, but rather it is to consider the economics of internalizing discrete bundles of resources.

Such an ordering of managerial preferences is traced by Ollinger (1994) in his study of the growth of firms in the US oil industry, with firms historically tending first to pursue richly linked horizontal and domestic expansion, before expanding into more weakly linked technologies and markets (such as petrochemicals, energy market, international markets), then finally moving into unrelated markets such as insurance, real estate, and office equipment.[4] This suggests firms will prefer to adopt strategies on the right of Fig. 4.3 when they are available, with a first preference for the specialization strategy.

This may help resolve the question of why firms may prefer to specialize. However, it raises an obvious further puzzle. Why do firms diversify? One obvious first answer to this is that they may be running out of specialized and richly linked expansion opportunities, just as Ollinger traced in the oil industry. This certainly may get us some of the way along the diversification trail, but it is not far enough. Diversification appears too extensive a phenomenon to be satisfactorily accounted for in terms of simply spilling over into more weakly related areas because more strongly related opportunities are not available. The conglomerate may be the most visible example of extreme diversification, but there appear to be many firms actively pursuing a diversification strategy that would not be characterized as conglomerates. We need to identify a logic for a diversification strategy, and we shall explore this possibility in the next section.

4.4. The Diversified Firm

From what has been discussed so far, we would expect economies to be characterized typically by highly specialized corporate strategies. To help explore further the question of why firms might actually want to diversify, Fig. 4.4 summarizes four strategies based on the earlier analysis of Figs. 4.2 and 4.3; the middle two strategies are both based on partial linkages, with one firm diversifying around common marketing resources, and the other diversifying around common technological resources. We presume that the marketing based diversification exploits common advertising, market research, marketing department, trucks, and sales force between the two business units; correspondingly the technologically based diversification exploits common plant, equipment, labour force, and research and development between its two businesses. The specialized strategy exploits both these linkages. Therefore, from left to right, we have a specialized strategy, two diversified strategies based on a major link, and a conglomerate strategy. In economic terms, the only relevant differences between the respective strategies is provided by the presence or absence of linkages.

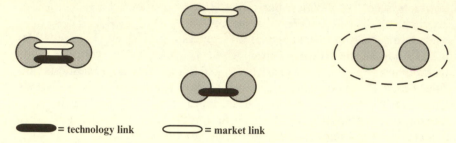

= technology link   = market link

Fig. 4.4. Specialization and diversification

Our analysis so far suggests that typically the specialized strategy would be preferred to the marketing based or technologically based strategies, which in turn would be preferred to the conglomerate strategy. *Ceteris paribus*, it would be irrational to sacrifice synergies by choosing a weaker linked strategy. So why would firms diversify? One route has been to suggest that separation of ownership and control in the modern corporation has given management some discretion in pursuing their own objectives, as opposed to those of the owners.[5] In those circumstances, they may stray from the path of profit maximization and pursue non-profit oriented goals; for example, the evolution of the conglomerate has been interpreted as reflecting growth maximization motives on the part of management (e.g. Mueller, 1969).

The problem with explaining diversification as a consequence of managerial motives is that the appropriate corporate strategy turns out to be remarkably consistent for a range of individual objectives, or mix of objectives. Consider again the four alternative strategies in Fig. 4.4 and suppose managerial objectives are either (a) profit, (b) monopoly power, (c) market share, (d) sales, or (e) growth. Our earlier analysis suggests that management are likely to pursue the synergy-rich strategy, which is consistent with profit maximization. But a firm seeking monopoly power or market share is clearly also going to be attracted to the specialized options, since diversification would tend to dissipate control of individual markets. At first sight it might seem that the four strategies illustrated in Fig. 4.4 are neutral as far as sales (scale) or growth objectives are concerned, but this is not the case. The richer the links in Fig. 4.4, the higher the profits, and the more internal resources that will be generated to help the firm pursue scale or growth objectives.[6] Whatever the objective, it will usually be best served by pursuing strongly-linked strategies compared to more weakly-linked strategies, *ceteris paribus*. The same conclusion follows for any mix of these objectives.[7] Similarly, Nickell (1995, pp. 36–9) lists three major categories of reason for acquisition; (a) synergies, (b) volatility reduction, and (c) managerial motives (advancement, power, hubris). It is interesting to note that apart from volatility reduction (which we discuss below), these categories of motive may be advanced by pursuing as richly linked a strategy as possible, *ceteris paribus*.

Thus, a particular strategy may be consistent with a wide range of managerial objectives. This is an interesting conclusion since it suggests that specialization is a highly robust strategy even when differences in objectives are recognized. Indirectly, it does tell us something about diversification since it suggests a wide range of possible influences should be excluded from consideration in this context. When this is recognized, it turns out that the circumstances in which firms will rationally pursue diversification processes typically require that: (a) either impediments are placed in the way of richly-linked strategies, or (b) richly-linked strategies have costs additional to those generally associated with transaction cost economics.

As far as impediments to richly-linked strategies are concerned, anti-trust policy may prevent or discourage firms from pursuing specialization. It may then have to consider less richly-linked alternatives. Similar considerations hold in the case of market saturation; finite or declining demand conditions may encourage the firm to switch its attention to alternative markets. However, while these influences may explain why the firm may switch from extreme specialization, they do not in themselves guarantee significant diversification; the pressures and rewards are still generally loaded in favour of exploiting the richest linkages possible, and the firm will have incentives to simply loosen linkages sufficiently to avoid the attention of anti-trust authorities, or to escape the saturation trap for individual markets. This means that firms will still wish to pursue strategies that are as strongly linked as possible, subject to anti-trust and market saturation constraints.[8] The target is still the same, even if the route is not as direct as it would be in the absence of impediments.

If more than minimal diversification is to be explained, then it seems that other influences need to be present. One reason may be described simply as availability; it may not be possible to find good richly-linked expansion alternatives. There may be no sound business opportunities available to which the firm could add strong market and/or technological linkages. Such considerations have influenced the conglomerate style expansion of many firms in the petroleum industry as described by Ollinger (1994) above. While some petroleum firms have chosen to exploit marketing linkages with alternative energy sources such as coal, nuclear, and solar power, each of these particular industries have specific problems that may reduce their intrinsic attractiveness as diversification opportunities. Consequently, many petroleum firms spilled over into completely unrelated industries in the post-war period as part of their expansion strategies.[9]

A consideration that may influence the availability of expansion alternatives is the time frame over which expansion is planned. Some companies (e.g. Cadbury Schweppes) plan expansion over a long time frame and carefully restrict acquisitions to those that fit their corporate strategy. Designing a synergy-rich strategy is easier if firms are prepared to wait for the right opportunity to become available at the right time. On the other hand, if firms are planning significant expansion over a relatively short period (like ITT in its heyday), their expansion strategy may have to be fashioned in a makeshift fashion out of the bits and pieces that happen to be available in the market place at the time, especially since rapid expansion would preclude internal expansion making more than a modest contribution to growth. Thus, the 'acquisitive' designation of many conglomerates may reflect time frame rather than strategy considerations, with the strategy of conglomerateness being formed by default as a consequence of the speed of expansion. The introduction of time frame considerations suggests that the conclusions of the previous section have to be qualified; growth objectives may indeed encourage significant diversification and even conglomerateness when speed of expansion overrides the ability of management to find synergy-rich acquisition possibilities. However, acquisitive conglomerates tend to require favourable and unusual capital market circumstances to evolve. Thus, so far we have only been able to identify *ad hoc* reasons for diversification. We have not identified any reason why the management of firms would prefer loosely-linked to strongly-linked strategies when the latter is available, *ceteris paribus*.

It is patterns of linkages that help explain why diversification may have intrinsically attractive properties for corporate management. Figure 4.5 shows a variety of strategies with simple two business strategies on the left, and more complex four business strategies on the right. The pattern of linkages correspond to the general categories of strategies described by Rumelt (1986). The specialized strategy operates a single business, as indicated by the double marketing and technological linkages over the length of its strategy; the conglomerate operates a series of unrelated businesses as indicated by the absence of linkages; the related-constrained case operates a single marketing or technological linkage over the length of its strategy; and the related-linked case alternates linkages over the length of its strategy such that all businesses are at least indirectly linked to each other. Now, suppose that management is facing a hostile environment that is capable of throwing up threats to the firm's existing activities. Such threats are indicated by a smoking bomb in Fig. 4.5. Bombs may take a variety of forms, including government regulation and resource depletion, but the most common and dangerous bomb is technological change; this can render specific marketing and technological skills obsolete overnight.

Threats may be concentrated on technological competencies, as happened some years ago when metal replaced wood in the construction of many sports rackets and bats, or they may be focused on the marketing side as many defence contracting victims of the peace dividend have found out to their cost. Some threats may attack both technological and marketing links.

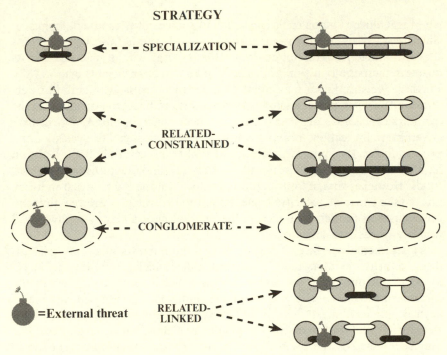

Fig. 4.5. External threats to strategies

This happened to the Swiss watch industry in the 1970s when the new, cheaper, electronic watches began to be retailed in a much wider range of outlets than those traditionally associated with watches. The Swiss lacked the technological, marketing, and distribution competencies to compete on equal terms with their new rivals, though they began a fight back later with the Swatch.[10] In each case the shared marketing or technological characteristics that could generate synergy across different products were also subject to attack or obsolescence. A firm may be able to ride the changes, as for example when its brand names smooth changes in patterns of distribution, or it may be seriously threatened by other kinds of external changes, such as fundamental changes in how products are distributed. For example many UK suppliers of financial services are currently finding that the direct selling of financial products by telephone is representing a major threat to many aspects of their business.

Whilst shared characteristics may allow competencies to be shared across businesses in the form of marketing or technological links, competencies may also be business specific, in which case threats could also be business-specific. The extent to which a threat extends across a firm's businesses will reflect the extent to which the competencies it attacks also extend. Localized competencies will restrict the scope of particular threats that attack them, while generalized competencies may extend vulnerability to attack from specific threats across a wide range of businesses. It should also be noted that shared characteristics do not guarantee that synergy will be generated across businesses, especially if similarities are minimal or superficial (Porter, 1987). Further, whilst linkages may point to areas of potential vulnerability, certain kinds of competencies may be perceived as being relatively immune from attack because of special circumstances (such as monopoly control, government protection, brand loyalty, or long product life cycles). Long product life cycles combined with brand loyalty has certainly helped sustain highly focused strategies on the part of certain manufacturers of branded foods. However, similar considerations helped lull the Swiss watch industry into a false sense of security, while some food companies are reappraising the robustness of their strategies in the light of increasing buyer power and trends towards own-labelling.

As with actual warfare, it is generally in the interests of protagonists to disguise their true intentions (Clausewitz, 1968) which is why the incidence, location, and timing of individual bombs is liable to be a surprise to the threatened firm. Here it is presumed that individual bombs are capable of destroying, or at least severely disabling, individual businesses or links. Bearing in mind that management is unsure of how, when, and where they may be bombed by the environment, a question that might exercise them in such circumstances is, how vulnerable is their present strategy to bombing? This can be expressed as a survival issue; if a substantial proportion of a firm's businesses are being bombed, then its very survival may be threatened. The ability of a firm to survive may depend on its being able to jettison disabled activities and build on the undamaged remainder. In Fig. 4.5 this question in phrased in terms of the maximum damage a single well placed bomb could inflict on specific strategies, and examples of such bombs are given for each of the strategies in Fig. 4.5.

Clearly if a bomb is dropped on any of the linkages in the specialized strategy, the firm is in considerable trouble. The related-constrained strategies illustrated in Fig. 4.5 diversify around one market or technology link, and while they move away from vulnerability to attack on one category of resource, they are still vulnerable to a single bomb dropped on their respective core linkages. On the other hand, the conglomerate strategy limits the maximum impact of individual bombs to specific businesses. The decoupling of businesses in the conglomerate strategy means that it provides a high degree of insulation from specific environmental threats. The conglomerate would appear to be a strategy designed for hostile, surprise-ridden environments, and this is consistent with its being found in disproportionate numbers in dynamic high technology contexts, with high degrees of technological innovation and short product life cycles (Kay, 1982). We shall describe such contexts as turbulent environments and it is hoped to show later that they play an important role in influencing patterns of diversification.

However, the critical determinant of strategic vulnerability turns out to be pattern of linkage rather than number of distinct businesses. The two related-linked strategies shown in Fig. 4.5 exploit single linkages across businesses just as in the related-constrained case, but the pattern of linkages is different here. Instead of exploiting the same market or technological link across the firm as in the related-constrained strategy, the related-linked strategy keeps individual links short range, and consequently limits vulnerability to external bombing. For the related-linked strategies in Fig. 4.5, individual bombs can hit no more than two linked businesses, despite the synergy-rich nature of the respective strategies. Thus, if management are concerned about the survival of the firm (and their continuing employment) in a potentially hostile and surprise-rich environment, an appropriate strategy would involve limiting the extent of individual linkages in the firm, or *de-linking*. De-linking may also be regarded as responding to the existence of creative destruction at the level of markets and technologies (Schumpeter, 1942) in attempting to inhibit creative destruction at the higher level of firms. This gives a positive rationale and incentive for firms to diversify, even if it involves the opportunity cost of sacrificing more closely related expansion opportunities. Therefore, links are double edged swords that can generate synergies *and* create vulnerability to external threats. Consequently, expansion strategies of management may involve both linking (or synergistic) and de-linking motives. Analysing the pattern of linkages helps uncover the fact that the related-linked strategy may be almost as effective in pursuing de-linking objectives as is the conglomerate strategy.

Survival and risk spreading motives have been ascribed to corporate management in the past, and de-linking may appear to have kinship relations with these previous interpretations. However, there are distinct features associated with the present interpretation. First, survival motives have proved notoriously difficult to operationalize, and it has proved difficult to distinguish them from other motives such as scale, growth, and long run profitability (Scherer and Ross, 1990, pp. 44–5 and 46–9). By way of contrast, de-linking gives a rationale and shape to corporate strategies which is not provided by more diffuse interpretations of the survival motive.

Secondly, de-linking is different from the risk spreading motive for conglomerateness as generally described in the economics and finance literatures.[11] The risk spreading motive is generally interpreted as concerned with earnings smoothing or stability. The supposed advantage provided by the conglomerate in this respect is that it puts together businesses whose returns are loosely correlated or uncorrelated, with a consequent reduction of the standard deviation of profits as a proportion of overall profits.[12] However, risk itself does not encourage de-linking in our analysis above; any of the businesses discussed above could have highly volatile returns and this would not be sufficient for it to diversify away from its core competencies in our analysis. There are few industries where volatile earnings pose a threat to survival, as long as the expected or average level of profits is stable. There may be costs to overdraft facilities or liquid reserves, but a competitive capital market should ensure the costs are less than the opportunity cost of sacrificing synergy opportunities by going conglomerate to smooth earnings. It is not risk in terms of standard deviation of returns that de-linking is designed for, but the uncertain possibility that the competititive advantage and the average profit levels associated with specific businesses and/or linkages might be threatened. De-linking is oriented towards long-term viability, not short-term variability.

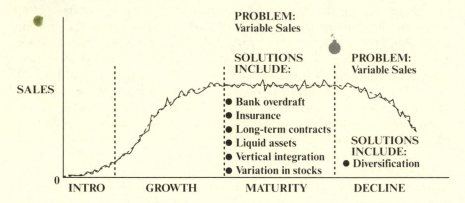

Fig. 4.6. Some options for dealing with variability and uncertainty

We can see this in the context of the product life cycle illustrated in Fig. 4.6. Suppose we have a firm making and selling this product, and it is its only product. As long as the product is in the maturity stage of the life cycle, there are a number of devices to deal with volatility that do not require the firm to move out of its specialized niche. If the firm (and the financial institutions that might support it) believe that the mean and variance of sales are fairly stable, then over the long haul the peaks will tend to balance the troughs, and then bank overdrafts or liquid reserves should allow rainy days to be passed without too much inconvenience. Further, insurance may compensate for some sources of variability (e.g. losses in transit), while a flexible stock-holding policy that compensates for peaks and troughs in sales may allow production facilities to run at or near full capacity. If the firm still finds volatility in sales unsettling, then long-term contracts with its suppliers may allow it to pass some of this risk down the line, alternatively vertical integration may be an additional means thorough which sales may be stabilized, as in the case of forward integration in retailing in the oil industry.

However, suppose an external innovation creates a further source of variability in firms sales as indicated by the bomb at the end of the maturity phase in Fig. 4.6. The innovation is a direct substitute for this product and sends the latter into terminal decline. In such circumstances, all devices to deal with risk at the maturity stage would provide only a very temporary stay of execution for this firm at best. Any firm trying to obtain recourse to the same risk smoothing devices that may be appropriate in the maturity stage is likely to find external and internal sources of funds rapidly drying up, stocks accumulating but not depleting, insurance companies writing them off as a bad risk, and the long-term contract/vertical integration solution merely tying them more deeply into a declining sector. As far as the long-term contract is concerned, the tension will be between the customer either wriggling out of the contract or going bankrupt first, while vertical integration in the face of technological threats can merely dig the hole deeper rather than provide an escape route, as a number of primary metals producers have found in the face of technological substitution by plastics.

So what is the 'solution' to the problem of variability (decline) in sales in the final stage of Fig. 4.6? The neoclassical solution is quite straightforward; if the assets do not provide value when put together as a collection within the firm, the firm should be broken up and individual assets dispersed to their next most valued usage in the market place.[13] Since this is likely to involve the loss of managerial jobs and salaries, it is not a solution that is likely to be attractive to this cohort, even if it is tendered as the efficient solution to a declining product-market. In fact, efficiency arguments can also be found in favour of maintaining the managerial coalition since it may be difficult to replicate effective team operation from scratch. In such circumstances diversification appears as the only realistic option for maintaining the managerial coalition, desirably diversification undertaken before the decline stage of the product life cycle sets in. As Penrose points out, diversification efforts demand and absorb significant resources from the firm. Since the decline phase of the life cycle also absorbs rather than generates resources, this is the worst time possible for a single product firm to be planning a diversification escape route.

Together with Chapter 3, such a perspective allows us to begin to explore why firms exist and why they set their boundaries where they do. The key here lies in analysing the pattern of links between businesses, the links themselves being capable of joining both synergies and threats. How the patterns of linkages associated with particular strategies evolve in practice may depend upon the exigencies of contingency and history.[14] In Chapter 7 we shall consider in some detail how different patterns of diversification may evolve in practice. The critical point for the moment is that synergy and de-linking are complementary concepts that depend on the nature and extent of links, and it is the nature and incidence of links that lies at the heart of questions as to why firms exist, and why they take the form they do.

4.5. Survival and the Firm

If diversification can insulate the firm from the possibility that an individual threat can threaten its survival, what are the implications for selection processes operating at the level of the firm? An obvious way to answer this question is to look at actual survival rates for corporations large enough to have been able to pursue de-linking if they so choose. However, this is not as easy as it might sound in principle, since what constitutes survival in this context has been subject to some debate. Here survival is defined to mean non-extinction; the firm has not been 'liquidated, dissolved or discontinued' (Chandler, 1977, p. 371).

This means that survival encompasses a firm merging with, or being acquired by, another firm. This can be justified on a number of grounds. First, if the particular bundle of resources that constitutes a firm has no further value as a productive entity, the logical strategy is simply to close it down and disperse individual assets to their next most valued uses. On the other hand, merger or acquisition indicates that the firm has value as a going concern. Indeed, almost all large corporations make use of a group structure (Lewis and Pendrill, 1994, p. 205) in which acquisitions may be made subsidiaries of the acquiring firm. An advantage of this structure is that it facilitates continuity of relations, including contractual relations, between the acquisition and its existing customers. In many such cases the customers may be unaware that a change of ownership has taken place at all. Secondly, Chandler noted that acquisition involving integrated US firms typically perpetuated hierarchies: 'normally the personnel and activities of the smaller or acquired firms were internalized by the core organization of the larger or acquiring megacorps' (Chandler, 1977, p. 371). Thirdly, if merger or acquisition marks the 'death' of a firm, we would expect some evidence to suggest that devices such as hostile bids are designed to help predators put an organization in terminal decline out of its misery. However, there has been a substantial amount of research into this possibility in recent years, and Nickell (1995, p. 50) concludes on the basis of this research that 'the evidence suggests that firms subject to hostile bids do not appear to be performing particularly badly'.

The conclusion that these various points lead us to is that merger or acquisition is generally designed to perpetuate the hierarchy that is being acquired. Survival is taken here to mean continuity of existence, and that continuity is typically preserved by merger and acquisition activity. These conclusions are important, because the question of what constitutes firm death has been an issue in the organizational literature for some years[15] and how firm death is interpreted has implication for our discussion of selection processes. In fact, there have been suggestions to the effect that merger can in fact be taken to signal firm 'death' in some cases, as has been argued in the population ecology literature (e.g. Hannan and Freeman, 1977, 1989). Hannan and Freeman (1989, pp. 150–2) acknowledge that treating merger as implying the death of the acquisition involves difficult conceptual issues and they recognize that there are cases where merger is consistent with the continued existence of both parties. However, they also suggest that three possible sets of changes following merger may be helpful in answering the question as to whether or not an organization's existence has been ended. The sets of changes are: (a) replacement of leaders, their subordination to new leaders, or radical changes in organizational form, (b) radical changes in the organizational task as when a health care firm changes its patient list to exclude those not covered by insurance, (c) changes in name and publicity associated with the organization.

The problem with these indicators of firm 'death' is that they would typically be accepted as consistent with the continuing survival of the firm if the firm was still independent. Individual firms are subject to boardroom *coups*, undergo radical changes of form (e.g. U-form to M-form) and task (e.g. the aerospace firms after the Second World War), radically change their publicity, and even their names (e.g. Esso to Exxon). None of these would normally be seen as signalling firm 'death' and indeed they would probably be seen in most cases as consistent with the survival of the firm. In general, associating merger or acquisition with firm death runs the danger of confusing survival with independence. Indeed, if merger counts as the 'death' of a firm, this would lead to certain paradoxes; if the acquisition is subsequently divested as an independent company, then presumably it would then spring to 'life', a curious reversal of the normal conceptions of mortality.

With these points in mind, what are the chances of survival for firms that are large enough to take advantage of the insulating properties of de-linking if they so wish? Studies by Navin (1970) and Hannan and Freeman (1977) provide useful evidence in this respect. Navin's study found that of the 278 largest US industrials in 1917, 264 (95 per cent) had still survived by 1967 in that they had not been liquidated, dissolved, or discontinued. If the survival rate is calculated for the large sub-group of 236 manufacturing companies, the survival rate in 1967 goes up to 97 per cent. Further, by 1917, all but 16 of the 236 manufacturing enterprises had adopted the U-form structure with integrated sales, purchasing, and manufacturing functions. The 16 laggards had stuck to more primitive single-function manufacturing structures. Of the 220 U-form manufacturing enterprises that had adopted a U-form structure in 1917, 216 survived until 1967, a survival rate of over 98 per cent. As Chandler notes with respect to the evidence of Navin's study, 'once an enterprise had set up a managerial hierarchy and once that organization had provided efficient administrative coordination of the flow of material through the processes of production and distribution it became self-perpetuating' (1977, p. 372).

In their study of survival rates, Hannan and Freeman (1977, pp. 959–60) compared the lists of firms on the Fortune 500 for the years 1955 and 1975 and found that 53.6 per cent of those on the 1955 list were on the 1975 list. Mergers had caused the disappearance of 122, while some slipped off the list, and one had been liquidated. Clearly relegation to a lower ranking or a secondary league is not equivalent to death, and Hannan and Freeman merely suggest that such patterns help to illustrate issues of 'volatility' and 'dominance'. However, consideration of predator–prey relations in biological environments would suggest that survival is not necessarily related to questions of volatility, dominance or size. If we remove merger as an instrument of firm death, then the sole example of firm death provided by Hannan and Freeman's study was of a firm specializing in Cuban sugar (Castro had come to power in Cuba in 1959). The best estimate that we would make here of the survival rate of Fortune 500 firms over the 20 year period surveyed by Hannan and Freeman is 99.8 per cent.

These results are both striking and counter-intuitive. The periods covered by both studies overlap and range from the October Revolution to the oil crisis of the 1970s. In between there were two world wars, the depression of the 1930s, and countless technological innovations that revolutionized the location of competitive advantage in individual sectors. For a hierarchy to survive throughout this period would seem a commendable feat. For about 97 per cent of large manufacturing enterprises to survive throughout this period is at the very least highly remarkable. It could be argued that an acquisition would be likely to bear little resemblance to the formerly independent firm by the end of this period, but again the same could be said of firms that had remained independent for all of this period. If survival has any meaning in this context, it in terms of continuity of existence, whether independently or as part of a larger combination.

This suggests that life-cycle theories of organizational development may draw on an inappropriate analogy. It is easy to argue that organizations grow, mature and die just like organisms. However, unless *ad hoc* and inappropriate instruments of death such as acquisition are invoked, life cycle descriptions of the firm are unable to account for the fact that large firms tend not to die, and so there can be no cycle. Penrose (1959) anticipated the difficulties in extending life-cycle analogies from the biological to the organizational sphere: 'the rudimentary biological theories of the growth of firms break down over merger: life-cycle analogies make no provision for abrupt discontinuities and changed identity in individual development; ecological analogies have trouble with sudden unpredictable changes in the very nature of individual organisms and the consequent changes in their relation to their environment' (p. 154). The unavoidable conclusion that these combination of difficulties suggests is that if the analogy is unhelpful it should not be used. However, this simply leads us into even deeper waters. Many analyses of competitive processes in economics depend on notions of firm failure and death as integral parts of the selection process. But if large firms tend not to die, what are the implications for the characterization of selection processes in economics? This is the next problem we turn to below.

4.6. Selection Processes in Economics

The first point that has to be emphasized in the context of selection processes is the importance of natural selection analogies in economic theorizing. As Scherer and Ross (1990) comment: 'when forced into the trenches of whether firms maximise profits, economists resort to the ultimate weapon in their arsenal; a variant of Darwin's natural selection theory. Over the long pull, there is one simple criterion for a business enterprise: profits must be nonnegative . . . failure to satisfy this criterion means ultimately that a firm will disappear from the economic scene' (p. 48). As Scherer and Ross indicate, the basic unit on which selection processes are presumed to operate in economics is the firm. However, as Gould (1993, p. 148) points out: 'a *struggle for existence* must therefore arise, leading by *natural selection* to *survival of the fittest*' (italics in original). In natural selection the corollary of selecting the fit is the weeding out of the unfit and actual failures (Gould, 1977, p. 11). But if natural selection operates on large firms as well as small, where is the evidence? As we have seen the industrial landscape is not littered with the carcasses of failed giants. Yet without failure there can be no natural selection, and if there is no natural selection the Darwinian analogy breaks down.

It order to deal with these problems, it is important to distinguish different levels of analysis. The selection processes impacting on firms may be quite different from those impacting on their constituent products. One difficulty with analysis of selection processes in economics is that it has tended to fuse together questions relating to the survival of product-markets with the survival of firms.[16] This is not surprising since, as we have seen, the neoclassical agenda and its theory of the firm is a theory of product-markets. But, while the gales of Schumpeterian creative destruction almost inevitably have a devastating effect on individual products over time, the same does not necessarily hold as far as the firm itself is concerned. Very few products produced by large firms at time of the First World War survive today in any form (other than museum pieces). The opposite is the case for the firms that produced these products. At the same time, the level of operation of Schumpeterian competition is wider than individual product markets; what such competition creates and destroys is not just product-markets, nor necessarily firms, but capabilities; the invention of the jet engine, nylon, and computer-aided design created new capabilities and rendered others obsolete.[17] However, firms may survive if the level of Schumpeterian competition is restricted to the level of capabilities and not to the level of the firm itself. The obsolescence of some capabilities is not in itself life-threatening for the firm as long as it has other capabilities it can draw on to maintain its commercial viability.

Yet the large diversified corporation can go further than simply localizing the damage posed by particular environmental threats, it can also internalize creative destruction. This is implicit in Nelson's argument (1959, pp. 302–3) that a diversified firm is better able to conduct research towards the basic research end of the spectrum, since a broad base can mean that the results may have application somewhere in the firm, whatever the outcome. However, this not only has the quantitative effect of potentially raising the value of radical innovative activity conducted by the firm, it has the qualitative effect of internalizing the major threat to corporate survival—technological change. As long as we are dealing with a population of specialized firms with creative destruction taking place in the external market, there will be a one-to-one correspondence between the death of technologies and the death of firms. There will also be a similar correspondence between life cycles of products and the life cycles of firms. What is commercial life for the new product-market (and its innovator) can mean death for the established product (and the specialized firms producing it). But if the forces of creative destruction can be locked up within the boundaries of the firm, then these sources of corporate mortality are removed. The death of one technology is matched (indeed caused) by the growth of another, and the viability of the firm is undisturbed. The internalization of creative destruction is the corporate equivalent of the elixir of life. Such internalization is certainly easier to develop and manage if you are a highly diversified company (e.g. 3M or General Electric), but it is a feat that even some fairly specialized companies have managed to achieve (e.g. Intel and Xerox).

4.7. Selection Environments and the Firm

The conclusion this discussion leads us to is that different levels of analysis within the firm are typically characterized by different selection processes. We argued in the previous chapter that it is important to look at the question of where the firm's boundaries should be set from the point of view of the firm, and the same arguments hold here with respect to the selection processes that the firm is subject to.

We can start by characterizing the typical representation of selection processes in economics as involving *hard selection*.[18] As with natural selection, by hard selection we mean cases in which elimination of individuals is an intended and integral part of the selection processes. This is the standard selection form in texts such as Tirole's *The Theory of Industrial Organization* (1988), which pursues a non-cooperative game-theoretic approach to problems in industrial organization and the theory of the firm. The analogies and terms employed typically imply hard selection as in 'wars' (e.g. Tirole, 1988, pp. 311–14), 'predation' (e.g. Tirole, 1988, pp. 37–76) and 'races' (Tirole, 1988, pp. 388–421). Other words which frequently appear in economic discourse and imply hard selection include 'tournament', 'auction', 'election', and 'lottery'; in such cases the eventual appearance of a winner implies the failure, and subsequent elimination, of a loser or losers. Indeed, when these various arrangements are considered as environments, the survival of the 'victor', is often taken to signify the termination of the environment which arranged for the continuance of the winning individual or system.

By way of contrast, the evidence of studies of survival rates in large firms suggests that selection processes operating at the level of the firm itself in such cases is typically characterized by *soft selection*. By soft selection processes, we mean cases in which elimination of individuals is abnormal or even pathological. Individuals are only removed from this environment in exceptional and unusual cases, the standard expectation is that they continue to survive indefinitely. The selection processes operating at the level of the firm in the typical large firm case would appear to display soft selection attributes. Other environments which appear generally to display soft selection characteristics looked at from the point of view of the individual or participating system include clubs, clans, families, associations, communities, and unions. There are usually a number of devices that can lead to the elimination of individuals in these various contexts, ranging from the calamitous (such as bringing disgrace on the good name of the social grouping) to the trivial (such as non-payment of fees in the case of the club). However, in each case it is generally presumed that the individual can continue to operate in this environment, subject to the attainment of certain standards. While hard selection environments tend to have finite life cycles, soft selection environments tend to have indefinite time horizons; the race may be ended, but the club continues.

This is not the only distinction between environments that can be made. For example, it is possible to identify cases where the elimination of individuals or systems from the environment in which they participate is neither a necessary (hard selection) nor a pathological (soft selection) feature of the environment in which they operate, but can instead be traced to performance related issues. These are termed *contingent selection* environments here, and they can include cases where individuals are members of teams and corporations, and possibly where firms are members of cartels. The important considerations here are the circumstances in which individuals or systems may be eliminated under the alternative regimes. In general, for the individual or system to continue under hard selection usually requires a winning performance, in contingent selection environments some degree or measure of adequate performance (possibly relative to others) is generally required, while soft selection environments generally only require some form of minimal performance.

It could be said that soft selection ideas were implicit in the managerial theories of the firm which entered the industrial organization mainstream for a brief period.[19] In these approaches, management maximized some objective function subject to a minimum profit constraint. However, these theories tended to leave no discretion as to outcome; once the objective function was specified there was usually a unique outcome that could be contrasted with the predictions associated with the neoclassical theory of the firm. These managerial models were consistent with Latsis' (1972) description of neoclassical theory as concerned with 'single exit' or 'straight-jacket' situations; once the situation has been specified, all discretion has been removed and there is only one rational possible course of action for decision-makers to take. It is ironic that industrial economists effectively dealt with the problems of discretion by denying its existence. However, taken as a whole, the various models illustrated some of the potential scope for discretionary behaviour on the part of senior decision-makers, with different models identifying a range of managerial objectives between them. It is also ironic that the range of outcomes associated with the models as a whole was generally regarded as a source of weakness, since they frequently made similar predictions and it was difficult to identify what was the 'correct' one. In fact, this variety of behaviour is indicative of the 'discretionary firm differences' that Nelson describes as the key to analysing the nature of the firm (1991, p. 62) with 'discretionary' implying 'a certain looseness of constraints, both in the short run and the long run, that gives room so that firms that differ in certain important respects can be viable in the same economic environment' (1991, p. 62). However, despite the promise that this route held, most mainstream industrial organization subsequently demonstrated a revealed preference for hard selection modelling.[20]

If we want to say something meaningful about the behaviour of firms in soft selection environment, we first of all have to recognize the possible implications of the particular characteristics associated with such selection processes. The management of such firms are likely to have substantial discretion over the design of their corporate environment; by way of contrast, some hard selection modelling built around maximizing implies 'one slip and out', contrary to the reality in which such firms operate. This does not mean that nothing can be said about behaviour in soft selection, and indeed the route chosen may reflect a variety of influences that may include design,[21] history,[22] personality,[23] chance,[24] or a combination of these. Also, a number of approaches in economics, organizational theory, and economic history reflect considerations which on closer examination bear the hallmark of soft selection; for example, Cyert and March's (1963) notion of 'organisational slack', reflects one device designed to facilitate organizational flexibility and adjustment as the environment throws up unexpected new challenges, and soft selection is implicit in much of the reasoning in (old) institutionalism and evolutionary theorizing. However having recognized that firms have discretion, how do they use it? Do we have anarchy and everything goes? Or do management try to pursue some form of coherence or pattern on the corporate strategies they pursue? As the title of the book suggests, the belief here is in the latter option. In the next chapter we shall look at the logic through which we might expect management to impose pattern and consistency in their pursuit of corporate strategy. The remainder of the book is concerned with exploring the implications of pattern in different strategic and hierarchical contexts.

4.8. Conclusions

In Chapter 3 it was argued that replaceability of resources influences the boundaries of the firm in the context of vertical integration. In this chapter it has been argued that the major determinant of the boundaries of the firm in the context of diversification is likely to be resource commonality or linkage across businesses. However, if the firm is pursuing horizontal or diversified moves through acquisition, it will internalize discrete bundles of resources. Similarly, if it was extending its boundaries through internal growth, the firm would have to create a whole new bundle of resources associated with the new business area. Apart from the special case of conglomerate expansion, there is usually a web of links connecting the new and old areas of the firm. Since these links or linkages trace the competencies shared across businesses in the firm, they may outline sources of synergy or internal economies. If competencies can obsolesce, they may also trace sources of potential shared vulnerability to particular environmental threats. The link can therefore serve as a double-edged sword, and it is reasonable to conclude that the firms' choice of strategy may be influenced by the balance and pattern of links associated with alternative strategies in different contexts. Although the firm would normally prefer richly-linked over weakly-linked strategies in the absence of pressures to move away from a specialized strategy, the threat of environmental attacks on particular links may encourage the firm to emphasize de-linking in its diversification strategy. While no conclusions have been reached yet as to what patterns of linkage are likely to obtain in practice (this will be the subject of Chapter 7), the soft selection characteristics of the environment in which the large diversified firm operates is likely to afford it a considerable degree of discretion over the precise design of strategy.

NOTES

1. Though the recent fashion for outsourcing would suggest a current trend for corporations to shrink rather than grow in this perspective.
2. See also Earl (1984) for analysis complementary to the discussion of this chapter.
3. This example was inspired by analysis of the BIC corporation but the discussion here is for expository purposes only. As far as is known, the company here bears no resemblance to the real world firm known as BIC.
4. As Ollinger (1994) shows, the subsequent restructuring and divestment of many of these unrelated moves helps illustrate potential conflict between managerial (growth-oriented) and shareholder (profit-oriented) interests.
5. There has been a considerable literature on managerial theories of the firm, which we discuss below, though it has tended to be superseded by the principal-agent literature in recent years. Much of the stimulus for the development of managerial theories in the 1960s was provided by Berle and Means' earlier work (1932) on the separation of ownership and control in the corporation. Major contributions were provided by Baumol (1962), Marris (1964) and Williamson (1964). For discussion of the principal-agent literature, see Tirole (1988, pp. 16–60).
6. The argument that a growth maximizing firm will also maximize profits was first made using a different model formulation by J. Williamson (1966).
7. A criticism made of the managerial theories of the firm was that it was difficult to discriminate between them since different theories often predicted the same or similar outcomes. However, if interest is in how robust strategy is in the face of different formulations of managerial objective functions, these 'problems' turn out to be positively advantageous.
8. However, Fligstein (1990, pp. 203–12) suggests that the severity with which anti-trust policy was interpreted in the US in the 1960s by some policy makers did actively encourage moves to conglomerate strategies. There may be cultures and periods where anti-trust policy does impose wide ranging constraints on even related diversification.
9. See also Measday (1982, pp. 56–8) for further discussion of diversification in the US petroleum industry.
10. See Ullman (1994).
11. See Hay and Morris (1991, pp. 522–4) for a survey of the literature on risk spreading and the conglomerate merger.
12. See Scherer and Ross (1990, pp. 127–8) and Hay and Morris (1991, p. 522) for discussion of this finding.
13. It may be that some sub-groups of assets may fetch more value if sold together, for example if the production process is tightly integrated and interdependent.
14. The evolution of corporations is likely to be a path dependent process, in the sense used by Hodgson (1993a, pp. 203–10).
15. For example, see the discussion in a number of articles in Nystrom and Starbuck (1981).

16. This can be seen in writers such as Marx (1976), Veblen (1925), and Schumpeter (1954).
17. This is not to say that the new development necessarily completely substitutes the old. The co-existence of safety, electric, and disposable razor technology in the same market is evidence that the innovation may only be a part substitute for the old.
18. Also, see Alchian (1950) and Friedman (1953) for early analyses explicitly associating the operation of competitive processes in economics with natural selection mechanisms. See Kay (1995*a*) for an analysis of differences in Alchian's and Friedman's viewpoints, particularly with respect to the role of profit-maximizing.
19. See Hay and Morris (1991) pp. 296–374 for a review of the major managerial theories of the firm.
20. Again, see Tirole (1988) for a review of many of these approaches.
21. For example, Hanson Trust's conglomerate strategy which was traditionally based around restructuring acquisitions in mature industries (J. Kay, 1993, p. 133). The recent decision of Lord Hanson to break up the corporation in the light of his imminent retirement in no way detracts from the rational design around which the Hanson empire was built.
22. IBM's long-term commitment to mainframe computers through the 1980s has been suggested by some commentators as a source of inertia in view of the competitive threat posed by PCs.
23. Edwin Land, the founder of Polaroid refused to consider significant diversification away from the company's narrow focus on instant technology, and it was only after he retired from the company presidency in 1975 that the company began to explore diversification opportunities seriously.
24. The emergence of extensive conglomerate strategies in Poland in the 1990s is due in part to a combination of circumstances. Just about the same time that Poland's privatized foreign-trade organizations lost their monopoly rights to international trade, their large foreign currency reserves suddenly made them cash rich due to their large foreign currency receipts. The result has been a fairly widespread buying spree by these companies, with sectoral boundaries being downplayed as far the question of whether or not to acquire is concerned.

5. Setting out the Framework

At this point it may be useful to take stock and draw a few threads together. It will be recalled from the discussion in Chapter 1 that Holmstrom and Tirole (1989) suggested that a theory of the firm should concern itself with questions of why firms exist, and what determines their boundaries. To this agenda we added questions of how the firm manages to survive, and how it organizes itself to pursue its chosen strategy. The previous two chapters have been concerned with how we should set up our approach to this fairly broad agenda, and were sensitive to how various spoke theories could be useful in framing this approach. However, before we go any further it is worth noting that even the basic Holmstrom–Tirole agenda for a workable theory of the firm goes beyond the limited agenda of the traditional theory. The neoclassical theory of the firm was developed to explain the behaviour of markets, not firms. The neoclassical agenda in this context was about how prices and outputs in the external market were determined (Machlup, 1967; Latsis, 1972, pp. 212–13; Blaug, 1992, pp. 150–7). The existence of firms was not a matter of interest or importance in its own right, but stemmed from the need to infer some supply side device involved in the behaviour of markets. There was no real concern with the scale or scope of the firm as such, with the possible exception of various debates arising over the role of decreasing returns or declining demand curves in limiting the size of the firm. Even here the concern was not really with the boundaries of the firm itself, but rather arose from a realization that unless increasing returns or declining demand curves existed, there was nothing to limit the scale of the firm and this in turn would lead to the breakdown of the ideal of perfect markets.[1]

Thus, there is no point in criticising the traditional theory of the firm for perceived inadequacies in dealing with the Holmstrom–Tirole agenda. It was designed to deal with quite another agenda and its performance must be judged on those terms. To the extent that the various spoke theories started from observation of actual firm behaviour, we should expect that they should be able to give a better account of how and why firms exist as institutions in their own right, as well as contributing to the analysis of the determination of the boundaries of the firm. It will be remembered that we identified four spokes coming off the neoclassical hub, and we shall summarize below where we think our analysis stands in relation to these spokes.

We shall start below in section 5.1 with the resource-based approach (spoke 2 theories) and then go on to discuss the relevance of spoke 3, spoke 1 and spoke 4 theories in sections 5.2, 5.3 and 5.4 respectively. Finally, we shall go on to develop other aspects of relevance to this approach, including system and pattern in the formulation of corporate strategies in section 5.5 and the role of history in section 5.6. We shall then elaborate our basic agenda by setting out eight fundamental issues that a theory of the firm should deal with in section 5.7.

5.1. Resource

In the transaction cost approach, it is the incremental transaction that is the unit of analysis as far as the internalization decision is concerned. Here the unit of analysis is the resource, but it would be a mistake to think of there being a corresponding internalization decision relating to the incremental resource, just as it would be a mistake to characterize the firm as a set of implicit or incomplete contracts. The firms in this perspective are essentially collections of resources organized in an administrative framework (Penrose, 1959) that 'know how to do things' (Winter, 1988, p. 175). In terms of corporate governance, the approach taken here is sympathetic to the perspective of (John) Kay and Silberston (1995) whose model of governance demands 'the evolutionary development of the corporation around its core skills and activities because it is these skills and activities rather than a set of financial claims which are the essence of the company' (Kay and Silberston, 1995, p. 91). One important issue which will not be pursued far here is how corporate governance may be affected by institutional and cultural considerations. For example, Nickell (1995) distinguishes between two stylized forms of financial environment and corporate governance: type I in which external control over managers is exerted by threat of takeover and replacement (e.g. US and UK) and type II in which long-term major shareholders exert control over managers (e.g. Japan and Germany). The suggestion here is not that these considerations may be unimportant; instead the suggestion is that there is sufficient commonality across different regimes of corporate governance in terms of the picture painted by Penrose (1959) and Nelson and Winter (1982) for us to neglect these differences in the present context.

Whether the capabilities associated with a particular resource (or cluster of resources) has more value inside the firm rather than out depends on its relationships with other resources, not the degree to which that resource may or may not have specialized uses. In the transaction cost approach, the boundaries of the firm are more likely to encompass a component if it is specialized to its use in the firm than if it can be obtained off-the-shelf in the market place. But, while asset-specificity may take us so far in analysing the boundaries of the firm, the problem is that this is not far enough. For example, a transaction cost analysis of the boundaries of Boeing in the early post-war period when it essentially produced warplanes would find that Boeing bought some of its components from outside suppliers, and made some components itself. It may well be the case that the company bought readily available, standardized components from outside suppliers, whilst making in-house those specialized components not available in the market place. However, if we use this as an explanation for the nature and existence of the firm itself, it proves extremely limited, even when we re-interpret 'asset specificity' in terms of problems of replaceability as we did in Chapter 3. Before we explain the boundaries of the firm in terms of the components it produces itself, we have to explain why Boeing produced the warplanes that use these components in the first place; this question prompts consideration of the firm's capabilities and history, not just the nature of its relationship to the components it uses.

However, analysis of the boundaries of the firm has to go further still. Any account of the growth of Boeing and the expansion of its boundaries has to explain why it subsequently diversified into civil aircraft, guided missiles, and space products. In each of these cases, the logic of diversification could be traced back to Boeing's expertise in aerospace technology and its marketing competencies in selling to a few technically sophisticated users. It is *non*-specificity of resources having alternative uses that helped fuel the expansion of Boeing's boundaries out of its base in producing warplanes. Indeed, instead of encouraging expansion of corporate boundaries as in vertical relations, specialized applications for resources served to limit it, as when Boeing found out that its technological and marketing expertise did not transfer readily into producing and selling mass market products.

The starting point of any analysis of the boundaries of the firm has to be with its resources, and the capabilities and competencies it generates. These features are more general and fundamental to the nature of the firm than are any notions of contract, incomplete or otherwise. To take one further example, the notion of a one-person firm is quite natural as long as we view the firm as a collection of capabilities—which in such a case would reside in one person. However, if the firm is a market replacing device as Coase and Williamson suggest, what market is such a firm replacing? (Fourie, 1993). We could go further and ask where are the internal markets and the hierarchical arrangements that transaction cost economics leads us to expect from the Coasian firm in the one-person firm case. Either such firms do not exist, or, as Fourie suggests, transaction cost economics cannot provide a fundamental explanation for the firm as a durable, cohesive entity.[2] We are inclined to the latter interpretation, and see the Penrosian interpretation of the firm as a collection of resources as the key to unravelling the nature of the firm and the reasons for its existence.

5.2. Hierarchy

One of the features of the economist's mental set discussed in Chapters 1 and 3 is the tendency to analyse resource allocation in exchange-based terms and indeed this is seen as a virtue by many economists: 'one of the attractive attributes of the transaction-cost approach is that it reduces, essentially to a study of contracting' (Williamson, 1986, p. 197). The usual interpretation of hierarchy is in terms of authority and responsibility for decision-making, but in transaction cost economics even hierarchy can be analysed in contractual terms: 'if one or a few agents are responsible for negotiating all contracts, the contractual hierarchy is great. If instead each individual negotiates each interface separately, the contractual hierarchy is weak' (Williamson, 1985, p. 221). Hierarchy in the organizational sense of an instrument for arranging decision-making tends to retreat into the background in transaction cost economics. Indeed, while the theory tells us individuals are known to be opportunistic, they are rarely seen to make a decision, and we are given few clues as to how they would make decisions when they get around to making them. Like the neoclassical theory of the firm, transaction cost economics is still essentially a theory of markets. Its approach to the nature of the firm is typically based on the relative efficiency of external markets versus internal markets, as in the case of markets for intermediate products (vertical integration), capital (the conglomerate) and labour (the employment relation). Even when hierarchy in the decision-making or organizational sense actually appears (as in Williamson, 1975, pp. 132–54), it is in the context of comparison of a hierarchy (U-form) with another hierarchy (M-form). Thus, as far as conventional definitions of hierarchy are concerned, the transaction cost approach tends to compare markets with markets and hierarchies with hierarchies, not markets with hierarchies (Kay, 1992*a*, 1993).

In Chapter 3 it was argued that the fundamental advantage that hierarchy had over markets was that it permitted the *deferring* of strategic decisions. Hierarchy implants decision-making capability at various places with individuals or groups having specified responsibilities for generating, responding to, or otherwise participating in future decisions. The creation of decision-making capacity associated with hierarchy is only needed when there is uncertainty as to what is going to happen in the future. However, this still leaves the parallel question of how hierarchy organizes and arranges this decision-making capacity in actual organizational forms, such as structures arranged by functions, by divisions, and so on. Hierarchy arranges and locates authority and responsibility for decision-making in the firm, and each organizational form constitutes one individual solution to the problem of bounded rationality. Since firms are clusters of resources and these resources may interact in a variety of ways, all hierarchical solutions favour some interactions between resources while impeding others. The hierarchical problem is to choose an arrangement that deals with these trade-offs as efficiently as possible. At the same time, choice of organizational form may be path-dependent and constrained by historical development; switching to a more efficient arrangement may be difficult, painful, and resisted until it becomes crisis-driven.[3] In Chapters 11 and 12 we shall focus on how hierarchy may develop to deal with patterns of links associated with alternative strategies.

5.3. Decision

The various spoke 1 theories associated with March, Simon and Cyert discussed in Chapter 2 were mostly concerned with the process of decision, and so far we have mostly been concerned with the subject matter of decision-making. Our starting point is that our typical firm is managerially controlled and growth oriented, with that growth limited by scarce managerial resources; at any one stage in its development the firm is likely to be faced with a number of alternative growth opportunities and has to choose between them. This is the type of situation represented in Chapter 4, in which the firm chooses from a limited number of discrete alternatives. Our firms can rank opportunities in order of preference, and may be directed by stable rules governing the selection of alternatives, but there is no sense that this may necessarily coincide with optimal choice rules (unless this is taken to be in the weak sense implied by Posner (1993, p. 85), in which more of a good thing is generally preferred to less). The nature of innovative threats to the firm's capabilities means that the firm is likely to be highly uncertain as to the possible nature and incidence of particular future threats. What it can do in such circumstances is audit the pattern of linkages represented by the corporate strategy, and assess vulnerability to specific 'hits' on individual linkages. Our firm's position in time period $t+1$ reflects where it has finished up in time period t and the opportunities it faces in that period; there is no notion of an optimal scale of firm, or a final equilibrium state for the firm.

This last point is consistent with the evolutionary perspective sketched by Winter (1988, p. 178) in which the size of a large firm is not to be thought of as the solution to some organizational problem, but instead reflects the cumulative effects of a series of events stretching back into the past. This does not mean that the firm will necessarily expand indefinitely; environmental pressures may mean that the firm can stand still or contract as well as expand in a given time period. Growth orientation can mean limiting shrinkage as well as pursuing expansion. As Grossman and Hart (1986, pp. 692–3) point out, the question of what limits the size of a firm has been a recurring problem in transaction cost economics that has never been satisfactorily resolved; however it is possible to analyse the issue as one reflecting corporate capabilities and history, in which case the idea of an 'optimal size of firm' ceases to make sense.

To what extent do managers have discretion to pursue their own objectives and make their own decisions? The answer from a variety of perspectives is that there is likely to be considerable discretion. First, our conclusion in Chapter 4 that the large modern corporation tends to operate in a soft selection environment removes a major source of potential inhibitors on discretionary behaviour. Schumpeter would not have agreed with Hick's dictum that the best of all monopoly profits is an easy life. Instead, he saw the 'soporific effect' of monopolization as being no basis for a general theory of firm behaviour, and argued instead that 'a monopoly position is in general no cushion to sleep on. As it can be gained, so it can be retained only by alertness and energy' (Schumpeter, 1954, p. 102). As long as we are in a world of single product firms, then potential competition in the product-market may indeed be sufficient to concentrate managerial attention wonderfully. However, the world of soft selection that was explored in Chapter 4 is one that may be consistent with management being afforded a degree of latitude over the design of corporate strategy. This does not mean that profit is unimportant, merely that it is only an element in decision-making.

Secondly, the shareholders of the modern corporation face substantial principal-agent problems in making sure that the management team are sticking to the straight and narrow of value maximization. Since Berle and Means (1932) it has become clear that there is an informational asymmetry between the professional management of the firm and the firm's shareholders which makes it difficult or impossible for owners to second guess and check the claims of the managers that they are maximizing the value of the firm on their behalf (e.g. see Stiglitz, 1985). The possible inconsistencies in objectives between management and shareholders in the particular context of diversification were demonstrated by Porter (1987). Porter studied the diversification records of thirty-three large, prestigious US companies from 1950 to 1986 and concluded that the corporate strategies of most companies have dissipated rather than created shareholder value.

Thirdly, there is little evidence that even the threat of hostile take-overs exercises strong discipline over management who do not maximize the value of the firm on behalf of the shareholders. Grossman and Hart (1980) have shown there are serious problems with the idea of hostile take-overs as a disciplinary device. If the shares in a company are dispersed into a number of hands, then a small shareholder may not be willing to accept a bid at an offer price that does not reflect the prospective increased profitability of the firm under the proposed new management. They may also judge that their individual decision will not be critical in deciding the success or failure of the bid). But if all shareholders reason this way, the bid will not go through for a share price that does not fully reflect these expected future profits, which should rather take away the incentive for the potential bidder. While there are ways that these effects may be muted in practice, Nickell (1995, pp. 48–50) concludes that the empirical evidence suggests that the hostile take-over mechanism is not very effective as a disciplinary device, except in the most blatant cases of inefficiency.

5.4. Technological Change

In our analysis, the key to understanding the effects of technological change is to understand its level of impact. If we have single product and single technology firms, then analysis is correspondingly simple. The destruction of technologies implies the death of products and the death of firms. The gales of Schumpeterian radical innovation sweep all before them, and any management complacent enough to believe that survival without adaptation is possible is either extremely fortunate or extremely foolish. Nor does it make sense to wait to change until the winds of Schumpeterian change have begun to blow. It is at such times that internal and external capital resources begin to dry up, just at the time when some slack is required. The wrong time to try to redesign the ship is when it is beginning to sink. Consequently, single-product firms that can ride out the obsolesence of their only business are either extremely clever or again extremely lucky.

The development of the diversified firm changed these rules. Firms do not obsolesce, capabilities do. If a firm is a collection of capabilities, then the obsolescence of some of its capabilities need not imply the demise of the firm. In general, the firm has three options for dealing with capabilities which are under attack. First, it can respond by upgrading the capabilities; basically a repair activity. Secondly, it can remove the capabilities altogether and substitute alternative ones (e.g. through acquisition); basically a replacement activity. Both these responses are consistent with the firm staying in the same business, but they do depend on the existence of other internal resources in the firm both to sustain the firm and undertake the repair and replace functions. Thirdly, the firm can accept that the attack on the capability is of sufficient severity that it brings the viability of the businesses to which it contributes under threat. In this case, the divestment option may be considered and the firm may jettison the affected businesses. Clearly, this last option cannot be carried out in isolation indefinitely, since the firm would eventually be reduced to a specialized rump and this would bring the original Schumpeterian scenario back into play. However, repair and replace activities should allow the firm to slow closure programmes compared to what would be the case with the specialized firm, whilst the internalization of creative destruction discussed in Chapter 4 should allow the firm to generate expansion opportunities to compensate for the shrinkage effects of divestment.

These issues have been of considerable interest in the strategic management literature, for example in the development of a variety of techniques and approaches by consultants such as Boston Consulting, Arthur D. Little and McKinsey, enabling top management to treat the corporation as a portfolio of investments (Miller and Dess, 1996, pp. 270–6). All of these approaches analyse the constituent businesses of the firm in terms of internal capabilities, relevant environmental conditions, and the business's position as a potential cash user or cash provider. The various repair, replace, and divest options can usually be grafted on to a portfolio analysis, if they are not explicit options already. Portfolio management approaches have been criticised as being rather mechanistic and only really useful as a complement to strategic analysis rather than as a substitute for it (Miller and Dess, 1996, pp. 275–6). For our purposes, the important point is that it is diversification itself which gives management the necessary degrees of slack and flexibility to decide whether to repair, replace, or divest. Whilst portfolio management may indeed be mechanistic, it helps to provide practical sketches of the processes through which the large diversified corporation continues to evolve and survive.

Capabilities can be double-edged; they may provide internal economies and a source of common vulnerability to obsolescence prompted by environmental attacks. Since links reflect patterns of capabilities, it follows that mapping these patterns should help to decipher underlying logic and coherence as far as the firm's strategy is concerned in terms of dealing with internal opportunities and external threats. Normally, the firm will choose these opportunities with which it could exploit the strongest potential linkages, though particular circumstances (e.g. absence of related opportunities, turbulent environments) may encourage it to pursue weakly linked opportunities instead. Normally, also, the firm operates in a soft selection environment, though hard selection may threaten in special cases, for example some smaller firms and larger diversified corporations in pathological crisis situations. The crucial point is that the modern corporation generally has the power to alter its general environment, and indeed has strong incentives to do so. Both individuals and firms have rational reasons for preferring soft selection environments over harder-edged alternatives, and we would therefore expect that these considerations should help to provide a useful guide to the strategies of the firm in practice. At the level of technologies, competition is Schumpeterian hard selection. At the level of the large diversified modern corporation, it is soft selection.

The level of impact we are concerned with is that of capabilities, or competencies within the firm. As Freeman (1994, p. 474) points out, one of the problems for analysis is the sheer variety and complexity of innovations. However, Malerba and Orsenigo (1993, 1995) provide a useful framework when they suggest a basis for analysing innovations in terms of four main categories. Their work reflects Penrosian as well as Schumpeterian sympathies in that they distinguish technological regimes in terms of opportunity (potential for innovation), appropriability (ability to protect from imitation), cumulativeness (of innovative effort) and properties of the knowledge base (tacit or codified, simple or complex, relation to science base, etc.). Pavitt (1984) and Pavitt *et al.* (1989) also distinguish between important types of innovative threats (e.g. science-based, scale intensive, etc.), while Tushman and Anderson (1986) focus directly on the issue of capabilities when they distinguish between competence-destroying and competence-enhancing technological shifts. In Tushman and Anderson's analysis, competence-destroying technological shift involves the creation of an entirely new class of product (e.g. xerography), a substitute for an existing class (e.g. diesel for steam locomotive) or a new process (e.g. float glass). On the other hand, competence-enhancing discontinuities are order-of-magnitude improvements in performance that build on existing know-how within a product class; they substitute for older technologies, but do not render obsolete the skills required to master the new technologies (Tushman and Anderson, 1986, p. 442).[4] Tushman and Anderson give as examples of competence-enhancing discontinuities the invention of the screw propeller for steamships, the fan jets for aircraft, and the electric typewriter (pp. 442–3).

These analyses are valuable and useful, but consideration of the potential implications of each of them from the particular perspective of the firm helps to simplify our problem somewhat. As Metcalfe (1995) points out, innovative possibility frontiers are not only technology-specific, they are firm-specific. In a sense, the critical point is not whether a new technology is strongly or weakly appropriable, science-based or not, competence-destroying or competence-enhancing. What really matters in this context is whether and how a firm can respond to a threat to its own competencies and capabilities. It is little comfort to know that you are being attacked by a weakly appropriable, competence-enhancing technology if you are unable to upgrade your competencies sufficiently to retaliate effectively.

As far as the possibility of external threat is concerned, the management of the firm have to decide whether, and to what extent, a de-linking strategy should be pursued. The threats that are important are the ones that may render particular competencies obsolete, and of course it may be difficult or impossible for the firm to anticipate the timing of a particular threat and the form it may take. Strategy formulation operates in a haze of uncertainty; individual threats may appear as surprises leaving the firm little time to respond. In such circumstances, the firm may not be able to predict the nature of individual threats, but it may be able to characterize environments in terms of degree of *turbulence*, or their propensity to throw up surprises. For example, high technology environments (such as electronics and information technology) typically exhibit higher degrees of turbulence than low technology environments (such as food and drink). While anticipating specific threats may be impossible in a world of bounded rationality, assessing environments in terms of degree of turbulence based on observation and experience of these environments would appear to be a much more reasonable and manageable information processing task. However, suppose the management can assess environments in terms of degrees of turbulence; what sort of rules are likely to be used to react to different levels of environmental threat? In the next section we shall start to consider the basis around which alternative strategies might be constructed.

5.5. Pattern

So far we have established that links may be double-edged, providing both internal economies and shared vulnerability to external threat. Also, if a firm operates in a turbulent environment, it may wish to operate some form of de-linking strategy in order to cushion itself from the impact of particular environmental threats. However, what form will such strategies take? Are they likely to be *ad hoc* and fairly arbitrary responses to particular situations? Or are they likely to follow some basic design rules and display consistency and pattern in their construction? We have three sets of justification for the idea that corporate strategy may not be randomly generated, but may be characterized by pattern, a conclusion which may have important implications for resource allocation in the firm.

The first argument relates to human cognition and is itself an important argument; traditional approaches to economics have tended to limit cognitive aspects to the ability of individuals to process information and then optimize or satisfice. However recent research in cognitive psychology and neuropsychology has suggested that human beings do attempt to construct patterns in processing and storing information. The idea that individuals may actively synthesize rather than just passively process information may seem uncontroversial, but it is not a view that has been traditionally encouraged in some quarters of mainstream psychology. Behaviourism has been an extremely influential approach in Western psychology, and there are interesting parallels between the role it has played in psychology and that played by neoclassical theory in economics. The early work of Pavlov into conditioned reflexes helped set the tone and context for much subsequent behaviourist analysis. Just as neoclassical theory started from the perspective of the firm as a black box processing inputs to produce outputs, so behaviourism in psychology saw the individual as a black box responding to stimuli to produce responses.[5] As well as helping to avoid the need to infer subjective processes such as consciousness, this helped to provide an atomistic unit on which analysis could be based; psychology's equivalent of the product-market in neoclassical theory. Gestalt theorists such as Koffka (1935) did provide an alternative perspective, popularly summarized as 'the whole is greater than/different from the sum of its parts', but it is probably fair to say that for much of the twentieth century, the obvious chasm that existed between the reductionist perspective of behaviourism and the systemic perspective of the Gestalt theorists was one that appeared too wide to bridge using the standard methods of experimental psychology. Also, while there has been a great deal of research into pattern recognition in cognitive psychology in recent years, this field is characterized by a number of competing theories and a variety of interpretations as to the nature of cognitive processes associated with pattern recognition (Matlin, 1994, pp. 27–41).

However, some striking recent results in neuropsychology suggest that human cognitive processes may generate both reductionist and holistic interpretations of the same phenomenon, and that the respective frames of reference may be influenced by different neurophysiological mechanisms. It has been known for some time that individuals with brain damage in the left hemisphere of their brain are more likely to respond poorly to the parts or details of a visual scene, while those with right hemisphere damage are more likely to respond to the overall pattern or Gestalt (Bradshaw and Nettleton, 1981; Robertson and Lamb, 1991). In turn, that has led to theories of brain function based on the idea that the left hemisphere functions analytically (emphasizing *local* elements, or detailed characteristics of phenomena), while the right hemisphere functions holistically (emphasizing *global* patterns, or system and Gestalt). The distinction between global and local in this context is illustrated in Fig. 5.1 which shows what Robertson and Lamb (1991) describe as a Navon-type diagram (after the work of Navon, 1977, 1981).[6]

Figure 5.1 shows a (global level) pattern which can be read as a large *M* composed of individual (local level) elements which are in turn small *z*s. A purely local level account of this figure would treat it as an aggregation of 24 small *z*s. In turn, a purely global account of Fig. 5.1 would read it as displaying a large *M*. Delis *et al.* (1986) found that when brain damaged individuals with lesions in the right hemisphere were asked to reproduce Navon-type diagrams from memory, they were more likely to miss global letters and geometric patterns, whilst those with lesions in the left hemisphere were more likely to miss the characteristics of local or constituent elements. In their wide ranging survey of neuropsychological studies of part/whole organization, Robertson and Lamb (1991) summarize investigations of individual recall of Navon-type diagrams as in Delis *et al.* (1986), and conclude that the evidence is consistent with two different cognitive mechanisms at work in the respective hemispheres, one responding to local level elements in systems, and one responding to global patterns. They also note that it is conceivable that brain damage itself could lead to a reorganization of cognitive processes and limit the generality of these findings, but they conclude later that the convergence between normal and pathological evidence is strong enough to reject that possibility.

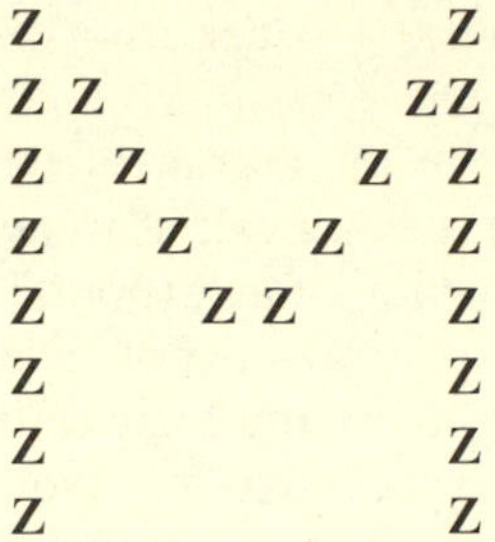

```
Z                    Z
Z Z                ZZ
Z   Z          Z   Z
Z     Z    Z   Z
Z       Z Z        Z
Z                    Z
Z                    Z
Z                    Z
```

Fig. 5.1. Navon-type figure

There are many interesting implications of research in this area of potential relevance to how individuals analyse the world and how this may influence their decisions. One whole line of research has been stimulated by Navon's claim (1977, 1981) of evidence for 'global precedence' in that individuals apparently process global information before local information *ceteris paribus*. There has been considerable debate over this conjecture (particularly characterized by amendments to the *ceteris paribus* condition), with the studies of brain damaged individuals referred to above representing one strand of research (Robertson and Lamb, 1991, pp. 302–10). Another line of neurophysiological research into attentional aspects of global versus local interpretations has employed explicitly efficiency-based criteria in their models, with attentional resources being reallocated between local and global levels according to perceived cost/benefit trade-offs (Robertson and Lamb, 1991, 312–18). However, for our purposes, the most important implication of research in this area is that global (systemic) and local (reductionist) perspectives are both natural and complementary features of human cognition. This is a conclusion which accords with experience and common sense. There are times when the chief executive of General Electric might wish to take an overview of the corporate strategy and get a feeling for the overall scope and balance of activities, and there are times when he may be more interested in business level profitability and the resultant aggregate performance. There are times when the editor of this book has asked for an overview of aims and objectives, and there are times when he has asked for a word count.

However, a quite separate line of experimental research in cognitive psychology suggests that individuals may not passively form patterns from stimuli provided by the environment, but that instead they may actively transform images into more regular, orderly, and symmetrical patterns than actually exists in reality.[7] The research is consistent with the idea of individuals seeking or even imposing patterns in trying to make sense of the world. The notion of the individual attempting to find coherence in the raw data around them is one that brings us closer to the world in which the strategic decision-maker can try to discern—or create—coherence in their corporate environment.

Our second justification for the argument that corporate strategies may be characterized by pattern is empirical; firms actually do appear to actively seek pattern in their construction of a corporate strategy: 'numerous empirical studies have shown that firms do not diversify in a random fashion. . . . There appears to be a pattern and logic to the diversification choices of most firms that is related to their base of resources, even though the variety of configurations across industry is very large' (Montgomery, 1994, p. 174). Further, Prahalad and Bettis (1986) argue that it is possible to identify the 'dominant logic' of a particular firm meaning a mind set or a world view or overall conceptualization of the business. In Prahalad and Bettis' view, the dominant logic is stored as a shared cognitive map (or set of schemas) among the dominant coalition and it is expressed in the form of learned problem-solving behaviour. Thus, not only do firms differ (Nelson, 1991), the differences do not appear to be constructed arbitrarily, but instead appear to reflect logical and coherent principles which may be peculiar to the firm itself. If such patterns do exist, and it is possible to establish some unifying design principles under which they operate, it opens up the possibility of being able to develop explanations of corporate behaviour in a wide number of areas.

Our third justification for the notion that patterns may exist in the specific context of strategic decision-making is that this can be an efficient way to direct resource allocation. Indeed, if this was not the case, then corporate strategy would be reducible to a simple aggregation of business level strategies, much like the cases above where local level features tend to be emphasized at the expense of global patterns. Instead, consistency or regularity in the characteristics across the firm permits economies to be achieved in scarce strategic decision-making resources and limits the possibility of a mismatch of rules and procedures developed in different contexts in the firm. This is something that we shall deal with at greater length when we look at diversification strategy in Chapter 7.

In the analysis that follows, we shall look at two basic patterns, weak patterns and strong patterns. A weak pattern is said to exist where a consistent rule applied to strategic alternatives can lead to variation in linkages, though in a consistent way. For example, the rule 'seek richest linkages' helps to explain a great deal of oil company expansion strategies as described by Ollinger (1994) in the last chapter, with companies tending to pursue richly linked horizontal and domestic moves first, then more poorly linked international and diversification moves, and then finally unrelated or conglomerate moves. The linkages thin out as the firm moves further and further away from its core technologies and markets. A strong pattern exists where consistent regularities persist over the whole of the corporate strategy. For example, a firm might base its expansion strategy around a double link, single links, or no links at all. We shall look at weak patterns in Chapters 8, 9, and 10, while Chapters 7, 11, and 12 will assume the existence of strong patterns for the most part.

5.6. The Role of History

A further important issue is that consideration of possible alternatives may be limited by history. An approach which has strongly influenced the arguments in the present work is evolutionary theory (e.g. Alchian, 1950; Nelson and Winter, 1982; David, 1985; Arthur, 1989). A concept which assists analysis here is lock-in by historical events (Arthur, 1989). For example, in the early stages of industry evolution, some initial accident can give a particular technology a lead over competing standards. This lead may in turn provide the technology with a first mover advantage through which it can further extend its lead. The process may be cumulative and characterized by positive feedback effects that further magnify the initial advantage that started the sequence off. The end result may be that a particular technology emerges as the dominant standard purely because of the initial accidental set of circumstances. Influences such as increasing returns and network externalities can give a technology incumbency advantages over alternatives, even when the alternatives possess attractive efficiency characteristics compared to the incumbent. The standard QWERTY keyboard is an example of a sub-optimal survivor (David, 1985). There are more efficient keyboard designs that allow for improved typing performance, but particular historical incidents led to the initial adoption and subsequent entrenchment of the QWERTY format. There is strong support in biology for the idea of evolutionary processes throwing up and sustaining sub-optimal solutions; for example the panda's 'thumb' looks like a finger and works like an opposable thumb, but is in fact a sixth digit fashioned out of a spur of wrist bone. The thumb in its carnivorous ancestors had joined the other digits in the function of clawing and stabbing, and was now too specialized in this role to help grasp bamboo shoots. As Gould points out, often 'an engineer's best solution is debarred by history' (1980, p. 24). Nature does not start with idealized blueprints and then optimize; it instead works with what is available and sorts out solutions that make do.

These outcomes reflect path dependency, in that the opportunities for future change are constrained by the particular developmental path the system has taken in the past. Once the possibility of path dependency is recognized, it can be seen in a variety of contexts. For example, some UK cities have a relatively affluent west end and a relatively impoverished east end. These developments were influenced by the prevailing winds and smoky chimneys; richer Victorians typically preferred to live in suburbs that were relatively unpolluted, and they could afford to pay the price for that privilege. Contemporary smoke control in cities means that the events that triggered such patterns of settlement have largely disappeared, but many of these historically determined residential patterns still survive today.

However, perhaps one of the most striking examples of path dependency is the vehicle through which beginning students are first introduced to neoclassical theory; the standard first year textbook. Compare any two first year textbooks, and a remarkable series of parallels in terms of topics may be observed, often contrasting strongly with the publicity about the uniqueness of the product on offer. One leading economics textbook writer has recently argued that the order in which microeconomics is taught could be much improved; for example, instead of a progression in the order consumer choice–competition–monopoly, a more appropriate ordering would be; monopoly–competition–consumer choice. It is difficult to communicate to students that price (P) = average revenue (AR) = marginal revenue (MR) in perfect competition is a particularly interesting or significant result until they have seen that P and MR can differ as in monopoly. In addition, students tend to accept the logic of a downward sloping monopoly demand curve as reasonable and sensible (what happens if the electricity company raises its price . . .?), while the idea of infinitely elastic firm demand as in perfect competition often appears counter-intuitive and unrealistic. It could make more pedagogical sense to introduce them gently to the world of monopoly first, before introducing competition and guiding them towards the more complex areas of long run firm and industry equilibrium in perfect competition. Also, the concept of marginal cost is easier to communicate than marginal utility; anyone who has tried to convince a first year class that 'utils' is a meaningful concept would probably agree with this. It could make teaching microeconomics more persuasive if the teaching of consumer choice was deferred until after the teaching of market structures.[8]

First year courses typically follow the standard approach in which the formats of the major components of microeconomics and macroeconomics are embodied in the acquired intellectual capital of lecturers' and tutors' teaching practice. Any author who wants their textbook adopted—or wants to keep it adopted—would ignore this at their peril. Jumping on to a 'better' path represented by an improved textbook structure could require nontrivial transition or conversion costs on the part of the users (in this case the teachers). In such circumstances, the relatively inefficient and inferior standard approach may continue to be adopted, while more efficient and superior versions fail to take off.

These processes are consistent with path dependent systems with lock-in effects. The survival of the standard textbook format with its inferior design has parallels in technology such as the QWERTY keyboard, and in biology as in the case of the panda's thumb. Schumpeter (1954) put the tendency of neoclassical economists to ignore the evidence of history well when he argued that 'the essential point to grasp is that in dealing with capitalism we are dealing with an evolutionary process' (p. 82) . . . 'they [neoclassical economists] accept the data of the momentary situation as if there were no past or future to it and think that they have understood what there is to understand if they interpret the behaviour of firms by means of the principle of maximising profits with reference to those data. The usual theorist's paper and the usual government commission's report practically never try to see that behaviour, on the one hand, as a result of a piece of past history and, on the other hand, as an attempt to deal with a situation that is sure to change presently' (p. 84). It seems we could go further; the usual economics textbook, as well as the usual theorist's paper and the usual government commission's report, may themselves be seen as products of path dependent processes in which traces of history can be found in their deficiencies and imperfections.

However, if the standard textbook design is imperfect, where did it come from? An obvious suspect is Samuelson's *Economics*, whose introduction revolutionized the teaching of economics. But if we go back to Marshall's *Principles of Economics* we find that the ordering of microeconomics topics in Samuelson largely followed Marshall. Go further back and the utility–competition–monopoly ordering can be seen in Ricardo's *Principles of Political Economy*, the same ordering that appeared in what is regarded as the foundation stone of modern economics—Adam Smith's *Wealth of Nations*.

The market that Adam Smith was aiming at was much wider than the eighteenth-century equivalent of Economics 101, and even the presentation of Marshall's *Principles* was influenced by the author's hope of being read by 'men of affairs' (Blaug, 1978, p. 442). The important point is that no economist starts with a blank slate in terms of textbook design, the pattern as well as the coverage of his or her work will be determined by what has gone before. To paraphrase Keynes, the textbook writer is the slave of if not a defunct economist, at least several dead ones. Indeed, all lovers of irony will probably enjoy the fact that the instrument used to communicate notions of optimal decisions and outcomes to beginning first year students is itself a highly sub-optimal device bearing all the hallmarks of path dependency and lock-in.

If economics textbooks, panda's thumbs, and typewriter keyboards are all imperfect designs reflecting history and contingency, we should not be surprised to find later that the same holds for the boundaries of the firm. Indeed, support for this is provided by North (1990, pp. 94–5), who argues that what Arthur is looking at in his analysis of competing technologies is only indirectly about technological standards, and more directly about decision-making in organizations. This raises the possibility that notions of path dependency may be of relevance to firms operating in soft selection environments of the kind discussed in Chapter 4. We shall explore this further at various points in later chapters.

5.7. Eight Fundamental Issues

The approach developed here leads to theories relating to the existence and nature of firms in eight specific areas: vertical integration, specialization, diversification, multinational enterprise, joint ventures, alliances, networks, and organizational structure. Conventional approaches to the theory of the firm have tended to focus on issues associated with individual product-markets, such as pricing, output, entry and exit, and vertical integration decisions. Analysing the firm in terms of its constituent links offers the possibility of widening the agenda. In the following chapters this agenda reflects the belief that analysing the nature of the firm means analysing both the strategies of the firm and the means or modes by which these strategies are achieved. Just as a traveller may be faced with a choice of alternative routes, and a further choice of alternative modes of transport associated with each route, a firm is typically faced with both 'where' and 'how' decisions in assessing alternative growth opportunities. Transaction cost economics typically focuses more narrowly on the 'how' questions as they relate to particular strategies. However, unless questions relating to choice of modes are framed within broader questions relating to choice of strategies, analysis will typically be restricted to questions of how to implement specific business level strategies. The agenda set out here is concerned with broader issues relating to the shaping of the boundaries of the firm. In each of the eight issues, the option under discussion is framed in a light shaded background, with other alternative solutions sometimes included for comparison purposes. Dotted lines between business units indicate cases where the link is exploited by creating hierarchy and provision for future decision-making *between* firms, for example when the two firms in Fig. 5.5 form a joint venture around the middle IBU (Individual Business Unit) in this example.

1. *Vertical integration*

Chapter 3 has already suggested that it is more helpful to analyse the reasons why firms vertically integrate in terms of the implications if a particular resource or resource combination were to disappear, rather than in terms of whether or not there are alternative applications for this resource in the

Fig. 5.2. Specialization

market place. It is an application of a resource-based perspective to the vertical integration question, and it helps to set the context for the fuller development of the picture of the firm as an integrated collection of resources in Chapter 4.

2. *Specialization*

The analysis of linkages in Chapter 4 helps to highlight the fact that when a firm chooses to specialize it is adopting both a strategy (specialization as opposed to diversification) and a mode by which to pursue that strategy (hierarchy versus market). Specialization serves as a basic reference strategy in our analysis; as Fig. 5.2 indicates, the specialization option tends to be characterized by richer potential linkages than diversification options (such as the option on the left), *ceteris paribus*. Chapter 4 also suggested that market alternatives (the option on the right) to exploiting synergy gains in-house are normally liable to be more costly than the in-house alternative. In short, exploiting specialization gains in-house would appear to be a very attractive option compared to less synergistic strategies and higher cost modes. This raises the question of why firms should ever opt for alternative strategies and modes, a question which is explored in different contexts associated with the next five fundamental issues below.

3. *Diversification*

As we saw in Chapter 4 the diversification option in Fig. 5.3 has to beat alternative strategies and alternative modes to be adopted. Why should a firm adopt more weakly linked diversification opportunities if the specialization option (the option on the left) is available? We shall explore diversification issues, including the conglomerate, further in Chapter 7 and this will also be the main subject of our analysis of particular corporate strategies in Chapter 6.

Fig. 5.3. Diversification and conglomerates

4. *Multinational enterprise*

As we shall see in Chapter 8, analysis of linkages associated with multinational enterprise raises the question as to why such a thinly linked option would ever be adopted. The only linkage that a multinational enterprise can easily exploit cross-frontier is usually know-how; other resources such as plant, equipment, distribution channels and labour tend to be specific to activities in particular countries. So why should firms ever exploit such thin linkages as indicated in Fig. 5.4 if domestic specialization or diversification (the option on the left) could share at least some of these know-how linkages, and add a substantial array of other marketing, technological, and country-specific linkages in addition? Chapter 8 explores these issues in some detail.

Fig. 5.4. Multinational enterprise

5. *Joint venture*

If the multinational enterprise appears paradoxical when analysed from the point of view of an option, a joint venture appears similarly paradoxical when analysed from the point of view of a mode for coordinating linkages. In Fig. 5.5, the dotted ovals indicate corporate boundaries with the middle IBU of the three IBU combination representing the joint venture co-owned by the two end firms. The joint venture exploits marketing synergies with one parent and technological synergies with the other. The single firm alternative (on the left) coordinates similar synergies to those exploited in the joint venture. Joint ventures tend to be associated with problems of dual managerial control, appropriability problems, and contractual costs. Since these are typically additional to the normal managerial costs associated with single firm exploitation of new venture opportunities (as on the left), it raises the question as to why joint ventures would ever be undertaken. Chapter 9 explores the implications of this basic question.

Fig. 5.5. Joint venture

6. *Alliances*

Chapter 4 considered the logic of firms clustering the exploitation of link-ages in-house by selecting one internalization opportunity compared to the alternative of dealing with many contracting opportunities simultaneously. The evolution of alliances in which firms cluster cooperative agreements with preferred partners would appear to echo such clustering of synergistic opportunities in a market context. However, since individual cooperative agreements do not face the same limited opportunities as complementary resources exploited within a specific firm, complementarity does not offer a guide to such clustering in the case of alliances; if firms must collaborate, why do they not simply seek the most suitable and highly valued collabo-rator on a case by case (link by link) basis rather than locking into one part-ner or a restricted number of partners? As Fig. 5.6 indicates, alliances are exclusive as well as inclusive, and Chapter 10 explores the circumstances and logic which may lead to alliance formation being triggered.

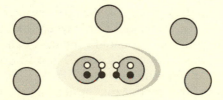

Fig. 5.6. Alliance

7. *Networks*

If alliances represent a clustering of cooperative agreements exploiting links or linkages between firms, then clubs or networks represent a clustering of firms involved in collaborative agreements as in Fig. 5.7. They raise similar questions to those posed in the context of alliances at the level of firms, though here the questions operate at the level of groups of firms. Chapter 10 also explores these questions further.

Fig. 5.7. Networks

8. *Internal organization*

The final fundamental issue to be discussed here is the implications of linkage for organizational structure. As with the question of alternative strategies and alternative modes of linkage coordination, the question of choice of organizational structures revolves around the opportunity cost of alternatives. All organizational designs involve costs, and the crucial question is, what is the least cost design for specific strategies and modes of coordination? Figure 5.8 illustrates two possible choices for a firm that has diversified along a technological link. If an M-form structure (or divisionalization by businesses) was adopted, then it would facilitate the grouping of complementary resources within businesses, but cut across (and possibly impede) the coordination of technological synergies. By way of contrast, a U-form structure built around functional departments such as marketing and production would facilitate the co-ordination of linkages (in this case the technological link), but separate out the complementary resources associated with the respective businesses, and possibly impede their coordination. Clearly the two solutions involve trade-offs, with an M-form structure favouring the coordination of complementary resources, and the U-form more favourable to the exploitation of synergistic opportunities. The strength and breadth of linkages should influence which form should be chosen in a case like this. Chapters 11 and 12 look at organizational design implications associated with such points.

Resource linkages play a central role in defining the resource allocation or organizational problem in each of these fundamental issues. The task for

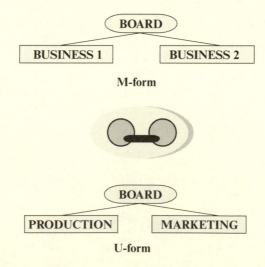

Fig. 5.8. Organizational structure

the remainder of the book is to try to explain patterns of behaviour in the respective cases. It is hoped to show that some simple basic principles transcend the analysis of individual topics, and help provide a unifying framework that allows us to make some general statements concerning the nature and behaviour of firms.

5.8. Conclusions

The four spoke theoretical routes coming off the neoclassical hub all contribute to an understanding of the nature and behaviour of the firm. Instead of focusing on optimal product-market price, the firm is seen as a collection of hierarchically organized resources in which decisions typically involve a limited number of discrete alternatives. The role of technological change is also important, both in terms of the ability of the large diversified firm to internalize the Schumpeterian forces of creative destruction, and in terms of the threats to particular links that may be posed by particular external innovations. Two important issues are raised, both of which will be the subject of further investigation in later chapters; first, corporate strategies appear not to be randomly constructed but are instead characterized by pattern and order in their formulation, and, secondly, strategies may be path dependent phenomena. Eight fundamental issues associated with the nature and behaviour of firms are identified; vertical integration, specialization, diversification, multinational enterprise, joint venture, alliances, networks, and the relationship between strategy and internal organization. It is hoped to show that the approach developed here can make a contribution in each of these areas.

NOTES

1. See particularly, Sraffa (1926), Kaldor (1934).
2. Hodgson (1993*b*) takes issue with Fourie's analysis suggesting that he and Coase were really talking about different interpretations of the firm. However, as Fourie makes clear, the real issue is not the one-person firm (which he uses as an illustrative device) but the 'attempt to derive and explain the typical and distinguishing nature of the firm exclusively in terms of another, typically different relation, the market' (Fourie, 1993, P. 47). In that respect, Fourie's analysis accords fully with the points which are being made here.
3. As Chandler's (1962) analysis of early switches from U-form to M-form demonstrated.
4. See Pavitt (1987) for criticism of Tushman and Anderson's (1986) taxonomy.
5. Earl (1990) makes a careful distinction between stimulus–response behaviourism

associated with the work of J. B. Watson (1924) and B. F. Skinner (e.g. 1969), and the behavioural approach to economics which tends to acknowledge the need to recognize intervening cognitive processes in decision-making.

6. See also Hofstadter (1980, pp. 310–36) for further examples and analysis of Navon-type diagrams.

7. See, for example, Hirtle and Jonides (1985), Moar and Bower (1983), Schiano and Tversky (1992), Stevens and Coupe (1978), Tversky (1981), Tversky and Schiano (1989).

8. Objections to these points could probably be made: for example, the convention of competition preceding monopoly allows subsequent market failure problems to be discussed together, and the revised sequence would disrupt this. Nevertheless, the point is that there are probably better ways of teaching economics than the current standard approach, and that there is little evidence of serious efforts to develop such alternatives.

6.   Mapping Strategy

In this chapter we shall apply an approach to mapping corporate strategy to an analysis of the recent strategies pursued by five large UK corporations. We shall start by looking at the basis for constructing maps at corporate level in section 6.1, before looking at five strategies in some detail in successive sections. The companies analysed here are Cadbury Schweppes (section 6.2), Thorn EMI (section 6.3), Ladbroke (section 6.4), Trafalgar House (section 6.5), and Hillsdown Holdings (section 6.6). Section 6.7 explores the possibility of using maps of the corporation as a basis for analysing possible sources of internal economies and external threats.

6.1. Mapping Strategy

In Chapter 4 we looked at the exploitation of synergy at a single level in the case of a simple two-business firm. However, in practice synergy is exploited at many levels within the large diversified firm. For example, brands may share plants and labour force, products may share marketing and distribution, divisions may share R&D, and groups of divisions may share legal and financial services. The exact pattern of synergy will depend on the particular corporation and its strategy, and some resources (e.g. advertising and R&D) might be exploited at any or all levels in the corporation. In addition, a given level may generate a rich set of resource linkages between areas (e.g. Ferguson *et al.* 1993, pp. 18–21 and 29). It might therefore seem a daunting task to set out to map the linkages that might give rise to synergy in particular firms. A full description of the synergy exploited by even a small, relatively specialized corporation, would require a map of considerable detail and intricacy. Any attempt to construct a full map of all the linkages involved in managing a large diversified multinational would commit the cartographer to a task of immense complexity. It is further questionable as to whether such a task would be worth the effort; just as a highly detailed map of a forested area might make it difficult to see the wood for the trees, so a complete mapping of synergy would be likely to make it difficult to see the strategy for the linkages.

In fact, the mapping of corporate strategy is facilitated by the hierarchical nature of corporate activity. A corporate hierarchy constitutes a nested series of layers with coordination of synergy taking place at various levels in the hierarchy. Management at all levels may have responsibilities for resolving interdependencies, and corporate strategy is largely concerned with the residual linkages which have not been resolved at lower levels. Further, nesting of decision-making may reduce the type as well as the number of linkages which have to be dealt with at corporate level. For example, in 1993, Cadbury Schweppes operated nearly 100 manufacturing and bottling plants in a variety of countries.[1] In such cases, operational questions of how best to coordinate capital and labour at plant level have to be largely resolved before they reach board room level if they are not to swamp top level decision-making capacity. In the extreme case of the conglomerate, all marketing and technological linkages may be coordinated at lower levels leaving only a few finance linkages to be coordinated at Headquarters level. An example of this is the conglomerate Hanson Trust, many of whose acquisitions had shared characteristics of having been weakly managed dominant firms in mature low technology markets. What Hanson added to its diverse portfolio of businesses was a skill in applying tight cost control and aggressive pricing strategies to such businesses.[2]

We shall look at how organizations organize nested clusters of resource linkages in Chapters 11 and 12, but for the moment we are concerned with the narrower question of what kind of resources are likely to generate synergies at the level of corporate strategy. Plant and hardware related synergies are likely to be exhausted at lower levels in most cases, as are labour skills and professional expertise related to a narrow range of technologies and markets. At corporate strategy level, the types of resource which tend to generate synergies typically fall into the general category of competencies. As Winter (1987) points out, the assets involved in corporate strategy are often denoted by such terms as 'knowledge, competence, know-how, or capability' (p. 160). At this level, the tangible assets associated with the traditional theory of the firm have typically been left behind at lower levels. The assets associated with corporate strategy tend to be diffused throughout various teams and coalitions, and it is the organizational task to draw upon them to formulate a coherent corporate strategy.

The nature and significance of competencies at the level of corporate strategy might be explored by considering what it would take to remove them. This turns out to be more difficult than might be first thought. It is easier to identify competencies than to establish where they are embodied. For example, it is clear that Boeing has developed technological competencies in producing complex high performance aerospace products, and marketing competencies in selling them to a few, technically sophisticated customers. However, it is less clear what it would take to wipe out Boeing's competencies in these areas, or indeed where they are located in the firm. It is usually difficult to identify a specific individual or group whose removal from the firm would also remove the firm's core competencies. Institutions such as firms tend to outlive the tenure of individual managers and managerial groups.

Perhaps the clearest clues as to where and how these competencies may be embedded is given by Nelson and Winter's (1982) analysis of organizational routines. Knowledge and skills are embedded in habits and routines in Nelson and Winter's analysis, and these in turn form the 'organizational memory' of the firm.[3] The concept of organizations having memory is one that is difficult to accommodate within the reductionist confines of traditional economics. In particular, it is difficult to reconcile such systemic concepts with the individualistic perspectives of neoclassical theory. However, it is even more difficult to make sense of concepts such as core competencies without recognizing that something, whether it is described as organizational habits, routines or memory, has to store these competencies. Consequently, if organizational memory (or something analogous to it) does not exist, it is difficult to see how we can talk of the competencies, and indeed the strategies, of firms. As we shall see, it is not only possible but natural to describe organizations in terms of their competencies, capabilities, strategies, and objectives. In turn, where these competencies are shared across businesses they may be expressed as links as we saw earlier. These links may indicate potential sources of economies or synergies from resource sharing. Further, as we saw earlier, these links may also represent sources of potential vulnerability to external threats, especially technological innovation.

In order to see if this mapping approach could be applied more generally to analysis of corporate strategy along the lines suggested in Chapter 4, five firms were selected for detailed analysis. The firms chosen were all large UK public companies. In each case there was detailed published information available stretching back some years. They were also chosen to be comparable in terms of size; in 1993, the largest (Hillsdown Holdings), had a turnover of £4595m and the smallest (Cadbury Schweppes) had a turnover of £3725m. Finally, they were seen to display an interesting variety of strategies seen from the point of view of mapping. The maps finally developed for the five companies are shown in Fig. 6.1.

Before we look at individual strategies, some points can be made about how the various maps were developed. To begin with, a decision was made to rely on published information as far as possible. This was assisted by there being a considerable amount of published material reporting the views of professional company and industry analysts on the coherence of each of the corporate strategies reported below. The *Financial Times* was a particularly valuable source of expert opinion on the logic and soundness of the respective strategies seen from the perspective of potential investors. The views of the companies themselves were also taken into account in this respect, especially as set out in their *Annual Reports*. It might be suggested that the exuberance with which companies pursued illusory synergy gains in the past might encourage treating recent claims in these regards with a degree of circumspection. However, there was little evidence here of major

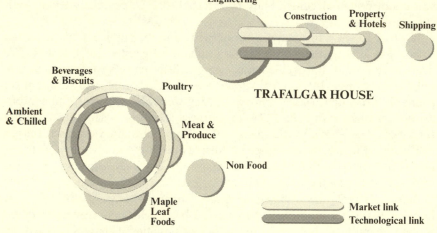

Fig. 6.1. Maps of various corporate strategies

disagreement between the companies' Boards and the wider investment community on the extent to which their respective strategies could exploit synergy.

The high degree of convergence of published views is not too surprising in retrospect. Any management that made what the investment community felt were unreliable or spurious claims concerning synergy gains in its product markets could invite an adverse reaction in the capital market. Also, the current emphasis on strategic focus would make management particularly cautious about making claims for synergy that went against stock market sentiment. It may be the case that managements' views have been forced more in line with independent opinion on the feasibility of transferring competencies across businesses, but it should also be remembered that conglomerate strategies have also been very popular with investment analysts in the past. It may be overly simplistic to regard management's views as converging on those of the investment community, since sentiment in this market has also been changing over time. However, whether management views and those of the investment community have been converging, or simply moving in parallel, these sources of information display a fair degree of consistency as far as analysis of potential synergy gains is concerned. This does not mean that shareholders and managerial objectives are necessarily consistent with each other. Consistency in terms of perceived effects does not necessarily imply consistency in terms of objectives; it is quite possible to agree on the length and time required for a journey and still disagree on its purpose and desirability.

In constructing the maps, some initial attempts were made to allow for varying the strength of linkages between businesses, for example in terms of strong, moderate, or weak linkages. However, this proved difficult to sustain. Analyses of particular strategies tend to focus on the perceived existence or absence of shared competencies across businesses, rather than more detailed auditing of the degree or strength of linkage. A second problem related to the construction of the maps. It is not difficult to represent complexity in terms of linkages as long as we are dealing with pairs of businesses as in Fig. 4.2. It is also not difficult to represent complexity at the level of a multi-business strategy as long as linkages are kept simple. However, representing complexity simultaneously in terms of both linkages and businesses turns out to be extremely difficult. There appears to be a natural trade-off in terms of representing complex linkages and complex strategies, in that analysis of one requires suppression of complexity at the other level. Similar trade-offs and partial suppression of complexity is carried out by economists moving back and forward between micro and macro levels of analysis, and the *ceteris paribus* assumption is a standard tool in this respect. Our earlier discussion of the hierarchical nature of linkages suggests that corporate strategy is concerned with a restricted number of know-how linkages in any case; attempts to fully map linkages exploited at all levels might obscure the nature of linkages involved in corporate strategy.

Therefore, in finally constructing the maps a simple question was asked: is there evidence of marketing or technological competencies shared across businesses? If it was reasonable to conclude that a non-trivial amount of expertise could be transferred across businesses, an appropriate link was recorded. If there was insufficient evidence, no link was recorded.

Marketing competencies were seen as reflecting sales and distribution expertise, while technological competencies reflected production and R&D expertise. The latter set of skills can be interpreted more generally as skills in operating a business, as in the case of retail operations for Ladbroke and Thorn EMI below. The most recently available *Annual Reports* were used in each case, which was 1993 for Cadbury Schweppes and Ladbroke, and 1994 for the others. The maps ignore minor business activities, which in this context means the few businesses recorded with less than £200m turnover.

Whilst the prime reason for simplifying the analysis of linkages at the level of corporate strategy was to reduce complexity and facilitate the manageability of the mapping process, it was felt that the end result provided a fairly good representation of corporate strategy in the respective cases. The maps echo fairly closely the broad conclusions of analysts in most cases, and when they were compared with maps that had attempted to incorporate more detail in terms of strength of linkage, it was felt that the latter did not add much to the audit of corporate strategy that the simpler maps did not also provide. There were clearly cases where a more detailed analysis would certainly have to acknowledge variation in strength of linkages, as in Hillsdown Holdings where the livestock divisions may have more in common with each other than with the other food divisions. However, this might be interpreted as inviting deeper analysis of groupings or clusters within the firm at a level below that of corporate strategy.

The corporate strategies of the five companies will be analysed below on the basis of the principles just outlined, after which some conclusions will be drawn concerning the application of the mapping technique in this context.

6.2. Cadbury Schweppes

Cadbury Schweppes plc manufactures, markets, and distributes internationally branded confectionery and beverage products. In 1993, out of total sales of £3725m, £2065m accrued from the beverages stream and £1660m from the confectionery stream. Trading profits from the streams were £228m and £208m respectively.[4]

Cadbury Schweppes was formed by a merger of the confectioner Cadbury and the carbonated drinks company Schweppes in 1969. Linkages between the two streams resulted in the consolidation of some operations, though not in distribution since bottling franchisees controlled local distribution in soft drinks.[5] There are other differences between the two streams. In beverages, some products such as Schweppes and Canada Dry are global brands, and some cross-country distinctions are nominal: for example, TriNaranjus in Spain and Oasis in France are identical orange drinks.[6] It is the world's third largest soft drinks producer, but its 4 per cent market share in 1993 was well behind Coca-Cola and PepsiCo.[7] The company has been exploring methods of exploiting potential scale economies in production and distribution, such as investing in its own bottling plants, though it also considers cooperative arrangements such as franchising as means of limiting commitment to particular areas.[8]

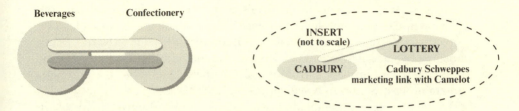

Fig. 6.2. Map of Cadbury Schweppes' corporate strategy

The company is fourth in terms of global market share in confectionery,[9] but this stream, in contrast to beverages, operates in a sector characterized by strong national differences. International brands such as Mars and KitKat are very much the exception in this market place. Even within Europe, Cadbury's UK products have to be re-formulated and re-branded locally.[10] Its 1989 European confectionery acquisitions were described as 'a boxed assortment rather than a continental network brimming with obvious synergy'.[11] However, the company has been able to consolidate some confectionery production, with cross-frontier sales within the European arena.[12] There are also technological differences between the two streams, and this is reflected in separate production with 38 facilities for beverage products and 57 for confectionery products. There is also a degree of separation in R&D, with the company operating a specialized beverages R&D facility in addition to other corporate R&D activities.[13]

While these differences do exist between the two streams, there are still strong linkages between them in terms of marketing, distribution and technological characteristics. Both streams are sold through a highly fragmented series of wholesale and retail outlets in which there is a high degree of overlap between the outlets of the two streams. Also, skills in food and flavouring technology run through the group's products as well as there being commonalities in some raw materials.[14]

Cadbury's original decision in the late sixties to diversify away from confectionery reflected a desire 'to hedge against . . . all our eggs being in one basket', areas of potential vulnerability cited including health propaganda, changing tastes, and dependence on raw cocoa (Rowlinson, 1995, p. 127).[15] Each of these could still be associated with possible threats at the level of the confectionery stream as a whole, with availability/price of raw cocoa hitting a technology characteristic widely shared within confectionery, and the other two possibly hitting market characteristics shared by confectionery brands. Vulnerability at corporate level relates to whether any of the company wide linkages are open to outside attack. For example, the widely shared ingredient sugar exposes the firm to a high degree of dependence on this in its operations, as well as to issues of tastes and debates on health on the marketing side. However, to date these links have not appeared to pose a focus for serious threats to the firm's corporate strategy. One other conceivable threat at corporate level is posed by the changing balance of power between large retailers and food manufacturers with the growth of own labelling by supermarket chains. It might be thought that Cadbury's brand strengths would insulate it from attack on these fronts, but the beverages stream at least is seen to be vulnerable to such threats.[16]

In 1993 the company hinted at possible (unspecified) moves outside confectionery and soft drinks,[17] and this was followed by its being a member of Camelot Group plc, the consortium that bid successfully for the right to run the UK's first National Lottery. The company identified its experience in impulse purchase markets and knowledge of retailing as providing the consortium with essential expertise in this market[18] (see insert to Fig. 6.2). This is a claim which appears more than justified in view of the critical role of marketing and retail distribution in what has turned out to be an outstandingly profitable venture in its first year of operation. Finally, in 1995 it purchased Dr Pepper, an acquisition which was seen as providing sales, distribution, and production synergies with its existing beverages stream, as well as moving the company up the world soft drinks league, 'within yodelling distance of Coke and Pepsi'.[19]

6.3. Thorn EMI

Thorn EMI is a company which has transformed itself in recent years in an 'amoeba-like'[20] fashion from a 'motley assortment of industrial interests'[21] to focus on its core businesses of retailing (mostly rental, such as TVs and other consumer durables) and music production. In 1994, turnover from its music business (EMI) was £1761m, from rental business (Thorn) it was £1512m, whilst for music retailing (HMV) it was £404m. There were a variety of businesses grouped under Thorn Security and Electronics (TSE), including plastic card technology, instrumentation, and fire detection systems (turnover £408m). Total turnover was £4084m, profits were £371m, with music accounting for two-thirds of profits.[22]

The company's music business, EMI, has attracted the interest of potential predators. The music business is highly concentrated with the five largest producers accounting for 60 per cent of global sales in 1994. EMI is the only one of the big five that analysts believe might conceivably be available for purchase,[23] and there has been corresponding talk of demerging the company.[24] There is perceived to be a 'lack of synergy between music publishing . . . and TV rental',[25] but they are linked indirectly. The music retailing business, HMV, has potential links with EMI in the music market, and with Thorn in retail operations.

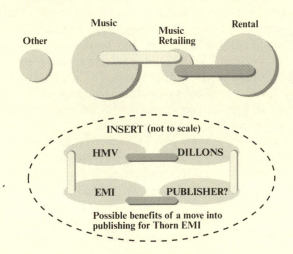

Fig. 6.3. Map of Thorn EMI's corporate strategy

Evidence of such linkage is indirectly provided by demerger speculation. A demerger of the company would cut across at least one set of these links, and there are differences of interpretation as to what would be the logical home for HMV in such circumstances. Some focus on its place in the music market, and would group it with EMI in the case of a demerger,[26] while others (including the company) emphasize its base in retail operations and would appear more likely to include it with Thorn in the eventuality of a breakup.[27] At the same time, the company has been pursuing further divestment possibilities of non-core businesses in the 'other' category (TSE).[28]

Two major recent strategic decisions, the sale of Rumbelows electrical stores and the purchase of Dillons, are consistent with a strategy of tightening up activities around strong core linkages. The moves were at first greeted with scepticism by some analysts since the apparent straight swap of one retailer for another suggested 'some inconsistency of management strategy'.[29] However, limited opportunities to purchase other record companies has encouraged the company to plan expanding into publishing and the purchase of a book retailer is a possible first step in this direction.[30] After conducting value chain analysis of a wide range of possible expansion opportunities within the media sector, the firm had concluded that book publishing and retailing were the only two sectors which offered it sufficient profit, growth, and synergy potential.[31]

The eventual purchase of a publisher is seen by analysts as a move which could build on EMI's skills in managing intellectual property rights[32] which include managing diverse outputs, handling copyright issues, and talent spotting.[33] Buying Dillons helps build up expertise in publishing, while broadening existing retail operations in HMV.[34] The insert to Fig. 6.3 (which excludes 'rental' and 'other' businesses) suggests how this strategy could therefore exploit at least four core competencies; operational linkages between HMV and Dillons in retailing (Dillons is to be run by the same management that runs HMV),[35] and between EMI and publisher in managing intellectual property; knowledge of the respective markets shared by EMI and HMV in music, and Dillons plus publisher in books. Additionally, analysts have also identified possible marketing similarities between EMI and Dillons' businesses (not shown in insert) as a possible source of synergies.

Apart from the attractive symmetry of such a strategy, it is worth noting that it would serve to tie core businesses together more tightly. This might increase vulnerability to specific external changes (e.g. multimedia and interactive technologies), but if the strategy is realized it should also make it more difficult for bidders to unscramble the omelette (or at least the non-Thorn part) through demerger. At the same time analysts believe it could open up opportunities for the company to become 'a multi-faceted entertainment group'.[36] Such moves could be regarded as adding value and/or as defensive moves against possible predation.

It might be regarded as ironic that the company has been moving out of electronics based businesses at the same time that other companies have been pursuing linkups between mass media entertainment and information, communication, and electronics technologies. However, it is questionable how much of the company's past expertise could have been readily transferred to these areas, and in fact EMI itself has been exploring investments and collaborative opportunities in areas such as digital, interactive, and multimedia technologies.[37]

Thorn EMI is an excellent illustration of how a company can completely transform itself over a period of a few years thorough a combination of internal development, acquisition, and divestment; it is difficult to recognize EMI as the company that was, 'a pioneer in television, a leader in computers, its music business was at the centre of a revolution in popular culture, and its scanner technology transformed radiology. Today only its music business survives' (Kay, 1993, p. 101).

6.4. Ladbroke

Ladbroke plc grew over four decades from a small private company providing credit betting for upper class clients in London's West End, to become a diversified multinational enterprise in the hotel, betting and gaming, retail (the Texas DIY chain), and property development industries. In 1993, out of a total turnover of £4269m, £894m accrued from hotels, £2539m from betting and gaming, £693m from retail, and £144m from property development (latter not shown on map, Fig. 6.4). Betting and gaming provided 59 per cent of turnover, but hotels, with only 21 per cent of turnover, provided almost half the group's profits of £238m.[38]

The company has rationalised a 'jumble' of leisure operations[39] that previously ranged through bingo halls, holiday camps, snooker halls, health clubs, and casinos to concentrate on its three major core businesses. Antitrust considerations precluded making major betting acquisitions in the UK and have encouraged the firm to turn its attention to expansion opportunities in these areas in the USA and continental Europe.[40] A major development of its hotels strategy was the acquisition of the Hilton International chain (Hilton hotels outside the USA) for US$1 billion in 1987.

In 1995, Ladbroke sold Texas to Sainsbury. Prior to the sale it might have been thought that Ladbroke could have exploited a reasonable degree of synergy between betting shops and DIY shops in terms of operational expertise, but analysts tended to disagree: 'it is difficult to see that Ladbroke brings much to retailing in the longer term'.[41] Analysts even expressed doubts that Sainsbury could exploit significant synergy benefits between its existing DIY business and Texas given their different market foci;[42] there are clearly even greater differences between a high street betting shop and a homecare superstore. Consequently, no linkages are indicated below between retailing and the rest of Ladbroke's businesses in 1993.

The acquisition of Hilton International was seen by management as providing substantial opportunities for linkages with its existing hotels division,

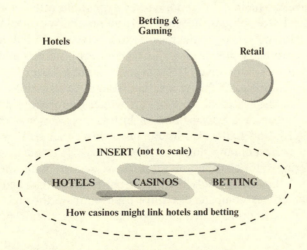

Fig. 6.4. Map of Ladbroke's corporate strategy

with Ladbroke providing competencies in areas of cost control, sales, and marketing, and the Hilton acquisition allowing the rebranding of a number of Ladbroke's existing hotels under the Hilton banner.[43] It is less clear what marketing or operational linkages may exist between the hotel division and the rest of the group. Interestingly, a failed diversification move by Ladbroke hints at what might have been in these respects. The original move into hotels took place in the 1970s at about the same time as moves into the casino business.[44] By 1979, casinos were supplying Ladbroke with about half its profits, but the company then lost its operators licence for breaking regulatory guidelines and was forced to withdraw from the business.[45]

Recently, managerial and regulatory changes enabled Ladbroke to move back into casinos[46] and explore the 'additional synergies'[47] they promised in association with hotels and gaming. This echoes ITT's recent purchase of Caesars World which creates the 'possibility of synergies between the casinos and ITT's Sheraton hotels'.[48] The operation of hotels and casinos may in fact become integrated concerns in locations such as Las Vegas. In addition, knowledge and expertise in betting and gaming might be exploited between casinos and Ladbroke's traditional businesses. These are represented as operational and marketing linkages respectively in the insert to Fig. 6.4, though further linkages might be exploited, for example in jointly marketing hotels and casinos to wealthy clientele, and operational economies between casinos and other betting/gaming businesses. Casinos may therefore represent the missing link in Ladbroke's diversification strategy.

The lack of strong company wide linkages historically limited the impact of most potential threats to specific businesses. At the same time, much of the group is particularly vulnerable to recessionary tendencies in the global economy, investment in DIY representing a possible attempt to build in counter-cyclical strengths, or at least limit vulnerability to economic slow downs. Unfortunately, each of the businesses has recently faced major problems, with recessionary pressures particularly affecting hotels and property, and an intensively competitive DIY market squeezing Texas Homecare.[49]

In addition, Ladbroke is facing a threat from a novel source. Early indications are that the National Lottery (for which Ladbroke bid unsuccessfully as a member of a consortium) is hitting conventional betting and gaming business, and Ladbroke, in common with other betting operators, is suffering a corresponding slump in these areas.[50] It is worth noting that novel marketing and distribution features associated with the National Lottery means that Ladbroke's betting activities are threatened by a consortium in which key competencies have been built up through experience in selling and distributing sweets and soft drinks (see section 6.2 Cadbury Schweppes).

6.5. Trafalgar House

Trafalgar House plc describes itself as an 'international diversified group'.[51] Over the past 30 years the firm has been involved in a wide range of industries ranging through oil and gas, newspapers, shipping, hotels, construction, engineering and property. Recently the company has been trying to shed the conglomerate label by repositioning itself as a construction and engineering group,[52] and has promised to continue to sell non-core activities, such as the hotels, as opportunities arise.[53] Out of a turnover of £3764m in 1994, £2227m came from the engineering division, £828m from the construction division, £319m from housebuilding, £42m from commercial property (including hotels), and £300m from passenger shipping (including the QE2). The company was in deep financial trouble at the end of 1992 due to the falling property market, a problematic acquisition, and a downturn in the core engineering and construction businesses.[54] It was rescued by a Hong Kong based developer becoming a major shareholder, and its ability to again contemplate major acquisitions is attributed to the deep pocket of that shareholder.[55] More recently, refitting the QE2 led to the public relations disaster of it sailing with the conversion incomplete.

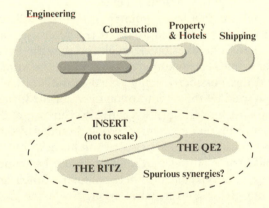

Fig. 6.5. Map of Trafalgar House's corporate strategy

Even though Trafalgar had built up a conglomerate strategy in the 1970s, it was still possible for analysts to find 'clear links between the various parts of the property/construction/shipping/leisure complex'.[56] Ironically, in view of recent emphasis on it as a core activity, the move into heavy engineering represented by the acquisition of John Brown in 1986 was regarded by analysts at the time as controversial and surprising.[57] However, the combination was seen by management as providing potentially strong synergies, with John Brown's design and project management skills and international orientation marrying with Trafalgar House's cost control experience in handling large projects.[58] Trafalgar House was positioned at the 'rough' or 'heavy' end of construction and had wanted to extend into engineering construction, an area which represented a major proportion of John Brown's activities.[59]

This is recognized in the map (Fig. 6.5) which acknowledges possible synergies between engineering and construction in both making and managing large project deals. In addition, the map suggests that knowledge and experience of the property market might have provided a link between construction and property. Construction therefore might exploit two sets of partially overlapping competencies with engineering and property respectively. However, in the case of engineering and construction, it was later acknowledged that 'there has been less synergy than expected',[60] one problem of integration being that large contracts often stipulate that the main contractor cannot award work to a subsidiary.[61] More generally, a recent change in senior management led to indications that the various elements in the company had been, at best, loosely coupled due to a general failure to properly integrate past acquisitions and a complex system of financial reporting.[62] More central management control and integration were promised, with the implication that, historically at least, links may have been more visible on paper than in practice.

A good example of this latter point is provided by Trafalgar House's ownership of prestige hotels such as the Ritz and cruise ships such as the QE2 in the Cunard Line division. It might be thought that skills in marketing and managing such luxury products would be transferable across these areas, and this possibility is illustrated in the insert to Fig. 6.5. This tends to be supported by the recent appointment of the former chairman of Rolls-Royce cars as the new chief executive of Cunard, and his comments that the experience of running a high profile branded product like Rolls-Royce would be more important for success in his new job than knowledge of the cruise industry.[63] However, Trafalgar House has concluded that the same cannot be said of possible links between luxury hotels and cruise ships: 'the hotels do not give rise to material synergy with the group's passenger shipping business'.[64] Consequently no links are shown between shipping and the rest of the group. The question of whether prestige products like the Ritz and the QE2 could have shared marketing competencies through tighter central management control is left open.

In late 1994, the company began a controversial and eventually unsuccessful bid for Northern Electric, a regional electricity company. Trafalgar had been planning moves into privatized electricity at least as far back as 1988, emphasizing potential links on the generating side with John Brown's construction and operating skills.[65] Analyst opinion was that Northern's expertise in power generation and distribution could combine with

Trafalgar's electrical engineering skills to open up some overseas markets, but that otherwise, 'the business fit is minimal'[66] and 'there is no synergy apart from finance'.[67] The bid was generally seen as an attempt to make use of its tax losses and offset Trafalgar's highly cyclical earnings with a stable stream of utility profits.[68] If successful, it would therefore have been widely regarded as a conglomerate type merger.

6.6. Hillsdown Holdings plc

Hillsdown Holdings plc was founded in 1975 and became a public company in 1985. By 1989 it was Britain's fourth largest food company[69] having built up its position mainly through acquisitions. It has about 200 independently operated subsidiaries focused particularly on selling to supermarket chains,[70] and it is the UK's largest producer of own label supermarket products.[71] In 1994, its activities were grouped into six divisions (turnover in brackets), European Ambient and Chilled (£672m), European Beverages and Biscuits (£293m), European Meat and Produce (£655m), European Poultry (£514m), Maple Leaf Foods (£1583m) and Non Food (£547m). Non Food contributed 20 per cent of profits (13 per cent of turnover) whilst Meat and Produce provided only 4 per cent of profits (15 per cent of turnover).[72]

Hillsdown's strategy has been to acquire and consolidate mature businesses in trouble, and combine decentralized operational management with strong financial controls. The head office itself only had 20 employees when the company itself had grown to 40000 employees. Acquisitions tend not to be merged, but compete in an internal market, even for the right to supply other Hillsdown subsidiaries.[73] Efficient scale and critical mass are important considerations for the company in its various businesses, and it emphasizes 'bolt on' or synergistic acquisitions.[74] Most of Hillsdown's UK products are unbranded, but this strategy puts Hillsdown in the commodity sector of the food business and makes it vulnerable both to the buying power of retailers and price competition from other suppliers. As a consequence, it has been placing increased emphasis on its branded products such as Typhoo tea and Cadbury biscuits in an attempt to differentiate products, add more value, and reduce vulnerability to cyclical competition.[75]

The company claims it can continue to 'achieve synergies between its extensive food operations'[76] and this is reflected in the map where linkages in food marketing and technology are run between the food divisions. However, the group is 'still evolving a corporate structure that brings synergy and communications to the disparate divisions'.[77] Clearly the potential linkages are stronger in some areas (e.g. between the agribusinesses) rather than others. Stronger integration of businesses was one factor in Hillsdown's April 1995 sale of its 56 per cent stake in Maple Leaf Foods, its Canadian based business. It had heavily restructured Maple Leaf after

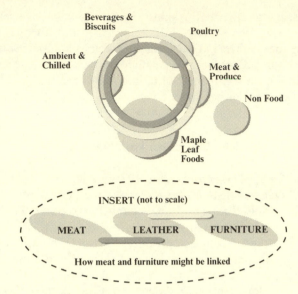

Fig. 6.6. Map of Hillsdown Holdings' corporate strategy

taking its first stake in 1987, but felt that without full control it could not maximize its potential.[78]

Analysts doubt the ability of Hillsdown to balance potential conflicts between the different competencies required in cost driven own label commodities and marketing driven brands;[79] performing well in both 'is a real strategic dilemma',[80] and it tends to be compared unfavourably to companies with a more focused corporate strategy, like Cadbury Schweppes.[81] It raises the question of whether Hillsdown could be 'stuck in the middle', caught between the two stools of cost leadership and differentiation (Porter, 1985). However, whether or not this is a real danger for companies in practice has been the subject of much recent debate.[82]

There are a variety of threats to Hillsdown's linkages. The BSE scare particularly hit red meat linkages,[83] whilst vegetarianism trends represent a broader threat to all animal products, including poultry. At the level of the food business as a whole, the growing power of large retailers and own brand sales are squeezing most manufacturers margins.[84] Hillsdown's move further into brands coincides with widening threats to branded products from own labels[85] (see also section 6.2 Cadbury Schweppes).

The non food division, (housebuilding and furniture), has no obvious synergies with the rest of the group.[86] Hillsdown points out that it could not easily replace them with a more profitable venture in food,[87] and that they counterbalance the volatility of food activity.[88] However, one recent divisional switch gives indications of interesting indirect linkages. The

Company's leather and by-products business was transferred from Meat and Produce into Non Food, where Hillsdown produces upholstered furniture for various customers such as World of Leather.[89] Leather's technical linkages with meat production and marketing linkages with furniture are indicated in the insert to Fig. 6.6. However, there are no indications as to how important these linkages might be in principle or in practice.

6.7. Mapping Links and Threats

Maps of the type outlined above may provide an organizing framework for a SWOT (strengths/weaknesses/opportunities/threats) type analysis of specific strategies. The cases discussed show how opportunities can be driven along the guidelines of linkages, whilst Fig. 6.7 is an exercise in pure speculation focusing particularly on how threats might hit specific businesses or linkages for some of the businesses we have already looked at. The potential threats illustrated for Cadbury Schweppes have already been discussed, and as Fig. 6.7 illustrates they may have an impact on linkages or specific businesses. For Thorn EMI, the vulnerability of all music related business to changes in tastes is indicated, while the company's expertise in high street retailing could conceivably be threatened by changing patterns of retailing in the future. The final example is based on the Hillsdown insert, and again suggests how some threats might hit competencies that are business specific, while others may attack linkages. For example, animal rights campaigns, new regulations, and competitors' innovations might all hit meat and leather as joint products, while the leather/furniture linkage could be vulnerable if a direct competitor establishes a reputation for improved design. There is no suggestion here that any of these conceivable threats might ever materialize; the point here is to demonstrate that they *are* conceivable, and to explore how they might be incorporated in the mapping approach. More detailed analysis of the nature of competencies in particular cases could also provide valuable input into analysis of corporate strengths and weaknesses.

An interesting way the mapping technique could also be applied is in terms of historical analyses of the development of particular corporations. Mapping the shifting boundaries of the corporation and the dominant linkages at particular points in time could provide a valuable illustration of the evolution of specific strategies. The analysis also suggests that the classic strategic management question 'what is our business?'[90] should be rephrased more accurately as 'what are our competencies?' Cadbury Schweppes' business is making and selling confectionery and soft drinks, but it was self-awareness of competencies which led to its joining the National Lottery consortium. Hotels and gambling are very different businesses, but Ladbroke's move back into casinos could link them indirectly through shared competencies. The crucial point is that it is competencies,

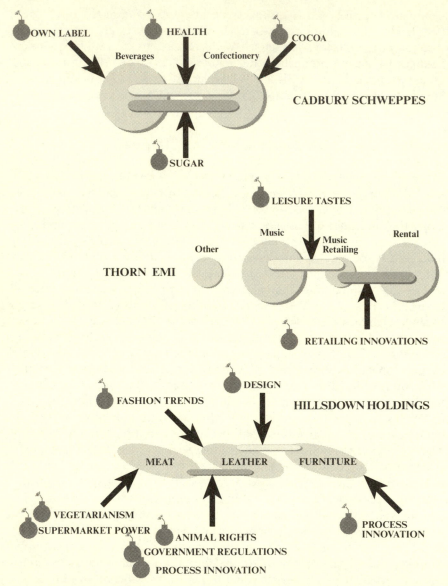

Fig. 6.7. Strategies and possible threats

not businesses, that help define both the nature of particular corporations and what they are capable of. The firm is interpreted here in terms of what it is, not what it does.

Finally, the cases also raise interesting instances where it is possible for firms to respond positively to potential threats by internalizing them as opportunities. Ladbroke attempted (unsuccessfully) to internalize the threat posed by the National Lottery by applying to run it as a member of a consortium. EMI is responding to developments in multimedia technology by investigating ways it can integrate such technology in its operations. And if Cadbury Schweppes was seriously concerned about the threat health issues posed to its sugar based products, an obvious response would be to explore diversification into products using non-sugar sweeteners. In each case, firms can try to neutralize or actively exploit that which passivity could permit to emerge as a threat. Such responses may be more difficult when the competencies required lie well outside the range of the firm's current competencies, as when electronic developments hit the Swiss watch industry. In such cases, firms may judge that merger, acquisition, or collaborative arrangements might allow them to respond more rapidly and effectively than could be the case with internal development.

6.8. Postscript

The maps in Figs. 6.2 to 6.6 were constructed during summer 1995. However, even by spring 1996 there had been a number of changes that could or would influence the maps. In February 1996, Thorn EMI confirmed its intention to demerge its music and rental businesses by the autumn,[91] confirming that the links between the two sets of businesses were tenuous at best. Ladbroke sold its retailing interests and signalled its intention to become more focused on its core hotels, gaming, and betting activities.[92] The company continued to suffer from competition from the National Lottery, but there was some good news for the company in that it won back the right to be a UK casino licence holder,[93] the potential 'missing link' in its strategy referred to above. Early in 1996, Trafalgar House was bought by Kvaerner, a Norwegian company. There was perceived to be a match between Trafalgar House's construction and process plant building skills, and Kvaerner's engineering interests. There were also perceived to be good fits between Kvaerner's and Trafalgar House's offshore energy businesses. Trafalgar House had already sold the Ritz[94] in 1995 and Kvaerner was expected to follow this by selling both company's shipping lines to improve the focus of the combined company.[95] In 1995, Hillsdown Holdings sold Maple Leaf Foods,[96] a divestment which would give its map more balance and focus.

Of all the five companies, Cadbury Schweppes continued to be the least surprising and newsworthy, perhaps reflecting its ability to beat the old Chinese curse 'may you live in interesting times'.

6.9. Conclusions

Each of the firms has undergone significant transformations in even the few years covered here, and the mapping technique has been useful in helping analyse the logic of the respective strategies. Here we have concentrated on the representation of the corporate strategy in terms of the pattern of links between the constituent businesses of the corporation. One contribution the technique makes is to provide a graphical representation of how expert opinion evaluates the competitive advantage of firms; as the discussion of individual cases above shows, it is the competencies of the respective corporations which tends to be the focus of such analysis. Where they exist between businesses, these competencies can generate synergy or economies of scope and are represented as links. However, since competencies can obsolesce, these links are also sources of potential shared vulnerability to environmental threats. The link can therefore provide both internal economies and shared vulnerability, and it is the tension between these two influences that can have strategic implications in many cases. What the mapping technique does is to provide an organizing framework around which the constituent businesses of the firm and their associated links can be represented, and the strategy of the firm interpreted.

NOTES

1. *Annual Report*, 1993.
2. See John Kay (1993, p. 133).
3. For discussion of the role of routines in organizational memory, see also Hodgson (1988, esp. pp. 124–44), and Kay, J. (1993, pp. 66–86).
4. *Annual Report*, 1993.
5. Mirabelle (1990, p. 477).
6. *Financial Times*, 4 March 1991, p. 11.
7. Ibid., 8 June 1993, p. 21
8. Ibid., 4 March 1991, p. 11; 8 June 1993, p. 21.
9. Ibid., 8 June 1993, p. 21.
10. Ibid.
11. Ibid., 4 March 1991, p. 11.
12. Ibid.
13. *Annual Report*, 1993.
14. Ibid.
15. Based upon internal company documents.
16. *Financial Times*, 14 October 1994, p. 8.
17. Ibid., 8 June 1993, p. 21.
18. *Annual Report*, 1993.

19. *Financial Times*, 24 January 1995, p. 19.
20. *Investors Chronicle*, 3 March 1995, p. 52.
21. *Financial Times*, 25 May 1995, p. 23.
22. *Annual Report*, 1994.
23. *Financial Times*, 25 May 1995, p. 23.
24. Ibid., 3 May 1995, p. 24; 24 May 1995, p. 20; 25 May 1995, p. 23.
25. *Investors Chronicle*, 9 March 1995, p. 52.
26. Ibid., p. 53.
27. *Financial Times*, 24 May 1995, p. 20; 25 May 1995, p. 23.
28. *Annual Report*, 1994.
29. *Financial Times*, 25 March 1995, p. 20.
30. Ibid., 25 March 1995, p. 20, and 3 March 1995, p. 20.
31. Ibid.
32. *Investors Chronicle*, 3 March 1995, p. 52; *Financial Times*, 25 March 1995, p. 20.
33. *Financial Times*, 3 March 1995, p. 20.
34. Ibid., 25 March 1995, p. 20.
35. Ibid., 3 March 1995, p. 19.
36. Ibid., 11 July 1994, p. 18.
37. *Annual Report*, 1994.
38. Ibid., 1993.
39. *Financial Times*, 30 August 1991, p. 14.
40. Ibid.
41. Ibid., 2 September 1994, p. 16.
42. Ibid., 25 January 1995, p. 21.
43. *Proposed acquisition of Hilton International*, Ladbroke plc, 1987, p. 5.
44. Mirabelle (1990, p. 141).
45. *Financial Times*, 30 August 30th, 1991, p. 14.
46. Ibid., 26 August 1994, p. 15, and 26 January 1995, p. 28.
47. Ibid., 2 September 1994, p. 16.
48. Ibid., 20 December 1994, p. 16.
49. *Annual Report*, 1993.
50. *Financial Times*, 23 May 1995, p. 20.
51. *Annual Report*, 1994.
52. *Financial Times*, 5 May 1993, p. 21.
53. *Annual Reports*, 1992 and 1994.
54. *Financial Times*, 4 April 1995, p. 25.
55. Ibid., 15 December 1994, p. 28.
56. Ibid., 22 August 1988, p. 20.
57. Ibid.
58. Ibid., 23 January 1995, p. 9.
59. Ibid., 22 August 1988, p. 20, and 23 January 1991, p. 9.
60. Ibid., 23 January 1991, p. 9.
61. Ibid., 25 January 1991, p. 9.
62. Ibid., 20 May 1995, p. 8.
63. Ibid., 19 May 1995, p. 12.
64. *Annual Report*, 1993, p. 3.
65. *Sunday Times*, 18 December 1988, p. D1.
66. *Financial Times*, 15 December 1994, p. 28.

67. Ibid., p. 1.
68. Ibid., pp. 26 and 28; 20 December 1994, p. 16; 4 April 1995, p. 25.
69. Mirabelle (1990, p. 513); *Financial Times*, 6 March 1992, p. 21.
70. Mirabelle (1990, p. 513).
71. *Financial Times*, 6 March 1992, p. 21.
72. *Annual Report*, 1994.
73. Miarabelle (1990, p. 513); *Financial Times*, 6 March 1992, p. 21 and 20 April 1995, p. 28.
74. *Financial Times*, 20 April 1995, p. 28.
75. Ibid., 6 March 1992, p. 21.
76. Ibid., 20 April 1995, p. 28.
77. Ibid.
78. Ibid.
79. Ibid., 6 March 1992, p. 21; 10 March 1995, p. 25; and 20 April 1995, p. 25.
80. Ibid., p. 28.
81. Ibid., 6 March 1992, p. 21.
82. For a summary of this debate, see Johnson and Scholes (1993) pp. 207–9.
83. *Annual Report*, 1994.
84. *Financial Times*, 7 October 1994, p. 21.
85. Ibid.
86. Ibid., 6 March 1992, p. 21.
87. Ibid., 8 September 1994, p. 24.
88. Ibid., 20 April 1995, p. 28.
89. *Annual Report*, 1994.
90. See, for example David (1991, pp. 5 and 92–5), following Drucker (1974, p. 611).
91. *Financial Times*, 20, p. 17 and 21, p. 19 February 1996.
92. Ibid., 26 January 1995, p. 28.
93. Ibid., 1 July 1995, p. 8.
94. *Annual Report*, 1995.
95. *Financial Times*, 5 March 1996, p. 20.
96. Ibid., 6 September 1995, p. 16.

7.   Diversification

As Montgomery (1994) points out (p. 163) conventional economic modelling is more comfortable with painting a picture which includes homogenous single product firms, but which excludes large diversified corporations. As we noted earlier, the reasons for this neglect are rooted in the neoclassical agenda; firms as institutions were not the subject of this agenda, and the notion of corporate diversification was one that simply did not enter into the neoclassical world of markets and single products. Despite the unpromising orientation of traditional theory, a number of writers have looked at the issue of corporate diversification at theoretical and empirical levels. Jovanovic (1993) and Montgomery (1994) summarize the economics literature, while Ramanujam and Varadarajan (1989) provide a comprehensive survey of the topic seen from the perspective of strategic management. Market power, scope economies, risk avoidance, creation of internal capital and labour markets, and managerial goals are amongst the major themes that have been explored in the economics literature, with mixed results (Jovanovic, 1993, pp. 199–204; Montgomery, 1994, pp. 164–8). We have already set out in Chapter 4 the basis for a theory of diversification, and in this chapter we explore this possibility further. The earlier analysis of the role of history in Chapter 5 also encourages an exploration of the possible influence of path dependency and lock-in on diversification strategies.

Whilst Chapter 4 was largely concerned with *why* firms might diversify, here we move on to the issue of *how* they might diversify. This chapter[1] explores the possibility that diversification strategies are characterized by certain patterns, and that some patterns may be more appropriate in certain circumstances than in others. Such notions are well established in the organizational literatures: Mintzberg states that; '*Strategy is a pattern*—specifically, a pattern in a stream of action . . . strategy is *consistency* in behaviour, *whether or not* intended' (Mintzberg, 1991, p. 13, emphasis in original). The idea of consistency or pattern in strategy is also implicit in the notion of 'coherence' of strategies, as discussed and analysed by Pettigrew and Whipp (1991, pp. 107–8; 239–68). We explore the notion of coherence and pattern in corporate strategy in section 7.1 before going on to look at the implications for design of corporate strategy in section 7.2. The implications of sections 7.1 and 7.2 are then compared with actual patterns of diversification in section 7.3.

7.1. Coherence and the Design of Strategy

Since our concern is the design of corporate strategy, we suppress business or product-market level considerations by assuming that our business units (IBUs) have similar characteristics in terms of scale, growth, profitability, and degree of vertical integration. We also assume that our firms either exploit or do not exploit market and technological linkages between IBUs. These are the basic building blocks for strategy. The next question is, what would constitute a coherent strategy in such circumstances? We can approach this issue by looking at a strategy that is plainly incoherent as in Fig. 7.1.

Fig. 7.1. Strategy and lack of coherence

Figure 7.1 shows a seven-IBU firm that has adopted a highly inconsistent and unbalanced diversification strategy. As far as linkage *strength* between IBUs is concerned, reading from left to right we have double linkages between the first pair of IBUs, and second and third, then a single linkage, then no linkage, then a single linkage, and then again a single linkage. However, as well as linkage strength varying, linkage *length* also varies. There are four links in Fig. 7.1, a four-IBU technological link, a three-IBU marketing link, and two two-IBU links, one marketing and one technological.

Should this matter? The firm appears to be exploiting a reasonable degree of linkage over the course of the corporate strategy, and it also combines this with the insulation benefits of de-linking. If it wishes *to* move in the direction of further linking or de-linking, then it can adjust its strategy accordingly. Granted this strategy appears rather erratic, why should this be important? We have already suggested answers to this in Chapter 5 in that there are cognitive and empirical justifications for the existence of pattern in corporate strategy, and we have also signalled the possibility in Chapter 5 that there may be efficiency justifications. We shall consider this latter possibility by looking at the implications of varying linkage strength and length respectively in the corporate strategy.

First, variation in linkage *strength* sends out confusing signals as to how the various businesses of the firm should be organized and managed. In general, if a firm is characterized by strong linkages between IBUs, the usual organizational response is to adopt a functional or U-form structure in which the various functions such as production, R&D, and marketing are organized together (Williamson, 1975). This facilitates the exploitation of strong marketing and technological linkages between IBUs. If, on the other hand, there are no significant linkages between IBUs, a multi-divisional or M-form solution is usually preferred with IBUs set up as separate profit centres (Williamson, 1975). In such a case, a firm would be organized around businesses and not functions. Further, in cases where there is a single link, firms often adopt a mixed solution in which all or a part of the link is organized as a separate and centralized function, with the rest of the firm's resources still organized in divisions. We shall look further at issues of organizational design in Chapters 11 and 12, but for present purposes it is sufficient to note that the firm in Fig. 7.1 would tax the ingenuity of organizational designers considerably. A U-form structure would put together dissimilar and incompatible technologies and markets. An M-form structure would cut across linkages and impede the coordination of economies at functional level, since all functional resources would now be split up and assigned to divisions. As for a mixed structure, there is no obvious candidate that suggests itself as a general solution to this rather messy strategy. Lack of pattern here is not just unsightly; it can make the whole enterprise unmanageable.

Secondly, variation in linkage *length* can also pose problems for the management of the firm. Here we have a four-IBU link, a three-IBU link, and two two-IBU links. Firms can, and do, make organizational adjustments to cope with linkages whose scope is less than that of the corporation as a whole. For example, task forces may be formed between IBUs to coordinate linkages, or groups may be formed around a particular technological or marketing link. The formation of a number of such groups within the firm can lead to two-tier divisionalization, with the first tier of divisionalization represented by the respective groups, and the second tier represented by their constituent divisions. General Electric is an example of a company which has adopted such an organizational design, the name of the group often giving clues to the kind of links that might be exploited by its constituent businesses, for example Medical Systems (linked by market) and Plastics (linked by technology).[2] This is a well established practice for dealing with partial or limited linkages. The problem here is that it is difficult to see on what basis the firm could form groups. Should a group be formed first around the four-IBU technological link, or the technology and marketing linked three-IBU combination? What about the three IBUs on the right: should the firm form two overlapping groups around the two links that exist here? How would these operate and how would they relate to the bigger group that would be formed on the left? Whatever solution is adopted, it is again likely to be messy and unbalanced requiring different integrative skills on the part of senior management in the different parts of the corporation. The basic principle here is that firms are likely to be able to cope with no linkages (IBUs make marketing and technological decisions), some linkages (form groups or task forces around links) and firm-wide linkages (take out a corporate level function such as corporate R&D or marketing). However, if senior management's perspective has to switch back and forward from short to long links over the course of the corporate strategy, this is likely to impede strategic decision-making. Again, while we shall look at these issues in more detail in Chapters 11 and 12, for the present it is sufficient to point out that the skills required to coordinate linkages in the corporation are likely to vary with length of linkage, just as the skills required to run a specialized firm are likely to be different from the skills required to run a conglomerate.

These problems suggest one definition of coherence in this context; a coherent strategy would be characterized by linkages of *constant* strength and length. Varying either the strength or the length of linkages could lead to problems of managing the firm as discussed above. On the other hand, replication of a given linkage strength and length throughout the system could allow the replication of integrative solutions throughout the system; for example, if all the links span only two IBUs, a task force design for coordinating a two-IBU link that works in one context may act as a template for similar solutions throughout the firm. Such templates may be less applicable if the number of IBUs linked together varies considerably; a solution that helps a duo work together may be less applicable to a quartet, and vice versa.

Clearly we are talking here about ideal types. It is probably fair to say that few, if any, large diversified firms have ever had the luxury of precisely designing their strategy to reflect the coherence principles outlined above. The opportunities available to the firm in the real world do not come neatly packaged in standard IBU sizes, nor is it reasonable to expect that marketing and technological linkages in a corporate strategy will be presented with consistent strengths and lengths. Our defence for suggesting that such ideal types may have potential relevance is that they may provide standards towards which actual strategies will gravitate. For example, the firm in Fig. 7.1 does not have to accept its fate, but can instead attempt to fashion a more coherent strategy through appropriately designed divestment, internal growth and acquisition strategies. The form this will take may depend on the opportunities and environmental pressures. These are issues that are looked at in more detail below.

With these caveats in mind, how many types of strategies can actually conform to such a definition of coherence by being able to display consistent linkage strength and consistent linkage length over the range of the corporate strategy? To answer this question, first assume a single-IBU firm shown at stage 1 in Fig. 7.2 and assume to begin with that all potential combinations of linkages are open to this firm. We also assume that the firm can only make one strategic move at a time. This is consistent with Penrose's (1959) concept of the receding managerial limit (pp. 42–64); for example, expansion strategies themselves consume scarce managerial

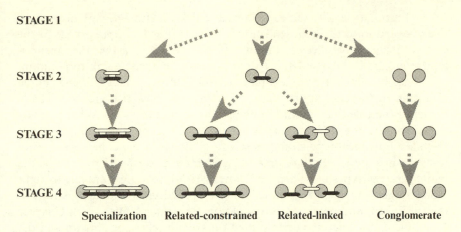

Fig. 7.2. Coherence and the evolution of strategies

resources, but these may be released to explore further expansion opportunities once the present expansion project is completed.[3] In these circumstances, if this firm wishes to expand, there are in principle three alternative routes open to it; the double-linked or specialized strategy, the no-link or conglomerate strategy, and the single link or related strategy. These are shown at stage 2 in Fig. 7.2. In reality, the firm has a fourth choice in that it could have pursued a single marketing link around which to base its diversification strategy. However, the coherent strategies which can be subsequently fashioned out of a single link do not depend on what form the link takes. Consequently, we shall look at only one of the single link strategies here, bearing in mind that if our single link at stage 2 was marketing and not technology, the analysis would lead to similar outcomes.

The firm now has limited options for expansion in stage 3 if it wishes to maintain coherence. If it has chosen the specialized (double-linked) strategy on the left at stage 2, it must continue this in stage 3. Pursuing a more weakly linked strategy in stage 3 would breach coherence. Similarly, if it has started off expanding as a conglomerate in stage 2, it is condemned to repeat this trick in stage 3; moving from no-links to one- or two-links in stage 3 would also breach the coherence rule on linkage strength. However, the single-linked strategy in the middle of stage 2 still has a couple of options. The most obvious is to continue to expand along the technological link as in the case second from the left in stage 3. However, if it now switched to a *marketing* link between one of its present businesses and the new IBU, this also would conform to the coherence requirement. Linkage strength would still be one link across businesses, while linkage length would cover two IBUs in both cases. Whilst this strategy certainly looks more erratic than the other three strategies, it is in fact just as consistent a strategy as the other three in terms of linkage length and strength.

The fourth stage only serves to illustrate that all strategies are now effectively locked-in to their chosen route if coherence is to be preserved. In the case we have just looked at, the firm has to switch to a two-IBU technological link with the new IBU. The link has to be a single link to maintain coherence in terms of linkage strength, and if this had involved the simple extension of the existing marketing link into the new IBU, it would have breached the rule that length of linkage has to be consistent. What is interesting about this exercise is that it has established from first principles that there are four ideal-type strategies which conform to the coherence restrictions on linkage length and strength, and these correspond to four of the major strategy types identified by Rumelt (1986); reading from left to right along stage 4 in Fig. 7.2, these are the specialized, related-constrained, related-linked, and unrelated or conglomerate strategy. We saw in Chapter 4 that these strategic categories all had different implications in terms of the opportunities and dangers they presented in terms of linking versus de-linking. What is noteworthy in the present context is that in the ideal type form displayed here, these apparently quite different strategic types all share one important trait; they are the only types to display coherence in terms of linkage strength and length. It has already been suggested that moving towards such coherence may be advantageous in terms of managerial efficiency; in the next section we shall suggest some possible influences on what might influence choice of actual strategy in actual cases.

7.2. Choice of Strategy

In the last chapter, we looked at the linking/de-linking implications of alternative strategies. In this chapter it has also been shown that there are only four basic 'strong patterns' which exhibit coherence in terms of linkage length and strength. What implications do these arguments have for design of corporate strategy?

The first and most obvious point is that if there is no reason to move out of a specialized expansion route, then the firm should rationally choose this option. Specialization will generate more economies compared to more weakly linked strategies, *ceteris paribus*, and these gains can in turn be drawn upon to help fuel further expansion opportunities. However, a number of influences may impede linking, or actively encourage de-linking. For example, linking may be impeded if a market is nearing saturation, if there is a possible threat of anti-trust investigation, or if there are no obvious links available to exploit. On the other hand, a firm may actively seek de-linking opportunities if it is worried about one link being attacked, for example through rival innovation. The reasons why a firm started off a particular strategy may be lost in the mists of time. However, once a strategy has been initiated the analysis above suggests that it may be very difficult to dislodge if coherence is to be preserved. A firm whose ideal type reference point is the related-linked strategy in Fig. 7.2 is unlikely to be able to make a sudden switch of reference point to, say, the related-constrained ideal type in the same figure.

This leads to a rather different interpretation of the evolution and stability of various strategies compared to some other analyses. For example, Dosi *et al.* (1992) argue that the conglomerate is generally an aberrant strategy which lacks 'coherence' (which in their case means linkage *strength*[4]). They argue that, 'as selection tightens, such as during recession, we expect this form to disappear' (Dosi *et al.*, 1992, p. 201). Evolutionary arguments are also used to support this prediction: 'Biologists have employed the term "hopeful monsters" to refer to new types arising as a result of a fundamental systematic mutation, among which a few occasionally have characteristics that are compatible with survival and result in the founding of a new species. . . . On average, there is not much hope per monster. The same may be true of large conglomerate corporations' (Dosi *et al.*, 1992, p. 206).

Dosi *et al.* present a persuasive critique of the evolution of corporate strategies, and certainly the decline of the conglomerate dinosaurs appears now to be well established in the conventional wisdom. However, the contrary view is taken here that is difficult to find credible evolutionary reasons as to why a conglomerate strategy should in fact disappear. It is true that there has been criticism of many of these conglomerates, especially those which first came to prominence during the 1960s when the mood of the capital market was unusually well disposed towards such strategies. It is also true that there has been considerable emphasis in the professional management literature in recent years on focus and 'sticking to the knitting'. However, what appears to be an obsolete left-over strategy seen from one perspective can turn out to be a viable path dependent phenomenon seen from another. Just because the genesis of the conglomerate strategy may be associated with an era long gone does not necessarily mean that it is in imminent danger of 'disappearing'. There are two main reasons for this. First, Chapter 4 analysed how corporations are generally subject to *soft selection*. If the management of a large conglomerate do not want to change the strategy, it can be difficult for the capital market to force them to do so. Since the skills involved in running a specialized or related strategy are liable to be quite different from those involved in running a conglomerate, it would be quite rational for conglomerate management to wish to avoid changing the strategy. Secondly, *lock-in* as discussed in Chapter 5 is likely to severely limit the conglomerate's room for manoeuvre even if management decided they did want to change strategy. The conglomerate in Fig. 7.2 cannot easily switch to a strategy characterized by linking. Internal generation of related opportunities would only be achievable over a very long time span, if at all, while putting together a strategy based on linkages through acquisitions is also extremely difficult to achieve as a number of empirical studies have shown. Further, the long interregnum involved in moving from a conglomerate to an alternative strategy would be marked by loss of coherence, and this alone could create major managerial problems for the firm.

However, this is not to say that conglomerate strategies cannot be adapted. The possibility of a structure of multiple tiers of groups and divisions discussed earlier may provide a basis for coherence to be expressed in different ways at different levels. For example, suppose the conglomerate at stage 4 in Fig. 7.2 decided to emphasize linkages, gave each of its divisions group status, and instructed each of these groups to pursue technologically related opportunities. Figure 7.3 indicates how the picture of the firm could change over the next two stages if all groups expanded at the same rate.

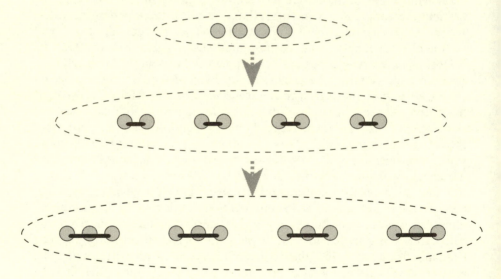

Fig. 7.3. Conglomerate and group focus

As far as corporate management is concerned, the firm is still a conglomerate although they now directly oversee unrelated groups rather than unrelated divisions. As far as group management is concerned, each have the responsibility of managing a technologically related group of divisions, in effect a related-constrained strategy within each group. Divisional management have the responsibility of running their particular IBU. The three levels of management (corporate, group, and divisional) each have clearly defined problem areas and can develop appropriate strategies and organizational designs to accommodate them. However, the conglomerate has not disappeared in this example, it has adapted. In short, we would expect to find a high degree of resilience in terms of conglomerate strategies among large firms, contrary to the conventional wisdom.

7.3. Empirical Patterns

The analysis above suggests that corporate strategies should evolve in a coherent fashion, following certain rules and displaying certain features. We shall look below at a number of issues to see if the behaviour and the patterns predicted actually occur.

1. *Patterns of diversification*

First of all, the idea that there are only four basic coherent strategies meshes quite well with the patterns discovered by Rumelt (1986) in his study of corporate strategies amongst the largest US corporations during the post-war period. Rumelt (1986, p. 99) describes five major strategies developed by large US corporations in the Fortune 500; the single business, dominant business,[5] related-constrained, related-linked and unrelated strategies. The single and dominant business categories are both specialized strategies in which the firm obtains the bulk of its revenues from a single discrete product market activity.[6] Rumelt identified the unrelated or conglomerate strategy, firms which had diversified significantly and with little concern for possible linkages between new business and current activities (1986, p. 32).[7] He also distinguished between acquisitive and passive types of conglomerates depending on whether or not they had an aggressive acquisition programme (1986, p. 32).

In analysing related diversification, Rumelt identified two categories; related-constrained, 'firms that have diversified chiefly by relating new businesses to a specific central skill or resource and in which, therefore, each business activity is related to almost all of the other business activities' (Rumelt, 1986, p. 32), and related-linked, 'firms that have diversified by relating new businesses to some strength or skill already possessed, but not always the same strength or skill' (1986, p. 32). Rumelt gave Carborundum as an example of a related-linked strategy: 'by adding new businesses in such a way that each was related to at least one—but often no more than one—of its current activities, the firm gradually became involved in a linked network of widely disparate businesses' (Rumelt, 1986, p. 19). In both cases, the related group had to cover at least 70 per cent of the revenues of the firm for the firm to be assigned to this class.

If, as seems reasonable, single and dominant business categories are combined together as 'specialization' strategies, then the major strategic categories identified by Rumelt reduce to four: specialization, related-constrained, related-linked, and conglomerate. By 1969, 52 per cent of Rumelt's sample for the Fortune 500 were still operating a specialized or dominant strategy; 24 per cent were operating a related-constrained strategy; 20 per cent were operating a related-linked strategy; and 12 per cent were operating a conglomerate or unrelated strategy.[8] These are also the four categories which were obtained through an entirely separate route by imposing coherence restrictions on the type of strategies that could evolve in our hypothetical sector. It is interesting that major strategies discovered through empirical investigation should correspond so closely to the categories of coherent strategies identified *a priori*. The correspondence itself lends support to the idea that strategic designers will attempt to develop a coherent strategy which in turn influences the setting of the boundaries of the firm.

However, it would be easy to overplay the correspondence between the two sets of strategies. For example, the related-linked strategy developed by applying coherence rules displays a neat and orderly alteration of marketing and technological linkages throughout its length. On the other hand, the related-linked strategy discovered in Rumelt's analysis typically displays a patchwork of linkages of varying length, strength, and importance. Whilst Rumelt's definition of related-linked would certainly allow for the coherent version as a special case, the coherent version is likely to be too narrowly defined to approximate many strategies in practice. If the correspondence does have significance, it is to be found in the notion of four broad strategic categories that firms will tend to gravitate towards. Each of these four different basic strategies call for quite different managerial and organizational solutions. In each case coherence may facilitate transferability of solutions throughout the organization, whether in terms of decision-making techniques or organizational design. The real world may indeed be messy and uncertain, but the designers of the firm will typically attempt to create patterns out of the available materials, and, as we have seen, such pattern-creating may be efficient. The fact that the four major strategies identified by Rumelt bear a family resemblance to the four coherent strategies identified earlier is consistent with pattern-seeking behaviour.

2. *Stages in the development of strategies*

The analysis here suggests that corporate strategies will tend to evolve through certain stages in their development. While the development of corporate diversification in other industrialized economies have tended to exhibit similar patterns to those identified by Rumelt (1986),[9] the US economy represents an obvious test case in this context given the breadth and depth of its industrialisation. The early beginnings of industrialisation in this context were characterized by a high degree of atomism and fragmentation, especially in some mill-based and extractive sectors (Chandler, 1977), while the merger waves of the turn of the century and the 1920s were largely characterized by rationalizations and consolidations intended to achieve gains from specialization and vertical integration (Scherer and Ross, 1990, pp. 153–6). Rumelt's analysis shows that it was not until the early post-war period that the related-constrained strategy began to appear in numbers, but Rumelt's estimates (1986, p. vi) make this the most frequently cited strategy for Fortune 500 firms by 1959, with 28.4 per cent of firms falling into this category by that year. Examples of firms cited by Rumelt as pursuing a related-constrained strategy in 1959 include Dow Chemical, Eastman Kodak, International Business Machines (IBM), and Lockheed. However, by 1974, the related-linked strategy had become the most frequently cited category (22.5 per cent of firms) in Rumelt's analysis of Fortune 500 strategies (Rumelt, 1986, p. vi). Examples of firms pursuing related-linked strategies in 1969 include Du Pont, General Electric, Minnesota Mining and Manufacturing (3M), and Time (Rumelt, 1986).

The sequencing of these strategies is consistent with firms consolidating from fragmented and inefficiently small bases to create IBUs in the first place, then moving on to the related-constrained category in some cases, with this strategy in turn feeding into the related-linked in some cases. This is consistent with the process described above, and as we shall see in Chapter 9, one of the most interesting aspects of this development is how it set up the conditions for the subsequent evolution of cooperative activity between firms, a process we shall look at in Chapter 9.

3. *Bimodal distribution of diversification strategies*

A phenomenon which has been observed repeatedly in firm diversification is bimodality in terms of degree of diversification. A number of studies (Wrigley, 1970; Goreski, 1974; Reed and Sharp, 1987) have observed that firms tend to prefer either low or substantial degrees of diversification, with relatively few firms opting for strategies involving modest diversification. Reed (1991) concludes that it is a phenomenon that appears to transcend both time and national economic boundaries. As Reed points out, despite the extensive literature on diversification, there has been a general failure to explain bimodality in diversification.[10]

It is therefore of interest that bimodality in diversification is likely to be a natural consequence of the pattern-seeking behaviour described above. A frequency distribution of firms arranged by number of businesses (ranging from 1 to 4) in the final stage of Fig. 7.2 would display a bimodal distribution (one specialized firm with one business, none with two or three, and three firms with four businesses). If we were to increase the number of firms (say by a factor of ten) distributed equally amongst the four strategies, then we would still have a bimodal distribution with ten firms running one business (first mode), thirty running four (second mode), and none between these two extremes. If we were to allow some variation in the expansion rates of individual firms in the latter thirty firm case, it might affect the location of the second mode and the frequency distribution of firms pursuing non-specialization strategies.[11] However, the first mode should still be composed of ten firms; the size distribution of the ten would vary if growth rates varied, but not the number of businesses (one) associated with this strategy. Capital market conditions should not affect the location of the first mode, but we would expect the location of the second mode to be a path dependent phenomenon related to capital market mood. Periods of loose ownership control should facilitate growth and diversification strategies, shifting the second mode to the right. Periods of tighter ownership control should shift the second mode to the left. Thus, while the location of the second mode may fluctuate, bimodality is likely to be a natural consequence of the coherence seeking behaviour described above.

4. *Diversified strategies and lock-in*

One of the issues suggested by the analysis surrounding Fig. 7.2 is that certain strategies (specialized and related-constrained) may continue unchanged or act as feeder strategies for other strategies, while other strategies (related-linked and conglomerate) are more likely to display lock-in. Once a related-linked or a conglomerate strategy has been chosen, coherence restrictions make it difficult to exit these strategies. This contrasts with Mintzberg's view (1979, p. 404) of the related strategy in general as a feeder stage *en route* to the development of a fully divisionalized conglomerate. Mintzberg uses Rumelt's discussion of Carborundum's related-linked strategy as an example of the related strategy[12] and then argues: 'As the related product firm expands into new markets or acquires other firms, with less and less regard for central strategic theme, the organization moves to the *conglomerate* form' (p. 412, italics in original). Our analysis here suggests that this is not the typical process by which corporations expand and that related-linked and unrelated strategies should be regarded as *alternative* routes for strategic development. If coherence is to be maintained, the related-linked strategy does *not* act as a feeder strategy for the conglomerate.

If specialized and related-constrained strategies are more likely to be transitory feeder strategies in many cases, whilst related-linked and conglomerate strategies are more likely to be characterized by lock-in, Rumelt's (1986) study should again provide relevant information. Rumelt looked at strategies adopted by Fortune 500 firms in 1949, 1959, and 1969. If we were to compare a firm's strategy in 1949 or 1959 with its strategy ten years later, the aggregation of firms' decisions as to whether to continue with a strategy or exit it should help provide evidence for lock-in, if it exists.

Analysis of Rumelt's raw data found there were 421 cases in which a firm's strategy in either 1949 or 1959 could be compared with its strategy ten years later. Most firms provided two time periods for comparison purposes, though merger and acquisition led to some attrition. There were 259 specialized, 107 related-constrained, 36 related-linked and 19 conglomerate starting points. When the starting strategy was compared with the strategy ten years later, 60 (23 per cent) of specialized starters had exited this category, 29 (27 per cent) of related-constrained starters had exited this category, 4 (11 per cent) of related-linked starters had exited this category, whilst none of the conglomerate starters had exited this category. It is difficult to place too much weight on the related-linked strategy in isolation in view of the small numbers, but the broad trends are as expected; in Rumelt's analysis, specialized and related-constrained strategies play active roles as feeders for more complex strategies,[13] while related-linked and conglomerate strategies display greater stability and continuity.

5. *Turbulence and the evolution of short-linked strategies*

As we discussed earlier, turbulence may be generated from a variety of sources such as changing regulatory regimes and changes in consumer tastes. However, the most widespread and powerful source of turbulence is technological change. In this respect, it is important to note a crucial difference between the two related strategies in Fig. 7.2. The related-constrained strategy could be effectively disabled by one serious hit on its technological link; in this respect it is potentially vulnerable across its length to a single threat from the environment, as the specialized strategy is on two fronts. However, short range linking of the related-linked strategy limits the potential damage that a single attack could pose to a link spanning two IBUs. This lies closer to the de-linking advantages of the conglomerate than it does to the tightly connected characteristics of the other two strategies. We would therefore expect that the two strategies providing de-linking advantages (related-linked and conglomerate) would be more likely to be preferred to specialized and related-constrained strategies in turbulent environments, with moves to a related-constrained strategy representing a transitory strategy.

In an earlier study (Kay, 1982) turbulence in the form of innovative activity was measured by industry R&D as a percentage of sales, for the sector the firm operated in. It was argued that large firms in the more technologically stable sectors would be under little environmental pressure to de-link. On the other hand, firms in the innovative high technology sectors were more likely to be bombarded by environmental changes and be subject to obsolescing competencies. These could easily destabilize the firm unless it had insulated itself from specific threats by adopting a related-linked or conglomerate de-linking strategy, and as we have argued a related-constrained move could also be a first step in this direction. Using Rumelt's database,[14] a statistically significant relation in the direction expected was found between propensity to adopt a non-specialized strategy (related or unrelated), and high/low technological environments. Low technology environments tended to be characterized by long-link specialization, whilst high technology environments tended to be associated with related and conglomerate strategies.

Rumelt argued that the technologically advanced industries such as chemicals and electrical[5] were based on extensible technologies which facilitated the diversification process. However, this does not explain why a strong clustering of conglomerate strategies were found in the high technology (and relatively turbulent) areas, since by definition these strategies are based on the absence of significant technological linkages. For the eight most R&D-intensive sectors, 23 per cent of firms adopted a conglomerate or unrelated strategy, while the percentage fell to only 6 per cent for the eight least R&D-intensive sectors. In all, 85 per cent of the conglomerate or unrelated strategies were operated by firms in the eight most R&D-intensive sectors (Kay, 1982, p. 100). Consequently, deliberate moves by firms in the direction of de-linking strategies appears to be a better explanation of patterns of diversification in the high technology sector over this period than is the extensible technology argument.

6. *The persistence of conglomerates*

As discussed earlier, some analysts see the conglomerate as an unstable, transitory phenomenon. The opposite view is taken here that it is a stable and coherent strategy which is likely to be a persistent feature of the industrial landscape. It is certainly the case that conglomerates are unfashionable and face a more hostile press than was the case some years ago, and they compare very badly when judged in terms of more fashionable concepts such as focus and down-sizing.[15] It also appears to be the case that strategies in practice reflect the new, restrained capital market mood; for example, Lichtenberg (1992) found using Census Bureau data that the degree of corporate diversification had indeed declined significantly in US industry in the late eighties due to a combination of divestment and the characteristics of firm entry/exit. At the same time there simply is not the evidence that we would expect to find if conglomerates were indeed an unstable, transitory phenomenon. Markides (1993) extended Rumelt's analysis of the Fortune 500 and analysed strategies of 250 of the Fortune 500 for 1981 and 1987. The biggest changes since 1974 were recorded in the 1974–81 period with the related business (related-constrained and related-linked) falling from 42.3 per cent to 21.9 per cent of the used sample of 210 firms. By way of contrast, the proportion of conglomerate strategies in the sample was relatively stable (20.7 per cent in 1974, 22.4 per cent in 1981 and 19 per cent in 1987). Actual observation of the Fortune 500 also confirms the persistence of conglomerates; the substantial majority of 1969's Fortune 500 science based conglomerates discovered by Rumelt (1986, p. 106) are still visible in the 1993 Fortune 500 listings.[16]

Further, Williams *et al.* (1988) analysed the *Forbes* list of conglomerates (all of which were publicly held US conglomerates with at least four distinct lines of business) over the period 1975–84. Of the 84 companies in the list, only one

(City Investing) was liquidated over the period, 13 others were acquired or went private.[17] On average the degree of conglomerateness was reduced, with the average number of distinct groups managed by the conglomerates rising from 4.82 in 1975 to a peak of 5.04 in 1979, before falling to 4.58 in 1984. Over the period as a whole, acquisitions by these conglomerates exceeded divestments. However, for the latter half of the period, there were 221 divestments by the cohort compared to 183 acquisitions. The bulk of acquisitions over the period as a whole were in horizontal or related directions, consistent with a move to group focus as indicated in Fig. 7.3. In short, the typical conglomerate trimmed, focused, and survived—as a conglomerate.

Even for firms that are undergoing radical restructuring, the conglomerate strategy demonstrates a high degree of resilience. Hoskisson and Johnson (1992) found that for a sample of 189 US firms voluntarily undergoing restructuring (defined as divesting at least two businesses representing at least 10 per cent of firm assets) between 1981 and 1987, that the related-linked strategy was the most unstable of all. Only 21 per cent stayed in this category after restructuring, compared to 73 per cent of dominant firms, 66 per cent of related-constrained firms, and 69 per cent of the 65 unrelated firms staying in their respective categories. However, not only did only 15 of the 73 related-linked firms before restructuring stay in this category after restructuring (38 exited to related-constrained and 9 to the dominant category), 11 of them actually exited to the unrelated category. Again, there is no evidence that the conglomerate or unrelated strategy is not at least as robust as alternative diversification strategies. We would expect soft selection and lock-in to lead to the persistence of this strategy, and this appears to be supported by the evidence.

7. *Divestment and instability of related-linked strategies*

There is a final set of research findings which appear to directly contradict the arguments of this chapter. Hoskisson and Johnson's (1992) conclusion above that the related-linked strategy is the most unstable of all the major strategic categories appears very reasonable. The findings raise a number of puzzling features. What has happened to the related-linked strategy lock-in that we apparently observed above? Why do so many related-linked firms exit to what Hoskisson and Johnson describe as a *more* diversified strategy (the unrelated option)[18] at the same time as a criterion for inclusion in the authors' sample of restructuring firms was that they had each signalled to the investment community that 'a strategic refocussing was underway' (Hoskisson and Johnson, 1992, p. 635)? Indeed, *how* can firms apparently achieve higher levels of diversification (and move to the unfashionable conglomerate category from a strategy based on relatedness), whilst simultaneously pursuing divestment and signalling intentions to refocus to the investment community?

We can suggest a simple resolution of these features of the restructuring process. The stable patterns and lock-in effects that we identified above are consistent with periods of steady and orderly change; where firms gravitated from one category to another, it was generally in a way that was designed to preserve coherence in the overall strategy of the corporation. Even if retrenchment became necessary, we would expect coherence considerations to encourage the firm to retrace its steps to its simpler beginnings. This can be seen visually in Fig. 7.2: if the related-linked firm was faced with having to shed businesses and move back stages from stage 4, coherence considerations dictate it would do so by selling off peripheral businesses. In the case of our related-linked firm this would involve end IBUs. In such circumstances the strategies would be related-linked, related-linked, related-constrained, before finally arriving back at the original specialization stage.

Short-term financial pressures can mean that the minority of firms that are forced into major restructuring (as in Hoskisson and Johnson's sample) are likely to have limited discretion as to which IBUs are to be divested. Other evidence on US firms divesting in the late seventies found that: (a) divesting companies have been performing poorly relative to non-divesting industry counterparts; and (b) divesting companies tend to reduce the gap in performance between themselves and their non-divesting counterparts after divestment (Montgomery and Thomas, 1988). A reasonable conclusion on the basis of this evidence is that for many of these restructuring firms: (a) there has been variable performance at IBU level; and (b) the least profitable IBUs are shed to improve short-term performance.[19] However, if IBU profitability is variable, there is no reason why the least profitable IBUs should be the end IBUs for our stage 4 firms in Fig. 7.2. If the least profitable IBUs are randomly distributed, some will be end IBUs, whilst others will be IBUs closer to the corporate core. In the case of the specialized and related-constrained firms, removing a central IBU would not alter the strategy since the three remaining IBUs would still be able to exploit the same links. Also, it would not alter the conglomerate strategy, except to reduce the number of IBUs. On the other hand, removing a central IBU in Fig. 7.2 would break up the related-linked strategy, turning it into a conglomerate in Rumelt's categorization with only two-thirds of the firm linked together; redesign by default. Removing peripheral IBUs is more likely to move the firm back to the related-constrained or specialized strategies.

The fragility of the related-linked strategy in the face of crisis-driven restructuring can be seen in Fig. 7.4. There are four six-IBU firms, a specialized, related-constrained, related-linked and conglomerate firm. Suppose each firm faces IBU-specific attacks on its strategy, such that the third and fifth IBUs in each case are attacked and subsequently divested. Clearly this does not alter the strategy of the conglomerate which still operates a series of unrelated businesses (now reduced to four). The related-constrained and specialized strategies are also unaffected, since the original technological or

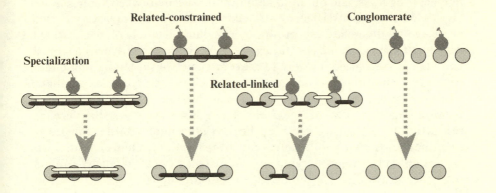

Fig. 7.4. Fragility of related-linked strategy

marketing links are still exploited by all four firms in the respective cases. However, attacks on the third and fifth IBUs in the related-linked case has shredded this strategy, leaving it a conglomerate by default. The central IBUs played a bridging role, holding this strategy together. Taking away these bridges leads to the related-linked strategy dissolving into a conglomerate as in Fig. 7.4.

Thus, in a crisis, long-term coherence may be sacrificed to short-term performance considerations. The complex interlinking of the related-linked strategy is the most vulnerable to redesign by default. Indeed, we have already seen such a crisis driven divestment programme in the case of Ladbroke (Chapter 6) when forced divestment of casinos turned Ladbroke from a related-linked company into a conglomerate. The possibility of redesign by default helps resolve the three puzzles discussed above. First, in a crisis, all strategies may face forced divestment, and the particular design features of the related-linked strategy makes it the most fragile of all strategies in such abnormal circumstances. Secondly, redesign by default is consistent with all companies genuinely refocusing on a more selected number of businesses, which is in turn consistent with the reported company signals to the capital market along those lines. Thirdly, redesign by default can shift the strategy from related-linked to unrelated, but contrary to Hoskisson and Johnson's (1992) interpretation, this move is to a *less* diversified strategy in terms of the number of distinct IBUs operated post-restructuring, not to a *more* diversified strategy.[20]

Finally, Hoskisson and Johnson (1992) argue that their results suggest that in terms of degree of diversification: 'there may ultimately be a trimodal distribution where firms focus on single or dominant business, a set of related businesses, or a set of unrelated businesses' (pp. 631–2). They base this conclusion on the revealed fragility of related-linked strategies in restructuring firms, and on the assumption that related-linked strategies are intermediate between related-constrained and unrelated strategies in terms of degree of diversification. However, our interpretation of the revealed fragility of the related-linked strategy is consistent with all types of related and unrelated strategies moving to a lower degree of diversification, and a consequent shift in the·second mode to the left as we argued above. Also, since the related-linked strategy is not an 'intermediate' category lying between related-constrained and unrelated, its fragility in the face of restructuring is not an argument for the development of a third mode in any frequency distribution of degree of diversification. Thus, contrary to Hoskisson and Johnson's arguments, we would expect bimodality to be a robust feature of diversification frequency distributions.

7.4. Conclusions

The starting point of this chapter was that there is likely to be efficiency advantages in terms of transferability of managerial skills if coherence in the corporate strategy is maintained, coherence being defined here as consistency in linkage length and strength. There were found to be only four strategies that could display coherence: the specialized, related-constrained, related-linked and conglomerate strategies. In turn, these were the major categories of strategy identified by Rumelt in his analysis of the development of the large US corporation in the post-war period. The analysis also helped provide explanations for a number of phenomena, including the bimodal distribution of diversification strategies; lock-in of related-linked and conglomerate strategies; the evolution of short-linked strategies in turbulent environments; the persistence of conglomerate strategies, and the fragility of related-linked strategies in periods of corporate restructuring.

NOTES

1. The chapter also develops points made in an earlier analysis in this area, Kay (1995a).
2. Source, company *Annual Report* for 1995.
3. Also, Penrose (1959, pp. 51–4) describes release of managerial services resulting from experience and routinization, or what today would be described as learning or experience curve effects.
4. 'A firm exhibits coherence when its lines of business are related, in the sense that there are certain technological and market characteristics common to each. A firm's coherence increases as the number of common technological and market characteristics found in each product line increases' (Dosi *et al.*, 1992, p. 188).

5. Rumelt also subdivided the dominant business into vertically and non-vertically integrated categories (pp. 28–32 and 99).
6. The cut-off points in the respective cases were: at least 70 per cent of revenues from a single product-market to be classified as a dominant business, at least 95 per cent of revenues from a single product-market to be classified as a single business (pp. 29–30).
7. This strategy was identified in cases where less than 70 per cent of the firms' revenues were from any group whose members were related in some way to one another (p. 29).
8. The percentages do not sum to 100 per cent because of rounding errors.
9. See especially, Channon (1973) and Dyas and Thanheiser (1976).
10. Reed does provide an explanation for bimodality in diversification based on the idea of jointly optimizing efficiency and effectiveness in diversification. However, we would suggest that our explanation is simpler in that it follows naturally from pattern seeking behaviour and does not depend on the idea of an optimal degree of diversification. Bimodality in diversification is also only one of a number of facts which we suggest our approach helps to explain.
11. For stochastic models of firm growth that help to explain the size distribution of firms in terms of size, see Simon and Bonini (1958) and Ijiri and Simon (1964, 1967).
12. The other related product strategy discussed here by Mintzberg (General Electric) was also classified as related-linked by Rumelt.
13. In the case of the specialized starters, 31 switched to related-constrained, 15 to related-linked and 14 to unrelated. In the case of related-constrained starters, 18 converted to related-linked, 9 to unrelated and 2 went back to a specialized strategy. While most of the firms exiting the related-constrained strategy either shifted into the related-linked strategy as predicted, or retraced their steps back to specialization, the 9 shifts to the unrelated category do not fit with expectations. One possibility is that our approach here limits expansion to an IBU at a time, whereas this was a period of intense merger activity which led to the assimilation of whole firms by others. A firm could move from the related-constrained strategy by acquiring other related-constrained firms and converting into a conglomerate that looks something like stage 2 or 3 in Fig. 7.3. This would ensure coherence at corporate level (conglomerateness) and at group level (related-constrained).

    It might be objected that if related-constrained firms can switch to a conglomerate strategy in this fashion, why should related-linked firms be more likely to display lock-in? An answer can be given by comparing the relative scale of the operations involved in shifting strategies in the respective cases (to control for scale only conversions to conglomerate status in the 1959–69 period were analysed, which is when most such conversions took place). In Rumelt's analysis, the median ranking in the Fortune 500 of the three conglomerates (FMC, GAF, and Litton) which evolved out of related-linked strategies was 77. The median ranking of the 9 conglomerates formed out of related-constrained strategies was 148, while the median ranking of the 9 which had evolved out of specialized strategies was only 288. As Fig. 7.2 indicates, related-linked strategies are likely to evolve later, be larger, and operate in more markets and with more technologies than many of their simpler related-constrained counterparts.

Maintaining coherence is likely to be much more difficult when conglomerates are being fashioned out of related-linked strategies rather than simpler building blocks, even when the merger route is adopted.

14. The source in this case was the first edition of Rumelt's work.

15. There are indications in the managerial literature that a body of opinion feels that down-sizing has been pushed too far in some cases.

16. Indeed, there is some evidence of a reaction in the managerial literature against fashionable concern for focusing and downsizing of conglomerate strategies; for example, Anslinger and Copeland (1996) argue that there is evidence that some companies successfully pursue conglomerate (non-synergistic) strategies.

17. See Wright *et al.* (1993) for a comprehensive survey of recent studies in this area.

18. See Hoskisson and Johnson (1992, p. 626).

19. For a survey of theoretical and empirical evidence on divestment, see Coyne and Wright (1985).

20. Hoskisson and Johnson based their assessment of strategic categories on a clustering analysis of the 2- and 4-digit SIC industry products operated by each company. However, Hoskisson *et al.* (1991) had earlier found that this method was highly correlated ($r = 0.82$) with the subjectively developed categories created independently using Rumelt's (1986) methodology (see Hoskisson and Johnson, 1992, p. 628). It therefore is reasonable to treat Hoskisson and Johnson's study as providing fairly good estimates of Rumelt's categorizations.

8.   Multinational Enterprise

In this chapter we shall extend the perspective developed earlier into the analysis of multinational activity. Multinationals are generally defined as enterprises that engage in FDI (foreign direct investment) and control value-adding activity in more than one country (Dunning, 1993, p. 3). It will be argued that the evolution of such firms can only be properly analysed by comparing them to alternative options for corporate expansion, and that relevant alternative methods may not be restricted to those that involve international expansion. The chapter itself provides a resource based framework that facilitates critical examination of a variety of approaches in this context, as well as providing a basis for further work into the behaviour of the multinational enterprise (MNE).

In section 8.1 we shall consider alternative perspectives to the question of why the MNE might evolve in the first place before developing a simple framework in section 8.2 for analysing the MNE and its alternatives in terms of resource linkages associated with particular options. This represents a development of basic ideas set out by Galbraith and Kay (1986), Kay (1991), and Kay (1992a). In section 8.3, the characteristics that would tend to be associated with the MNE in a resource based approach are identified, and section 8.4 examines the extent to which these characteristics appear consistent with the empirical evidence.

8.1.   Analysing the MNE

There have been a number of different approaches to the theory of the MNE, though sometimes the notionally distinctive theories display significant overlap when examined closely (Casson, 1987, p. 32). Major candidates have included the Hymer–Kindleberger account (Kindleberger, 1969) of multinational expansion in terms of firm-specific advantages, Vernon's theory (1966) which saw the MNE as reflecting a particular stage in the product life cycle, Aliber's theory (1970) of the MNE as a currency area phenomenon, and Knickerbocker's theory (1973) of foreign investment as oligopolistic rivalry. Each of these have been subject to analysis and criticism, most commonly in that they are, at best, partial explanations of multinational activity (Casson, 1987, pp. 1–49).[1] However, if there is a major theme around which a number of researchers in this field have gravitated in recent years, it is the notion of internalization as represented in the various analyses of Buckley and Casson (1976, 1991), Rugman (1981), Hennart (1982), Williamson (1985, pp. 290–4) and Teece (1986*b*).

As Caves (1982, pp. 1–2) points out, a natural starting point for any analysis of the evolution of MNE is provided by Coase's 1937 article in which he raises the question of what determines the setting of the boundaries between firm and market. Coase's answer is that the operation of markets may involve transaction costs which may be reduced in some cases by incorporating the transaction under the umbrella of the firm.

It would seem reasonable to presume that transaction cost economics may provide an explanation for the development of the MNE, and Williamson does indeed suggest one in a brief discussion of why the MNE might evolve:

A more harmonious and efficient exchange relation results from the substitution of an internal governance relation under those recurrent trading circumstances where assets, of which complex technology transfer is an example, have a highly specific character (Williamson, 1985, p. 294).

This description of why MNE evolves is consistent with Williamson's transaction cost argument that market contracting is likely to be 'efficacious' in circumstances where asset specificity is absent, even if transactions are otherwise characterized by problems of bounded rationality and opportunism on the part of the contracting parties (1985, pp. 31–2). Williamson argues that the fact that many contingencies cannot be foreseen in the case of technology transfer can make parties to a market mediated transfer vulnerable to opportunistic action by their trading partners in cases where asset specificity locks in transactors. By substituting corporate organization for costly market exchange in such circumstances, MNE may evolve as an efficient and rational response to potential transaction costs.

However, this explanation does not accord with the facts. Like transaction cost economics in general, Williamson's arguments are designed to deal with particular internalization issues raised by vertical integration and its alternatives, as exemplified by make-or-buy decisions. As we have seen in Chapters 3 and 4 the framework cannot explain horizontal integration which deals with assets being *non*-specific in terms of application and usage; technology transfer in MNEs tends not to take place in a *vertical* context as in crude oil transfers from field to refinery, but in a *horizontal* context in which the sharing of an input (in this case R&D) is extended to new applications (markets) as in cases of product diversification.[2] While there has certainly been some interest and research into the topic of vertically integrated MNEs in recent years, it has attracted far less attention than have issues surrounding horizontal MNEs (Caves, 1982, pp. 15–24), which appears only reasonable given the greater frequency with which horizontal expansion is cited as an MNE strategy.[3] In this respect, the focus on vertical transactions in Williamson's explanation of the growth of MNEs merely extends the restricted scope of the transaction cost approach into the multinational sphere.

Additionally, as we have seen, if there is one asset package that is likely *not* to be specialized to potential uses or users, it is transfers involving what Williamson describes as 'technology and associated knowhow' (p. 293). These fall into the category of intangible assets (Caves, 1982, pp. 3–4), one feature of which is that they are likely to have public good characteristics to some degree at least: 'once an idea has been developed and applied in a certain location, it can be put to work elsewhere at little extra cost and without reducing the "amount" of the idea available at the original site' (Caves, p. 5). Such potential flexibility and mobility of application is clearly at variance with Williamson's conceptualization of complex technology transfer in terms of a high degree of asset specificity. Indeed, it is the possibility that the potential flexibility and mobility of such assets may be reflected in know-how leaking to competitors that leads many firms to adopt MNE organization instead of licensing technology (Caves, 1982, pp. 205–6). Thus, it is asset *non*-specificity rather than asset specificity that encourages corporate expansion in such instances.

If we are to find explanations for the evolution of the MNE, it is clear that transaction cost economics does not provide a satisfactory starting point. This is not to say that transaction costs in the more general sense may not be important, only that the theoretical perspective as outlined by Williamson appears to have limited applicability in this context. Analysts of MNE behaviour such as Buckley and Casson (1976, 1991) have developed transaction cost explanations of the MNE that recognize the importance of appropriability issues and are not dependent on concepts of asset specificity.[4] Buckley and Casson provide an excellent and comprehensive analysis of the sources of failure in the market for knowledge, but there are indications that the problem of limited comparators discussed in Chapter 4 may be a problem here as well. Buckley and Casson argue that the nature of multinationalism is essentially driven by the need to internalize transactions involving a global network of plants:

There is a special reason for believing that internalisation of the knowledge market will generate a high degree of multinationality among firms. Because knowledge is a public good which is easily transmitted across national boundaries, its exploitation is logically an international operation; thus unless comparative advantage or other factors restrict production to a single country, internalisation of knowledge will require each firm to operate a network of plants on a world-wide basis (Buckley and Casson, 1991, p. 45).

One problem with this argument is that to the extent that R&D can indeed be treated as a public good with low transmission costs within the firm (Buckley and Casson, 1991, p. 35), it should not have an impact on the location of production; if R&D turns out to be in the wrong place in terms of potential internal usage, it can be cheaply relocated to where it is needed. The location of R&D then becomes irrelevant as far as its exploitation in production is concerned since it is effectively available on tap anywhere within the firm. The servicing of global markets and the location of production then becomes a matter of how best to distribute and locate production resources. Buckley and Casson argue (rightly) that imperfections in the market for knowledge may mean that there may be circumstances in which it is more efficient to internalize a market for knowledge by choosing a multinational option for servicing an overseas market rather than licensing the knowledge to a host country based partner (1991, pp. 36–45). While this is correct as far as it goes, the problem is that it may again be a limited comparator. This may explain why a particular *mode* of servicing overseas markets is undertaken. It does not help to explain why the particular *strategy* of servicing overseas markets has been chosen given that there is likely to be an opportunity cost in terms of alternative strategies foregone. As we shall see, the MNE tends to be one of the weakest linked options when analysed in resource terms. It is therefore likely to be the case that multinationalism is only likely to be stimulated in special circumstances.

However, Buckley and Casson (1991, p. x) and Casson (1987, p. 32) make it clear that their theory is not presented as a general theory, which makes it unfair to judge it on these grounds. It is certainly an improvement on the transaction cost interpretation of Williamson since their approach recognizes the non-specific nature of technical know-how. If the problem can be specified in terms of the form of the decision to enter a foreign market in cases where the export option is impeded, then Buckley and Casson's approach provides an excellent and exhaustive account of the considerations that may be relevant in these situations. However, if we are to make further inroads into the question of what determines the scale and scope of the MNE, we need to broaden the analysis beyond the confines of the internalization decision itself.

In this context, a useful perspective is offered by Dunning's Eclectic Paradigm, (Dunning, 1993, pp. 76–95). Dunning argues that it is necessary to examine the development of the MNE in terms of possible ownership-specific (O), internalization (I), and location-specific (L) advantages that may be involved in multinational expansion. O advantages generally refer to a sustainable competitive advantage over firms of other nationalities conferred by a firm's privileged possession of intangible assets.[5] I advantages reflect market failure conditions and mean that the firm may find it advantageous to add value itself, rather than contracting out activities to foreign firms. L advantages exist when the interests of the firm may be served by operating in a foreign location. According to Dunning, it is the interplay between these three sets of influences that drive the development of the modern corporation. The approach leads to some clear predictions, for example, 'at any given moment in time, the more a country's enterprises—

relative to those of another—possess *O* advantages, the greater the incentive they have to internalize rather than externalize their use, the more they find it in their interest to exploit them from a foreign location, then the more likely they are to engage in outbound production' (Dunning, 1993, p. 80). Thus the development of the MNE is determined by firm, market, and territorial considerations.

As Dunning points out, the contribution that the Eclectic Paradigm makes may be less in terms of providing a theory itself, and more in terms of a framework in which alternative theories of the MNE may be couched and compared (1993, p. 85). Certain theories are more consistent with the Eclectic Paradigm than are others, and Dunning's framework provides a basis for sorting and organizing alternatives. A criticism of the framework has been that the variables identified by the framework are so numerous that its predictive value is nil (Dunning, 1991, p. 125), which may be another way of suggesting that it is essentially non-refutable and does not constitute a genuine theory. However, Dunning points out (1991, p. 133) that it is not presented as a theory, but as an organizing framework and so such criticisms are misplaced.

It will be argued here that the Eclectic Paradigm makes invaluable contributions in helping ensure that the right questions are asked, as well as providing a useful starting point for a comparative analysis of corporate options. For example, it helps to demonstrate that the development of the MNE requires special circumstances to operate and should not be regarded as necessarily inevitable or inexorable. If home country firms do not possess some ownership advantage that gives them a competitive edge over host country firms, we would not expect home country firms to locate some of their activities in that country; inward investors are likely to operate at a disadvantage to established host country incumbents unless *O* advantages more than compensate the difficulties of playing away from home. Furthermore, if internalization advantages do not exist, we would not expect to see 'away' investments in the form of multinational overseas subsidiaries when the more efficient solution would be to conclude a market agreement with incumbent host country firms. Also, if location advantages do not exist outside a particular firm's home base, why impede the exploitation of economies of scale and incur extra coordination problems by fragmenting corporate activities on an international basis?

Thus, a world without ownership advantages that transcend national boundaries is likely to be one characterized by domestically specialized firms. A world without cross-frontier internalization advantages would likely be characterized by international contracts such as licensing, franchising, and sub-contracting agreements rather than multinational expansion. A world without location advantages would tend to favour consolidation of corporate activities, and see access to foreign markets gained through exporting rather than direct foreign investment. Each of these scenarios favours alternative strategies to the MNE. It is only when O, L, and I advantages coincide that the MNE begins to emerge as a rational form of economic organization. Analysis of the MNE is likely to be incomplete and misleading unless the complementary role that each set of advantages plays in multinational development is recognized.

However, one difficulty in analysing the development of MNEs has already been alluded to. Once specific reasons begin to be sought for the development of MNEs, analysis quickly encounters a myriad of O, L, and I advantages that may influence the development of MNEs. Dunning (1993, p. 81) suggests about two dozen O, a dozen I, and 9 L categories of advantage that may represent some of the more important in the respective cases. Further, many of these categories are extremely broad (e.g. the O advantage of 'synergistic economies . . . in production . . . purchasing, marketing, finance, etc.') which raises the prospect that more disaggregated analyses could lead to such listings being considerably expanded. When possible interactions between O, L, and I variables are recognized, the potential complexity of the problem expands considerably. Even if a theory was to focus on one broad category of O advantage (e.g. 'favoured access to inputs'), one broad category of I advantage (e.g. 'to compensate for absence of future markets') and one broad category of L advantages (e.g. trade barriers), there would be 2592 possible OLI combinations to choose from.[6] Once the analysis begins to be disaggregated (e.g. trade barriers as quotas, tariffs, etc.), and alternative conduct or strategic variables fed into the analysis (game theoretic modelling can help here in expanding possibilities indefinitely), then there should be enough scope to keep a theorist specializing in just one set of OLI combinations employed in years of model building.

Such prospects signal a possible dilemma. Whilst there may be dangers of over-generality posed by sticking at the level of the broad perspective offered by the Eclectic Paradigm, there are clearly countervailing dangers of particular theories being too restricted in scope to provide an adequate explanation for the development of MNEs. In fact, we shall suggest that there may be a middle way that helps provide a systemic basis for analysing the evolution of MNEs by helping to highlight those issues that may be important in this context, while eliminating others. In the next section we shall develop an approach to the MNE that builds on points raised by Dunning's Eclectic Paradigm and treats the MNE as a complex system in which the nature and pattern of resources determine choice of multinational solution over alternatives.

8.2. The MNE and its Alternatives

It is the variety and complexity of real world processes that make analysis so difficult in the case of the MNE. As we did with diversification, we simplify the analysis by abstracting from business unit level and assume that our firms are concerned with IBUs which are identical in terms of scale, profitability, and growth characteristics.[7] This again allows us to concentrate on the implication of resource *linkages* while holding other factors constant. Expansion of each firm (e.g. by merging two IBUs), may lead to exploitation of economies of scale (e.g. single product-market expansion) or scope (e.g. diversification). We also assume that there is a strong propensity towards devious, opportunistic, and self-interested behaviour (Williamson, 1985). This means that co-operative options such as strategic alliances, joint ventures, and licensing are only considered as devices of last resort; internalization of expansion opportunities within the firm to protect know-how and curb potential opportunism is normally the first preference. Treating co-operative options as devices of last resort allows us to set them on one side in this context. This does not mean that they are not potentially important issues, and indeed we shall extend the analysis into these areas (and reintroduce questions of hierarchy versus market alternatives) in Chapters 9 and 10. It *does* mean that we can focus on alternative wholly-owned internalization options in developing an approach to help explain the nature of the MNE, which is the primary objective of this chapter. The treatment of co-operative options as devices of last resort in a global context is supported by arguments developed in Kay *et al.* (1987), Hennart (1988*a*), and more recently in Hennart (1991) and Kay (1991). To some extent this anticipates discussion of collaborative options in the next chapter, which will be more fully concerned with these issues.

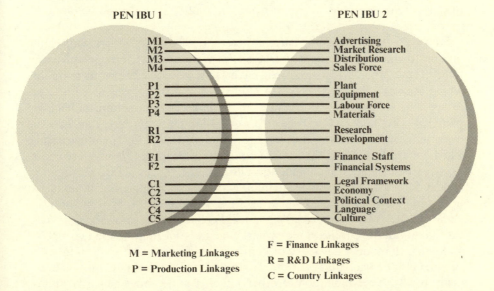

Fig. 8.1. Specialization and resource sharing

Now, suppose we also have two countries, North and South. Both country differs from the other in terms of political, economic, legal, social, and linguistic traditions. There is a Northern firm (Dispen) that manufactures disposable pens and is considering four possible expansion strategies. Two involve domestic expansion (specialization, diversification), and two involve international market entry into the South (exporting, the MNE). We shall start by outlining the resource implications of pursuing a specialization strategy. Dispen would pursue the specialist route by setting up a new IBU producing and selling its product in its Northern base. Figure 8.1 identifies the major *categories* of resources which may be shared across IBUs. Wherever a resource can be shared, economies may be generated and costs reduced. As can be seen from Fig. 8.1, the specialization option opens up a long menu of resource sharing possibilities. With the possible exception of C-links, most of the linkage categories are self-explanatory, and consistent with those discussed in earlier chapters. Wherever a resource (say, a truck or a marketing manager) can be shared by IBUs, indivisibilities may be more effectively exploited or specialization and division of labour facilitated.

The C-linkages are perhaps less obvious. Domestic expansion of any kind means that Dispen can take advantage of the wide range of country-specific knowledge that accumulates with experience of operating in a particular country. Dispen's knowledge of Northern legal, political, economic, social, and language characteristics is not something that has to be learnt afresh in starting up and running the new IBU. Instead the new IBU can exploit Dispen's existing capabilities in this area, a less obvious form of economy that only really becomes apparent when international expansion involves its sacrifice.

However, there is a particular characteristic of C-links which, whilst not unique to them, are perhaps displayed in more extreme form in this case than in any other. Most resources have fairly obvious homes in terms of what category of linkage they are likely to be most associated with. For example, a salesman may generate an M-link, an accountant an F-link, plant a P-link, and an R&D scientist an R-link. Some resources may cover more than one category of link (e.g. strategic planners). On the other hand, when we are looking at the level of individual resources, C-links are most likely to be exploited in conjunction with other linkages. Thus, marketing, production, R&D and financial managers can all exploit the benefits of operating under common C-links as long as domestic expansion only is being pursued. There are clearly potential economies when marketing specialists do not have to learn a new language in co-ordinating the two IBUs, and when the same knowledge of contract law can be used in dealing with suppliers to the two IBUs. For the most part, exploitation of C-links is bundled up with the exploitation of other linkages and cannot be easily disentangled from them. There is no separable C resource called 'language' that can be disengaged from the rest of the firm's resources and even treated as a make-or-buy problem in the same way that resources such as trucks, equipment, and components can be. Yet such common knowledge can generate economies here just as surely as can these other resources.

In Fig. 8.2, we simplify the first diagram to illustrate the broad categories of linkages obtainable from resource sharing in the specialization case. The subscript 's' indicates linkages associated with specialization. The reasons for continuing to distinguish between production and R&D resources will become clearer later.

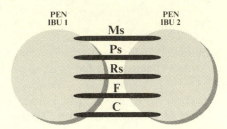

Fig. 8.2. Specialization option

The specialization option represents a limit case of economies of scale in terms of cost savings from resource linkages. However, other options to expand are also being considered by Dispen. One option is the diversification option, which in this context would mean starting up a new IBU to make and sell disposable razors in the North.

Dispen would expect this expansion strategy to exploit economies from shared resources in all major categories. Compared to disposable pens, disposable razors would be sold to similar market outlets using similar production techniques and much common R&D into light metals and plastics. However, while some shared resources would generate economies here as in the specialization option, other linkages would be sacrificed. For example, some distribution channels may be shared between IBUs, some may be different; some labour skills may be readily transferable to the new IBU, others may have to be developed; some materials R&D may be applicable to both IBUs, some may be IBU-specific; and so on. Consequently, while the diversification option may also exploit M-, P- and R-linkages, the linkages are likely to be weaker compared to the specialization option and the potential economies accordingly less. These weaker links we identify by the subscript 'd' for diversification in Fig. 8.3.

However, it is in the nature of C-links that they are not product-specific, and domestic diversification is expected to exploit them just as in the specialization option. Dispen also expects the economies achievable from shared financial resources to be the same under diversification as in the case

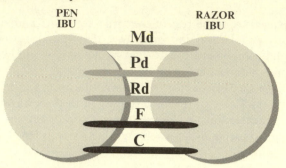

Fig. 8.3. Diversification option

of specialization, for similar reasons. Collectively, the M_d-, P_d-, R_d-, C- and F-links help generate cost savings associated with economies of scope in the diversification case.

We are now in a position to consider all of Dispen's alternative options since the various linkages of potential relevance in each case have already been introduced. Figure 8.4 represents the four basic options and shows how they compare in terms of potential linkages. We are looking at the implications of alternative options solely in terms of potential gains from resource sharing, and for the moment ignore any other possible influences on corporate strategies, such as transport costs and government policies.

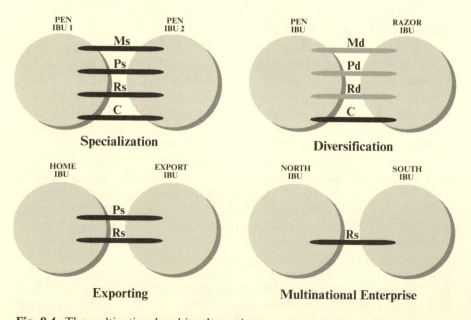

Fig. 8.4. The multinational and its alternatives

In addition to the specialization and diversification strategies discussed above, Fig. 8.4 introduces exporting and MNE and analyses them in terms of the categories of common resources that each may exploit. Since F-links are common to all options we drop them from the analysis for the moment; it is only *differences* in resource linkages which are important for the purposes of our analysis.

Each of the new options has different implications in terms of potential resource linkages. As far as the exporting option is concerned, Dispen is considering exporting pens from North to South. Since the product is identical this means the IBU for the export market could exploit fully the R&D associated with the IBU for the home market (the R_s-link), while the consolidation of production activities in the North means that this option could achieve the same production economies that specialization exploited (the P_s-link). However, the exporting option involves a different country (and consequent sacrifice of C-links), with separate and distinctive marketing and distribution activities compared to the North (no M-links). A variety of export modes may be available to Dispen,[8] but all of them will have to deal with the issue that such market entry cannot draw upon Dispen's market, distribution and country experience which is specific to its Northern operations. Consequently, exporting exploits only P_s- and R_s-links between IBUs in Fig. 8.4, and separate bundles of C- and M-resources have to be reproduced in the two countries to reflect the particular needs in the respective cases.

But while the exporting option involves some sacrifice of potential economies that domestic expansion would have exploited, the MNE option fares even worse as a potential source of economies from resource sharing. If Dispen is considering setting up a production facility in the South to service this market, not only would this involve similar sacrifices of potential M- and C-links to the exporting case, but the splitting of production between North and South entails a further sacrifice of resource sharing possibilities in the area of production (P) economies.[9] The only major category of resource that MNE Dispen can share between North and South operations is technology in the form of R-links.[10]

For the four options, some clear points emerge from this exercise. First, the specialization option exploits more linkages than any other. This is not surprising and simply confirms the general principle of gains from specialization discussed in Chapter 4. Whilst we are ignoring demand side considerations in our analysis, it should be noted that introducing them would simply reinforce the advantages of specialization to the extent that such expansion facilitated increased market power on the part of the firm. It is the relationships between the other three options in terms of potential gains from resource linkages that have more interesting implications. It is clear that the exporting option would allow more resource linkages than the MNE option. It not only exploits the same R_s-links that the MNE would exploit, but opens up P_s-links as well. Thus, there is a clear ranking running from specialization to exporting to the MNE, since the higher ranked options can exploit all the resource linkages that lower ranked alternatives can exploit and add more besides. The rankings are more ambiguous when the diversification strategy is brought into consideration. At first sight, diversification offers a richer set of linkages than either exporting and the MNE. However, while exporting and the MNE do not exploit the breadth of linkages associated with diversification, the limited technological linkages they do exploit are exploited more intensively than in the diversification option ('s' versus 'd' subscripts).

There is however a less obvious potential disadvantage of multinational-ism. Figure 8.5 compares specialization and MNE options in terms of their vulnerability to external shocks. The dotted lines in the case of the MNE join resource bundles in which the host market and technology are simple clones of those in the home country, but do not provide linkages that can generate economies through resource sharing. In Fig. 8.5 the MNE strategy involves different bundles of C-resources with its host country activities rep-resenting a straightforward replication of home activities.

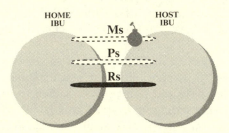

Fig. 8.5. Multinational specialization

This illustrates a problem with the MNE option in that it exposes the firm to most of the potential dangers of vulnerability to external environmental shocks associated with a specialist strategy, with the exception that it may allow diversification away from country specific shocks. At the same time, the MNE fails to exploit the corresponding economies that a specialist strat-egy could exploit, with the exception of R&D economies. In some respects the MNE option may offer the worst of all worlds in such circumstances, with global dispersal of assets impeding the exploitation of economies while still generating simultaneous vulnerability in all sectors to single external shocks such as technological change or changing consumer tastes (Kay, 1982). One innovation by a competitor could threaten Dispen's pen tech-nology and attack it in all the markets in which it makes and markets pens. It is not difficult to identify real world parallels of MNEs that have faced simultaneous threats of this nature, such as Wang (word processors), Singer (sewing machines), and IBM (mainframe computers).

Compared to the two international expansion options, diversification trades linkage depth for linkage breadth, but it has the additional benefit of reducing the vulnerability of the firm to specific external environmental shocks. Whether breadth or depth of linkages will generate more economies in practice will depend on circumstances. What such analysis does provide is clues as to where our firm might look if it is to investigate the conditions which should favour the choice of one option over another. In the next section we shall consider the circumstances that are likely to result in firms adopting the multinational route.

8.3. The Multinational Option

The analysis of the previous section has clear implications regarding the conditions in which multinational expansion is likely to be entertained by a firm. The MNE is inferior to both domestic specialization and exporting in terms of potential economies. Also, while it is conceivable that its R_s economies could be sufficient to beat the broader range of economies afforded by domestic diversification in particular circumstances, at first sight this would appear to call for an unusual combination of conditions. It should also be noted that we have given the MNE the benefit of the doubt in assuming that its R&D may be transferable without modification to the host country. In practice, technology may have to be adapted to host country conditions, further reducing the range of shared resources. Therefore, it is not sufficient to simply identify advantages of MNE expansion to explain its existence. Something must be wrong with alternative forms of expansion for it to be seriously considered.

With this in mind, we can now begin to trace the circumstances in which our firm may choose the MNE route. Our starting point is that it would clearly be rational for Dispen to choose that strategy which generates the highest level of economies. Whilst this holds obviously if Dispen is pursuing profit oriented objectives, in this analysis it is also consistent with non-profit objectives such as scale or growth of the firm. Choosing less profitable options would sacrifice internal economies that could have been used to support growth or other managerial objectives. In this respect, choice of option is likely to be consistent over a wide range of objectives as we saw in Chapter 4.

Our firm has a clear first preference for domestic specialization through simply cloning its original IBU. There must be some negative influence at work that impedes this strategy, and the most obvious are market saturation or the threat of anti-trust intervention. Certainly market saturation limits will be encountered sooner or later, and when they are, alternative

strategies to domestic specialization may be considered. Diversification is
the obvious alternative next best strategy for an expansion minded Dispen.
Only if richly linked diversification alternatives are not available does international expansion become a serious possibility. Otherwise Dispen will continue to choose the cheaper and more profitable options associated with
staying at home.

The circumstances likely to favour international expansion are therefore
those in which diversification offers only limited or weak linkage opportunities. If potential M-, P-, C-, and R-economies from diversification are
weaker than the technological economies achievable from international
expansion, then the firm may turn to the latter set of options. However,
within this set of options there is an unambiguous preference for exporting
on the basis of resource linkages. Some other negative influence is needed
to encourage the firm to adopt the less preferred MNE option if international expansion is being pursued.

There are a variety of pressures that might affect the export option and
encourage the MNE solution even though the latter is weaker in terms of
potential linkages. For example, transport costs and trade barriers may
impede cross-frontier trade and encourage switching to direct MNE investment to enter foreign markets. Through such influences, the lowly rated
MNE solution may emerge as a rational option to exploit technological
linkages, but only after a variety of blocks have been placed in the way of
exploiting option that would normally be expected to be more highly rated
in terms of resource linkages. It is important to bear in mind that a particular option must beat all contenders to be adopted. It is not sufficient to
point out that barriers to foreign trade may encourage the MNE over the
exporting option. MNE still has to beat diversification, which means
MNE's rather narrowly constrained R_s economies must be sufficient to
overcome the latter's generally broader linkage opportunities.

The picture this implies is of a firm specializing until it is forced to diversify, then diversifying until it is forced into international markets, and only
then choosing the MNE option when barriers close out the exporting
option. Such a perspective lends itself naturally to a stages interpretation of
multinational development. In most sectors, there are specialization and
diversification opportunities for firms. However, pursuit of specialization
eventually encounters market saturation limits, which means the firm turns
to diversification opportunities. The most richly linked diversification
opportunities are exploited first, the weaker later. Eventually the residual
diversification opportunities fail to beat the R&D economies from MNE
expansion in sectors in which impediments to trade preclude or impede
exporting. The picture this paints is of the development of weak patterns as
described in Chapter 5, with the firm progressively exploiting weaker linkages as it expands. Also, the role of history as discussed in Chapter 5 is seen
to be important. Unless analysis of the multinational option is embedded in

the context of the firm's historical development, the logic and impetus underlying multinationalism is likely to be obscured.

In such circumstances, the MNE is typically therefore large and diversified compared to non-MNEs. This is not because there is a particular advantage in being large and diversified in becoming an MNE, but rather the opportunities encourage becoming large and diversified *before* becoming an MNE. Whilst this distinction may appear subtle, it is nevertheless important and consistent with the low rating of MNEs in terms of resource linkages. Domestic diversification also has the incidental benefit of helping to compensate for the vulnerability to external technological and market shocks that an undiversified MNE strategy entails. A further characteristic this suggests of MNEs is that they tend to be more research intensive than non-MNEs. Where firms have little R&D activity, there are no obvious economies exploitable from MNE expansion. It is when the firm is loaded up with a high level of potential R_s-economies that the MNE is more likely to appear as a substitute option as diversification opportunities are exhausted.

Thus, this suggests a picture of the MNE as typically large, diversified, and technologically progressive. Such characteristics are likely to place the MNE in the league of the most successful corporations. Its multinationalism may be seen by some commentators as a symptom of that success, which would be ironic given that the MNE option here is born of weakness. It is market saturation, limits to diversification, and barriers to trade that force the MNE option. In the next section we shall see if this picture is of relevance to patterns of multinational activity that actually obtain in practice.

8.4. Empirical Patterns

As in the last chapter we shall consider whether the expected patterns are consistent with the empirical evidence.

1. *Domestic clustering of MNE assets*

The first issue we shall consider is the incidence of multinationalism in the global economy and the location of assets. The conventional definition of an MNE as an enterprise that engages in foreign direct investment and controls value-adding activities in more than one country (Dunning, 1993, p. 3) can be somewhat misleading. On that basis virtually all corporations beyond a fairly modest threshold level in most sectors are MNEs. It is akin to describing a firm as diversified if it has any interests, however minor, in more than one product.

Since our approach is a resource based approach, a fairer measure of multinational activity would reflect the balance of resources between domestic and foreign bases. Dunning (1993, p. 47) sets out some vital statistics for some of the world's largest industrial companies in 1989 that provides some useful information in this respect. For the thirteen non-petroleum companies for which a breakdown between domestic and foreign assets is available, not one had a majority of assets accounted for by foreign affiliates.[11] For the thirteen firms as a whole, the figures ranged from 8.8 per cent in the case of General Electric, to 48.6 per cent in the case of IBM, with a median figure of less than 25 per cent of assets accounted for by foreign affiliates. These figures suggest a strong propensity for these corporations to cluster assets in their domestic bases. If this clustering of assets related to products rather than countries, we would describe most of these firms as reasonably or highly specialized. This holds even for the European MNEs in Dunning's survey where narrower country bases compared to the USA might have been expected to encourage increased investment spillover beyond domestic frontiers. Also, it would be fair to assume that a proportion of these foreign investments were only undertaken as a consequence of host country restrictions on market access, (or positive inducements to locate in the host country) and that, absent host country intervention, these company's first preferences would have led to an even greater concentration of assets within domestic bases.

This domestic clustering holds even more strongly for assets associated with innovative activity. Patel (1995) surveyed recent studies of the propensity of firms to locate technological resources abroad (a variety of measures being used in the studies) and concluded that most put the proportion of foreign technological activities at between 10 per cent and 30 per cent (p. 143). Patel also compared the percentage of R&D conducted overseas by 243 of the largest US firms, with the percentage of patenting activity undertaken overseas by the rather wider survey of all US firms covered by the NSF R&D survey. The results showed that the US firms conducted less than 8 per cent of their R&D and patenting activity abroad during the 1980s. In comparing the percentage of technological activity (measured in terms of patenting activity) conducted outside national boundaries for his sample of the world's largest firms, he found that the percentage was only 1 per cent for Japanese firms, to between 10 per cent and 15 per cent for Italy, France, and Germany, with only large firms from the smaller European countries of the Netherlands and Belgium averaging over 50 per cent of technological activity outside national boundaries in this study. Freeman (1995) also points out that the foreign R&D activities of MNEs tend to represent either modifications to meet local requirements, or monitoring of local science and technology and notes the overwhelming concentration of the more original research in the home base.[12]

While we should add the caveat that there are indications that in some sectors firms appear to be locating a higher proportion of their assets abroad, including technological activities (Patel, 1995), these studies still indicate a strong preference for MNEs to cluster their resources (especially their technological resources) in their home base, and are also consistent with Porter's (1990) arguments concerning the importance of home base for the formulation of competitive strategy. Multinational activity is only the foreign investment tip of the corporate investment iceberg, and the size of the tip is itself largely a consequence of external governmental pressures, not internal corporate objectives. To the extent that trends towards liberalisation of global trade are successful, we would expect this to reinforce such parochial tendencies on the part of corporations, with exporting substituting FDI possibilities in many cases. In short, even a high degree of sensitivity to global *markets* does not necessarily imply a global *corporation*, at least where its resource base is concerned. The picture this suggests is of reluctant multinationalism and one which is quite consistent with our earlier discussion.

2. *MNE activity and research intensity*

The next set of issues of relevance refer to the R&D characteristics of MNEs. How do they relate to the picture developed here of MNEs as research intensive corporations? The picture we have painted of multinationalism is observed at two levels in connection with research intensity: first it tends to be associated with research intensive *sectors*, secondly it tends to be associated with research intensive *firms* within particular sectors. The clearest way to interpret this is in terms of the opportunity cost of going multinational for sectors or firms that are not research intensive. For these cohorts, even if there are no further M-, P-, or R-links from domestic expansion, a domestic conglomerate strategy would have C-link advantages over the MNE option and would be preferred to it. There appear to be no circumstances in this picture in which multinationalism can evolve unless R-links allow it to beat even this weakly linked strategy. R-linking is a necessary but not sufficient condition for multinationalism here. Thus, the association of multinationalism with research intensive sectors and firms in this view should not be seen in terms of research intensity somehow making this option more attractive; it more accurately reflects the fact that it is only in those sectors that multinationalism is ever likely to evolve at all, and only then after sector- or firm-specific weaknesses (such as trade barriers or exhaustion of domestic alternatives) lead to it being turned to by default.

Empirical studies of MNEs tend to be broadly consistent with these patterns. As far as research intensity is concerned, at least a dozen studies have looked at the relationship between measures of technological intensity and propensity to undertake multinational activity. The general conclusion to be drawn from these studies is generally of strong and positive relationships between R&D activity and the propensity to go multinational,[13] both between sectors and at the level of the firm, with some caveats in the case of Japanese and UK FDI.[14]

3. *Marketing-based MNEs*

The basic framework developed here does not explain vertically integrated MNE strategies, and indeed it is not designed to deal with such intra-business tactics. This is the territory of vertical relations within individual product-markets that has been well trodden by the conventional *IO* literature (e.g. see Tirole, 1988, pp. 169–203) and transaction cost economics (e.g. see Williamson 1985). Whether or not such approaches provide a reasonable description of the reasons for the evolution of the vertically integrated MNE is really beyond the scope of this present analysis which is concerned with more usual cases of resource *sharing* (horizontal relations) and corporate strategy, rather than resource *transfers* (vertical relations) within individual product-markets. At the same time, we would expect that the analysis of vertical integration developed here in Chapter 3 could also be helpful in explaining the evolution of the vertically integrated MNE.

However, there are other non-vertical MNE strategies that have been discussed in the literature which have not been dealt with so far. These include MNEs to exploit marketing know-how. This is illustrated in Fig. 8.6 and compared to a reference case of the MNE strategy discussed earlier.

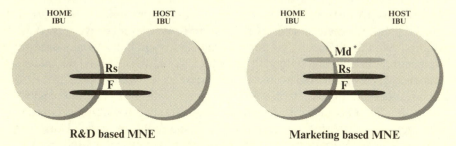

Fig. 8.6. Alternative multinational strategies

For simplicity, we have assumed so far that no marketing knowledge is transferable across frontiers. Such an assumption is reasonable to the extent that much marketing know-how is country- or even region-specific. Even products that are technically identical may be sold in very different ways in different countries depending on national characteristics and the products' identity in respective countries.[15] However, a proportion of marketing know-how may be communicable cross-frontier, the proportion depending on the extent to which product marketing has to be adapted to the host market. For example, if user needs for a particular brand of PC can be identified in the USA, a great deal of this knowledge may be transferable to the UK context. In the latter case, marketing know-how economies may be exploitable by the MNE across home and host markets, just as are technical know-how economies. Such possibilities are illustrated in Fig. 8.6 where the partial transferability of marketing linkages is indicated by the 'd*' subscript.[16] If firms are loaded with a high level of potential economies in terms of marketing know-how, this may eventually lead to the development of marketing based MNEs in analogous fashion to the development of R&D based MNEs. As Dunning (1993, p. 151) points out, a number of researchers have investigated this possibility, commonly using advertising expenditure as a percentage of sales as a proxy for this form of potential ownership advantage, and they have generally found positive and significant relationships between advertising intensity and FDI activity.

These points are captured in Fig. 8.6, but there is another issue which our resource based approach helps to raise which might not be apparent from consideration of marketing considerations in isolation. Is marketing know-how a substitute or a complement for technical know-how in the evolution of the MNE? This issue arises because it is quite clearly the case that R&D economies can be exploited cross-frontier even if there are no similarities between home and host markets to permit sharing of marketing resources. It is less clear that marketing economies can be exploited cross-frontier between home and host countries unless there are strong technical similarities between the respective products. Even if all marketing linkages are not country-specific, many, if not all, may be highly product-specific—for example advertising, user manuals, market research, and so on. Whilst the extent of product-specificity of marketing know-how may only be established by further research, and to the extent that such know-how is product-specific, we would expect that it would only be extractable by the MNE where it is operating technically similar or effectively identical products in home and host markets. In this respect, we would expect that marketing know-how economies would depend on technical similarities in a way that technical economies do not depend on marketing similarities.

4. *Size, diversification and MNE activity*

A further set of issues relates to the impact of size and diversification on multinationalism. Sectors vary in terms of the opportunities they offer for economies from specializing and diversifying. In some cases, the minimum efficient scale of production is quite low and diversification opportunities are weak or limited. In such instances, the MNE option appears on the corporate agenda sooner than in cases where there are significant economies of scale and abundant opportunities for diversification. Thus, the influence of size and diversification varies from sector to sector. What is clear in the view developed earlier is that for a given sector, the larger and more diversified the firm the more likely it is that exhaustion of richly linked domestic options will encourage multinationalism. Smaller more specialized firms in a given sector are more likely to have significant unexploited opportunities for domestic expansion than do their large diversified peers, *ceteris paribus*.

The empirical evidence in this context is again generally consistent with these expectations. Dunning (1993, pp. 151–2) and Pearce (1993, pp. 31–2) survey a number of studies in which the relationship between firm size and propensity to undertake foreign direct investment (FDI) has been investigated. Pearce found that positive relationships between size and multinationalism tended to prevail (Pearce, 1993, p. 151). The general conclusion to be drawn from these studies is of a positive relationship between the respective variables. Bergsten *et al.*'s (1978) findings for US firms is of particular relevance in this context: 'size is critical *within* an industry but not *between* industries. Within any given industry large firms tend to be the foreign investors, but in some sectors, average firm size is large but [degree of FDI is] small' (Bergsten *et al.*,1978, p. 243).

One difficulty with the studies is that size itself may be a proxy for other variables (Dunning, 1993, p. 151), and one variable which size may be representing in some of these studies is diversification. A recent study which has attempted to separate out the effects of diversification is Pearce's 1993 study of the world's 792 largest industrial enterprises. Pearce examined the association between industrial diversification and the percentage of a firm's sales attributable to foreign production. He found evidence of a strong and positive relationship between firm level diversification and internationalization tendencies on the part of the firm. This was even more pronounced in the case of FDI than it was in the case of exporting, and Pearce concluded that there was evidence of strong complementarities between diversification and multinationalism (Pearce, 1993, p. 147), consistent with the arguments developed here.

5. *Industrial concentration and MNE activity*

Finally, a further issue suggested by the approach developed above is that there may be links between domestic sectoral concentration and propensity to go multinational. Unlike some conventional explanations, the reasons do not involve market power or barriers to entry considerations, but rather the likelihood that increased concentration may reflect the fact that firms in such circumstances may be running out of domestic room to expand, either because resource linkages have been exhausted or because anti-trust considerations inhibit further domestic expansion. Again, as with the other influences on multinationalism, the connection between the stimulus and multinationalism is a negative one; here it is not that concentration opens up options or induces strategies such as multinationalism through enhancing oligopolistic corporate power as in many conventional interpretations of this possible relationship (Pearce, 1993, p. 35). Instead, concentration may signal that other options have been closed down and that the MNE route has been chosen by default.

Lecraw (1983) found that there tended to be a significant and positive relationship between US and European FDI and the degree of industrial concentration, though the Japanese case produced contrary (negative) relationships, as did results for developing country FDI. However, as Dunning (1993, p. 429) points out, when MNE activity as a whole is looked at, 'the average concentration ratios of the sectors that account for the greater part of MNE activity are considerably higher than for the rest of industry'. On the other hand, Pearce found no relation between industrial concentration (generally measured as the three largest firms' share of the top twenty firms' sales) and propensity to undertake overseas production for his study of large global enterprises. He leaves open the issue of whether this reflects a refutation of the possibility of a link between concentration and multinationalism, or a weakness in his concentration measure (Pearce, 1993, p. 78). In fact, Pearce's use of global large firm concentration measures leads to almost all industries with above average concentration levels being located in the low technology sectors[17] (drink; tobacco; building materials; rubber; shipbuilding, railroad and transportation equipment), the only exception being office equipment, including computers (Pearce, 1993, p. 9).

It is in contexts such as these that the resource based approach developed here may be especially valuable in interpreting results. Pearce uses multiple regression analysis to separate out the effects of different candidate causal variables (such as size, diversification, and concentration), on propensity to undertake FDI. However, to the extent that the highly concentrated industries in Pearce's analysis are clustered in the low technology sectors, we would not expect concentration to have a major impact on FDI even at extremely high concentration levels—as our earlier analysis suggests, there would be no major R-links to exploit. It is concentration *together with* technological progressiveness that might stimulate FDI in the resource based context, not concentration *separated from* technological progressiveness as in a multiple regression analysis. This suggests a potentially highly satisfactory route to help resolve differences in empirical findings in this area, as well as signposting how theoretical predictions might be reformulated in the future.

8.5. Conclusions

Much of the literature in this area tends to analyse the decision to go multinational in terms of the advantages of internalizing markets. However, overseas expansion is typically only one of many options facing the firm at a given time. Analysing the MNE from a resource-based perspective reveals it as one of the weakest linked of expansion options. Instead of seeing the growth of multinationalism as natural and inexorable, the resource based approach applied here paints a picture of reluctant multinationalism, an option only resorted to when other more richly-linked expansion opportunities are blocked. Firms will typically prefer to specialize, diversify, or export before they are tempted into the weak-linked multinational option. This perspective helps account for a variety of phenomena, including the domestic clustering of MNE assets; the close relationship between MNE activity and research intensity; the tendency for MNEs to be large and diversified compared to non-MNEs; and the apparent absence of a relationship between industrial concentration and MNE activity. The special case of the marketing-based MNE was also dealt with.

NOTES

1. Surveys of work in this field include Buckley and Casson, (1976, 1991), Kay (1983), Casson (1987) and Dunning (1993). Melin (1992) surveys the business literature on the evolution of international business.
2. Strictly speaking, the term 'technology transfer' is quite misleading since 'transfer' implies that something shifts across boundaries and vacates the previous space it occupied, whether it is a passenger changing aircraft, or a barrel of oil being shipped ('*transfer* . . . to change or go or cause to change or go from one thing, person, or point to another', *Collins English Dictionary*). If technological know-how was in fact displaced in this fashion, we would indeed be talking about vertical transfers and vertical integration. However, 'technology transfer' typically falls into the category of activities associated with resource *sharing*, and horizontal or synergistic relations as discussed in Chapter 5. This is to be expected given the public good characteristics associated with knowledge based assets (Caves, 1982, pp. 3–4) which enables R&D costs to be spread over a larger level of output (home and host), just as shared distribution and production activities can assist the diversified firm to exploit economies of scope. In this respect, a less misleading term for technological transfer would be technology sharing; this would reduce the possibility that it would be mistakenly interpreted as a simple extension of vertical integration issues as in Williamson (1985, pp. 290–4).
3. See, for example, Dunning's adaptation (1993, p. 147) of the Group of Thirty (1984) analysis of FDI decisions by 52 leading firms. Companies were asked to rank the six most important influences on new FDI in industrial countries and less developed countries. Market seeking reasons (which would tend to be associated with horizontal integration) appeared frequently in the top three reasons, e.g. access to host country's domestic market 87 per cent of respondents, access to markets in host country's region 34 per cent, avoidance of tariff barriers 43 per cent, avoidance of non-tariff barriers 28 per cent. On the other hand, resource seeking reasons (which would tend to be associated with vertical integration) were

cited infrequently as a motive for FDI, i.e. access to raw materials 11 per cent of respondents, comparative labour costs 13 per cent, and comparative material costs 4 per cent.

4. For surveys of a variety of transaction cost perspectives, see Caves (1982) and Dunning (1993). I am also grateful to Kieran McCaldin whose Honours dissertation at Strathclyde University first brought to my attention the relative neglect of the exporting option in the internalization literature. McCaldin's thesis may be regarded as exploring the problem of limited comparators in this context.

5. Casson points out, correctly, that possession of an ownership advantage is not necessary to explain multinational operations since internalization itself may provide the firm with the necessary competitive advantage (Casson, 1987, pp. 33–4). Similar points have been made here in Chapter 2 concerning the misplaced emphasis on 'distinctive competencies' and 'unique assets' in these other contexts. More properly, the notion of ownership advantage should be replaced with some notion indicating firms' distinctiveness (Nelson, 1991) and an acknowledgement that in some cases internalization may both reduce transaction costs *and* generate a competitive advantage.

6. This may be overstating the case to the extent that some OLI advantages are similar or duplicate each others effects. Against this mitigating factor must be set the variety of ways that certain other advantages can manifest themselves and affect the behaviour of firms.

7. Cave's (1982, p. 6) employs a similar type of mental experiment when he explores the implications of transferring technology in an imaginary situation involving seven different plants (firms) in seven different countries.

8. Young *et al.* (1989) summarize a variety of methods of exporting, including direct and indirect forms of foreign sales representation.

9. We are assuming the extreme case where production operations are quite separate in the two countries, though in practice Dispen may try to exploit some production economies and protect its technological advantage by limiting the local content of its Southern subsidiary, requiring it to take components from the North. To the extent that this is successful, it may generate a proportion of the P-links and associated economies that could have been obtained by exporting. However, it does not change the ranking of exporting versus MNE options in terms of their ability to generate economies through resource sharing.

10. It could be argued that whilst technology represents the most obvious form of know-how linkage, it is not the only one. We shall consider this possibility below.

11. Sales figures by overseas affiliates might appear to be an alternative basis for estimating degree of multinationalism, but these typically include goods imported from the parent for resale and would overstate the resource commitment to foreign bases.

12. Though he does note important exceptions in the drug and electronic industries, where specialized pools of scientific expertise can be important.

13. See Dunning (1993, pp. 149–50) for a summary of these results.

14. Thus, in a pooled cross-sectional analysis for 1965, 1970, and 1975, Clegg (1987) found that whilst R&D expenditure was the most significant determinant of outbound FDI for US, Swedish, and West German MNEs, the relationship was negative and significant in the case of Japanese MNEs, and negative but

insignificant in the case of UK MNEs. Pearce found similar tendencies for R&D intensity to be linked to propensity to engage in FDI in the cases of US and European multinationals, with the UK again proving an exception. He found that for Japanese firms, although propensity to undertake FDI was positively related to the research intensity of their sector, there was some tendency for the less research intensive firms within sectors to show a higher propensity to undertake FDI. Dunning (1993, p. 149) comments that the results for the UK may reflect the higher level of UK FDI in resource intensive sectors.

15. Examples include the very different images and target markets for particular beers and whiskies in different European countries.

16. We have asterisked this subscript to indicate that whilst this case extracts partial marketing linkages as in the diversification case, the linkages here are not necessarily the same ones.

17. Pearce (1993, p. 9). The comparisons discussed here are for the latest figures available, that is for the year 1982.

9.   Joint Venture

The proliferation of cooperative activity between firms in recent years has been widely noted and commented on. First, however, another puzzle. If cooperation is such a good thing, as so many writers in this field appear to argue, why did firms generally wait until relatively recently before pursuing such activities so enthusiastically? We shall be concerned with this fundamental question in this chapter, as well as a number of related issues.

There have been a number of the reasons for cooperative or collaborative activity cited in the managerial literature. For the particular case of joint venture (a jointly owned subsidiary between two or more firms), Harrigan (1988a) lists 28 different motivations which can generally be reduced to benefits from sharing resources (e.g. finance, plant, distribution, technology, information, management practices) or demand side considerations (e.g. reducing competition). Similarly, Contractor and Lorange (1988a, pp. 9–10) argue that joint ventures, licensing, and other types of cooperative agreements can achieve at least seven or more objectives: (a) risk reduction; (b) economies of scale and/or rationalization; (c) technology exchanges; (d) co-opting or blocking competition; (e) overcoming government mandated trade or investment barriers; (f) facilitating initial expansion of inexperienced firms; and (g) complementary contributions of partners. Further, Hergert and Morris (1988) identify some recurring themes behind international collaborative activity as (a) capital requirements; (b) excess capacity; (c) modular design facilitating splitting of responsibilities; (d) economies of scale; (e) emergence of global products; (f) risk reduction; (g) foreign market entry.[1] On a rather different tack, Ring and Van de Ven (1992) explore the implications of risk and reliance on trust for the formation of cooperative relationships.

One problem with studies of cooperative activity between firms (including joint venture) is that if there is one area which has been particularly marked by the problem of limited comparators, it is this one. All too often, analysis of reasons for conducting a specific type of activity implicitly or explicitly relate it to a do-nothing alternative. Indeed, it is often difficult to discern significant differences between checklists produced by different analysts to account for mergers, joint ventures, strategic alliances, and contractual alternatives such as licensing. There should be no surprise that checklists for various strategic options often display a strong family resemblance with key phrases such as 'market access', 'R&D economies', 'reduction in competition' recurring from list to list. Rather, there should be surprise if the respective options did not display strong similarities. The reason for this is that strategic options are not typically different ways of doing different things, as the drawing up of checklists often implies. Instead, they tend to be different ways (modes) of doing the same thing (direction).

In this chapter we shall introduce and develop a set of principles for analysing the development of collaborative activity. It will be suggested that these principles are useful in helping to develop an efficiency rationale for the evolution of collaborative activities and that they are also consistent with a broad span of empirical evidence on these issues. It is argued that cooperative activity may impact at business, corporate, and group level. The key to understanding 'the complex and inter-locking clusters, groups and alliances which represent co-operation fully and formally developed' (Richardson, 1972, p. 887), lies in recognizing the implications of the inter-play between multiple levels of analysis. Our primary focus will be on the form of cooperative activity characterized by joint ventures, though some of the analysis will generalize to other forms of cooperative agreements.

The basic ideas here have their genesis in an earlier paper by Kay *et al.* (1987) and Kay (1992*b*) and is also consistent with points developed separately by Hennart (1988*a*) and Buckley and Casson (1988). Kay *et al.* (1987) pointed out that merger between two large diversified firms to exploit a limited venture opportunity could be akin to using a sledgehammer to crack a nut. In a similar vein, Hennart comments, 'Besides the obvious case when governments restrict mergers and acquisitions, joint venture will be preferred when the assets that yield the desired services are a small and inseparable part of the total assets held by both potential partners or when a merger or a total acquisition would significantly increase management costs' (Hennart, 1991, p. 99). Buckley and Casson (1988, p. 41) suggest that one reason why partners may enter into a joint venture rather than merge may be managerial diseconomies arising from the scale and diversity of the resulting enterprise. Kogut (1988, p. 176) suggests that it is reasonable to assume that acquisition may be ruled out as an option if the technology being transferred is only a small part of the total value of the firm, and Lewis (1990, p. 16) argues similarly that acquisitions are logical only if the value of the resources sought is a large part of the purchase.

This captures the essence of the case for joint venture, and this chapter develops a framework in which points such as these are set in context. It shows that analysis is likely to be flawed when based on the assumption that joint ventures can be low cost over the domain of the joint venture itself, or based on the assumption that joint ventures can generate gains that otherwise cannot be achieved by other options. It is argued that an efficiency rationale for joint venture must show that it can obtain the same gains as other options but at lower cost subject to governmental restraints such as in anti-trust or market access areas. Such a rationale must simultaneously reconcile this with a recognition that organizing ventures through split ownership is itself typically unambiguously more costly and less efficient than single ownership options. From this is developed the analysis of collaborative activity that builds into an analysis of alliances in the next chapter. A number of elements in the chapter may be seen as following from, or consistent with, Richardson's 1972 paper, including his 'triple distinction' (p. 896) between firm, cooperative and market modes of resource coordination; the role of complementary activities in collaboration; the role of *future* decision in stimulating cooperative arrangements; and the picture of the firm as a bundle of capabilities represented by appropriate knowledge, experience, and skills.

In section 9.1 below, we make some initial points regarding the nature of collaboration that sets the agenda for what an analysis of joint venture activity must achieve. Market arrangements, hierarchical arrangements, and joint venture arrangements to coordinate complementary assets are looked at in sections 9.2, 9.3, and 9.4 respectively. Section 9.5 examines how the evolution of sectors may create the essential preconditions for the development of joint ventures. Section 9.6 compares the analysis of this section with actual patterns of joint venture and other collaborative activity.

9.1. Collaborative Activity

The role of complementary activities or assets has been recognized and analysed as a major stimulus to collaborative activity (Richardson, 1972; Teece, 1986a). Richardson and Teece argue that to bring complex projects to fruition, a variety of skills or resources may be required, not all of which may be possessed to the requisite degree or quality by one firm. Collaborative activity between firms providing different but complementary assets is one way that such resources can be combined to produce efficiency oriented economic activity. The significance of complementary assets in collaborative activity is clear, with numerous examples provided by Teece and other writers to support this point. However, there are points following from the arguments of the previous section that are required to set it in context.

To start with, complementary assets refers only to a sub-category of advantages from resource interaction. Complementary assets depend on heterogeneity of firms, but both market power and scale economies from resource sharing depend on some degree of homogeneity of interest or resources across firms. For example, Dunning (1993, pp. 256–7) surveys studies on cross-border cartels, and concludes that this form of collaborative activity is most likely to be successful where products are homogeneous and the ownership specific advantages of firms are similar. Also, on the supply side, many joint ventures in the extractive sector have traditionally been characterized by the desires of firms to share capital or spread risk, while the development of R&D clubs or consortia has been generally stimulated by the collective motive of replicating the exploitation of R&D economies that otherwise could only be achieved by a prohibitively large and diversified firm. The key question here is 'are differences between partners essential for this form of collaborative activity to exist?' If the answer is no, then the objectives of the collaboration are more likely to be found in market power or scale reasons, rather than complementary assets. One important issue that relates to these points of clarification is that it helps confirm that the different types of competitive advantage that may be generated by collaboration is a simple one-to-one mapping of the types of competitive advantage that may be generated by merger. Collaboration can fashion market power, economies of scale and economies of scope from the same basic ingredients as merger activity. It can exploit synergistic as well as complementary relations.

Thus, consistent with the points made in the last section, the important issue is not what collaboration can do. Collaboration can do more than just exploit complementary assets, but even the extended list is a simple replication of sources of competitive advantage that may be exploited by alternative modes such as merger or internal expansion. Figure 9.1 builds on these points to help provide a focus for analysis of collaborative activity. The circles in Fig. 9.1 represent IBUs, and as before, each unit, considered as an independent unit, is assumed to be identical to all others in terms of profitability, growth, and scale. This simplifying assumption allows us to suppress product-market considerations here and concentrate instead on the implications of business unit linkages along the lines opened up in Chapter 4. We shall also focus here on efficiency oriented economies from sharing and leave issues of competition on one side.

The top left of Fig. 9.1 illustrates the reference case of stand-alone or abstention modes, with three single unit firms engaged in head to head competition (C). No linkages in the form of economies from shared resources exist between the firms. Arranged along the top are two alternative options. In (S), one unit exploits complementary assets provided by the two other units. One link is market related and could represent, for example, shared assets in marketing, distribution, advertising, and/or reputation. The other link is technological and could represent, for example, shared assets in plant, equipment, work force, and/or R&D. Given that all business units are presumed equal in value terms when operated as independent units, any market or technological synergies or economies of scope exploited in arrangement (S) means that it is efficiency and value enhancing compared to (C). However, the same argument holds for (E). Here the respective units share identical or similar resources. If it is a collaborative arrangement, it could be a farmers' cooperative, oil companies co-developing an oil field, or electronic companies participating in an R&D club. As with (S), the value of the combination when a resource link is coordinated exceeds the value of the three-unit competitive scenario in (C). Berg *et al.* (1982, pp. 21–2) point

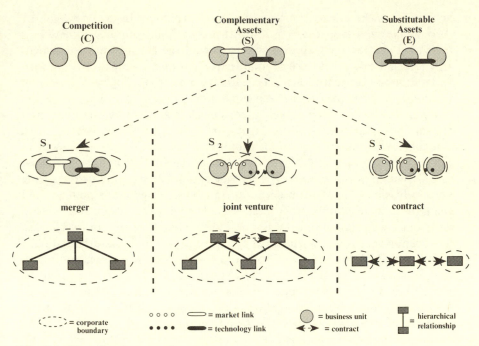

Fig. 9.1. Coordinating complementary assets

out that joint ventures to share scale, finance, and risk are a common feature of the mining and metals industries.

Both complementary and substitutable asset cases may be exploited by a variety of options and institutional arrangements. However, in Fig. 9.1 we concentrate on the case of complementary assets for illustrative purposes. The dotted circles or ellipses represent corporate boundaries. Figure 9.1 illustrates three possible options to exploit the (S) case of complementary assets, S_1, S_2, and S_3. The collaborative option in this case (S_2) is a joint venture with overlapping corporate boundaries thrown around the middle business unit indicating co-ownership and co-direction of this unit by the two firms associated with the other respective units.

A myopic checklist approach to the collaborative option might compare arrangement (C) with combination (S_2) and conclude that a rationale for (S_2) would be that it beats (C) on value enhancing grounds. However, not only are there varieties of collaborative options but there are also alternatives to collaboration in the form of co-ownership. For example, combination (S_1) represents a full-scale merger with corporate boundaries thrown round all three linked business units, while S_3 represents an extreme case of market organization in which all linkages are exploited by market contracts. As Richardson (1972) points out 'co-ordination (of complementary activities) can be effected in three ways; by *direction*, by *co-operation*, or through *market transactions*' (p. 890). If merger, joint venture, and systems of market contracts are all available to exploit the gains from complementary assets in case (S), choice of mode can focus on the comparative advantage of the respective options. This leads to some interesting conclusions on the comparative merits of the respective modes displayed in Fig. 9.1.

Figure 9.1 displays some likely hierarchical arrangements for the respective options with dotted ellipses again indicating the boundaries of firms. The contractual arrangements for exploitation of complementary assets do not involve any additional hierarchical arrangements over those that exist already within business units. The merger option here is presumed to create a multidivisional or M-form corporation (Williamson, 1975) built around the three units responding to a single HQ. The joint venture option leads to with joint ownership of one division as indicated by the overlapping ellipses. The hierarchical arrangement for the joint venture may look rather strange, indeed awkward. It is not usual to find a two-division M-form corporation, and, in fact, small, relatively specialized firms as in this example might be more likely to continue to operate functionally organized unitary form or U-form structure (Williamson, 1975). The strange representation is a consequence of two related issues; it is true that joint ventures typically tend to be coordinated between divisionalized business units operating with an M-form corporation, but, as pointed out above, usually at least one (and often both) firms are large diversified systems[2] in which the domain of specific collaboration of the type described in Fig. 9.1 above is limited to a fairly localized region of the overall firm. This means that Fig. 9.1 provides a partial or incomplete picture of corporate systems involved in collaboration.

As we shall argue below, it is the fact that representation of collaborating firms as in Fig. 9.1 tends to be incomplete that holds the key to understanding the evolution of joint ventures. However, consistent with most conventional treatments of this subject, we shall first look at the efficiency and cost implications of joint ventures by considering the administrative and contractual issues associated with units directly involved in coordinating complementary assets. Since merger and joint venture both involve the creation of hierarchy to coordinate complementary assets, we shall start by considering why a hierarchical option may be preferred to a contractual solution, and then assess the relative efficiency implications of joint venture versus the merger alternative. Both parent companies now operate two divisions, their original IBU and the new (joint shared) venture.

9.2. Market Arrangements to Coordinate Complementary Assets

The issue of whether a contractually based solution will tend to be preferred to a hierarchical (merger or joint venture) solution is likely to depend on the nature of the assets being transferred. Contractually based coordination tends to come into play when the services provided by the assets being coordinated tend to be fairly standardized and well specified. Complexity of assets is not likely to be an issue as long as the other conditions are satisfied. Expensive, complex and technologically indivisible assets such as computers, satellites, and space shuttles can all be simultaneously exploited by multiple users using variants on standard market contracts. Where contractual solutions tend to encounter problems is more commonly in situations involving ambiguity, uncertainty, and novelty, as in the case of technological innovation and market entry.

Thus, contractually based coordination of complementary assets is most likely to be adopted where we observe well established and stable technologies conducive to standard, off the shelf solutions such as licensing, rental, leasing, and franchising (as we saw in Chapter 3). Some researchers have fused asset complexity with contractual uncertainty, but in fact the concepts are quite distinct. Arnold Schwarzenegger was able to hire Harrier jets from the Pentagon for US$1600 an hour, but the Post-it concept for adhesive notes was invented, developed, produced, and marketed by personnel working in-house with the 3M corporate hierarchy.[3] Few would dispute that Post-it technology is intrinsically simpler than jet fighter technology, yet, like most advanced high technology corporations, 3M relies mostly on internal R&D for its innovation search rather than contracting out. The hierarchical imperative 'find new products' is fundamentally much more problematic than the contract 'lease existing technology'. The critical point being made here is that when elements that are the subject of the contract are innovative, then these transaction costs are likely to be especially marked and indeed the contractual option may breakdown completely and fail to coordinate the potential gains from complementary assets. As we argued earlier, contractual arrangements work best when there are few decisions left to be made concerning the cross coordination of complementary assets between business units that cannot be resolved by reference to the terms and conditions of the respective contracts themselves.

The tendency for coordination costs to fall as uncertainty and incompleteness of specification are removed from contractual situations may help to explain why a contract may cope well with stable, established technologies. However, it does not explain why contractual arrangements may cope *better* than hierarchical arrangements such as merger and joint venture in such circumstances. As discussed above, anything a contractual arrangement can do, in principle a hierarchical arrangement can do also. Only if contractual arrangements involved lower coordination costs than hierarchical alternatives would we then have an efficiency rationale for coordination by contract in such cases.

In fact, it is not difficult to develop such a rationale, since it is no more than the standard defence and justification for the market system. If hierarchical alternatives are chosen to coordinate complementary assets, then the range of assets to be drawn from is limited by the boundaries of the hierarchies involved, whether single firm or joint venture. By way of contrast, contract opens up the possibility of matching assets to their highest valued uses as we saw in Chapter 3, not just to the constrained uses to which they may be put within a specified hierarchy. Also, as Williamson points out (1985, chapter 6), hierarchies may have intrinsic bureaucratic and incentive disadvantages compared to contract, including a possible tendency to more easily 'forgive' poor performance that would not be tolerated in a market environment. This is the realm of privatization, contracting out, outsourcing, and downsizing arguments that has been well trodden by management theorists and politicians alike since the 1980s. Consistent with such arguments, if contracts can be well specified then we would expect to find no justification for the evolution of hierarchy to coordinate the exploitation of complementary assets, as we saw in Chapter 3. Commodities such as base or precious metals tend to be standardized and well specified and so their exploitation tends to be coordinated by systems of market contracts.

9.3. Hierarchical Arrangements to Coordinate Complementary Assets

The costs and disadvantages inherent in hierarchical arrangements do not disappear as more innovative and incompletely specified elements are introduced into asset coordination between business units. Indeed, control problems and administrative costs are likely to increase as senior management find themselves less experienced and less familiar with the tasks being carried out by lower level personnel, and consequently less able to police and coordinate activities. The only argument in favour of hierarchy is that the effect of introducing incomplete specifications into market contract alternatives is typically much worse.

As we observed in Chapter 3, hierarchy begins to exert absolute advantage over market coordination alternatives where significant decisions still remain to be made in the future concerning the coordination of assets between business units. This is likely to be the situation where the relevant activity involves innovative elements, and where specifications of particular assets are poorly developed, or as yet absent. The coordination of complementary assets cannot then be adequately regulated by a pre-set contractual recipe. Where contractual arrangements rely heavily on the important resource relocation terms and conditions being decided in the *present*, hierarchy allows for such situations involving incompletely specified assets by creating decision-making capacity to make strategic *future* decisions. Such capacity can help to both generate and clarify asset specifications, and coordinate the exploitation of assets across business units in the future once their characteristics are more fully known. Interestingly, both market contracts and hierarchy rely on repetition to facilitate coordination, though in very different ways. Market contracts frequently rely on standardization and homogeneity of goods to specify closely what is to be provided by particular goods and services, while hierarchy often uses continuity and repetitious employment of individual managers to make overall assessments of their performance. It may be possible for individual managers to conceal poor performance or opportunism on a one-off basis, but more difficult to do so on a continuing basis.

Thus, the evolution of single firm or joint venture hierarchy as in Fig. 9.1 is a recognition that significant strategic decisions remain to be made concerning cross unit asset coordination. This follows from the argument of Chapter 3 that the need to defer future strategic commitments in cases where assets are incompletely specified is the fundamental reason for the evolution of hierarchy. Unless provision is made to renegotiate contracts, market solutions tend to compress strategic decision-making into present commitments to future action. However, it is also worth noting that hierarchy facilitates the protection of property rights by giving the asset holder more direct control over their use and development. This has been argued as being particularly important in the case of intellectual property rights where legal safeguards to protect licensing agreements (e.g. patent law) may prove difficult or too expensive to invoke. Doing it all yourself and/or keeping developments secret can be an attractive option where technology could leak to other firms.

Such arguments may be plausible in the context of the single firm hierarchical solution in Fig. 9.1, but it leaves us with a puzzle. If hierarchy is a means of retaining control, why do firms create joint venture hierarchies where the method of coordination involves the dual system of hierarchical control illustrated in Fig. 9.1? In the next section we shall explore more fully the difficulties associated with the joint venture option.

9.4. Joint Venture to Coordinate Complementary Assets

In Fig. 9.1, there are two hierarchical alternatives available to enable the coordination of complementary assets—the single firm solution (S_1) and the joint venture solution (S_2). Again, it bears repeating that both forms can achieve the same gains from facilitating the sharing of resources across business units. Accordingly, an efficiency explanation for the evolution and choice of joint ventures must focus on its associated costs relative to the single firm option.

These relative costs may be analysed with the help of the hierarchical arrangements illustrated in Fig. 9.1 for the respective merger (S_1) and joint venture (S_2) modes. Both the merger and joint venture cases here involve the operation of three business units controlled and coordinated by higher level HQ decision-making. However, there are three significant differences between joint venture operation and merger, each of which may have a bearing on relative costs: (a) *dual control* by two HQs in joint venture (the middle 'V' portions of the joint venture hierarchy in Fig. 9.1); (b) *contractual aspects* of joint venture (the double headed arrow in the joint venture hierarchy in Fig. 9.1); (c) *overlapping ownership* in joint ventures (the area of overlap between the dotted ellipses spanning the joint venture hierarchy in Fig. 9.1). We shall discuss each in turn; none of the points are contentious, since the elements of each are already well recognized in the literature as confirmed by Hennart's (1991) arguments concerning possible cheating, divergent goals and control problems in joint venture.

1. *Dual control* Being the servant of two masters is not a problem if the masters share the same objectives, the same strategies regarding the attainment of these objectives, and share common views regarding the nature and timing of actions to pursue these strategies. Unfortunately, such happy and ideal coincidence of interests is unlikely to be observed in practice, and the joint venture literature provides much evidence of the existence and consequences of differing objectives and strategies of partners.[4] If procedures for conflict resolution do not exist or do not work adequately, costs are imposed on the joint venture operation. However, even if procedures for conflict resolution do work well, they will inevitably impose costs on the joint venture by involving the commitment of managerial time and resources. Consequently, dual control will tend to add costs to joint venture operation compared to the merger or single firm option (Madhok, 1995, p. 126). Kogut (1988) reviews a number of studies in which parental conflict led to instability in the joint venture itself. Also, after interviewing managers involved in thirty-five joint ventures in North America and Western Europe, Killing concludes that because of dual control, 'if one asks any manager, North American or European, which is more difficult to manage, a wholly owned subsidiary or a joint venture, the chances are high that the joint venture will get the nod' (Killing, 1983, p. 8).

2. *Contractual aspects* These exist in joint venture where no corresponding regime of contracts exist in single firm operation. There may be substantial transaction costs following from managerial and legal resources required to search for a partner, negotiate the contract and police the agreement. Berg *et al.* (1982, p. 42) report that one steel joint venture with multiple partners required documents nineteen inches thick to spell out the rights and obligations of all the parents. Since such costs follow from the splitting of ownership rights that are otherwise consolidated in single firm operation, these must also be counted as an additional cost of joint venture relative to the merger option illustrated in Fig. 9.1.

3. *Overlapping ownership* The contractual aspects above are likely to involve direct resource costs and associated efficiency losses. However, there

is a further contractual issue that may or may not involve efficiency, but is likely to be perceived as an uncompensated cost by at least one partner and accordingly discourage or impede joint venture formation. This is the issue of appropriability problems regarding the use of intangible assets such as intellectual property and managerial know-how. The problem here is that partners may exploit such intangible assets in areas not covered by the joint venture contract without compensating their partners, and might even use the know-how obtained through the joint venture to become a direct rival to its existing partner in future strategic moves (Richardson, 1972). From an economic perspective, such diffusion may be efficient and desirable, since knowledge tends to have public good characteristics that should generally encourage its dissemination to any users for whom it has value.[5] However, such considerations should also encourage parents to restrict or slow transfers of sensitive technological information to the child, which should in turn impair the performance of the joint venture relative to that of wholly owned alternatives.

These three issues—dual control, contractual aspects, and overlapping ownership (appropriability problems)—are interrelated and partially interchangeable in normal conditions. For example, joint venture partners may commit a great deal of resources to establishing and policing the contract in attempts to mitigate possible dual control and appropriability problems. Correspondingly, firms may skimp on contract costs and trade them off for possible dual control and appropriability problems.

However, what we are left with is a remarkably clear and unambiguous conclusion. The implications of dual control, contractual aspects, and appropriability problems all point to joint venture being a less efficient method for coordinating complementary assets than is single firm operation as in the merger case in Fig. 9.1. The existence of one set of problems would have been sufficient to allow this conclusion to be drawn; the existence of all three merely serves strongly to reinforce the conclusion. If joint venture as described in Fig. 9.1 could offer some category of efficiency gains relative to single firm alternatives, we would have a basis for comparing the relative merits of joint venture versus unified hierarchy in different circumstances, and predicting conditions which would encourage the evolution of joint venture in preference to single firm solutions. However, the consistency with which joint venture appears to be an inefficient solution compared to single firm operation closes off such options. Although Fig. 9.1 represents a standard type of joint venture arrangement, it seems to signal that there is no obvious efficiency rationale for the evolution of joint venture activity. On this basis, single firm operation would typically be preferred to joint venture coordination of complementary assets. This is consistent with much of the organizational and managerial literature. For example, from interviews of executives involved in joint ventures in the chemicals industry, Berg *et al.* found that 'joint ventures were often viewed as a last resort, dominated by other forms of intercorporate activity such as mergers' (Berg *et al.*, 1982, p. 39).

The discussion here also suggests that it may be extremely misleading to think of joint venture as a mixed or hybrid mode which occupies an intermediate position between hierarchy and contract on some hypothetical spectrum, drawing elements from both polar modes. However, this has become the standard transaction cost interpretation of cooperative activity in general, and joint venture activity in particular (Zaheer and Venkatraman, 1995). For example, Williamson (1985, pp. 83–4) identifies a dimension arrayed in terms of the degree to which parties to deals maintain autonomy, with discrete transactions located at one extreme, centralized hierarchical transactions at the other, and hybrid transactions (including joint ventures) located somewhere in between. He also argues that

roughly speaking, transaction cost economics predicts that there will be a shift out of markets (which have the stronger incentive intensity properties) into hierarchies (which feature adaptability) as the condition of asset specificity builds up. Hybrid modes of organization (joint ventures, franchising, regulation, various form of long term contracting), are interpreted as governance structures for which an incentive intensity/adaptability compromise has been reached (Williamson, 1990, p. 68).

The idea of cooperative agreements such as joint ventures being a 'hybrid' or a 'compromise' appears to involve some idea of there being a trade-off in terms of market/hierarchy characteristics in this perspective. Also, Lorange and Roos (1993, p. 3) begin their discussion of strategic alliances by identifying joint venture activity as lying midway on a spectrum of degree of vertical integration between the polar extremes of free market activity at one end, and hierarchy (and mergers and acquisitions) at the other.

The concept of hybrid implies a selective fusion of elements from different sources, as in the case of plant hybrids, with the implication that hybrids might trade-off some features of one mode in exchange for aspects of another. However, the idea that joint ventures occupy some intermediate point on some organizational form spectrum is misplaced. An analogy might be drawn with someone carrying either a 1kg bag of sugar or a 3kg bag of flour. If he or she carries both, the burden is 4kg, not 2kg; the weight is augmented, not averaged. Similarly, joint venture carries the burden of both hierarchical *and* contractual arrangements, and indeed the respective market or hierarchy costs may be greater than in the corresponding pure form; for example, it is difficult to see how the complicated dual control hierarchy of joint venture could be more efficient than the simpler conventional structures associated with the wholly owned alternative. We are dealing with a phenomenon that lies outside conventional market and hierarchy modes, not some simple fusion of them.

Of course, just because we cannot find an efficiency rationale for joint venture around the circumstances represented in Fig. 9.1 does not mean that it is impossible to find such a rationale. We may have missed something, or could have constructed a straw man to justify our conclusions. However, whilst our way of constructing the analysis may be novel, the elements of our argument are not. The arguments concerning dual control, contractual, and appropriability problems are well documented in the literature. If there are serious objections to our arguments, it is more likely to come from outside the consensus of research findings in this area. Alternatively, it could be argued that efficiency rationales may not be necessary or appropriate to explain the evolution of joint ventures. For example, some theorists have argued that power rather than efficiency objectives may influence the development of the corporation.[6] However, it is difficult to see how such arguments may be easily applied to cases of joint venture activity being preferred to single firm operation, since it performs badly on power as well as efficiency criteria. Control is diffused and often scrambled in joint venture arrangements compared to single firm options.

Yet it is not difficult to find examples of joint venture activity where it is adopted, even where it is appears less efficient than the single firm option. The clearest examples are cases where Third World governments require joint venture with a local firm as a prerequisite for market access. Here the inward investor faces Hobson's choice if it wishes access; the choice is restricted to (C) versus (S_2), with (S_1) taken out of consideration. Additionally, inefficiency is not necessarily a guarantee of joint venture failure. If collaboration results in a degree of monopoly control and competitive advantage in the domain over which the joint venture operates, the joint venture may survive comfortably and indefinitely, even though its costs of operation may be higher than if a single firm solution had been adopted.

Thus, our provisional conclusions above regarding joint venture inefficiency have to be qualified by recognition that such inefficient solutions may be sustainable in certain situations. The problem is that such a qualification does not take us very far in helping to develop a coherent and logical explanation of joint venture activity, and it certainly does not help to account for the proliferation of joint venture agreements between progressive high technology companies in developed countries in recent years.

In the next section we shall look at the relationship between diversification and collaboration options and suggest that this holds an important key to analysing the evolution of joint venture activity in the firm.

9.5. The Evolution of Collaboration in the Diversified Firm

A fundamental problem with conventional approaches to collaborative activity between firms is that they tend to take the agreement as their basic unit of analysis, and then they analyse possible motives firms may have for pursuing individual agreements. Just as analysis of product-markets in isolation may obscure patterns of diversification, so analysis of collaborative agreements in isolation may obscure patterns of collaboration and fundamental reasons for their existence. Very few current analyses of collaborative activity could be said to provide a satisfactory explanation as to why they evolve in particular contexts and at particular times. In most studies, the various objectives ascribed to collaborative activity generally do not differ from those that have been traditionally attached to merger activity, and it is typically not clear why one mode should be preferred over another.

In this section we shall extend the analysis of previous chapters into a simple mental experiment to explore conditions likely to be associated with the emergence of collaborative activity amongst firms. We shall start with a population of sixty-two IBUs constituted as separate firms, and assume that each is pursuing growth opportunities. As in Chapter 7, such opportunities may or may not involve sharing market or technological links. However, we shall not worry about imposing strict coherence conditions on our firms, not because coherence is not deemed to be important in practice, but because it is an unnecessary restriction in this case. The firms will still be recognizably related-constrained, related-linked, and conglomerate, and it is these attributes which will drive the development of the system in our example, irrespective of whether or not the firm displays the strict coherence and strong patterns associated with the analysis of Chapter 7. We shall focus throughout on decisions from the point of view of a particular firm, or group of firms (indicated with a background mat as in earlier analysis).

If we were to draw parallels with evolutionary biology, Fig. 9.2 is an economic equivalent of the primordial ooze. The firms in Fig. 9.2 are simple specialized IBUs operating in a fragmented, unstructured environment. There is nothing to differentiate any firm in Fig. 9.2 from any other in terms of scale or profitability. Now, suppose the firms begin to explore growth

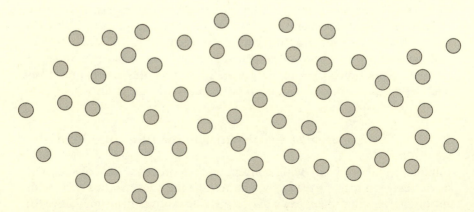

Fig. 9.2. Stage 1. Atomism

opportunities. In our experiment, this will involve either merger or joint venture, with merger involving the combination of existing firms and joint venture involving the setting up of a new IBU jointly owned by two firms. For simplicity we shall ignore the possibility that the firms may expand using wholly owned internal expansion and/or multinational options. To begin with we shall ignore possible implications of environmental turbulence and conglomerate strategies, but we shall deal with these issues later. So, what strategies and modes are likely to emerge in such a process?

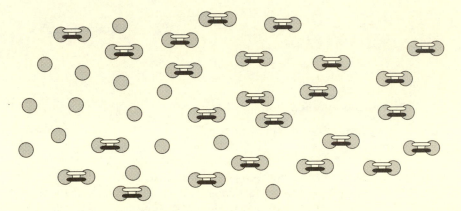

Fig. 9.3. Stage 2. Specialization

As our analysis in Chapter 4 suggests, the first preference for growth purposes is likely to be specialization strategies in which both market and technological links are exploited. Thus, in Fig. 9.3 firms have sought and merged with IBU twins to pursue this strategy. As Chapter 4 also suggests, problems of coordinating the linkages involved in such strategies through market transactions are likely to encourage the adoption of the internalization (merger) option. In Fig. 9.3, forty-eight firms have merged to form twenty-four new firms formed around IBU pairs to exploit double linkages associated with specialization. Fourteen IBUs have been unable to find suitable partners to merge with at this stage.

At some point firms will run up against barriers to further specialization. The most obvious barrier is simply running out of room for further expansion opportunities for a particular business, although the possibility of antitrust intervention may impose barriers to such expansion at an earlier stage. In this experiment we assume that such saturation takes place in each case after the merger of two IBUs. If the firms now seek further expansion opportunities they can exploit single links at most. In the figure, we have also added shaded background mats to help in the identification of certain strategies. In Fig. 9.4 eleven pairs of firms have combined to form 4-IBU related-constrained strategies. There are three firms on the middle two mats

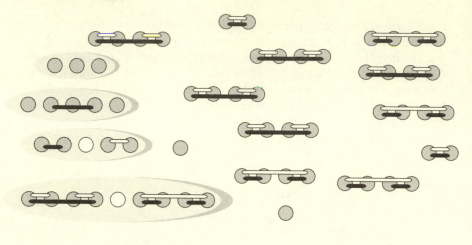

◯ = New business opportunity

Fig. 9.4. Stage 3. Related-constrained strategy

which have been formed around single links to form one 3-IBU and two 2-IBU related-constrained firms. Outside the mats, two single and two double IBU firms have been left behind in this expansion process. On the mats themselves, a series of firms are considering further expansion opportunities. The top two mats both have three firms considering ways of coordinating potential marketing and technological linkages, whilst on both of the two bottom mats there are pairs of firms negotiating starting a new IBU (the white IBU in both cases) which would draw upon the marketing expertise of one company and the technological expertise of the other. Again, these processes of expansion are consistent with Ollinger's (1994) study of the historical growth of firms in the US oil industry, with firms pursuing strongly linked (horizontal and domestic) growth opportunities to begin with, then into more weakly linked petrochemical technologies, energy, and international markets, and then finally into unrelated technologies and markets as opportunities for further related growth opportunities became scarcer.[7] This would be consistent with a weak pattern of linkages in the sense described in Chapter 5, with the firm progressively moving into areas of weaker linkages as it expands over time.

Just like specialization (or double-linked) strategies, individual linkages are likely to encounter saturation limits eventually. It is reasonable to assume that the opportunities associated with individual marketing and technological competencies can only be stretched so far at any point in time. In Fig. 9.5 we assume these limits are reached after two, four, or six IBU combinations, depending on the particular market or the technology. The fourteen related-constrained firms from Fig. 9.4 have still been seeking growth opportunities, and in Fig. 9.5 all but two of them managed to find merger possibilities. The six 8-IBU firms can still exploit linkages though combination, but linkage saturation limits have forced each of them into a related-linked strategy. Figure 9.5 shows that the firms on the top three mats from Fig. 9.4 have merged to coordinate potential linkages and have emerged as related-linked firms in each case. The firms on the bottom mat in Fig. 9.4 have also merged to internalize linkage opportunities, and now form the 9-IBU combination on the left of the bottom mat in Fig. 9.5.

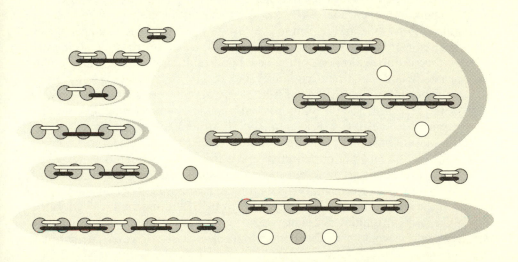

Fig. 9.5. Stage 4. Related-linked strategy

The firms on the largest two mats in Fig. 9.5 are now considering starting new IBUs that could draw upon their marketing or technological expertise in the respective cases. On the bottom mat, a single IBU firm possesses a technological expertise that could be married with the marketing expertise of the two larger firms to produce a new IBU in the respective cases. Again, these new opportunities are indicated by white IBUs on the bottom mat. On the large mat at the top, the middle firm is similarly exploring new IBU opportunities that could draw upon complementary expertise to be provided by itself and the other two firms in the respective cases. The merger option is still the most obvious mode to coordinate these new opportunities, but now some problems are becoming apparent if this option is to be continued with. If the firms were to merge to exploit the emergent IBU opportunities in the respective cases, it would create a 20-IBU firm on the bottom mat, and a 26-IBU monster on the top mat. At the moment, no firm covers more than nine IBUs and 13 per cent of those in this sector. If the amalgamations take place, the two new firms would cover two-thirds of the IBUs in this sector.

What is happening here is that merger opportunities at each stage carry with them the baggage of the past. It raises the possibility that the evolution of cooperative activity may be a path dependent phenomenon, and this is something we explore in more detail in the next chapter. The four new business opportunities on the two large mats draw upon market and technological links provided by separate firms, just as in the cases of the firms in Figs. 9.4 and 9.5 that combined to form the firms on the two smaller mats in Fig. 9.6. However, in these earlier cases the new opportunity represented a significant proportion of the economic activity of the combined firm (as much as one-third of the firm in the case of the 3-IBU combination on the smallest mat in Fig. 9.6). By way of contrast, if two of the firms on the top mat merged to exploit one of the new opportunities, this major shift in corporate boundaries would be undertaken to coordinate the exploitation of an opportunity that would constitute only about 6 per cent of the activity of the new firm. Such a solution would be tantamount to taking a sledge-hammer to crack a nut (Kay *et al.*, 1987). More precisely, merger to exploit the venture possibility may have serious efficiency and regulatory implications for the separate or collective operation of business units in the combined firm that go well beyond the business strategy implications of coordinating complementary assets for the new business opportunity.

If the effect of merger was restricted to the IBUs directly involved in the linkage opportunities associated with the new business opportunity, these scale effects would pose absolutely no problem at all. However, merger may

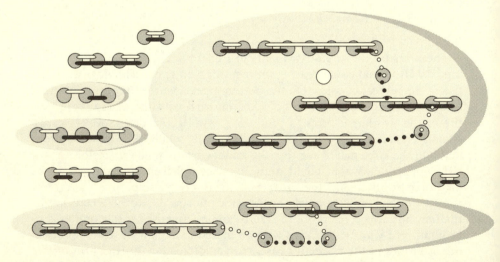

Fig. 9.6. Stage 5. Collaboration

well have knock-on effects on corporate performance in two major categories. The first and most obvious implications follow from the scale of the merged firm if two large diversified firms are involved. Against the gains from coordinating complementary assets with the new opportunity must be set any additional costs of bureaucracy in running a considerably enlarged enterprise. Unless these are zero, which may be taken to be a possible but unlikely situation, merger to exploit the new business opportunity will incur costs that are externalities from the perspective of the IBUs involved with the new opportunity (and consequently ignored in analyses like Fig. 9.1), but which may have significant and adverse efficiency implications seen from the perspective of corporate strategy. In such circumstances, the firms may pass up exploitation of the common venture opportunity, or consider alternative forms of hierarchical control such as joint venture. The second major category of problem is the more units the respective firms operate, the more likely it is that merger may raise competition or anti-trust issues. If any two units that had been formerly operated separately within the respective firms are now likely to jointly control a significant portion of a market post-merger, then merger itself may be discouraged or prohibited. A possible solution could be to divest one of the offending units, but this would entail sacrifice of the gains from complementary assets that the divested unit would otherwise have exploited with neighbouring units before merger took place. Such reorganization creates further opportunity costs of merger to set against the local gains from exploiting complementary assets with the new business opportunity. Thus, the firms in the large mat in Fig. 9.6 decide instead to opt for joint ventures to coordinate linkages (indicated by white dotted lines for marketing links and black dotted lines for technological links).

Thus, when the focus changes from the new *venture* to the new *firm* (and from business strategy to corporate strategy), it becomes apparent that single firm or merger solution to exploiting complementarities may generate significant additional costs or prohibitions that are ignored if attention is paid only to the direct costs and benefits associated with the new business opportunity. This is indicated in Fig. 9.6 with the four new business opportunities being coordinated through joint venture in the respective cases. Whilst joint venture is certainly likely to be more expensive than the merger alternative *over the region of the relevant collaborating IBUs* in the respective cases, it may well be a cheaper or more acceptable alternative *at the level of the respective firms.*

What about the single-IBU firm considering new venture opportunities with the two larger firms on the bottom mat in Fig. 9.5? Clearly merger to exploit both opportunities would create an extremely large 20 IBU firm and this could lead to the same problem of quantum jumps in the scale of firms discussed above. However, if the single-IBU firm were to merge with one of its potential partners (say the 8-IBU firm) on the bottom mat, this would mean that one new venture was internally coordinated within the enlarged 10-IBU firm, whilst still leaving the opportunity to exploit the other venture opportunity with the 9-IBU firm through a collaborative agreement. This internalizes one of the two potential agreements within corporate boundaries with only a modest increase in the scale of one of the firms.

One reason why this solution may not be adopted is that assimilation of the single IBU firm by one of the larger firms might compromise the other potential agreement. The two larger firms on the bottom mat may be content to cooperate with the small independent firm, but they may also be rivals that would not wish to enter into collaborative agreements with each other. The large number of businesses in which they operate may bring them into conflict in more than one area. The firms may therefore maintain a cooperative umbrella over *both* venture possibilities as indicated by the dotted lines on the bottom mat in Fig. 9.6. Whilst this may be expensive, it may also be the only way to ensure that both opportunities are pursued. Merger with one could sacrifice cooperation with the other. As we shall see in the next chapter, this may be an important issue surrounding the continuing independence of small firms in the biotechnology sector.

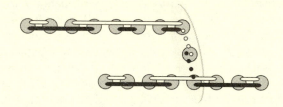

Fig. 9.7. Joint venture and coordination cost hot spot

These arguments clearly pave the way for a rationale for joint venture activity based on efficiency criteria, and this may be illustrated more clearly with Fig. 9.7 which shows the joint venture set up by the two top firms in the top mat in Fig. 9.6. The mat in Fig. 9.7 shows the region associated with the joint venture in this case, covering the donor IBUs from the respective firms as well as the jointly owned venture itself. The domain of the joint venture is likely to be an area of intense administrative and contractual activity as discussed earlier. Just as unusual activity in the sun's corona in the form of a solar flare is associated with a rise in the temperature over the local hot spot, so intense managerial activity channelled into the joint venture will be associated with higher coordination costs compared to the single firm option. However, while there may be a flare up of heightened coordination costs across the joint venture hot spot, collaboration also helps prevent significant spillover of costs into other regions of the participating firms. The scale of the respective firms is only marginally greater than before, (expanded by their respective shares in the new IBU), and any anti-trust implications that would have followed from full blown merger are likely to have been defused. The joint venture option can therefore be preferred over the merger option.

Thus, joint ventures are indeed locally costly relative to single firm options as earlier analysis suggests, but it is the systems-wide costs of coordinating the respective alternatives that matters, not just the direct costs involved in this local hot spot. Just as it would be a mistake to infer the average temperature of the sun's surface from that of the region of solar flares, so it would be a mistake to infer the overall costs of institutional arrangements by focusing on the local costs of specific ventures.

One further point that requires emphasis here is that the *form* of diversification is likely to be an important influence on the development of collaborative activity. The arguments of Kay *et al.* (1987) and Hennart (1988*a*) are based on the idea that it is difficult to decompose or disengage the various business assets in a firm pursuing related diversification, whether related-constrained or related-linked. Hennart uses the expressive phrase 'tangled assets' to capture this notion. However, there is one diversification strategy in which untangling or disengaging assets is relatively straightforward—the conglomerate. If the bottom firm in Fig. 9.7 was a conglomerate, then we would have an arrangement as in the conglomerate joint venture of Fig. 9.8. Such an arrangement is unnecessarily complicated; the conglomerate could simply decouple its contributing business unit and sell it to the other firm for a price that allows both to share in the resulting enhanced value, with the top firm continuing its related-based strategy. This is the asset trading option in Fig. 9.8. The sale of the donor IBU by the conglomerate to the collaborating firm results in the latter fully internalizing linkages that would otherwise have been coordinated by joint venture. The three IBUs that would have been involved in the joint venture are indicated by the mat in this case.

Conglomerate decomposability would facilitate asset transfer and coordination that reflects their highest valued uses. A possible brake on this process is that, carried to its logical conclusion, it might tend to shrink conglomerates as in Fig. 9.8 to an unsaleable rump composed of elements of little strategic value or interest to other corporations. Such a fate may not be entirely palatable to conglomerate management whose objectives may include seeking to maintain the corporate system and managerial coalition. A managerial limit on asset trading could be reflected in the collaboration option being pursued even for the conglomerate case in some instances.

We can summarize our position so far as suggesting there are three conditions for the evolution of joint ventures. If analysis does not recognize each of them as necessary elements, then it is liable to be incomplete or misleading, and indeed one of the problems of limited comparators in this area is that the three conditions have not always been recognized. *First*, there

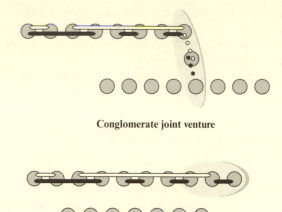

Conglomerate joint venture

Asset trading

Fig. 9.8. Conglomerate decomposability and joint venture activity

must be gains from complementary assets compared to the competition or abstention option. In Figure 9.1, this is represented by the (S) option versus the (C) option in the top row. This prerequisite is uncontroversial, the problem is that many of the checklist based approaches stop at this prerequisite. *Secondly*, the *hierarchical* option [(S_1) and (S_2) type options in Fig. 9.1] must be a more efficient way of coordinating complementary assets than are contractual options. Contract is more efficient when strategic decision-making concerning the nature and integration of complementary assets is effectively complete, as is the case when dealing with commodity-type markets. 'Where buyer and seller accept no obligation with respect to their future conduct however loose and implicit the obligation might be, then co-operation does not take place and we can refer to a pure market transaction' (Richardson, 1972, p. 886). As we have argued, hierarchy is more efficient where important strategic decisions concerning the nature and integration of complementary assets remain to be made in the future, as in the case of market entry and technological innovations. New markets and new technologies are both likely to necessitate creating and maintaining capacity for managerial decision-making capacity (and so hierarchy) with managers occupying space that would otherwise be occupied by contract in stable, established situations. It is this need for future decisions that creates hierarchy. Hierarchy buys time by providing a bridge to the future that would otherwise be constrained by premature contractual commitments.

Thirdly, joint venture must be a more efficient way of coordinating complementary assets than are single firm options, subject to regulatory restrictions being fulfilled. The problem here is that over the region of the joint venture, any gains that can be made by joint venture can typically be made more cheaply by single firm alternatives; it is this localized costliness that must be compensated for if joint venture is to be justified. 'Regulatory restrictions' refers to constraints such as anti-trust policies or governmental restrictions on multinational access to local markets. This prerequisite means there may be two major categories of joint venture: (a) joint ventures that help deal with tangled asset problems in pursuing specific new business opportunities. This is more likely to be the case with large diversified firms than small specialized firms, as we have seen above; (b) joint ventures that are resorted to by firms if government restrictions preclude single firm operation or place too high a cost on such options. This prerequisite means that it is not necessary to identify the spurious gains that a joint venture can achieve and a single firm cannot. Also, it is entirely consistent with the joint venture domain itself remaining a coordination cost hot spot.

Some studies have attempted to justify joint venture on the basis that the venture itself may be low cost if trust and mutual forbearance exists between partners.[8] But, even though goodwill may lower the coordination cost temperature of the joint venture hot spot, it is unlikely that such dual control systems could ever be reasonably expected to operate as simply and efficiently as conventional unified hierarchies. Similarly, efficiency gains from joint venture that have been identified in the economics literature include a sharing of knowledge, risk, and capital.[9] However, as long as the concept of the joint venture coordination cost hot spot holds, these studies do not explain why joint venture is more efficient than single firm operation in these regards. It is only when the joint venture hot spot is set in the context of the wider corporate systems that efficiency rationales for joint venture evolution begin to emerge.

Before we look at actual patterns of joint venture activity, it should be noted that arguments made here concerning coordination of complementary assets tend to apply similarly to cases involving substitutable assets as in Fig. 9.1.

9.6. Empirical Patterns

We have a nested set of prerequisites for the evolution of joint ventures. Exploitation of shared assets must be more efficient than abstention or do-nothing alternatives, In turn, for the range of institutional arrangements that can exploit shared assets, hierarchy must be more efficient than contractual alternatives. Finally, for the range of hierarchical arrangements than can exploit shared assets, joint venture must be more efficient than single firm operation after allowing for regulatory restrictions. We have argued that systems most conducive to the evolution of joint ventures are likely to be those in which systems wide efficiency implications dominate

considerations that hold over the limited domain of the new venture opportunity itself. We have argued that this is most likely in circumstances involving large diversified firms. Joint venture tends to evolve where there is a
need to implant hierarchy to enable future strategic decision-making in
cases where single firm alternatives are inferior or prohibited.

This perspective allows us to make sense of various patterns of joint venture evolution.

1. *Stages in practice*

Joint ventures to facilitate access to Third World markets by host governments have been a feature of international business for many years.
However, Dunning (1993, p. 257) notes that the proliferation of joint venture activity between technologically progressive and sophisticated partners
is a relatively recent post-war development, while Harrigan (1987, p. 195)
estimates that joint ventures (and other forms of cooperative agreements)
have only become particularly widespread since 1980. This phenomenon is
understood most easily by standing it on its head and asking why such patterns of collaboration had not been observed in earlier periods if they are
indeed efficiency enhancing and desirable.

However, we need to note first that cooperative or collaborative agreements cover a wider set of modes than just joint venture. For our purposes,
the important distinction is between cooperation agreements that; (a) make
provision for future decision-making with strategic content between the parties, and install appropriate hierarchical controls with this in mind, and (b)
effectively treat the agreement as contract with all important strategic decisions established to begin with, and little, if any, provision for future strategic decisions in relation to the area of cooperation. Joint venture is likely to
fall into the first category, while a straightforward licensing agreement
would be more likely to fall into the second category, though of course the
degree of hierarchical provision for future-related decision-making may
vary from case to case. A problem is that whilst we are interested in the
extension of hierarchy as represented by cooperation agreements such as
joint ventures, databases have an unnerving habit of aggregating the two
types together in their analysis of general trends.

In this context, Hagedoorn and Schakenraad (1991, p. 6) make an
extremely helpful distinction between cooperative agreements that are
aimed at the 'strategic, long term perspective of the product market combinations of the companies involved and cost-economizing agreements which
we think are more associated with the control of either transaction costs or
operating costs of companies'. These distinctions appear to closely parallel
our type (a) and type (b) distinctions. Hagedoorn and Schakenraad (1991)
further distinguish between two groups of modes, finding that the first (joint
ventures, research corporations, joint R&D agreements, and equity invest-

ments) are over 85 per cent strategically motivated, while only a small proportion of the second group of modes (technology exchange agreements,
one-dimensional technology flows, and customer-supplier agreements) are
strategically motivated. In some cases, Hagedoorn and Schakenraad (1991,
pp. 7–8) suggest that this latter group of agreements may be analysable in
transaction cost terms, following Williamson (1985).

It is the long-term strategically motivated agreements that may require
provision for future decisions (and the creation of joint administrative or
hierarchical arrangements) that we are interested in. A separate paper by
Hagedoorn and Schakenraad (1990) provides information that may be helpful in assessing the relative importance of cooperative agreements that are
likely to be oriented towards long-term strategic positioning, compared to
those that are more likely to be concerned with short-term cost economizing. They studied the development of alliances and inter-firm agreements in
three core technologies (new materials, information technology, and
biotechnology) up to 1989 using the MERIT-CATI database which logged
4619 agreements in these areas (out of over 7000 cooperative agreements).
Of the 4619 agreements in the three core technologies, group 1 type agreements (joint ventures, research corporations, joint R&D, and equity investments) accounted for 2739, or 59 per cent. The proportion of group 1 modes
was well above 50 per cent in each of the three sectors. In all three sectors,
over 90 per cent of agreements had been established in the 1980s. This is
consistent with other studies of the incidence of cooperative agreements.
Analysing the INSEAD database on international collaborative agreements
reported in the *Financial Times* and *Economist* over the period 1975–86,
Hergert and Morris (1988) found that over the period they grew from
'almost zero to the point where new ventures are announced on a daily
basis' (p. 99)[10] whilst in a wide ranging review of a number of empirical
studies, Hagedoorn (1993*a*) concludes that cooperative agreements on a
large scale first appeared in the 1970s (p. 134). This is also broadly consistent with results from the LAREA/CEREM database (Mytelka, 1991)
which collected 1086 inter-firm agreements (1980–87) in biotechnology,
information technology, civil aeronautics, and the auto industry, involving
at least one European based collaborator. Mytelka (1991) shows that the
average number of agreements per year rose from 67 in 1980–82, to 133 in
1983–5, to 243 in 1986–87.[11]

This allows us to make three points. First, it is possible to distinguish
between cooperative agreements in terms of their likely emphasis on hierarchy versus market coordination, as Hagedoorn and Schakenraad (1990,
1991) have done. Some (like licensing) may be heavily characterized by market exchange characteristics and contractual arrangements. Others like joint
ventures are likely to add provision for future strategic decisions (with
implications for extension of hierarchy into the area of the agreement).
Secondly, it appears that strategically-oriented agreements constitute a

significant proportion of cooperative agreements. As a first approximation, it would seem that about half of the cooperation agreements in the core technology sectors surveyed by Hagedoorn and Schakenraad (1990) are likely to invoke some degree of continuing strategic decision-making, while the other half are likely to be largely contractually oriented. Thirdly, whilst most measures of cooperative agreements between firms tend to fudge the distinction between those that are strategically oriented and those that are short-term agreements, the evidence is that both broad categories of cooperative agreements have achieved their present importance from a base close to zero in the 1970s.

These patterns are consistent with our expectations that it was the diversification strategies pursued by large corporations in mature economies in the first half of the post-war period (Rumelt, 1986; Channon, 1973; Dyas and Thanheiser, 1976) that provided the crucial set of triggers required for the evolution and proliferation of cooperative activity in the second half of this period. We would expect these trends to have stimulated the growth of all types of cooperative ventures, since large diversified firms considering the potential exploitation of linkages (whether strategically oriented or cost economizing) are likely now to be forced to turn to modes other than merger to do so. In particular, the coordination solutions provided by options such as joint venture were more easily provided by merger options in earlier decades. Before the Second World War, even large corporations tended to be small and specialized when compared to the larger and diversified corporations that evolved later. Where firms found areas of overlapping interest, as in the cases of complementary and substitutable assets in Fig. 9.1, merger was typically the obvious solution (up to the limits provided by regulatory constraints on expansionary zeal). Systems wide effects of the type associated with related-linked expansion were likely to be nonexistent or of minor importance. It was the post-war diversification boom that created the conditions that really stimulated the growth of joint venture activity.

. Further, in a study of the evolution of cooperative agreements in the biotechnology industry, 1971–89, Barley *et al.* (1992) concluded that as the creation of new subsidiaries of diversified firms and new freestanding firms began to decline in the early eighties, so the rate of formation of new cooperative agreements markedly increased. Again, this is consistent with the early phase of diversification triggering subsequent cooperative activity in this particular sector.

2. *Size, diversification, and joint venture activity*

Cross-sectional analysis tends to display a link between size of firm and propensity to form joint ventures (Boyle, 1968; Berg and Friedman, 1978).[12] Since, *ceteris paribus*, large firms also tend to be more diversified, these results are consistent with joint venture being stimulated by prior diversification activity. It would be useful if we could separate out the effects of diversification from size, and Berg and Hoekman (1988) provide extremely useful evidence in this respect. They analysed joint venture activity in the Netherlands as of 1981 and again confirmed that size of firm had a stimulating effect on joint venture activity (noting also that similar patterns appeared when comparable Swedish, US and German data were analysed). They then analysed propensity to undertake joint venture activity for the 150 largest Dutch corporations separated into those that (a) stayed close to a specialized base with less than 10 per cent of its turnover outside its core business, and (b) diversifying or vertically integrating firms (DIV/VI firms), with more than 10 per cent of turnover outside their core business. The corporations were ordered in groups of 25, ranked according to turnover. For the first group of 25 (i.e. the largest corporations), DIV/VI firms were only 48 per cent of this cohort but accounted for 89 per cent of the 209 joint ventures formed. For the second group of the next largest 25 firms, DIV/VI firms were only 25 per cent of the cohort but accounted for 75 per cent of the 105 joint ventures formed. DIV/VI firms were 24 per cent of the third cohort, but accounted for 73 per cent of the 74 joint ventures, they were 8 per cent of the fourth cohort but accounted for 40 per cent of the 51 joint ventures, they were 16 per cent of the fifth cohort but accounted for 76 per cent of the 50 joint ventures, they were 12 per cent of the last cohort of 25 (the smallest firms here when ranked by turnover), but accounted for 64 per cent of the 25 joint ventures. In this case the stratification of the corporations into groups of like-sized firms helps to suggest a clear association between diversification activity (or more generally, movement away from a core business) and subsequent joint venture activity on the part of the firm. The evidence is generally consistent with prior diversification triggering subsequent joint venture activity. Thus, the suggested relationships between joint venture, diversification, and merger appear to hold over time and at a point in time, consistent with the perspective developed here.

3. *Merger/joint venture relationships*

The relationship between merger and joint venture is more involved than is generally acknowledged. It is usual to think of them as substitute options, but merger can also serve as the crucial source of diversification that triggers subsequent joint venture activity. For example, Scherer and Ross (1990, p. 92) point out that the diversification of US corporations 1950–75 was carried out to a considerable degree through merger and not internal growth. Consequently, not only does merger stand as a nominal alternative to specific joint ventures, merger activity served as the precursor to later joint venture activity by creating the pre-condition of diversification that helps foster joint venture activity.

4. *Joint venture stability and frequency*

Williamson (1985, pp. 83–4) supposes transactions to be arrayed along a dimension representing the degree to which parties to a trade maintained autonomy, with conventional market contracting at one end, and centralized hierarchy at the other. Cooperative agreements, such as joint venture, would be located in between. Whereas before he had earlier regarded cooperative agreements as both infrequent and inherently unstable (1975, pp. 108–9), with a bimodal distribution of transactions clustering around the extremes of the market and hierarchy dimension, Williamson later modified this position in the face of empirical evidence to the contrary to acknowledge that the distribution was typically more uniform than he had earlier conceded (1985, pp. 83–4). He concludes 'whatever the empirical realities, greater attention to transactions of the middle range[13] will help to illuminate an understanding of complex economic organisation. If such transactions flee to the extremes, what are the reasons? If such transactions can be stabilized, what are the governance processes?' (Williamson, 1985, p. 84).

However there is no mystery concerning the proliferation of joint ventures in the view developed here. There is no tendency for cooperative agreements such as joint ventures to flee to the extremes of pure market or hierarchy, nor a need to stabilize them, for the simple reason that the mistake is to conceive of them as representing some form of hybrid or intermediate state somewhere between pure market and pure hierarchy on some hypothesized dimension. As far as the individual venture opportunities themselves are concerned, the trigger for the adoption of the joint venture mode is not to be found in the characteristics of the ventures themselves, but in the context in which they are set. Unless the role of previous corporate diversification is identified, the joint venture will remain an enigma inviting spurious explanations based on the supposed merits and demerits of the mode considered in isolation. In fact, joint ventures lie outside traditional market and hierarchy modes and are not simple hybrids produced by selectively fusing elements from market and hierarchy extremes. As argued above, joint venture is the extension of hierarchy by a less direct route, and is triggered when the natural evolution of firms and sectors produces blocks to simpler hierarchical alternatives. This helps to explain the increased frequency and persistence of joint venture activity, despite these phenomena representing puzzles when viewed from the perspective of conventional transaction cost economics.[14]

5. *Joint venture and product-life cycle considerations*

We would expect to find hierarchical solutions such as multinational expansion and joint venture used at earlier stages in the product life cycle than contractual alternatives such as licensing, given that innovative stages tend still to have significant strategic decisions to be made in the future. This is both consistent with an internalization extension of the stages of development approach (Young *et al.*, 1989, p. 33), and with empirical work by Davidson and McFetridge (1985) who studied 1200 intra-firm and market technology transactions by US firms 1945–78. They concluded that the probability of internal intra-firm hierarchical transfer was greater for R&D intensive companies and for newer technologies and technologies with few previous transfers.

9.7. Conclusions

As with the analysis of diversification and multinationalism, the key to understanding the phenomena of joint ventures is to maintain the firm as the basic unit of analysis. Studies which have analysed the joint venture in isolation have tended to miss the point that the joint venture is an extremely expensive device through which to coordinate resource allocation, and that it is typically only resorted to as a device of last resort. Whilst this may include host governments' requirements for a local partner, in recent years it has increasingly been associated with large diversified firms imposing hierarchy through joint venture solutions because a merger of the two firms is costly and impracticable. It is not the characteristics of the joint venture that typically poses problems in these respects; it is the variety of businesses and linkages that merger would bring together that is the problem. The resource-based perspective helps bring these issues centre-stage, and hopefully contributes to an analysis of a variety of phenomena: these include reasons why joint ventures have proliferated only relatively recently; relationships between firm size, diversification and joint venture; the role of previous merger activity in triggering later joint venture activity; joint venture stability and frequency; and the place of joint venture in the product life cycle.

NOTES

1. See also Hagedoorn (1993*b*) for an extensive audit and associated bibliography of cited motives for inter-firm technological cooperation.
2. Indeed Williamson points out that size, and especially diversity, tend to be prerequisites for the adoption of the M-form structure by individual corporations.
3. Schwarzenegger's film company hired the aircraft from the Pentagon for the making of the 1994 film *True Lies* (*The Sunday Times*, London, 21 August 1994, p. 19). The development of the Post-it has become the stuff of legend in the

innovation literature, and it could be argued that much serendipity surrounded the eventual commercial impact of this innovation and that neither market nor hierarchical arrangements could have anticipated the initial development or subsequent phenomenal success of this product. However, the important point here is that serendipity, uncertainty, and surprise are all concepts which can be difficult or impossible to handle in a contractual context, but which may be more appropriately handled within a hierarchy. Mintzberg (1979, pp. 273–7) also points out that environmental complexity differs from stability or uncertainty and develops implications for bureaucratization and decentralization.

4. This is not to say that multiple objectives and conflict resolution techniques are not observed in a unified, single firm hierarchy (e.g. Cyert and March, 1963, analyse the implications of multiple objectives in managerial coalitions and discuss associated conflict resolution procedures). However, the point being made here is that dual control is likely to add a further layer of cost elements in this respect, compared to those associated with unified hierarchy.

5. The general argument here is that knowledge (such as R&D) tends to have high fixed costs of generation, but once generated it can frequently be provided to a new user at low additional cost per user. In this respect it can be similar to other public goods; it may cost a great deal to construct lighthouses to service just one user, but a second user can use the services provided at zero marginal cost. Since allocative efficiency obtains where price equals marginal cost, the allocatively efficient price is zero when marginal cost is also zero. Consequently, there is an efficiency argument for the free and unfettered dissemination of knowledge.

   Obviously, such principles would dim or eliminate the private incentives to search for new technologies, since innovators would not be able to protect their intangible assets from appropriation by others. Consequently, systems such as patent law tend to reflect a balance between private incentives and public good arguments.

6. See Pitelis (1993) for a number of readings dealing with this issue.

7. Ollinger sees the subsequent restructuring of firms and shedding of unrelated assets in this sector as shareholder interests (and profitability concerns) asserting themselves over growth-oriented managerial interests. If anything, this suggests that what may be a failed investment in terms of shareholder interest may be satisfactory from the point of view of managers—in the absence of shareholder intervention.

8. See Kay (1992*b*) pp. 205–6.

9. See ibid. pp. 206–7.

10. Though this trend may be overstated to the extent that this phenomenon only became one of general interest in the 1980s and so may have been underreported in these sources in the early part of this period. International collaborative activity was certainly not invented in the 1970s; for example Gomes-Casseres (1988) traces a broadly increasing trend in the relative incidence of joint ventures in new manufacturing subsidiaries formed by US MNEs 1900–75, with a sharp *decrease* in the relative incidence of joint venture formation in the 1960s. Gomes-Casseres attributes this latter behaviour to cyclical phenomena.

11. See Dodgson (1993, p. 18) for a useful survey of a number of empirical studies and databases in this area.

12. Boyle's results were especially striking, finding with his US based sample that

joint ventures had parents from the top 100 of the Fortune 500 in 42 per cent of cases, whereas parents from the next 100 only occurred in 4 per cent of cases.

13. That is, cooperative agreements such as joint ventures.

14. It is important to distinguish questions of persistence of solutions at the corporate level from those at the business level. Cooperative agreements may become established as stable and continuing phenomena pursued by corporate management, whilst the lives of individual cooperative agreements are more likely to be tied to (and curtailed by) lower level product life cycle considerations. The difference lies in the level being looked at; as discussed in Chapter 3, higher level institutions may reveal a stability and permanence that is not visible if the focus is solely on the characteristics and behaviour of constituent elements.

10.   Alliances and Networks

In this chapter we shall first of all be concerned with an extension of the question which we raised in the last chapter: if cooperative activity is such a good thing, why has it apparently only become so prevalent in recent years? In the last chapter we were concerned with cooperative activity at the business level, particularly joint venture. We widen the scope here to look at patterns of cooperative activity involving alliance or partnership between two firms (involving a multiplicity of cooperative agreements), and the possibility of network or club-like behaviour involving groups of firms.

Whilst we have seen in the last chapter that there has been a considerable amount of interest in the economic literature in terms of modelling business-level cooperative behaviour, the same cannot be said of cooperative activity at the level of alliances and networks. To some extent this neglect is understandable, and indeed inevitable. If the focus is still on the product-market aspect of the neoclassical agenda, then consideration of the efficiency implications of alternative modes of organizing that product-market (such as joint venture) may not be too difficult to add on to that agenda. However, alliance at the level of large diversified firms is not something that the neoclassical perspective is well disposed to recognize, let alone analyse. The idea of networks involving multiple firms with multiple businesses is even more difficult to comprehend from the single product perspective of traditional theory. Jarillo (1988) has suggested that networks of firms may be efficient if networking helps economize on Williamson's conception of transaction costs, and has suggested that trust may help to reduce these transaction costs. Again, the role of trust in smoothing transaction costs can be conceded, but this does not help us to explain why networks involving strategic decisions have apparently proliferated in recent years, and once more we have implicit limited comparators. On the presumption that strategic managers can usually trust their own organization more than outsiders, this would make even a 'high trust' relation with an outside firm a relatively inefficient proposition. The 'high trust' explanation is also vulnerable to the question raised in the context of joint ventures: if they are such a good thing, why did management not discover them earlier?

Notions of alliances and networks are now well established in the strategic management and organizational literatures.[1] However, there is often a tendency to regard networks of organizations as analogous to individuals forming networks. This can be misleading since it may obscure a fundamental difference between networks of individuals and networks of organizations. Network interaction at individual level can be a natural reflection of physical or cognitive limits at individual level, and constitutes a device for facilitating the exploitation of gains from specialization and division of labour; individuals cooperate because they need other individuals and cannot do everything themselves. Even if a club or network of individuals is characterized by rich interactions, individuals do not internalize these interactions and take each other over or merge if they wish to retain their status as individuals. But if networks of organizations wish to internalize interactions, merger or takeover might simply involve a redrawing of their boundaries rather than a qualitative change in status; the transmutation of organizations into other organizations is generally more straightforward than the transmutation of groupings of individuals into an organization. The fundamental question then becomes why networks composed of organizations do not choose the obvious alternative. If network interactions have major economic significance to participant organizations, why do they not merge? The question is given added emphasis by the observation that some networks (such as in the biotechnology sector) handle the kinds of innovative decisions that our earlier analysis suggests would appear to be more naturally conducted within a firm's boundaries.

An immediate problem is that the concepts here appear to be difficult to define and pin down. Dunning defines strategic business alliances as 'alliances deliberately designed to advance the sustainable competitive advantage of the participating firms' (Dunning, 1993, p. 250). However such an objective could be said to apply to all three business solutions in Fig. 9.1. Consequently such interpretations do not take us very far, but Dunning's definition is not atypical of approaches to the problem of what is a strategic business alliance. Porter and Fuller go a little further in defining coalitions as 'formal, long-term alliances between firms that link aspects of their businesses but fall short of merger' (Porter and Fuller, 1986, p. 315). Thus, such alliances are seen by Porter and Fuller as being (a) relatively durable; (b) between firms and not just specific business units (and therefore involving questions of corporate strategy and not just business strategy); and (c) involving limited and partial interconnection (aspects only of the respective firms are connected). This last point appears to imply that the participating firms are likely to be involved in multiple activities (whether of a multi-product, multi-process or multi-region nature is left unstated). Porter and Fuller suggest that strategic business alliances may encompass joint ventures, licensing arrangements, supply agreements and marketing agreements amongst other arrangements. There is a consensus in the literature that the types of collaborative acts involving alliances can be highly varied as Porter and Fuller suggest. Porter and Fuller also point out that such 'coalitions' can only be understood in the context of a firm's overall global strategy, which may involve multiple coalitions (Porter and Fuller, 1986, p. 316) and the opportunity cost of other options must always be compared to that of coalition formation if it is to be justified as the preferred option (p. 327). We shall take up these points below in looking at issues arising from coalition formation in practice.

Porter and Fuller argue that partnerships, alliances and coalitions must be looked at from the perspective of corporate strategy, which appears eminently sensible. However, we also have observed that *acts* of collaboration take place at business strategy level, at the level of specific business units. We have one piece of valuable information concerning collaborative behaviour to take with us as we now travel up the higher level of corporate strategy; diversification stimulates collaborative behaviour. In other words, a pattern found at corporate strategy level may influence choices at the lower business strategy level. We should not be surprised to find the relationship operates in both directions, that is that actual or potential acts at business strategy level may exert influence over choices at corporate strategy level, in this case the formation of an alliance.

We can also extract another element from our earlier arguments. At the level of corporate strategy, the multiproduct firm is also faced with three major categories of option to exploit potential linkages. For single product firms these options were the wholly owned (merger), cooperative (joint venture), and market contract solutions. In principle, these options still exist at the level of corporate strategy for the multiproduct firm, though at this level alliance can replace (or encompass) specific collaborations such as joint venture as the relevant mixed mode. It is still obviously a hierarchical solution in that alliances can provide for new decisions and activities that could not be fully specified in a contractual solution. As a hierarchical solution, our earlier arguments lead us to expect alliances to be preferred to contractual options in areas involving poorly specified problems and decisions such as new markets and new technologies. Porter and Fuller's (1986) and Dunning's (1993) surveys confirm that these tend to be the major factors underlying coalition formation. An example of a recent alliance which reflects these issues in that between Daimler Benz and Mitsubishi. The partners now collaborate in a variety of business link ups, Daimler Benz reportedly offering access to mechanical technology and European markets for Mitsubishi, and Mitsubishi offering access to electronic technology and Japanese markets for its European partner (*Financial Times*, 7 March 1990, p. 1 and 31 December 1993, p. 49).

Bearing these points in mind, in section 10.1 we shall extend our analysis of the evolution of a sector in the last chapter to explore how alliances and networks might evolve in practice. In section 10.2, we shall see how the patterns predicted in the previous section compare with the actual development of alliances and networks in practice.

10.1. The Evolution of Alliances and Networks

So far the mental experiment we started in the previous chapter has identified five discrete stages in the evolution of the firm; atomism, specialization, related-constrained, related-linked, and collaborative stages. In this chapter we shall push our analysis a couple of stages further and suggest what patterns of behaviour are likely to evolve eventually in our hypothetical sector as our firms continue to seek growth opportunities. In the early stages our sector was fairly fluid with firms having a fairly wide range of strategies and expansion possibilities to choose from. By Fig. 9.6 (in the last chapter) the sector had matured into a fairly stable pattern involving thirteen firms, six of which had a joint venture arrangement with another firm in the sector. Now, suppose the top firm in the large mat of Fig. 9.6 is considering extending one of its technologies into a new market. The new IBU possibility (the white IBU in Fig. 9.6) could be set up with complementary marketing resources from the middle firm on the top mat in Fig. 9.6, or from either of the other two large related-linked firms on the bottom mat. As far as the three options are concerned, there is nothing to choose between them in terms of the suitability of the marketing resources they could bring to the new venture opportunity. In each case the preferred mode to coordinate linkages would be collaboration rather than merger for the same reasons that led to this firm starting to collaborate in stage 5. Are there any further considerations that might persuade our firm to prefer one potential collaborator over another?

If there is no difference in the potential gains from exploiting linkages

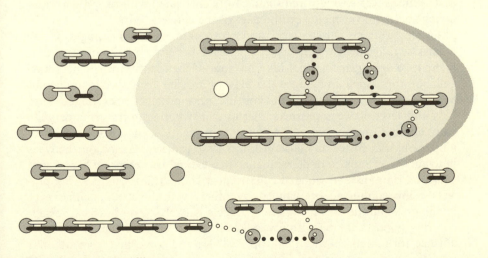

Fig. 10.1. Stage 6. Alliance

with the new IBU whichever collaborator is chosen, then the efficiency implications of which collaborator should be chosen boil down to a question of coordination costs. In this respect the fact that this firm already collaborates with the middle firm on its mat may reduce such costs. If there is a likelihood that a collaborator might act opportunistically (Williamson, 1985), then the existence of another agreement between the two firms may act as a hostage to encourage or ensure good behaviour on the part of the other firm. This source of security could allow our original firm to reduce search, negotiation and monitoring costs associated with the new venture. Accordingly, our firm forms the new joint venture with its existing collaborator as indicated in Fig. 10.1.

However, the efficiency implications from clustering collaborations between firms go well beyond this set of gains. The argument is symmetrical in so far as the *other* firm can also reduce coordination costs associated with the new venture compared to the level they would be if the firm were collaborating with a stranger. If the first firm can use its existing collaboration to ensure good behaviour, then so equally can the second firm with whom it shares this agreement. Further, the coordination costs associated with the *original* joint venture may be reduced for both firms by the new agreement insofar as the new venture can itself adopt the role of hostage to help dissuade opportunistic behaviour with respect to the original agreement. Thus, preferring the existing collaborator over a new collaborator can result in reduced coordination costs for *both* collaborative agreements for *both* firms. The effect is to turn the business level collaboration of Fig. 9.6 into the corporate level alliance of Fig. 10.1.[2] Consistent with this, Zaheer and Venkatraman (1995) found in a study of 329 independent insurance agencies in the USA that cooperative activity between insurance carriers and agencies was strongly and significantly correlated with reciprocal transaction-specific investments on the part of the carrier.

Therefore, there can be clear and strong efficiency advantages for an alliance arrangement which clusters agreements between pairs of firms over alternative arrangements that take no note of the identity of business level collaborators. Such an alliance can help to provide an umbrella to encourage and sustain a variety of collaborative arrangements operating at business unit level between partners, just as can twinning agreements between pairs of cities or universities. Twinning agreements at the level of the overall systems can foster and sustain lower level projects carried out between individuals, groups and departments located in the respective partners. Cheating on a distant, isolated collaborator is one thing; endangering projects being conducted or planned by others within your system due to knock-on reputational or retaliatory effects is likely to represent a hostage ensuring good behaviour. Equity stakes in the other firm can be a part of alliance formation (Lewis, 1990, pp. 108–27) and these involvements may further limit the scope for opportunistic behaviour. Therefore, there are likely to be strong coordination cost pressures leading to firms clustering their collaborative agreements between a limited number of selected partners. It may even be the case that the efficiency gains from sticking with existing partners for new collaborations may be sufficient to more than compensate for any resource deficiencies or weaknesses relative to other firms at the level of the venture opportunity itself. Taken venture by venture, it may be more efficient to prefer a weaker partner over a stronger stranger if the former allows firms to economize on coordination costs.

A feature of this perspective is that it highlights interdependencies between relationships at business and corporate levels. The (corporate level) diversification of the firm through the first four stages eventually encourages (business level) collaborative agreements in stage 5. In turn as past diversification encourages a switch of emphasis from merger to collaboration, the proliferation of (business level) collaborative agreements encourages the formation of (corporate level) alliance arrangements in stage 6. Thus corporate strategy influences business strategies, which in turn feed back to influence corporate strategy. The relationship between collaboration at business level and alliance at firm level is symbiotic; as collaborative possibilities are created, they are likely to stimulate alliance formation, and as alliances are created they are likely to stimulate and facilitate further collaborative agreements at business level.

However, the analysis can be taken at least one stage further. In Fig. 10.1, the top firm on the mat is now exploring setting up a new IBU that draws upon another one of its technologies, and is searching for a firm with complementary marketing expertise. In this case potential collaborators with relevant expertise again include the two large related-linked firms below the mat in Fig. 10.1, as well as the bottom firm on this mat. For the reasons discussed above, if the firm has to collaborate it would prefer to collaborate with its existing alliance partner, *ceteris paribus*, but in this case its existing partner simply does not have appropriate expertise. If we again assume that there is nothing to choose between the three potential collaborators in terms of the marketing resources they can bring to the possible new venture, are there any efficiency-based reasons why our firm should prefer one potential collaborator over another?

A start may be made here by noting that while the top and bottom firms on the mat in Fig. 10.1 do not presently collaborate with each other, they are indirectly linked in that they both collaborate with the middle firm. If the top firm was to form a joint venture as in Fig. 10.2 with the bottom firm on this mat, the middle firm would have the hostage of its existing joint venture with the bottom firm to encourage responsible behaviour on the part of the latter in this new venture. Why should it be prepared to exercise this potential power? One answer is that such mediation need not be altruistic but could be entirely self serving; the top firm itself has its own potential hostage in the form of its collaborative agreement with the middle firm, and

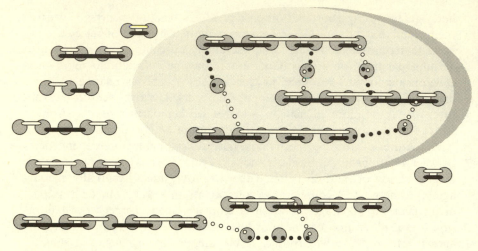

Fig. 10.2. Stage 7. Network

this might be used to lean on the middle firm to encourage it to lean on the bottom firm. Further, the middle firm now also has an indirect interest in the wellbeing of its collaborators; if they are damaged it may affect their ability to contribute to their existing joint ventures with this firm. Indeed, the more the partners share interests, the more the welfare of the other partner becomes an issue of mutual interest. Also, the network can make opportunistic behaviour more visible; as Powell and Brantley observe in the case of the biotechnology industry, 'the relevant biotech community is tightly knit through communication networks: news about malfeasance spreads rapidly' (Powell and Brantley, 1992, p. 378). For these reasons if the top firm were to choose the firm at the bottom of the mat as collaborator, the existence of potential hostages should contribute to a reduction of the coordination costs in this case when compared to the two other alternatives, *ceteris paribus*. The central point is that in industrial networks actors can influence each other, not only directly, but also indirectly through other actors in the network (Hakansson and Johanson, 1988, p. 376).

The hostage threat is weaker and more indirect in this case than it was in the case of alliance in Fig. 10.1. *Ceteris paribus*, the top firm should still have encountered lower coordination costs if it could have made a similar deal with its existing partner (with whom it has a direct hostage) rather than having to find a new collaborator. None the less, it does provide a rationale for preferring one potential collaborator over another, and indeed the efficiency gains here once again go well beyond the cost savings to the top firm. We can see this by first noting that we have looked at the story so far from the point of view of the bottom firm as potential opportunist, top firm as potential victim, and middle firm as potential mediator. However, by completing the joint venture in Fig. 10.2 each of the three firms on this mat are now indirectly linked to each other, and each could adopt any one of these three roles depending on circumstances. For each firm on this mat, every collaborative agreement now has at least one indirect hostage to back it up. By introducing just one new joint venture a network has been created with efficiency gains from reduced coordination costs diffused throughout the network. An example of such a network in practice is given by Lorange and Roos (1993, pp. 246–7 and 248–62) with Hitachi, Fiat, and John Deere operating a network based around links in the hydraulics area. In this area, each of the parties takes primary responsibilities for marketing in their home trading bloc, while each takes on particular R&D responsibilities, the results of which are shared with the other two parties. Other links include joint ventures to manufacture hydraulic excavators in North America (Hitachi/Deere), and in Europe (Hitachi/Fiat), and an agreement to jointly develop a backhoe loader based on joint research (Fiat/Deere). In such a tightly knit network, opportunistic behaviour by one partner with respect to another is likely to be of concern to the third party.

If the transition though stages 4, 5, and 6 are characterized by symbiotic interdependencies between business and corporate strategies, then the interdependencies here are likely to extend to symbiotic interdependencies between business/corporate level considerations and considerations at the level of *groups* of firms.[3] Proliferation of collaborative and alliance possibilities help to create the conditions for the evolution of networks or clubs; the networks or clubs themselves provide the umbrella protection that may extend back down to corporate and business levels and further stimulate the development of new collaborative and alliance agreements within their boundaries. Business, corporate, and network levels are likely to interact in mutually supportive ways, with the deepening or strengthening of cooperation at one level helping to stimulate cooperative activity at higher and/or lower levels. Focusing entirely on business level considerations (as in a neoclassical perspective) obscures the role of system-wide relationships operating at corporate or even higher levels. This also helps explain why much economic analysis of cooperative activity has tried to square the circle by trying (contrary to reason and evidence) to find efficiency explanations at the business level for cooperative activity relative to merger alternatives where none is justified. A neoclassical perspective would not take us very far in understanding the interactions and relationships that have evolved in this example. The perspective here is also quite clear on the role of trust in alliances: in our experiment firms do not cluster agreements in particular alliances *because* they trust their partners, but *in order to* trust their partners. If a firm has numerous ties with one firm, and only one tie with another, it is more likely to be able to rely on the former's good behaviour than the latter, *ceteris paribus*. In our experiment the identity of collaborators (over and above issues of potential complementarities at business level) only becomes an issue of relevance after initial collaborative agreements have been struck. Here, trustworthiness depends on context, not personality.[4]

An implication of this experiment is that particular strategies and modes may be triggered at different stages in the evolution of a firm and a sector, and may be profoundly influenced by what has happened at the previous stage. Thus, the exhaustion of specialization opportunities in stage 2 triggers more loosely linked related-constrained strategies' expansion strategies in stage 3. The exhaustion of the single core marketing or technological link exploited by the related-constrained firms in stage 3 triggers the less consistent chaining of links in the related-linked strategies of stage 4. In turn, the pursuit of related-linked strategies though merger contains the seeds of its own (scale or anti-trust) blockages to further such expansion, eventually triggering collaborative activity in stage 5. As collaborative opportunities become increasingly emphasized, so the proliferation of these arrangements triggers alliance arrangements as a protective umbrella for collaborative activity in stage 6. Finally, intensification of alliance and collaborative activity triggers the formation of networks or clubs in stage 7. At each stage a crucial change in the feasibility or opportunity cost of various alternatives triggers a new strategy or mode of coordination. The story of the seven stages is generally one of firms turning to alternatives that had previously been less valued or more costly compared to their first preferences in the earlier stages.[5] Figure 10.3 summarizes the shifts through the various stages described in our experiment from the perspective of the top firm on the mat in Fig. 10.2. The figure shows the firm moving from its highly specialized and synergy-rich base into others involving progressively weaker or more costly linkages as it expands. The consequence is the creation of weak patterns of linkage along the lines described in Chapter 5.

There are three other aspects which may be of relevance to our experiment, and these are issues of stage skipping, environmental turbulence, and path dependency respectively. As far as the possibility of stage skipping is concerned, it may be noted that in stage 7 the bottom firm on this mat has skipped the alliance stage and gone straight into a network relationship with the other two firms. Stage skipping is something which may reflect the balance of opportunities at the previous stage; for example, this firm's potential collaborators may be unavoidably dispersed, with few opportunities for concentrating collaborative agreements in alliances. Plausible scenarios can be constructed for stage skipping in the case of other strategies; for example, the firm in the related-constrained stage in Fig. 10.3 may find that it can extend this strategy on its single market base by further diversifying into a variety of technologies. This firm may face no pressure to move into a related-linked strategy until eventually scale and/or anti-trust pressures trigger the collaborative stage to pursue further expansion possibilities. Whilst stage skipping may reduce the number of stages a firm may go through, it does not affect the ordering of these stages as implied by our analysis.

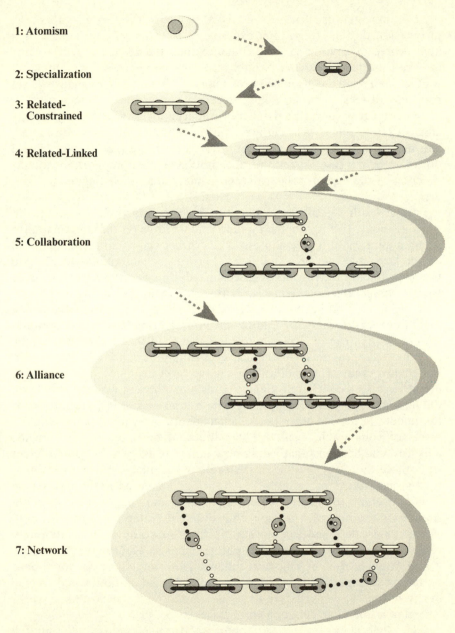

1: Atomism

2: Specialization

3: Related-
Constrained

4: Related-Linked

5: Collaboration

6: Alliance

7: Network

Fig. 10.3. Seven stages of corporate growth

Environmental turbulence, as discussed in Chapter 3, may also affect the progression through stages. For example, if a sector is characterized by a high degree of environmental turbulence then the related-linked strategy may be triggered sooner than would otherwise be the case. Firms may not wait until all related-constrained expansion opportunities are exhausted, but may instead seek to avoid linkage dependence by shifting into a related-linked strategy at an earlier point. In turn, such diversification may rapidly create a tangled asset problem if merger possibilities are being considered, and in turn may trigger the collaborative stage more quickly than would otherwise be the case. Again, this does not have direct implications for the ordering of the various stages, though it may affect their timing and incidence.

Further, path dependency is likely to be of considerable importance in such processes. In Fig. 9.6, the top and middle firms on the large mat have set up a joint venture. But suppose at the earlier stage that the middle firm on the large mat had been indifferent between collaborating with the top firm and either of the two large related-linked firms on the bottom mat, each having comparable marketing strengths that could be married with this firm's technological strengths. Chance events (e.g. conference encounters, illness, unfounded rumours) lead to this firm agreeing its first collaboration with the 9-IBU firm on the bottom mat rather than with the top firm on the large mat. In turn, many subsequent events may be contingent on this initial chance event. The middle firm on the large mat now has a positive incentive to seek collaborative agreements and alliances with the cohort on the bottom mat, while the top firm now has no reason in future to prefer the middle firm over other potential collaborators with resource endowments of comparable quality. The pattern of collaborative agreements, alliances, and networks that would now unfold is likely to be very different from those that were feasible or desirable in the analysis here. What happens at each stage is contingent on what has happened in the past. If we could somehow re-run the evolution of particular sectors all over again from early beginnings, it is likely that different patterns of linkage would emerge as accident and contingency tip firms on to different evolutionary routes compared to their original paths, much as Gould (1989) has suggested would happen in biological spheres. However, whilst we would have no reason to expect that the same patterns of collaboration would emerge in any re-run, we would expect to see collaboration, alliance, and networks emerging at the same developmental stages as before.

Like stage skipping and environmental turbulence, path dependency influences the patterns that emerge at each stage, not the logic underlying the developmental ordering of these stages. Richardson points out that 'firms form partners for the dance, when the music stops, they can change them' (Richardson, 1972, p. 896); however, clustering may introduce elements of stability that binds partners together when the music stops.

Consistent with this, Kogut *et al.* suggest that switching networks may not only mean firms having to redesign existing ventures, but it may mean sacrificing a member with whom they have learnt to cooperate (Kogut *et al.*, 1993, pp. 76–7) and they suggest there is likely to be a corresponding degree of inertia associated with networks in practice (p. 81). In a separate work analysing cooperative activity in the biotechnology industry, Kogut *et al.* find evidence that over time, 'cooperative choice appears to be significantly nested within the cumulative pattern of previous decisions by individual actors. It is the structure of the network, rather than the attributes of the firm, that plays an increasingly important role in the choice to cooperate' (Kogut *et al.*, 1992, p. 364). Using the MERIT-CATI database, Hagedoorn (1995) also found that evidence of networks tended to involve relatively stable groups of cooperating companies.

These influences are likely to be major forces shaping the evolution of networks in practice. For example, there was nothing pre-ordained about the emergence of Silicon Valley and Hollywood as major specialized industrial centres or districts. If, in the 1930s, Frederick Terman had not been Professor of Electrical Engineering at Stanford, if he had not encouraged some of his brightest students to stay in the area by forming their own companies on an industrial site owned by the university, and if two of the first students to take up this offer had not been called Hewlett and Packard, then the absence of these critical historical events might have led to a very different future. A history in which, say, Hewlett and Packard had moved with him to a different university could mean us talking today about Silicon Hill, or even Silicon Beach, and not Silicon Valley. In the case of Hollywood, the location really took off in the early twentieth century as independent film makers tried to put as much distance as possible between themselves and the clutches of the established film producers' trust or cartel based in New York (San Francisco, Florida, and Cuba also developed as early centres). An edge that Los Angeles had over San Francisco was that it was close enough to the Mexican border to allow independent producers to easily flee injunctions and subpoenas prompted by the East Coast trust.[6]

However, while path dependency and contingency may strongly influence the particular direction in which a sector develops, it does not alter the logic underlying the process or ordering through which the various stages unfold in the analysis here. If the middle firm on the large mat had begun to cooperate with those on the bottom mat instead of the top firm, the pattern of networks in this sector could have developed very differently. Yet in our analysis this in itself would make no difference to the pressures and influences which lead to the firm first pursuing diversification strategies, then collaboration, then alliances, then networks. History constrains rationality and efficiency, it does not negate them. The triggers that influence the ordering of stages should still operate in a similar manner in this alternative story.

Finally, attention can be drawn to an important feature of this description of the evolution of collaborative agreements, alliances, and networks. There is an *ad hoc* feel to many current explanations of such phenomena. First, studies typically note that such agreements have proliferated in recent years and this leads to a search for causes. Then, a reductionist perspective usually prompts a search for causes rooted in recent external changes or in the venture itself; for example, it has been variously argued that cooperation is stimulated because technology is more complex, is more expensive, is changing more rapidly, is more risky, and so on. Alternatively, such a perspective may encourage a search for reasons why joint venture itself may generate higher revenues and/or lower costs than the wholly owned subsidiary alternative (e.g. Contractor and Lorange, 1988*a*, pp. 21–2).[7] However, such a line of argument is difficult to sustain in view of the innate coordination cost disadvantages of joint versus wholly owned alternatives at the level of the venture itself, discussed earlier in Chapter 9. As long as perspective is limited to the levels of individual businesses and product-markets as in conventional industrial economics, it encourages a search for such causal factors located in the environment or in the venture itself. Here we have argued that there is no need to invoke such mechanisms to explain the evolution of the varieties of strategies and modes associated with our seven stages of corporate and sectoral evolution. Instead, it is the natural evolution of the firm itself at each stage that constitutes the crucial trigger stimulating the unfolding of the next stage.

When we look at actual patterns of behaviour in the next section we shall give particular attention to such phenomena in view of the fact that the existence of small firm networks would appear to contradict the patterns predicted here.

10.2. Empirical Patterns

Once again, we shall examine the extent to which the kinds of patterns we would expect to obtain actually accord with empirical reality in a variety of contexts. One issue we shall bear in mind from the previous chapter is that cooperative agreements are often taken to represent a large array of actual modes of cooperation and what is meant by 'cooperative agreement' may include a very diverse set of arrangements. Another problem here is that the apparently simple question 'What are the boundaries of the network?', is not so simple to answer.[8] It is one thing to know that a network exists, but it is quite another to analyse the breadth and depth of particular networks, especially in cases where rapid change creates fluid and volatile patterns of relationships. Much of the research in this area has focused on the relative strength of ties between participants (e.g. Granovetter, 1973; Burt, 1992), whilst our analysis is more concerned with why networks evolve in the first place. Relatively speaking, it is easy in principle to count cooperative agreements, joint ventures, and alliances; it is more difficult to measure networks. We *can* say at this juncture that our analysis above helps to explain why networks do appear to have become important phenomena in recent years. However, at this stage we shall focus more narrowly on empirical evidence for the evolution of alliances, and we shall look at networks in the context of evidence for small firm networks.

1. *Patterns in the biotechnology industry*

We may get more detail on the latter stages of corporate evolution by looking at actual patterns of cooperation in biotechnology. This is an industry in which alliances and networks have evolved as major features in recent years, and which has been one of the most intensively studied of sectors in this regard. A study by Barley *et al.* (1992) provides useful information in this context.

We have already noted above and in Chapter 9 the barriers to merging highly diversified systems. As far as small firm involvement in alliances is concerned, if a small specialized firm has multiple actual or potential knowledge-based links with other small specialized firms, multi-firm merger to create a multi-business firm is the obvious solution. Alternatively, if a small specialized firm has multiple actual or potential knowledge-based links with *one* partner, then merger with its partner is still the obvious solution, whether or not the partner is large and diversified.

However, if a small firm has multiple partners, some of whom turn out to be large and diversified, then cooperative solutions may be turned to. We saw in the discussion of the single-IBU firm on the bottom mat in Fig. 9.6 that having venture opportunities with two large diversified firms may create barriers to merger solutions to coordinate these opportunities. When a small firm has multiple alliances, these problems are multiplied many times over. In such circumstances, if a small firm was to merge with only *one* of its existing partners, this would only fully internalize one set of agreements whilst leaving the rest still to be exploited through co-operation agreements. Against the limited gains that such partial internalization offers must be set the potential impediments to existing and future collaboration in cases where loss of independence, and assimilation within a potential or actual competitor, is seen to matter. This analysis suggests that patterns of alliance formation would tend to be characterized by cooperation involving large diversified firms, and that where smaller specialized firms are involved, this would be in instances in which they form a number of alliances with a number of partners (otherwise we would have an unstable situation in which focusing cooperation on one partner could be a prelude to merger).

Barley *et al.* (1992) studied nearly 2000 organizations involved in the US biotechnology sector. They found that the types of organizations that tended to cooperate with a larger number of other institutions than any other type of organization involved in the industry were diversified corporations and the smaller dedicated biotechnology firms formed to pursue biotechnological R&D (such as Biogen, Genentech, and Cetus). As Barley *et al.* (1992, p. 337) comment, 'by diversifying both partners and ties, a firm . . . remains relatively autonomous with respect to any one of its partners. This was the strategy pursued by Genentech'.[9] They also note that the majority of the enterprises that form alliances with smaller dedicated biotechnology firms are large diversified corporations (p. 343). These findings are consistent with our expectations that (a) alliances will tend to involve large diversified firms; (b) where small firms are involved in alliances, they will tend to have multiple partners; (c) small firms' partners tend to be large diversified firms, not other small firms.

2. *Timing of alliance development*

As one of the last stages in the evolution of the firm, we would expect to find alliances making a belated appearance on the sectoral scene. In the last chapter, we noted Hagedoorn and Schakenraad's (1990) study of the development of alliances and inter-firm agreements in three core technologies (new materials, information technology, and biotechnology) up to 1989 using the MERIT-CATI database. In all cases, over 90 per cent of agreements had been established in the 1980s. At the same time, Hagedoorn and Schakenraad's analysis not only indicates the apparent existence of alliances and networks in the 1980s, but the tendency for their numbers to increase substantially during the latter part of the eighties. Their analysis of the pattern of cooperative agreements indicates that what we define here as alliances (two firms having two or more cooperative agreements between them) had a relatively modest increase from 31 in 1980–84 to 42 in 1985–89 in biotechnology (Hagedoorn and Schakenraad, 1990, pp. 22–3), but went from 5 to 16 in new materials over the same period (pp. 24–5). In information technology, alliances had become so widespread by 1985–89 that any mapping of alliances would have led to just 'one big jumble of lines' (p. 22). However, the number of alliances in this industry with four or more agreements increased from 9 in 1980–84 to 43 in 1985–89, while those which involve what Hagedoorn and Schakenraad define as 'very strong' tie-ups (with six or more cooperative agreements over the relevant periods) increased from none in 1980–84 to 14 in 1985–89.

A word of caution is in order here. It has to be pointed out that an increase in collaborative activity would be likely to lead to an increase in the number of alliances just by chance. None the less, there appears to be convincing information provided by the work using the MERIT-CATI database that alliances are non-random directed phenomena that can have degrees of intensity and stability that are difficult to explain in reductionist terms when analysis is restricted to the level of individual cooperative agreements.[10] These sectors are characterized by extremely large numbers of cooperative agreements, with alliances typically not appearing until extremely late in the day in terms of sectoral evolution. This is generally consistent with the arguments above that alliances will generally not be triggered until firms have gone through various earlier stages of growth, diversification, and cooperation.

3. *Small firm networks and atypicality*

Our analysis emphasizes the role of diversification and scale as a trigger for collaborative activity, and then on to networks through the alliance stage. This perspective does not explain the existence of small firm networks; in our approach if small specialized firms started to find venture possibilities of mutual interest, merger would be the most obvious mode to coordinate linkages. We have seen that small firms may be involved in networks if they collaborate with bigger, more diversified neighbours, but this is not the same thing as a network composed mostly or entirely of small firms. Yet there has been considerable interest in recent years in this possibility; for example, the Commission of the European Communities (1988) sees cooperation between small firms as often being required to supplement their limited resources, and has developed policies to encourage such cooperation. There has also been significant interest in the notion of industrial districts, often characterized as involving active networks of cooperating small firms (You, 1995, pp. 448–50). Much of the recent interest in this area was stimulated by Piore and Sabel's analysis of flexible specialization, one form of which involves industrial districts 'composed of more-or-less equal small enterprises bound in a complex web of competition and cooperation' (Piore and Sabel, 1984, p. 263). Amin (1993) also suggests that there are parallel trends towards localized small firm networks and globalized networks of large transnational corporations.

The first point that can be made is that the interest by scholars and policy makers in small firm networks has not been matched by evidence of their widespread existence or economic importance, even after allowing for any scale bias against observing and reporting agreements between small firms. Perrow (1992, pp. 455–7) first points out that while small firm networks have been apparently identified in a variety of industries, and while networks (and presumably small firms) appear to exist in most cases, it is not clear that this always involves networks of small firms. He suggests there is excellent evidence of successful small firm networks in Northern Italy, but only patchy evidence from other European countries and Japan. Silicon Valley was the only small firm network he could identify in the USA, while there was no evidence of small firm networks in Britain or Ireland. He concludes that small firm networks are both a minor phenomenon, and theoretically implausible in conventional terms (Perrow, 1992, p. 459). The first point may be taken as broadly in line with the arguments of this chapter, but we shall try to go further and suggest circumstances conducive to the evolution of small firm networks.

4. *Small firm networks and non-critical exchanges*

Bearing the previous point in mind, one route to examine small firm networks is first to note that our starting point in this and the previous chapter has been that collaborative activity is likely to emerge when new ventures are small relative to the scale of the firms that are donating complementary resources. We then held the scale of ventures constant, and considered how the evolution of large scale diversified firms can stimulate collaborative activity. However, the argument is symmetrical; if we were to hold *scale of firm* constant and reduce the scale of the resource or activity which is being shared between respective firms, then we might expect to observe collaborative activity between small firms. This means that we would expect to find that collaborative activity between small firms is likely to involve either peripheral or occasional activities—otherwise merger would be the more likely outcome if the sharing possibilities covered significant areas of the respective firms' value chains.

Usefully, Von Hippel (1987, 1988) looked at one such small firm network involving informal know-how trading in the US steel minimill industry (there were about 60 minimill plants and 40 firms in this industry in 1988). He found a general willingness on the part of engineers to assist engineers in other firms in the industry (even sometimes direct rivals) by volunteering proprietary knowledge or referring them to other engineers in the industry network—providing the information was not crucial to the original firm's competitive position, and on the assumption that reciprocal help may be provided by the recipient to the donor (or to another referred by the donor) at some point in the future. The non-critical nature of the information exchanged in such networks is consistent with behaviour in the aerospace industry where informal trading of information between rivals tends to be stifled when an imminent government contract is in the offing. After the award of the contract, the same know-how that had been closely guarded will apparently again be freely traded (Von Hippel, 1988, p. 87). Such aspects of small firm networks are consistent with their focusing on exchanges of relatively minor, peripheral, and occasional importance, as in industry association and Chamber of Commerce type networks and clubs (for example, the Chambers of Crafts described by Grabher (1993*a*), for small craft firms in the Ruhr district). This is not to denigrate such associations, merely to place them in the context of relative impact on the firm's competitive advantage. Indeed, Nohria (1992) explicitly describes the 128 Venture Group (a monthly forum for those with possible complementary interests relevant to new high technology firms in the Route 128 region around Boston) as 'a weak-tie generator where participants with different affiliations within the network may create bridging ties with one another' (Nohria, 1992, p. 256).

Further, one of the most publicized small firm networks in recent years has been the Italian knitwear industry based in Modena. However, Lazarson's (1993) analysis of the ties that bind together these small firms relate essentially to informal cooperation in *vertical* relations between supplier and customer (pp. 217–18). The fashion based Italian knitwear exploits economies of scale at the level of one or two machines, not whole factories, and with many discrete production processes at different stages (Lazarson, 1993, p. 211). As in the case of informal know-how trading our analysis here is consistent with even horizontal cooperation—as long as the opportunities are minor or occasional. However, if these small firms in Modena were to establish opportunities or needs to coordinate *horizontally* and share resources on anything other than an occasional basis (e.g. because of standardization of designs) then we would predict that the appropriate first response would be horizontal integration, and not continued maintenance of this cooperative but atomistic structure. Interestingly, Italy also provides an example of exactly such an arrangement in the same industry. In the Veneto region, Benetton dominates the production stage in knitwear and pressures subcontractors to work for it exclusively (Lazarson, 1993, p. 217).

Once again, the critical issue in the internalization/cooperation question appears to be, how significant are the cooperative opportunities relative to the scale of the parties involved? The more important the opportunities from coordinating opportunities relative to the overall level of activity of the relevant firms, the more likely it is that a single firm solution will emerge through merger, acquisition, or internal expansion. The same logic comes through, whether we are looking at networks of global multinationals, or of small scale local firms.

10.3. Conclusions

This chapter represents an attempt to extend the resource-based approach developed earlier into the area of alliance (multiple cooperative agreements between two firms) and network (in which a number of cooperating firms may be involved). The essential prerequisite for making sense of the evolution of alliances and networks is again keeping the firm in focus as the basic unit of analysis; the analysis above suggests that it would be difficult or impossible to explain the evolution of alliances and networks without analysing stages and characteristics in the prior evolution of firms. The resource-based perspective provides explanations for a number of phenomena, including patterns of alliance formation between large and small firms;

the extremely recent rise to prominence of alliances and networks; and the general restriction of small firm networks to special cases involving minor or non-critical exchanges.

NOTES

1. For example, see the various readings in Axelsson and Easton (1992) and Nohria and Eccles (1992).
2. A contrary point of view is given by Badaracco in his study of GM and IBM's alliances: 'at bottom, cooperative agreements are not fundamentally links between one firm and another, nor do they connect firms and labor unions or firms and government agencies. Such abstractions do not exist, and they cannot have relationship with another. Only individuals and small groups can. Hence the success of a collaboration depends on whether specific individuals in separate organizations can work together and accomplish joint tasks' (Badaracco, 1991, pp. 141–2). As in the case of neoclassical theory, this is an extreme reductionist position. In it, the Daimler Benz alliance would be simply the aggregation of the individual cooperative agreements at business unit level. Also, if cooperative relationships operate only at the level of business units and not firms, it is difficult to explain moves like Ciba-Geigy's purchase of an equity stake in Spectra-Physics, a West Coast laser firm, as part of a broader alliance to pursue joint developments (Lewis, 1990, p. 119).
3. Indeed, Gomes-Casseres (1994) goes so far as to suggest that networks themselves may compete directly, and gives the example of the RISC computer field with four separate constellations of firms and alliances.
4. However, see Fukuyama (1995) for an excellent account of how differences in trust relationships in different societies can influence forms of economic organization. Also Kay (forthcoming) considers some aspects of the economics of trust.
5. An exception to this general trend may be the move between stages 5 and 6. In our experiment, shifts from single collaborative arrangements to alliances are likely to lead to an across the board reduction in costs of coordination at venture level for each firm.
6. In time other advantages provided by Los Angeles helped to reinforce its status as a base for film-making, such as the weather, availability of cheap labour and the variety of nearby locations for film-making (Jacobs, 1939, pp. 84–5). The important point here is that the conjunction of transient historical events (the East Coast trust and the independents' fear of litigation) with a geographical feature (proximity of the border) helped to spark off the positive-feedback process that led to the establishment of the Hollywood film industry. Different historical events might have meant that today we could be talking about the Palo Alto or the Brooklyn film industry.
7. Contractor and Lorange do recognize that benefits from the joint venture may diffuse to other parts of the company. However, this in itself does not explain why the same added value could not be realized by acquisition or appropriate asset swapping.

8. Burgers *et al.* (1993) confirm the difficulties of defining the boundaries of networks in practice. See also their work for an analysis of possible networks and sub-networks in the global auto industry.

9. However, the authors add that this strategy did not prevent Genentech from being taken over by Hoffman-La Roche. Presumably the potential gains to Hoffman-La Roche from internalization in this case were perceived to be sufficient to compensate for the threat to Genentech's other (actual or potential) cooperative agreements. However, the considerations discussed here may help to explain why the acquisition was only partial (60 per cent) and why Genentech continued to be independently listed on the stock exchange (Powell and Brantley, 1992, p. 370); such quasi-autonomy, real or perceived, might make it easier for Genentech to sustain and create cooperative agreements with rivals to Hoffman-La Roche. For a survey of Genentech's numerous linkages in the biotechnology industry, see Freeman and Barley (1990).

10. See Hagedoorn and Schakenraad (1991) for a more extensive analysis of patterns of alliances using the MERIT-CATI database.

11.   Complexity and Hierarchy

The concept of 'complexity' is frequently cited as a major influence on the behaviour of decision-makers and organizations. Indeed it is sometimes difficult to find analyses of strategic decision-making, innovative activity or organizational forms in which the terms 'complex' or 'complexity' do not make an appearance at some point. That complexity is an important determinant of the behaviour of institutions is typically taken for granted to the extent that many writers neglect to consider what the term actually means and how it may be defined.

A further assumption that is generally made is that complexity of decision-making has actually increased in recent years. Escalating R&D costs, shortening product life cycles, and increasing political turbulence, are all examples of issues that have been identified as sources of increasing complexity, and as we saw in the last chapter, increased complexity has been identified as a contributory factor in the evolution of phenomena such as joint ventures. In fact, it is as easy to identify trends towards increasing *simplicity* of tasks and decisions. It is difficult to argue that navigating and running a lightly manned and push-button controlled supertanker is a more complex business than was the operation of an eighteenth-century sailing ship. Modern materials and mass production techniques have considerably simplified the production of beer barrels, a task which some years ago in Britain involved an apprenticeship of up to nine years for coopers. Also, modern engineers have generally abandoned the intricacies of a slide rule for the rather more straightforward calculator.

In this chapter we shall suggest that there are important inconsistencies in the way that complexity is treated by many writers in the organizational literature, and that organizations handle complexity in a rather different manner from that generally accepted in the literature. We shall also begin to look at different aspects of hierarchy in this chapter. So far we have largely been concerned with hierarchy as a device for implanting decision-making capability for future decisions. Here we start to explore the role of hierarchy in arranging and layering such capabilities. The chapter will also help to set the context for a fuller analysis of organizational structures in Chapter 12. In particular, the frequently stated view that complexity of decision-making tends to increase as we move up the hierarchy will be shown to be misleading. It will be argued instead that complexity of decision-making generally diminishes as we move up the hierarchy, that this is essential for organizations to function normally, and that these points are consistent with findings in the empirical literature. We shall focus particularly on arguments by Jaques (1990) in developing these points. In section 11.1 we shall first examine the relationship between task complexity, novelty, and routinization, before looking at some implications of research in cognitive psychology for hierarchical structures in section 11.2. In section 11.3 we shall examine how clustering of related activities within hierarchical levels helps organizations handle complexity.

11.1. Complexity and Task Performance

Consistent with many writers in the organizational field, Jaques (1990) regards complexity as a fundamental determinant of patterns of layering in corporate hierarchies:

The complexity of the problems encountered in a particular task, project, or strategy is a function of the variables involved—their number, their clarity or ambiguity, the rate at which they change, and overall, the extent to which they are distinct or tangled. Obviously, as you move higher in a managerial hierarchy, the most difficult problems you have to contend with become increasingly complex. The biggest problems faced by the CEO of a large corporation are vastly more complex than those encountered on the shop floor. The CEO must cope not only with a huge array of often amorphous and constantly changing data but also with variables so tightly interwoven that they must be disentangled before they will yield useful information. . . . That the CEO's and the lathe operator's problems are different in quality as well as quantity will come as no surprise to anyone (Jaques, 1990, p. 129).

At first sight these conclusions do appear obvious and unremarkable, and consistent with the conventional wisdom: 'As we move upwards in the supervisory and executive hierarchy, the range of interrelated matters over which an individual has purview becomes larger and larger, more and more complex' March and Simon (1958, p. 150); 'As we move up the hierarchy, managerial decision making becomes more complex' Mintzberg (1979, p. 145). Jaques goes further and makes a direct link between hierarchical level and cognitive capacity: 'As we go higher in a managerial hierarchy, the most difficult problems that arise grow increasingly complex, and, as the complexity of a task increases, so does the complexity of the mental work required to handle it' (Jaques, 1990, p. 132). This requires enhanced decision-making capabilities at higher levels: 'effective value-adding leadership of subordinates can only come from an individual one category higher in cognitive capacity working one category higher in problem complexity' (Jaques, 1990, p. 131).

Jaques is a highly respected and experienced researcher into the behaviour of organizations who has made important contributions to this area of study.[1] However, Jaques' linking of task complexity to hierarchical levels is misleading, and based on a misinterpretation of the relationship between the complexity of decision-making, cognitive capabilities, and the nature of hierarchy. Hierarchy does not, as Jaques suggests, simply sort out complex problems to higher and higher levels along 'a continuum of complexity from the bottom of the structure to the top' (Jaques, 1990, p. 130). Instead, hierarchy plays an active role in transforming the nature of decision-making such that new problems and tasks appear at different levels in the organization. This transformation takes place whether we are looking at changing perspectives generated by moving from lower to higher, or from higher to lower levels. While task complexity may change from level to level, there is no organizational law that dictates that tasks must become more complex at higher levels in the corporation. We shall instead argue that the reverse is the case, and that not only does task complexity tend to diminish as we move up the corporate hierarchy, but that this is a normal and indeed essential condition for the effective functioning of organizations. This argument follows directly from research in cognitive psychology and the behaviour of organizations.

We shall start by considering two examples of decision-making at opposite ends of an institutional hierarchy. Jaques defines complexity as being a function of the number, clarity,[2] rates of change, and inter-relationships of elements. This appears a reasonable definition, broadly consistent with Hodgson's point (based on arguments in the economics and biological literatures) that while complexity requires *variety* (i.e. variance of a characteristic, or number of distinguishable elements), it also involves the idea of some kind of *structured interaction* between the various elements (Hodgson, 1993*a*, pp. 82 and 276). While operational measures of complexity may vary from case to case, these are broadly consistent with what most writers on complexity mean by the term.

One guide to developing measures of complexity along these lines is provided by Flood (1987) who interprets complexity as arising from the number of elements, the states they may take, and the possible relationships between these elements. We shall draw upon this interpretation to compare imaginary choices facing two individuals. One is a Chancellor of the Exchequer deciding whether or not to raise interest rates by 1 per cent. The only information she regards as relevant is that her inflation target is 2 per cent, and that her advisers tell her that holding interest rates (at 5 per cent) will lead to an inflation rate of 3 per cent, while raising interest rates by 1 per cent will hold inflation at 2 per cent. Next door her typist is about to type the word 'organization'. How do these tasks compare in terms of degree of complexity?

If we restrict the typist's potential choices to the 26 letters of the alphabet, then each letter typed can take one of 26 possible states. This means that for a twelve letter word there are 26^{12} possible combinations. Taking possible states as a measure of the complexity of this task, the typist has to choose one combination out of one hundred thousand million million possible choices (to a first approximation), or about 10^{17} possibilities. By way of contrast, the Chancellor's task is rather different. She may be regarded as facing a metaphorical keyboard, one with only two keys marked '2 per cent inflation' and '3 per cent inflation' respectively. Taped to the side of this metaphorical keyboard is a reminder 'keep inflation at 2 per cent'. Again, taking possible states as a measure of complexity, the Chancellor has to choose one combination out of two possibilities, a much less complex task than the 10^{17} possibilities associated with the typist's task. As a rational actor, she chooses the 2 per cent key and raises interest rates.

Measured in such terms, the typist's task is clearly the more complex. Such a conclusion may appear counter-intuitive, even nonsensical. A competent typist might be expected to skate over the word in a second, while the Chancellor might be reasonably expected to hesitate and agonize over even the restricted choice on her metaphorical keyboard. However, it is important to recognize that the importance of a decision is not necessarily the same thing as intrinsic complexity; also, whilst it could be argued that the decision is unlikely to be so straightforward for a politically aware Chancellor who must likely take other considerations into account, it could equally be noted that the measure of complexity in the typing example could be expanded to recognize choice sets that include numbers, punctuation marks, fonts, etc.

Interpreting the Chancellor's decision as a complex one would be to misinterpret the significance or importance of decisions (an *output* measure) as somehow representing complexity (an *input* measure). Similarly, it is easy to confuse subjective features of the decision *process* itself with intrinsic complexity. For example, the Chancellor's inclination to regard the interest rate decision as being intrinsically difficult or uncertain may be influenced by her own personality, experience, and capabilities. A hesitant or insecure Chancellor may assure her colleagues that she finds the decision extremely complex, while ironically an ignorant, inexperienced, or stupid Chancellor may treat the decision as a simple one, even if her advisers' multi-equation econometric models do not.

One interesting aspect of this examination of complexity is that it helps demonstrate that, paradoxically, uncertainty may reflect and require a great deal of knowledge on the part of decision-makers. Suppose the typist is unsure whether she is expected to type 'organization' with an s or a z. While this may be interpreted as an ambiguous, unclear, uncertain situation, it has been, in fact, by this stage reduced to a remarkably simple choice between two alternatives, comparable to the yes/no choice facing the Chancellor, and incomparably simple when contrasted to the complete set of alternatives that the word has to be selected from. As Loasby (1976, pp. 8–9) points out, conventional economic interpretations of uncertainty tend to assume implicitly so much knowledge on the part of decision-makers as to represent only minor qualifications of the assumption of perfect knowledge. A considerable weight of knowledge lies behind such expressions of uncertainty, and it would be a mistake of the first order to confuse this with ignorance, or the absence of knowledge. Uncertainty, confusion, and ambiguity may actually serve as indicators that the decision-maker is coping with complexity and has moved away from a state of complete ignorance.

Whilst the casual outside observer might judge the task facing the typist as being as simple as the task facing the Chancellor is complex, to do so would be to confuse novelty, uncertainty, difficulty, or task importance with innate complexity. Standardization and routinization helps individuals and organizations to handle complexity, not to eliminate it. For example, few people would be surprised to find robots making bicycles or 6-year old children riding them, and it might seem a reasonable next step to conclude that both sets of tasks are inherently simple; as easy as riding a bike, in fact. However, the sight of robots riding bicycles and 6-year old children making them would be likely to be greeted with astonishment and disbelief. This reflects the fact that both making and riding bicycles are highly complex tasks that require the manipulation and integration of a large number of inter-related variables for successful completion (and it could be added in passing that the same may be true for Jaques' lathe operator: shaping, cutting, facing, and boring can be complex tasks of an order of magnitude closer to that of typing than to interest rate determination in our above example). The behaviour of experienced and skilled operators may serve to disguise complexity by making tasks appear simple; ironically task complexity may be more clearly revealed by the failures and problems faced by inexperienced operators in specific instances. Appropriately, studies cited by Child (1984, pp. 73–7, 79–84) point out that length of training to perform a task competently may be taken as one indicator of task complexity.

Jaques interprets a variety of political, economic, social, and technological issues as potentially contributing to the strategic complexities facing CEOs, such as European Union, Pacific Rim, Eastern Europe, Middle East, and Third World developments. However, the major task facing strategic planners is not to *encompass* such complexity, but to *reduce* it to manageable proportions. A variety of devices can be enlisted for this purpose by placing filters on the quantity and quality of information allowed on to the strategic planning agenda. These include standardization of information, such as financial information from divisions; the use of specialist advisers or teams to analyse and summarize issues for strategists; quantity restrictions, such as requiring advisers to restrict briefing papers to no more than one side of paper; standard programs or routines to simplify decision-making; and converting potential choice situations into less informationally demanding search situations that only require attention when certain targets or aspiration levels are not achieved.[3]

The role of hierarchy as informational filter and task transformer can be seen most strikingly in the case of conglomerate management. Since conglomerates are a form of diversification that involves unrelated businesses, this form of corporate strategy generates a greater variety of market and technological problems and issues than corresponding related or specialized strategies. Yet large conglomerates can be managed by a small core group of strategists focusing on standardized financial information and plans from divisions, with many complex market and technological inter-relationships shoved down to lower levels. Financial manuals and courses can be drawn upon to help the conglomerate planner make efficient decisions. In view of the potential for routinization and programming of financial decisions, it would not be surprising if the manuals drawn upon by some conglomerate CEOs were shorter than the corresponding manuals available for the typing of the present document using a word processing package. There is therefore no conflict between the idea of highly diversified firms tending to operate in technologically dynamic environments (as observed earlier), and the non-technological bias of conglomerate management.

Once again, such an interpretation invites comment and criticism. Conglomerate management has been widely, and possibly deservedly, criticized in some quarters for taking the mechanistic approach described here. The characterization of conglomerate management above might similarly be criticized for reinforcing such perspectives and over-simplifying the inherent complexities and subtleties of strategic management. Such a criticism would again confuse complexity with significance. The decision to build a new plant will be of much greater economic significance than the machining of any individual part comprising it, though at the level at which the respective decisions are made the decisions may be equally simple—or equally complex. The planners may compare expected rates of return, whilst the lathe operator may push buttons. Both tasks would be revealed as highly complex if they could be fully specified, with the planners being aided by analysts and the lathe operator by a computer.[4] The fundamental point remains that new problems and new forms of complexity certainly appear as we shift levels in the hierarchy—but that new complex relationships may appear in *both* directions, whether involving shifts up or down the hierarchy.

An analogy may be drawn with fractal geometry in which complex patterns may become apparent and then disappear as the level of resolution and magnification seen from the perspective of an outside observer changes. This process occurs whether the resolution increases towards micro levels (revealing patterns nested within other patterns), or decreases towards macro levels (with new patterns emerging out of lower level building blocks).[5] Task complexity may certainly vary up and down the hierarchy, but it does not do so in the predictable, uni-directional fashion suggested by Jaques. In the next section we shall discuss how these points link with experimental evidence from cognitive psychology.

11.2. Cognition and the Effects of Experience

If, as Jaques suggests, effective leadership of subordinates can only be achieved by superiors 'one category higher in cognitive capacity working one category higher in problem complexity' (Jaques, 1990, p. 131), then organizations would simply become unmanageable. It is not obvious how we would measure cognitive capacity in such cases, but Jaques makes it clear it has to match the 'sharp discontinuities' (p. 127) in problem complexity encountered moving up the hierarchy. However, the logic of Jaques' position requires this category shift in problem complexity and associated complexity to be progressive and cumulative as we move up multiple levels in the hierarchy. Jaques argues against over-layering of hierarchies and claims that seven hierarchical levels reflecting different orders of task complexity is enough for all but the largest corporations (pp. 131–2). He illustrates this with an example of a company with seven hierarchical levels ranging from technicians, operators and typists at the bottom to the CEO at the top.

Concepts of compound growth help clarify the difficulties involved in Jaques' position. If every upwards shift in Jaques' hierarchy meant enlisting superiors with enhanced cognitive capabilities 'a category higher' compared to their subordinates, and if we start at the bottom with ordinary mortals and decision capabilities, then by the time the CEO's office is reached we shall either observe or require a race of super-mortals. If the distinction between superiors and subordinates is non-trivial in terms of cognitive capabilities as Jaques suggests, then just seven levels would be sufficient to accumulate a level of cognitive capability at CEO level that bears no relation to that normally associated with the species *Homo sapiens*. We can demonstrate this with a simple example: suppose we have some measure of cognitive capacity associated with normal or average cognitive capabilities at base level in the corporate hierarchy. Call this base measure *1*, and assume that superiors working 'a category higher' than their subordinates as we move up the hierarchy means that cognitive capacity doubles with each new level. For the nth level in the hierarchy, cognitive capacity would have to be enhanced to the level $C = (1 + i)^{n-1}$, or 2^{n-1}, where $i = 1$. Even with only seven levels this would require the cognitive capacity of the CEO to be 64 times normal levels. However cognitive capability is measured, doubt might be expressed as to whether such super-normal abilities could be found in the typical modern corporation, let alone be part of an implicit job description for senior management.

In fact, the purpose of hierarchy is not to sort out and arrange individuals in terms of *variation* in cognitive capabilities. Hierarchical ordering and layering of tasks is designed to reduce the level of complexity facing individual decision-makers. Indeed, if any residual tasks remain that lie well

beyond the capabilities of normal human beings, then the designers of hierarchy are not doing their job properly. It is hierarchy that responds to cognitive capabilities, not the other way around. Further, novel elements in a
decision should *reduce* the degree of complexity that can be handled. This
is a crucial point in view of the tendency of many writers to associate
novelty with complexity. For a decision-maker of given capabilities, *complexity of decision must be reduced as the number of novel decision elements
increase*. This is a corollary of general principles concerning performance
improvement through task routinization and learning.

These points are reinforced by experimental results from cognitive psychology showing a striking tendency for capabilities to converge towards
average or standard values for performance in cognitive activities such as
concept attainment and short-term memory (e.g. see Miller, 1956, and
Simon, 1981, pp. 62–127, and discussion above). Simon (1981) argued that
certain cognitive processes display such a degree of constancy across individuals that they may be measured in terms of parameters. Earlier, Miller
had established that the amount of information that may be stored in short-
term memory is about seven items, and that this limit is independent of the
form in which the items are presented (for example, whether the items are
letters or words). Such a finding at first sight appears paradoxical, since
obviously individual words contain more information and are more complex than individual letters. However, Miller explained this in terms of the
phenomenon of *chunking* in which individual letters were integrated and
combined into a single word item in short-term memory; a word like 'baby'
is not usually remembered as being composed of four separate letter items,
but instead can itself form a single concept and item for those who are
familiar with it. Chunking, or the coding of multiple items into a single item,
considerably expands the information processing capacity of individuals
since the informational content of individual 'chunks' can be enormous.
Subsequent research has helped show the influential role that experience and
familiarity play in chunk formation and individual performance[6] and
chunking has been investigated and established for a wide variety of cognitive items besides letters and words, such as numbers, pictures, and chess
positions.[7]

In his wide ranging and provocative essay on the psychology of thinking,[8]
Simon argues that the limits or bounds to rationality are generally expressible in the form of parameters; through a great range and variability of
tasks, 'only a small number of limits on the adaptability of the inner system
reveal themselves—and these are essentially the same limits over all the
tasks' (Simon, 1981, p. 72). Miller's parameter seven in the case of item or
chunk capacity in short-term memory is only one example identified by
Simon, another is the five seconds of fixation it typically takes to commit a
chunk to long-term memory.[9]

Simon refers to a large body of experimental work in a variety of contexts and topics and concludes: 'The artificiality—hence variability—of human behavior hardly calls for evidence beyond our observation of every-day life. The experiments are therefore mostly significant in what they show about the broad commonalities in organizations of the human information-processing system as it engages in different tasks' (Simon, 1981, p. 96). Such a conclusion has profound implications for the design of organizations. If the boundedness of cognition is expressible in the form of universally applicable parameters, then cognitive capacity must dictate hierarchy rather than (as Jaques argues) hierarchy dictating cognitive capacity. It would seem reasonable to suppose that the implications of this would be regarded as major issues in the organizational literatures.

In fact, such an assumption would be mistaken. Whilst the relevance of the concept of bounded rationality, and Simon's own contributions in this context (both individually and with collaborators) are widely recognized, there is little evidence of recognition of the remarkable degree to which basic cognitive capabilities may approach the status of a standardized asset. If such recognition were widespread it is unlikely that arguments such as Jaques' could be entertained, or at least be allowed to pass without sub-stantial comment and criticism. The reasons for this neglect may lie partly in the tendency for academic disciplines to compartmentalize,[10] and also partly in the tendency for cognitive psychology to focus more explicitly on hypothesis testing rather than parameter estimation.[11] The evidence for Simon's arguments exists, but it is not evidence that is always easily decipherable even for cognitive psychologists, let alone for other social scientists.

Interestingly, the modern findings from cognitive psychology reported by Simon are consistent with the philosophy of what Hodgson (1993*a*, pp. 54–72) terms the Scottish School, associated perhaps most strongly with the work of Adam Smith and David Hume:

Both Smith and Hume presume that each human being at birth is broadly similar in ability. Smith assumes that variations in skill arise from learning-by-doing in the process of production itself. As Smith himself writes in the *Wealth of Nations*: 'the difference between the most dissimilar characters, between a philosopher and a com-mon street porter for example, seems to arise not so much from nature as from habit, custom, and education' (1976, pp. 28–9). Consequently, skill differences are not 'so much the cause as the effect of the division of labour'. For Smith it is the division of labour that alters character, not character that determines the allocation of tasks . . . the riches of industrial organisation are seen to flow ultimately from market relations, not preexisting diversity. This is in marked contrast to Darwin's theory of natural selection, where *ex ante* differences in character are the evolution-ary fuel (Hodgson, 1993*a*, pp. 59–60).

At first sight Jaques' position would appear to be more consistent with the latter tradition than it is with the Scottish School, but it must be immedi-ately noted that his view of the wide range and diversity of innate abilities necessary for normal organizational functioning is not a feature of Darwinism. Indeed, natural selection typically operates through the accretion *over numerous generations* of variations that are small at individual level relative to the extent of evolutionary differences between species (Gould, 1977, p. 12). In practice, the findings cited by Simon are as consistent with Darwinism as they are with the beliefs of the Scottish School, none of which provides comfort or support for Jaques' views on variation in cognitive abilities and its implications for hierarchy.

One last issue remains to be settled at this point. What, if anything, can be said about the degree of task complexity dealt with by individual decision-makers as we move up the hierarchy?

Our conclusions on this point are clear and unambiguous. Performance depends on learning, which in turn depends on familiarity and repetition. The extent to which situations can be programmed and repeated will influence the extent to which increasing orders of complexity can be coped with by individuals (e.g. through chunking) and the extent to which task performance may improve. Repetition builds up skills with observable effects on performance as in the cases of learning and experience curves. However, programmed decision-making tends to be concentrated at lower (operational) levels in hierarchies and non-programmed innovative decisions tend to cluster at higher (strategic) levels. As a consequence, strategic decision-makers will be unable to transfer experience to the same extent as in programmed situations. The amount of complexity strategists can deal with must be reduced accordingly, and for radical innovative decisions this reduction will be in the region of several orders of magnitude compared to standardized procedures. Such a perspective can build on Thompson's (1967) argument that a hierarchy will tend to be arranged into basic units sharing 'reciprocal interdependencies' (where work is fed back and forth between tasks), with higher level groupings picking up residual interdependencies.

The role of learning in expanding the ability to cope with complexity can be observed in the improvement in terms of words per minute typed as a typist progresses from novice to skilled status. The intrinsic complexity of individual words remains the same, and it is reasonable to assume that the inherent cognitive capabilities in a physiological sense of most typists do not suffer significant degradation or augmentation over this period. It is repetition and learning opportunities which account for the transformation in the ability to handle and process complexity in such cases, and the familiar QWERTY keyboard is an essential standardized component in this process.

By way of contrast, the strategic decision-maker may be regarded as feeding decisions into a keyboard controlled by a mad programmer. It may be impossible to rely on the format of the keyboard from one time period to the next; the wiring, positioning and even the number of keys may vary in unexpected ways. Consequently, the strategic keyboard player has to spend considerable time uncovering relationships which could otherwise be taken for granted if the keyboard format remained unaltered from one time period to the next. Such a strategist never has a chance to travel down any learning curve, but is condemned to remain stranded in its upper reaches, struggling with basic relationships like a novice typist encountering a keyboard for the first time.

Clearly such a description overstates the case to the extent that elements are transferable from one strategic decision to another. If no such generic elements existed, managerial experience and training would count for nothing, and general management training such as MBA degrees would have zero value in the market place. There must be some common elements across strategic decisions if corporate strategy is to have any coherence and direction. Indeed, Penrose's (1959) analysis of expansionary strategies in the firm depends on strategy-formulating resources being released from current activities through experience and the effect of routinization. Nevertheless the basic argument holds, and the strategist's ability to cope with complexity will be affected whether the mad programmer manifests himself as demonically sadistic or only mildly mischievous. In general, the mad programmer's efforts will be more disruptive the more radical and novel a strategic decision is. In general, also, a strategic decision-maker will only be able to cope with levels of complexity several orders of magnitude lower than that typically dealt with at lower levels in the hierarchy. In the next section we shall consider how such issues of complexity and standardization may be incorporated into analysis of hierarchy.

11.3. Complexity, Standardization and Hierarchy

In this section we shall put together a view of hierarchy that benefits from perspectives developed in organization theory, cognitive psychology, and strategic management to examine further how organizations deal with complexity. We start with the precept that grouping of individuals and activities within the corporate hierarchy can be viewed as a process of progressive clustering. For example Conrath (1973) developed an analysis in which individuals or groups are combined into bottom-level or first-order clusters, which in turn are grouped into larger clusters, and so on up to the highest level cluster encompassing the whole organization. Such an approach sees the organization as a system of nested relationships in which sub-systems form elements in higher level systems. As we move up through the levels in such an analysis, lower level linkages disappear. Such absorption of lower level linkages as we move up the hierarchy is both natural and necessary; linkages between particular lathe operators are unlikely to be much discussed at boardroom level, but if they were it would most likely be a signal that something was wrong with this firm. Further, the linkages that emerge and are evident at higher levels in turn disappear for administrative purposes as we move down through the levels in the organization. This is simply a corollary of the previous point concerning the emergence of higher level relationships. The relationship between the Marketing Director and the R&D Director is unlikely to form integral aspects of the day-to-day scheduling of lathe operations, and can reasonably be ignored for such purposes.

What these points signify together is that shifting levels in the hierarchy brings new relationships into focus. Most crucially, the process is symmetrical, with new linkages appearing and others disappearing whether the shift in levels is in an upwards or a downwards direction. This symmetry is an integral part of the operation of organizations and meshes with our earlier arguments concerning complexity and hierarchy.

In practice, our earlier arguments suggest that there would be a general tendency for complexity to decrease as we move up levels. Hierarchies and nested clusters are means by which this reduction in complexity can be achieved. Research on the span of control of managers (i.e. how many individuals should report to each manager) is generally consistent with these points, with Mintzberg (1979, pp. 143–5) reporting research that indicates that unit (cluster) size tends to *decrease* at higher levels in the hierarchy. Consistent with the earlier arguments developed here, Mintzberg points out that this reflects the increased opportunities for standardization at lower levels. Higher level units will be more likely to be faced with novel situations and therefore less able to deal with the number of subordinate units that are manageable at lower levels. However, Mintzberg (1979, p. 145) also argues that this means that managerial decision-making becomes more complex as we move up the hierarchy. Our earlier discussion suggests that this confuses complexity with novelty or uncertainty. Novelty in fact forces *reduction* in levels of complexity that can handled by decision-makers (e.g. as reflected in the reduced span of control at higher levels), while standardization and routine facilitate an *increase* in the degree of complexity that can be handled (e.g. the learning curve and increased individual task performance over time at lower operating levels).

As Mintzberg points out (1979, pp. 106–7), groupings such as those implied by Conrath create bases for co-ordinating work by helping to provide common supervision, common resources (to an extent at least), and joint performance measures, as well as facilitating the interaction of complementary individuals and activities at any given level. If there is also a symmetry in terms of how linkages may emerge and then be absorbed as we move up and down the hierarchy, what do such nested groupings look like in practice?[12]

Whilst the nested clusters may represent a basis for the development of hierarchy, there is not necessarily a one-to-one correspondence between clusters and hierarchical levels. A cluster may have more than one

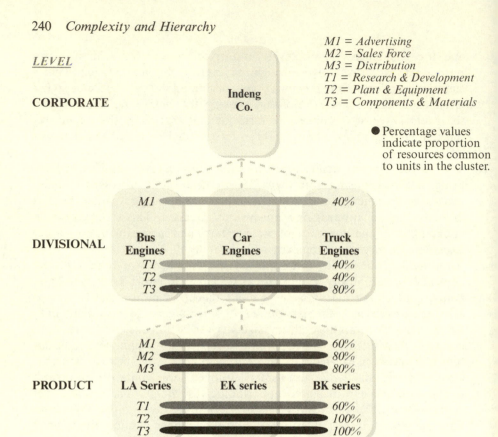

Fig. 11.1. Hierarchy and cumulative linkages for Indeng

hierarchical level if it makes heavy demands on managerial decision-making, whilst one hierarchical level may cover more than one stratum of lightly managed clusters. As Minzberg implies above, it is the features shared by elements within a cluster that help to discriminate the cluster from others at higher and lower levels. In Fig. 11.1 we pursue this point by first identifying various categories of marketing and technological resources. Again to simplify analysis, we have been highly selective regarding the categories of resources chosen. A fuller analysis would identify other categories of marketing and technological resources as well as various categories of support staff such as legal, personnel, and planning services. We then ask the same question for each category of resource and each cluster: 'in value terms, what proportion of this category of resource is standardized across units in the cluster?'

We apply this approach in Figure 11.1 which shows the case of Indeng, a manufacturer of vehicle engines. We assume the firm is organized into three divisions (bus, car, and truck engines), of equal size and value, and each of these three divisions in turn operates three products of equal size and value, an assumption which simplifies the question of assignment of value or resources across divisions and products respectively. Now, if the question is asked: 'in value terms, what proportion of T3 (components and materials) is standardized across clusters?', the answer is 80 per cent by value at divisional level, whilst at product level the proportion rises to 100 per cent. The strength of the linkage in the respective cases is indicated with appropriate shading, black indicating 100 per cent. Thus, the bulk of components are identical across *all* the activities of the firm, whilst a fifth is shared between products within the respective divisions. Similar exercises are carried out for the other category of resources, and Fig. 11.1 shows the resource commonalities deepening as we move down the firm. This is to be expected. At corporate level, there may be very little in common between the various groups or divisions of the firm, especially if the firm is highly diversified or even a conglomerate, whilst at the lowest level of the corporation, brand variations on a product theme may imply almost 100 per cent sharing of resources. Thus, the measures for levels of linkage increase as we go down the corporate hierarchy, as Fig. 11.1 indicates. There is still some need for customization of resources to the level of individual products, which is why M1, M2, M3, and T1 do not reach values of 100 per cent at the product level.

However, it is not the figures for *cumulative* linkages between activities that matter for organizational design purposes as we go down the hierarchy, but figures for additional or *incremental* linkages. In the case of components, 80 per cent of components are already shared between divisions before we begin to talk about additional sharing of components at product level. In fact this leaves only 20 per cent of components to share at this lower level, as Fig. 11.2 shows. However, if 80 per cent of components are shared between divisions, at what level in the firm should the coordination of these resources take place? An obvious solution might be to leave it to divisional management to sort out. But this solution might lack a clear integrative mechanism, leaving conflicting interests and sub-groups within the divisions to distort resource allocation. The usual solution in such circumstances is to provide mechanisms for coordinating the allocation of shared or identical resources a level *above* where the incremental linkages are observed. Thus, since 80 per cent of components are shared at the level of divisions, there is likely to be an active purchasing policy at *corporate* level, the level above where the bulk of component sharing is observed. The remaining 20 per cent of components are identical between products within the respective divisions. Again, divisional managers could leave product managers to sort out this residual component purchase between them. However, it is the divisional managers that are best placed to oversee and integrate a unified purchase policy for the remaining components that are common to products within their respective divisions. In this context, the

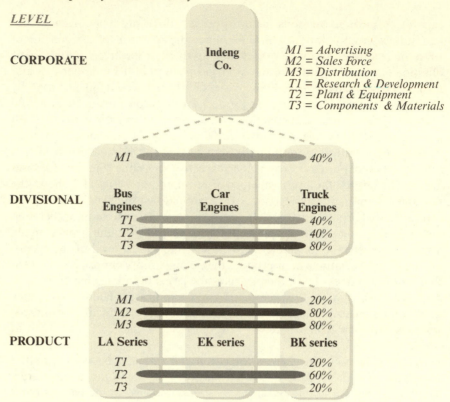

Fig. 11.2. Hierarchy and incremental linkages for Indeng

role of hierarchy is to integrate and coordinate the additional linkages that appear a level just below them.

We can demonstrate the importance of incremental linkages by modifying our example. Suppose we replace the bus engine and car engine divisions in this firm with two businesses of equivalent scale and value, food and drugs respectively. We now assume that there are no shared components between the respective divisions. What would this mean for cumulative and incremental linkages respectively? As far as cumulative linkages in components is concerned, we now have 0 per cent shared between divisions, but we still have 100 per cent component sharing between products within the car division. As far as the incremental linkages that appear as we move down the hierarchy is concerned, we now have 0 per cent at divisional level, and again 100 per cent at product level. It is the change in the incremental figures that carry the important messages as to how and where to coordinate shared resources. Whereas before the bulk of shared components appeared at the divisional stage as we moved down the hierarchy, now no shared components appear at this level, and there is no corresponding invitation signalled of the need for corporate management to coordinate activities between divisions. On the other hand, within the car division there is now 100 per cent sharing of components. The responsibility for coordinating the purchase and use of components is likely to be that of the management team whose role is to integrate product activities, that is divisional management.

Similar exercises are carried out in Fig. 11.2 for the other resource categories. Again, the strength of linkages (here measured incrementally) is indicated by the depth of shading. It is interesting to compare the strength of incremental linkages in the respective levels as we come down the hierarchy. There are strong advertising, R&D, plant and equipment, and components and material linkages appearing at *divisional* level as we descend this hierarchy, suggesting the need for *corporate* level coordination of some marketing and technological activity, including some R&D. At product level, the strongest incremental linkages are in sales force, distribution, and plant and equipment. Again, the coordination of resources commonalities is likely to take place a level above where the sharing of resources takes place. For example, given that 80 per cent of sales force and distribution networks is shared between products, divisional level is the appropriate level to coordinate most of these activities. If each product management team had its own sales force and distribution channels, this could lead to considerable duplication of effort, or at least would make it difficult to coordinate and exploit economies from sharing. Therefore, the strength of incremental linkages helps to indicate the important areas for resource coordination as we move down the hierarchy. As we have seen, each level has its own areas of responsibility which can be quite differentiated from levels above and below, much as the working agenda of a lathe operator and a strategic planner may bear no resemblance to each other.

At this point a warning flag must be raised. Even though the impact of a particular activity may be felt at a particular level, that does not necessarily mean the activity will be organized at that particular level. If this happened in our example this would result in advertising and R&D being disbursed throughout the various levels, dissipating marketing and R&D effort and potentially impeding coordination of these functional activities. In such cases there will be a trade-off between intra-level and intra-functional coordination which may lead to organizational solutions such as matrix management to deal with simultaneous interactions of this nature. With this caveat, Fig. 11.2 identifies linkages that are additional and specific to respective levels as we move down the corporate hierarchy. The picture that emerges is quite different from Fig. 11.1 where commonalities are identified on a cumulative basis. There is no consistent trend for incremental linkages to increase or decrease in intensity as we move through the various levels.

It is also worth noting that Fig. 11.2 shows how organizations handle complexity. Linkages emerge and then submerge as we move through levels in the corporate hierarchy. It is the disappearance as well as the appearance of linkages that permits complexity to be managed. Without the absorption of lower level linkages as we move up hierarchical levels, higher level management would indeed require the supernatural cognitive capabilities implied by Jaques. Nested clusters and incremental linkages instead help organizations function in a world of normal people and standard capabilities. Clustering and nesting together with the standardization and routinization of complex tasks at lower levels means that Jaques' 'continuum of complexity' runs in the opposite direction to that suggested by him. In the example here, we have restricted the number of levels to three for simplicity, but further levels could be added in practice, for example, by identifying 'groups' between corporate and divisional levels, or even through delving down to the deeper levels of 'brands' below product levels. Such complexities were felt unnecessary at this stage, but we would expect the same principles that inform the discussion here to be applicable in an extended hierarchy.

Analysing the organization in this way also helps to reveal parallels and correspondences that run right through the organization. Each level has its own clusters with their associated linkages and relationships. Questions of which level or levels play dominant or more important roles do not arise since each plays an integral part in the normal functioning of the organization. Also, it is relevant that such analysis helps to illustrate the specific domains traditionally covered by particular economic analyses of competitive strategies and linkages. For example, Rumelt's (1986) analysis of market and technological linkages in corporate strategy focuses on relationships involving group or divisional levels, Porter's (1985) coverage of value chain determinants of competitive strategy focuses especially on value chain analysis and linkages at lower levels in the corporation, while Williamson's (1975) analysis of organizational forms is particularly concerned with the development of organizational arrangements for the middle (divisional) level. Inevitably analysis has to be selective in terms of which domains can reasonably be covered by a given analysis, but the above discussion suggests that there may be deeper issues involving nested clusters and linkages between elements that may be common to all levels of analysis.

11.4. Conclusions

The function of hierarchy is not to separate out individuals into layers of cognitive ability, with the most able at the top, and the least able at the bottom. Instead the function of hierarchy is to reduce the amount of complexity facing individual decision-makers in recognition of the tendency for individual cognitive capabilities to cluster around standard parameters. Results from cognitive psychology demonstrate what Simon describes as the 'commonalities' of the human information processing system such that the bounds of rationality across individuals can usually be expressed in the form of parameters that hold over a wide range of individuals and a variety of tasks. Furthermore, the amount of complexity an individual can handle is directly related to familiarity and practice opportunities, and inversely related to unfamiliarity and novelty which means that the complexity of individual tasks at lower levels is typically significantly higher than the content of tasks at higher levels. These considerations will typically swamp any effects of differences in cognitive capacity of decision-makers that may exist at individual level. Consequently, there is a 'continuum of complexity' running from the bottom to the top of organizations as Jaques suggests, but it operates in the opposite direction to that identified by him. Finally, organizations handle complexity by arranging resources in nested clusters of linked activities. In moving down the hierarchy, incremental linkages that appear at each stage dictate the managerial agenda to be set at each level.

NOTES

1. See, for example, discussion of Jaques' work in Child (1984, pp. 27, 62, 88).
2. We suppose this variable 'clarity' to be related to uncertainty. However, as we discuss below, uncertainty has to be distinguished from complexity, and indeed the existence of uncertainty may serve as an indicator that the complexity of a decision-making situation has actually been reduced.
3. See March and Simon (1958) and Nelson and Winter (1982) for discussion of the role of programmes and routines in organizational processes.
4. In the interests of symmetry, it could also be pointed out that since the background of many CEOs tends to be in finance and marketing, they might find initial encounters with a lathe as confusing as lathe operators might find DCF techniques.
5. Developments in fractal geometry made by mathematicians such as Mandelbrot have been drawn on as bases for new research programmes in various areas of science and engineering. The analogy drawn here should not be pushed too far, certainly at this stage, since one feature of fractal analysis, as in the widely publicised Mandelbrot set, is that highly complex patterns at various levels of resolution can be generated from the same simple elements and functions. However, the patterns in such cases tend to be endogenously determined by the underlying mathematical relationships, while in organizations any patterns observed are likely to be at least partly determined by interaction with the environment. There is no guarantee that the environment plays according to the same rules at different levels, and indeed the increasing emphasis on non-programmed decision-making at higher levels may be just one factor impeding neutrality of scale effects across levels. The important point is that a new pattern may become apparent as

the level of resolution varies, irrespective of whether variation is in a micro or macro direction.

6. See, for example, Marks and Miller (1964) and Bower and Springston (1970) for studies showing the effect of experience on the formation of word chunks.
7. For example, see Egan and Schwartz (1979) for chunking in recall of drawings.
8. See chapter 3, 'The psychology of thinking', in Simon, 1981, pp. 62–98.
9. Simon cautions that these parameters should not be regarded as measurable to two decimal places—or even one (p. 78). The full title of Miller's 1956 article gives a flavour of the degree of approximation that may be involved in these calculations. Simon argues that variability may reflect variation in experimental conditions that conceals a genuine parameter whose value may be ascertained once it is known what conditions should be controlled for (p. 78).

   It is not clear what room (if any) such arguments leave for variability in individual cognitive ability as determinants of performance, and Simon points out that questions relating to the stability and precision of parameters typically invite much further work. The important point for immediate purposes is that it is reasonable to argue that such parameters exist and represent limits that generally constrain and shape cognitive performance.
10. See, for example, Mintzberg (1979) and Child (1984), two leading texts that survey the literature on organizational structures and processes. Referencing is heavily biased towards administrative and organizational journals in both cases rather than towards cognitive psychology research. This reflects the research agenda in this field rather than any author bias.
11. This is a criticism made by Simon (1981, pp. 77–8).
12. See, for example, organizational charts of General Electric, Intel, and Hewlett Packard (Mintzberg, 1979, p. 411; Mintzberg and Quinn, 1991, pp. 191 and 468–9, respectively). In each case the analysis of headquarters, group, and divisional activities shows the layering and clustering effects discussed below.

12.   Strategy and Structure

In this chapter, we shall outline an approach to issues of organization design that helps to develop an integrated perspective dealing with a variety of organizational forms. These include hybrid structures such as matrix organization, as well as standard functional and divisional forms of organization. We shall look particularly at problems involving multinational enterprise, not just because of an interest in international activities *per se*, but also because organization design issues in the multinational tend to operate at an order of complexity greater than those involving purely domestic strategies. We shall focus particularly on relationships between the various resources utilized by the firm. It will be suggested that it will be helpful to distinguish between just two basic kinds of resource relationships, and that in conjunction with a simple rule these can help to provide a basis for analysing the logic of various forms of organization.

In the previous chapter, we looked at the role of hierarchy as a device for handling complexity and arranging decision-making capabilities in levels or layers within the firm. In this chapter we extend this analysis and look at how hierarchies may evolve in practice, and especially the role of linkages in influencing these patterns. The starting point is that the expansion of the organization and bounded rationality considerations can mean the sub-division and delegation of activities to permit the organization to function effectively. In turn, this progressive slicing up of activities leads to the elaboration of hierarchy and evolution of organizational layers of decision-making as we saw in the last chapter. One problem can be characterized in terms of the decision as to *when* to slice, which involves questions of span of control (or number of subordinates reporting to a manager), which in turn raises questions of how deep or shallow the layering of tasks in an organization should be (Williamson, 1967; Mintzberg, 1979; Child, 1984). This has implications for how flat or tall the organization should be. Whilst there has been a considerable degree of interest in recent years in terms of how new information technology may 'de-layer' and flatten organizational hierarchies, in practice large organizations are still organized around hierarchical principles. A second major problem involves *where* to slice, and the question of how best to group activities potentially affected by the slicing process. Slicing does not necessarily prevent integration of separated activities, but it does make it more difficult.[1] Efficiency considerations suggest that the slicing process should cut along lines characterized by relatively weak interactions, whilst keeping together areas where there are relatively strong interactions.

We shall be looking at the question of where to slice in this chapter. As far as the hierarchy of the firm is concerned, it is the early work of Chandler (1962) as interpreted by Williamson (1975) which has helped to shape and inform debate in this area. The major concern here has been with the efficiency implications of unitary or U-form structures (sliced into functions) versus multidivisional or M-form structures (sliced into divisions based around products, regions, or processes). Williamson's multidivisional hypothesis states that: 'the organization and operation of the large enterprise along the lines of the M-form favors goal pursuit and least-cost behavior more nearly associated with the neoclassical profit maximization hypothesis than does the U-form organizational alternative' (1975, p. 150). Williamson (1975) points out that adoption of the M-form structure can help separate out strategy-formulating from operational activities, and can help free up top management to specialize in the former role. It may also permit the creation of an internal capital market within the firm, and enhance auditing and control of the various businesses operated by the large diversified firm.[2] A number of empirical tests of the M-form hypothesis have been carried out (e.g. Steer and Cable, 1978; Armour and Teece, 1978; Thompson, 1981).[3] In addition, there have been parallel studies in the managerial literature concerned with the relationship between strategy and structure, again typically focusing on the implications of divisionalization for the performance of firms (e.g. Channon, 1973; Dyas and Thanheiser, 1976; Rumelt, 1986). The results have typically been consistent with the general conclusion that adoption of a divisionalized structure does lead to enhanced performance in the large diversified firm. A further line of research whose origins can also be traced back to Chandler is concerned with the strategy and structure of the multinational enterprise: Egelhoff (1988) and Habib and Victor (1991) provide surveys of this literature.

These studies and results provide valuable evidence, but a problem with the transaction cost perspective is that it is difficult for it to say much about organizational design beyond comparison of the relative merits of M-form organization over U-form organization for the large diversified firm. We have noted earlier that the emphasis on asset specificity limits the applicability of the transaction cost framework in the area of strategy, and the same point holds in the context of structure or hierarchy. The emphasis on asset specificity as a foundation stone for Williamson's version of transaction cost economics means that it is not applicable to the case of the large diversified firm exploiting market or technological linkages (asset non-specificities) between its various businesses. Since it is difficult to conceive of any large firm that does not attempt to exploit such linkages (possibly within divisions in the case of a pure conglomerate), such self-imposed restrictions may be regarded as limiting the relevance of the framework.[4]

In this approach, we shall again focus on the two basic relations between resources discussed and analysed earlier; synergy and complementarity. *Synergy* and corresponding economies of scope may be obtained by sharing resources between different economic activities. It has been defined as the 'effect which can produce a combined return on the firm's resources greater than the sum of its parts' (Ansoff, 1987, p. 82). Ansoff's use of the concept makes it clear that it is intended to apply to situations in which different activities exploit economies through shared resources, such as common marketing and distribution effort; shared plant, equipment, materials or labour force; joint R&D; or transferable managerial skills (Ansoff, 1987, pp. 82–3). The comprehensive listing by Ansoff (pp. 82–3) of the types of resources that might provide synergy suggests that virtually any resource may be a source of synergy. *Complementarity* exists when different resources contribute in combination to economic activity. This is similar to Teece's (1987*a*) use of the concept of complementary assets in the context of generation of technological innovation. However, complementary relationships between resources are more general and not restricted to innovative activity. Here, complementarity means different resources can contribute to the conduct of a specific business; synergy means a specific resource can contribute to the conduct of different businesses. Gains from complementarity and synergy may both need coordination, which provides us with the starting point for our analysis of hierarchy.[5] Further, in Chapter 5 we introduced the notion of strong patterns involving consistency in linkaging over the whole of corporate strategy; we shall see that organizational design is generally facilitated if strategies exhibit strong patterns. More specifically, it will be found that slicing rules are simplified if linkages are coherent along the lines discussed in Chapter 7.

In section 12.1 we shall look at the issues of synergy and complementarity and introduce a simple principle that will help make sense of a variety of organizational structures. We then look at the problems involved in the decomposition of various strategies into different organizational designs in section 12.2. Section 12.3 reviews some problems posed by the evolution of multinational enterprise for organizational design and section 12.4 looks at the matrix solution in this context.

12.1. Interactions between Bundles of Resources in the Firm

An example may help illustrate the role of synergy and complementarity in coordinating resources. Suppose a sports goods manufacture producing and selling sports goods in the UK has three main products; soccer balls, rugby balls, and volleyballs. Each of the company's three product-markets draws upon resources that can be labelled sales, production, or R&D resources. There are therefore nine possible discrete categorizations or bundles of resource activity if they are broken down both by product-market and

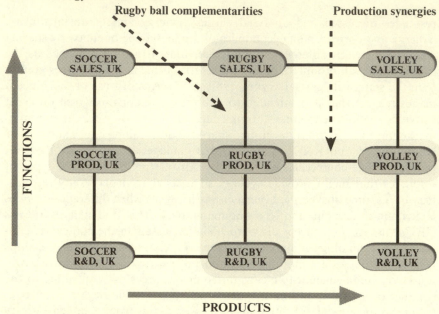

Fig. 12.1. Synergy and complementarity

functional orientation, for example soccer sales, volleyball R&D, and so on. These breakdowns are shown in Fig. 12.1.

As Fig. 12.1 illustrates, there are two major ways that resources can inter- act with other resources. First, producing a particular product will gener- ally require co-operative activity at various stages between functional specialists, for example rugby R&D and rugby production may need to jointly plan the implementation of new designs into production, while rugby R&D and rugby sales may have to coordinate how best to develop and market innovative designs. These *complementary* relationships obtain through the interaction of resource categories within the columns in Fig. 12.1, with the shaded column illustrating the range of related resources that might provide complementary relationships, for the example of rugby balls. Secondly, there are potential interactions within functional categories that may generate synergies or economies; for example economies in production may be exploited across all three product-markets through the sharing of plant, equipment, labour force, and production management skills. These relationships based on *similarity* in resource characteristics obtain through the sharing of resources in Fig. 12.1, with the shaded row illustrating the range of resource categories that may provide shared resources in the exam- ple of production synergies for the three product-markets.

In the early stages of the development of an organization, these interac- tions may be dealt with on an *ad hoc* basis. If the firm is little more than an entrepreneur and some assistants, then coordination can be facilitated by one individual having the overview necessary to give appropriate weightings to the priorities and trade-offs involved in attending to the more significant complementary and synergistic relationships, as needs arise. However, as the organization expands, bounded rationality considerations encourage the development of hierarchy and delegated decisions if the top decision-making level is not to be swamped by information overload (Simon, 1981; Williamson, 1975). This is a well established argument for the development of hierarchy (Mintzberg, 1979, pp. 1–2); the issue that concerns us here is not whether corporate expansion leads to a development of hierarchy, but *how* the hierarchy should develop.

One obvious decomposition of the various bundles of resources in Fig. 12.1 would be to provide a section manager for each of the nine bundles of resources in Fig. 12.1, and have him or her report directly to the chief executive. However, the price of such extreme decomposition would be to cut across two sets of interactions for each resource bundle; complementary relations with other functions, and synergistic relations with other products where similar resource characteristics exist. This does not mean that such relations cannot now be coordinated, but the effect of separating the respective resource bundles into separate sections is generally to place barriers to such coordination and integration. Coordination of resources is generally easier within sections rather than between. An extreme decomposition of this kind would also still leave top management having to coordinate the various interdependencies between sections, or set up mechanisms for doing so.

A further possibility would be to decompose around one category of relations. For example, three sections could be created around functions (the rows in Fig. 12.1) to exploit synergistic relations and form a functional or U-form structure (Williamson, 1975) as in Fig. 12.2(a). This would reduce the information load on top management as far as these decisions are concerned, but it would also cut across complementary relations and could impede the coordination of decisions at product level. Alternatively, three sections or divisions could be created around products (the columns in Fig. 12.1) to coordinate complementary relations, and so form a multidivisional or M-form structure (Williamson, 1975) as in Fig. 12.2(b). The M-form also provides particular advantages over the U-form in terms of the separation of senior management from functional concerns. They now have the capability to focus on strategy formulation and oversee the operation of an internal capital market based around divisions as profit centres (Williamson, 1975, pp. 132–54). However, these gains are predicated on the assumption that the diversified firm can be treated as a highly decomposable system, an assumption which may be reasonable in the case of the conglomerate but not necessarily in the case of other diversified strategies. In the case of related diversification, the M-form solution would cut across synergistic relations and impede their coordination.

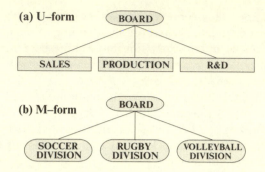

Fig. 12.2. Two organizational solutions for the sports goods manufacturer

The fundamental point is that whatever form of hierarchy is imposed on a richly interacting system as in Fig. 12.1, there is generally a price to pay as a consequence of the erection of barriers to potential interaction between sub-systems. This is a point that is well recognized in organization theory; as Mintzberg (1979, p. 119) points out (following Thompson, 1967) in any hierarchical decomposition 'residual' interdependencies are likely to remain that are not picked up within the chosen groupings. One solution suggested by Thompson and Mintzberg is that these residual interdependencies must be picked up in higher level groupings, and this is considered below. However, it may also be the case that a particular grouping means that the firm never gets around to integrating residual interdependencies at any level in the firm; for example, divisional competition may make it impossible or too costly to coordinate potential synergy connections across different divisions within the M-form internal capital market. Whether a particular grouping prevents or simply impedes the coordination of residual interdependencies, the point is that residual interdependencies contribute to the price of any specific decomposition.

Thus, the U-form facilitates the exploitation of synergistic relations within functions, but is not well adapted to deal with complementary relations; correspondingly, the M-form is well suited for exploiting complementary relations within divisions, but can impede the coordination of synergistic relations. Such a conclusion accords with the general economic observation that there is no such thing as a free lunch; the price of any form of hierarchical arrangement includes the opportunity cost of any interactions it may impede. However, while much of Williamson's analysis of the problems of the expansion and growth of corporations can be read as confirming the price of U-form organization, the parallel proposition that there is also a price to pay for M-form organization is not well developed in this approach (see Williamson, 1975, pp. 132–75; and 1985, pp. 273–97). This is understandable given the emphasis on the conglomerate as the archetypical form of diversified firm in transaction cost economics; by definition, synergistic interactions between divisions are weak or non-existent in such a strategy, and therefore the opportunity cost of sacrificed synergy is correspondingly low or negligible. If the only large firm strategies recognized are weakly interacting in terms of synergy, then it is not surprising that the opportunity costs of M-form organization are relatively neglected in transaction cost economics.[6] However, even for extremely large diversified firms, the conglomerate is a relatively unusual strategy. Rumelt (1986) found evidence of conglomerate strategies in the USA over the early post-war period, but even large diversifiers tended to emphasize related rather than unrelated expansion.[7]

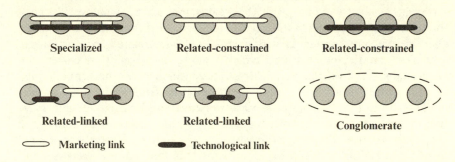

<table>
<tr><td>Specialized</td><td>Related-constrained</td><td>Related-constrained</td></tr>
<tr><td>Related-linked</td><td>Related-linked</td><td>Conglomerate</td></tr>
</table>

⊂⊃ Marketing link   ⬤➡ Technological link

Fig. 12.3. Large firm strategies

Figure 12.3 provides an interpretation of the major varieties of large firm strategies found by Rumelt that we have discussed earlier. So far we do not have a basis for predicting what form of organizational structure would be appropriate for the various strategies outlined in Fig. 12.3. We have argued that whatever hierarchical decomposition is used, there is likely to be a price to pay. However, what is likely to influence the choice of organizational structure in particular circumstances? For example, Fig. 12.2 outlines two possible decompositions for the sports goods manufacturer. Both will involve cutting across one or other set of relationships; what is likely to influence organizational design in such a case?

The principle that we shall start with here is that in terms of adding value to the firm, *when activities are strongly related, synergistic relations will dominate complementary relations.* For example, if we can assume that there are strong marketing (sales) and technological (production and R&D) linkages between all three businesses operated by the sports goods manufacturer, then there will be more interactions within functions (and between products) than within products (and between functions). A given functional specialist is likely to have more need to coordinate decisions on a day-to-day basis with colleagues within the same function, than with colleagues from other functions but responsible for the same business. This suggests that the resource bundles along the rows in Fig. 12.1 can be treated as richly interacting, whilst the resource bundles along the columns can be treated as weakly interacting, relatively speaking.

12.2. Organization Design and the Decomposition of Strategies

The implication of the 'synergy dominates complementarity' principle is that it suggests that organizational design will be driven by the existence or absence of potential synergy. Complementarity is likely to be a standard feature of corporate organization; the different functions responsible for a particular product would typically be weakly interacting, whatever the corporate strategy. Businesses still need to be run and functions coordinated, whether they are conducted within conglomerate, related, or specialized strategies. On the other hand, synergy may vary from non-existent to strong, depending on the particular strategy pursued by the firm. In Fig. 12.3 this would mean that each of the four businesses run by the six firms would exhibit (weak) complementary relations at business or product-market level. At the same time, there are veins of market or technological relatedness in all but the conglomerate strategy that encourage strong synergistic interactions within the relevant functions (and across businesses). If pressures on top decision-making levels also require the development of hierarchy, then these considerations suggest that the appropriate basis for hierarchical decomposition may vary from strategy to strategy.

Fig. 12.4. Conglomerate strategies and the M-form

The simplest possible case is represented by the conglomerate strategy. In view of the fact that the conglomerate is generally regarded as a complex strategy that appears in the later stages of corporate evolution (Mintzberg, 1979, pp. 412–18) such a conclusion might seem surprising at first sight, and it might seem strange to begin with this strategy. However, whilst the conglomerate is complex relative to specialized alternatives as in Fig. 12.3 when viewed in terms of the *varieties of competencies* required to operate it, it is extremely simple relative to the same alternative when analysed in terms of the *interactions between resource bundles*. The only interactions that are of relevance in this context are the weak complementary relationships between functions and within businesses. Since relatedness is absent, so also is potential synergy; consequently the weakly complementary functions become (if only by default) the dominant consideration in organizational design, and the natural foci around which to form decision making units. This is illustrated in Fig. 12.4. The decomposition of the firm into business units puts together the resource bundles that do need to interact, and the result is the formation of an M-form structure as described by Williamson. M-form organization may also enable top management to assess the performance of each component division within the wider internal capital market of the corporation, as Williamson (1975) suggests. In terms of the opportunity costs of hierarchical organization discussed above, the conglomerate M-form structure comes the closest to a free good since its decision units cut across little, if any, linkages and relationships.

Fig. 12.5. Specialized strategies and the U-form

The specialized strategy adds synergy relations to the complementary relations involved in the conglomerate strategy, with the added complication discussed earlier that each resource bundle is now involved in two sets of potential relations; synergistic and complementary interactions. In this case, our assumption that synergy dominates complementary considerations in strongly related strategies suggests that the first preference in such circumstances would be for a decomposition around functions rather than businesses, the U-form solution of the type illustrated in Fig. 12.5. Such a breakdown would facilitate the exploitation of strong synergy relations within such functions as sales, production, and R&D for the specialized strategy in Fig. 12.3. The price of such a decomposition in the case of the specialized firm is that it would cut across complementary relations and impede product level coordination. However, a decomposition according to M-form principles would only create decision units around the weaker complementary relations, and there would be a higher price to pay in that an M-form decomposition by businesses would cut across the rich synergy links. Consequently, in the case of the specialized firm, the M-form alternative would be likely to generate less benefits and involve a higher price than the U-form solution. The U-form structure is therefore likely to be preferred in such circumstances.

The picture is less clear when we consider the related-constrained and related-linked strategies, and we shall consider both in turn. The related-constrained strategy exploits a major linkage such as the marketing or technological linkages illustrated in Fig. 12.5. However, unmodified M-form and U-form solutions would both encounter difficulties in accommodating such a strategy. For example, in the case of the related-constrained strategy that exploits marketing linkages across businesses, the M-form structure would assist the coordination of complementary relations, but it would also cut across the marketing linkage. Also, in this case, the U-form structure would facilitate the exploitation of the marketing synergies, but in addition to cutting across complementary relations, it would also lump together a disparate and unrelated bunch of technological competencies in the production and R&D functions. Similar problems exist for the related-constrained strategy linked together through a shared technological theme; the M-form structure again cuts across a strong synergistic linkage, while the U-form structure puts together an agglomeration of activities with no common sales or distribution characteristics within the one marketing function.

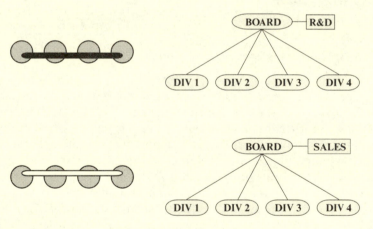

Fig. 12.6. Related-constrained strategies and hybrid organizations

One possible solution is a hybrid form of organization that selectively incorporates features drawn from M-form and U-form structures, as in Fig. 12.6. This bolts a specialist functional department reporting directly to top management on to a basic M-form structure. In the case of the marketing based related-constrained strategy, this could be a corporate level sales or marketing department, while in the case of the technologically based related-constrained strategy it could be a corporate level department concerned with technological development. Such solutions are reflected in the various divisionalized firms which have given corporate level marketing or R&D departments responsibility for activities spanning a substantial proportion of corporate activities. In principle, such a solution offers the possibility of firms having their cake and eating it, with at least some complementary relations being coordinated within product-market divisions, and strong synergistic relations being coordinated by the specialist corporate level department. In practice, there is still likely to be a price to pay; the removal of all or part of one major function from divisions will make it difficult to coordinate the complementary relations in which it should be involved, whilst the introduction of a function shared across businesses will make it more difficult to separately assess the performance of each division within the M-form internal capital market. Nevertheless, the widespread adoption of corporate level marketing and R&D departments by many firms suggests that this is deemed to be a price worth paying in certain circumstances.[8]

However, if the related-constrained strategy poses problems for design of hierarchy, they are minor compared to the issues raised by related-linked strategies. First of all, it must be borne in mind that the related-linked strategy is one which has been extremely popular amongst large corporations (Rumelt, 1986), and it has intrinsically desirable properties seen from the perspective of design of strategy (Kay, 1984). It is when consideration is given to design of organizational structure that potentially severe problems become apparent. This can be seen from the perspective of the two related-linked firms discussed earlier, and reproduced again in Fig. 12.7.

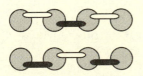

CORRESPONDING ORGANIZATIONAL FORMS?

Fig. 12.7. Simple related-linked strategies and the problem of organizational form

The fundamental problem involved in designing a structure for a related-linked strategy is that it is richly linked, but erratically so. The two firms in Fig. 12.7 exploit a series of short range links that extend over a limited domain of the respective firms businesses in each case. First, an M-form solution in either case would cut across rich marketing and technological links in each case and impede the coordination of synergistic relations. However, any U-form solution would finish up with an assortment of unrelated competencies within each function, as well as cutting across complementary relations. Further, the hybrid structures (Fig. 12.6) that may be applicable in the case of the related-constrained strategy turn out to be no solution in this case, since no single linkage extends far enough over the corporate strategy to make it worthwhile taking out at corporate level. There are no simple or obvious organizational solutions to the related-linked strategies outlined in Fig. 12.7.

However, the related-linked strategy observed by Rumelt is one that was adopted by extremely large corporations. This raises a further possibility that may not be appropriate for the simple four-business strategies outlined in Fig. 12.3; the expansion of the firm may require the addition of further levels in the corporate hierarchy, which in turn may provide opportunities for the exploitation of limited or localized linkages at group level within the firm. Such possibilities are illustrated in Fig. 12.8 for a nine business related-linked firm in Fig. 12.8 in which a technological link extends over four businesses, a marketing link extends over another set of four businesses, and a further technological link joins three businesses. Two businesses joined by the marketing link also have technological bases that bridge the rest of the firm to the technologically linked businesses.

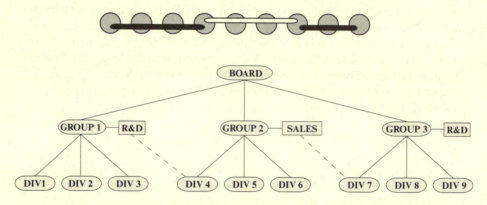

Fig. 12.8. Complex related-linked strategy and hybrid organization

Figure 12.8 shows one possible approach to the problem of this related-linked strategy. The essence of the solution is that clusters of businesses are treated as related-constrained strategies at group level within the corporation. This permits each group to adopt hybrid solutions of the type outlined in Fig. 12.6 at group level; this version shows three sets of divisions forming three separate groups, with the three different synergistic linkages reflected in specialist functions reporting to the respective group management. There are therefore three tiers of management illustrated in Fig. 12.8; corporate, group, and divisional levels. One additional problem is what should be done with the two divisions (divisions 4 and 7 in the organizational chart) that share both marketing and technological linkages with other clusters; in this version, division 4 is assigned to the marketing-linked Group 2, while division 7 is assigned to the technologically-linked Group 3. It may be possible to set up some formal or informal mechanisms to coordinate the synergy link being cut across by group formation in the respective cases, and these possibilities are indicated in Fig. 12.8 by dotted lines connecting the relevant sections.

This solution is consistent with Thompson's (1967) and Mintzberg's (1979, p. 119) observations that once a particular decomposition is chosen, residual interdependencies may be dealt with by shifting them upstairs to become the responsibility of a higher level grouping within the corporation. It means that the groups can operate as modified M-forms along the lines of solutions outlined in Fig. 12.6, facilitating the coordination of some complementary relations, as well as the synergy-rich link in the respective cases. In turn, the groups can themselves be treated as higher level divisions in their own right, the result being the formation of a super M-form at corporate level. The logic of M-form organization can therefore be imposed on two tiers in this corporation. Such an approach builds on the nesting of related-constrained structures at group level within groups reporting to corporate level. This is similar to the nesting of U-form structures within M-form divisions (Williamson, 1975, pp. 136–7),[9] and indeed if the hierarchical level one below divisions was opened up in Fig. 12.8, it would reveal divisions composed of complementary functions arranged into U-form structures. The formation of groups simply takes the layering possibilities of hierarchy one stage further as the expansion of firms encourages the parallel development of complex hierarchy. We would expect layering to follow the principles set out in Chapter 11.

As with most of the other solutions discussed above, this does not eliminate cutting across synergistic or complementary relations, but it does provide a basis through which hierarchical layering can keep such barriers within manageable bounds. The crucial issue is the opportunity cost of the best alternative solution; the tiered solution may be costly to administer, but if it is more effective than alternatives such as single tier M-form and U-form structures, then we would expect to see it being developed by large diversified corporations. An example of such tiering is provided by Hewlett Packard, which in 1982 had several tiers ranging up from operating divisions, through groups[10] to corporate level (Mintzberg and Quinn, 1991). As in the example above, some specialist functions reported to management of lower level clusters of divisions or groups (e.g. Instrument Marketing spanning both Microwave and Communication Instruments, and Electronic Measurements), while some functions spanned sufficient of the firm's interests to report to corporate level (e.g. HP Laboratories).

The fundamental problem of organizational design that tends to recur in these examples is that resource bundles tend to need to interact with more than one other set of resource bundles in the typical organization. As a consequence, whatever decomposition is chosen, it will create barriers to coordinating interactions across the sections created by the particular decomposition. In the next section these problems will be seen in their most extreme form when we look at multinational enterprise and the role of organizational structure.

12.3. Multinational Enterprise and Organization Design

The problem of the appropriate organizational structure for the sports goods manufacturer discussed in Fig. 12.1 raised the issue of how conflicting demands and relations can best be resolved by different hierarchical alternatives. Each resource bundle or section in Fig. 12.1 had sets of complementary and synergistic relations that hierarchy may both facilitate or impede. These were analysed in two dimensions in Fig. 12.1. However, suppose the sports goods manufacturer now decides to pursue a multinational strategy and sets up facilities in both the USA and France to supply these markets. This adds a further dimension to corporate activity, and Fig. 12.9 provides an outline of the potential interdependencies that may be involved in such a case. The original domestic activities for the sports goods manufacturer now represent the front of the cube in Fig. 12.9, whilst the new multinational activities extend the firm's activities along the regions dimension.

There are three dimensions in Fig. 12.9. The *vertical* dimension arranges resource bundles by types of function, and traces potential complementary relations. The two horizontal dimensions trace potential synergistic relations that may be exploited through resource sharing. The *lateral* or products dimension traces the types of synergistic relations that may be exploited

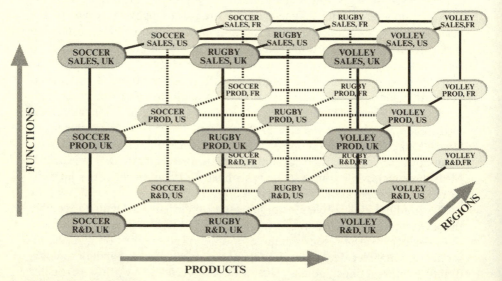

Fig. 12.9. Multinational enterprise and the matrix structure

domestically, while the *interior* or regions dimension traces the categories of know-how or competencies that a multinational can transfer internationally. To the extent that a great deal of country-specific customization is required, the various boxes representing individual country resource bundles will be quite active. On the other hand, in cases where there is a high degree of resource sharing, some of the region boxes may be virtually empty; for example, many multinationals concentrate R&D activities around home country headquarters. Here we assume that there is a non-trivial amount of activity associated with each of the twenty-seven possible resource bundles or sections broken down by products, functions, and regions. In those circumstances, Fig. 12.9 indicates that each resource bundle has three possible sets of interactions with other resource bundles; complementary relations along the vertical dimension for a given product and country, domestic synergistic relations along the lateral dimension for a specific function, and international synergistic relations along the interior dimension again for a given function. Figure 12.10 shows the coordination problem that this involves for two selected resource bundles, US rugby ball production and French volleyball sales.

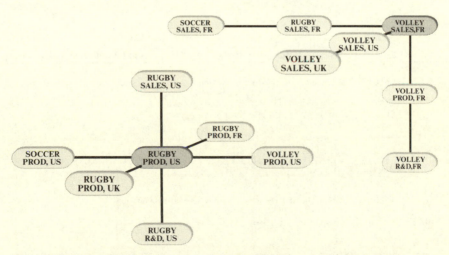

Fig. 12.10. Relations involving two selected sections in a matrix structure

In the case of rugby ball production in the USA, managers may have to coordinate complementary relations with other US based functions responsible for rugby balls (the vertical dimension), whilst there may be domestic synergies available from coordinating all types of sports ball manufacturing (the lateral dimension) and advantages in sharing know-how internationally in how to produce rugby balls (the interior dimension). Similarly, those responsible for French volleyball sales may have need to coordinate activities with other complementary French functions responsible for volleyballs, while there may be economies from synchronizing sales activities with other French sports products, and in transferring expertise internationally in how to market volleyballs. Similar exercises can be conducted for the other bundles of resources in Fig. 12.9.

Just as there was a need to coordinate resources along different dimensions in Fig. 12.1, so there is a corresponding need for the various resource bundles represented in Fig. 12.9. The difference in this case is that there is a need for coordination to take place over three dimensions rather than two. One set of solutions would simply give priority to the most significant linkages as in the M-form and U-form solutions in Fig. 12.2, recognizing that some weaker linkages may be impeded. For example, one solution that the sports goods manufacturer might find attractive in the early stages of multinational expansion is to give an international division responsibility for the firm's overseas activities. This division is simply pasted on to the existing home based U-form or M-form structure as in Fig. 12.11. It requires that activities cleave naturally into 'home'/'not home' categories, which may be a particular problem in practice.

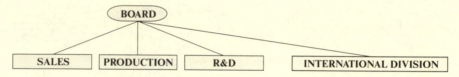

FIGURE 12.11a: The U-form structure with international division

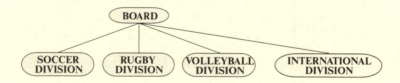

FIGURE 12.11b: The M-form structure with international division

Fig. 12.11. The international division

The ability of the international division to cope with its responsibilities is likely to be strained by product and regional diversity. It may work as a holding measure as long as overseas activities are of minor importance compared to the firm's home based activities.[11] However, whether the international division is grafted on to a U-form structure or an M-form structure, multinational expansion is likely to pose problems for the international division. In the case of the sports goods manufacturer, a U-form or an M-form solution as in Fig. 12.2 would have split the firm into three units comprising three domestic resource bundles from Fig. 12.1. Adopting the international division solution to deal with the multinational case shown in Fig. 12.9 would leave the domestic groupings essentially undisturbed, but would require the international division to mop up the other eighteen resource bundles. In this case, such a solution can militate against transfers of know-how to overseas businesses, as well as putting a large and diverse range of responsibilities under the 'international' umbrella. Dunning (1993, p. 217) gives Xerox, Bristol Myers, and DuPont as examples of corporations that continue to organize their foreign activities primarily by way of an international division.

Based on a study of the expansion strategies of 187 multinationals, Stopford and Wells (1972) put forward a stages model for multinational expansion. At low levels of overseas sales, the international division solution may be adopted as an interim measure. As the multinational expands, the scale and diversity of overseas activities eventually put too high a strain on the ability of the international division to cope with its responsibilities. At this point, multinationals tend to opt for one of two options according to Stopford and Wells; regionally based international divisions, or global divisions based around products. In the case of the sports goods manufacturer, this is tantamount to slicing the cube in Fig. 12.9 in two alternative directions, rather in the manner of slices of salami. If the organizational salami slicer cuts in an interior (regions) direction, we have slices by area or country. This is illustrated in Fig. 12.12. Here we are dealing only with the important first cuts; clearly the full organizational design will require further decomposition within particular regional boundaries.

The region slices may constitute divisions or groups in their own right, and each may answer directly to senior management within the reconstituted firm. As Stopford and Wells (1972) indicate, area or region salami may be preferred if there is relatively low diversity of foreign products, and this is consistent with its relative popularity in the oil, tobacco, food processing, and branch banking sectors (Dunning, 1993, p. 217). In our example of the sports goods manufacturer, there probably would be a high degree of product relatedness between the various products operated by the firm in an area or region, and this synergy consideration might dominate the direction of slicing in favour of region salami. Region salami is sensitive to product level synergies in that it puts potentially strongly interacting products into the same basket. On the other hand, region salami cuts across cross-regional relationships within the same function and product, and may impede international transfers of know-how by function or product. As an example of an area based division structure, Channon and Jalland (1979, pp. 36–7) give the example of Ford which adopted the form in the late sixties, after first basing overseas expansion on an international division structure. Dunning (1993, p. 217) also gives Pfizer, CPC International, and Barclays Bank International as examples.

The alternative major route to multinational expansion is global divisions based around products. Here the salami slicer operates in a lateral (products) direction as in Fig. 12.13. The logic here is that the resulting

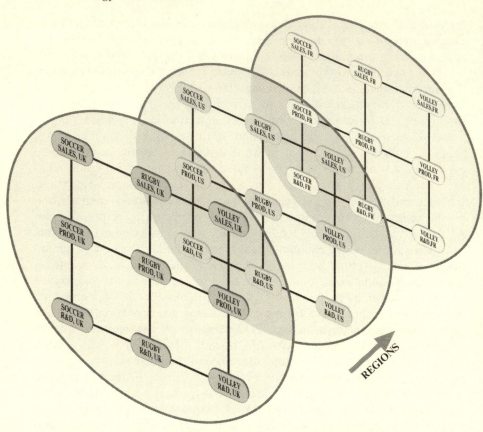

Fig. 12.12. Area salami: regionally based international subsidiaries

slices facilitate the integration of functional and international relationships for a given product. However, it cuts across the potentially synergistic relationships that may exist between products, and makes it hard to coordinate these on a country by country basis. That is why this solution tends to be adopted when there is a high degree of diversity of overseas products operated by the multinational; it is not that there is a sudden need to coordinate relationships operating at product level, rather that the cross-product synergistic pressures that dominated organizational design considerations in Fig. 12.12 tend to be much weaker in such circumstances. The focus of organizational design accordingly switches to the residual product-oriented complementary and international relationships as the multinational extends its M-form structure to incorporate overseas activities within the respective product divisions. Channon and Jalland (1979, p. 33) give the early example of RCA who made the transition from an international division to a worldwide product division structure in the late sixties. Contemporary

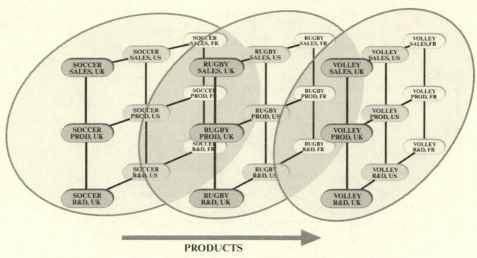

PRODUCTS

Fig. 12.13. Product salami: global product or integrated structure

examples of firms that have adopted worldwide product division structures include Rockwell International, Colgate, Sperry, Thomson Brandt, and General Electric (Dunning, 1993, p. 217)

However, it will be remembered from earlier discussion that the M-form cuts across intra-functional linkages, and the same is true of an M-form operated on an international basis. If the multinational is so specialized that a U-form structure is still appropriate for its domestic operations, then it may extend this function based logic into its overseas operations. In these circumstances, the organizational salami slicer cuts in a vertical direction and its first cuts keep all resource bundles for a given function together. The global functional structure is dominated by synergy considerations, and complementary relations may be subverted to the drive to coordinate synergy internationally. Function salami cuts across the complementary relations involved in operating any product and may impede integration of product level activities. A global U-form as in Fig. 12.14 is the exception rather than the rule amongst multinationals (Dunning, 1993, p. 217), probably because they tend to be large and diversified with a natural bias towards M-form structures. Firms that adopted the global functional structure have included John Deere (Channon and Jalland, 1979, p. 29), SKF, Caterpillar Tractor, and Lockheed (Dunning, 1993, p. 217).

As discussed earlier, there is a price to pay for each organizational solution. Each of the three salami cases are intended to decompose the corporation around those resource bundles displaying the most significant interactions in the respective cases. In each case the decomposition cuts across relations that run between the groupings that have been created by the first set of cuts. The most efficient solution will partly depend on the

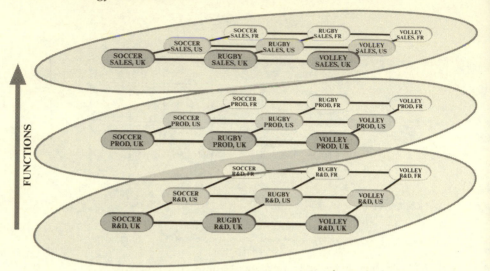

FUNCTIONS

Fig. 12.14. Function salami: global functional structure

relative intensity of the complementary and synergistic relations in the respective cases. However, in the stages model, the continued expansion of the multinational is likely to be accompanied by further diversification, both at product and geographical levels (Bartlett, 1986, p. 368). If the firm has opted for region salami, this is likely to place further strain on product level integration; if it has opted for product salami, it may find integration of activities within regions increasingly difficult. Whichever form of cut has been chosen, the price (in the form of the opportunity cost of impeded relations) tends to rise with multinational expansion. One structure which appears as a candidate solution to such circumstances in the stages model is matrix organization (Bartlett, 1986, p. 368). We shall look at this alternative in the next section.

12.4. Multinational Enterprise and the Matrix Structure

Matrix organization introduces new principles of hierarchical decomposition in addition to those discussed above. Each of the three salami cutting exercises discussed above made their cuts along *one* specific dimension. Further cuts at lower levels may shift the axis of slicing; for example, region salami may first form area groupings, each of which may be cut into product divisions, each of which may then be sliced in turn into functionally organized departments. Complex organizations may cut along any or all of the different dimensions as moves are made up or down the hierarchy. However, in such cases, there tends to be a consistent direction in terms of salami slicing at a given level in the hierarchy. What distinguishes the matrix from all the other solutions discussed above is *simultaneous* cutting of the organization along different dimensions at a given level.

In Figs. 12.12, 12.13, and 12.14 the salami slicer works in one consistent direction before possibly switching dimensions as it moves through lower levels in the respective cases. However, suppose integration of relations involved in all three dimensions were regarded as being of sufficient importance to justify salami slicing in their favour in each case; how could this be done, and how could the organization operate in such circumstances?

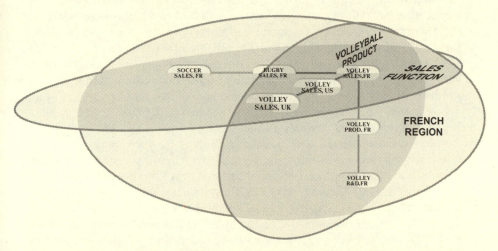

Fig. 12.15. Matrix management from the perspective of an individual section

In the case of our multinational sports goods manufacturer, a matrix solution could involve slicing the cube in Fig. 12.9 along all vertical, lateral, and interior dimensions simultaneously. Figure 12.15 illustrates this for the case of the volleyball/sales/France resource bundle; similar exercises could be carried out for all the other resource bundles in the firm. The figure traces the function, product, and region slices specific to this particular resource bundle. Each slice will have its own structure and system of coordinating the nine resource bundles it is responsible for. However, whatever structure is adopted within slices, the volleyball/sales/France section now has three 'homes' within the firm: function, product, and region homes. The management of this section are answerable to three different lines of authority, the particular pattern of reporting reflecting the form of organization adopted within each of the three relevant slices. Further, the areas of responsibility overlap; for example 'Volleyball Product' has responsibility for volleyball sales, as does 'Sales Function'. The benefits of simultaneous slicing in the matrix form is that it avoids separating richly interconnected resource bundles as in area, product, and function salami. The problem for lower level sections such as the volleyball/sales/France resource bundle is that they now report directly to different streams of overlapping authority within the firm. Such a complex organizational structure is costly in terms of managerial time and resources, and can create confusing and ambiguous lines of authority.[12]

An example of a three dimensional matrix structure operated by Dow Corning is provided by Mintzberg (1979, p. 173). Dow Corning also cut its matrix into product, function, and region dimensions with region and product slices acting as profit centres, and the function slices acting as cost centres. This echoes the typical treatment of area and product divisions within the M-form, and function treatment within the U-form. A similar product, function, and region matrix structure is operated by Ciba Geigy (Dunning, 1993, pp. 219–20). However, this does not exhaust dimensional possibilities, with Shell in the 1990s reportedly running a matrix structure cut into region, product, function and operating company dimensions (Johnson and Scholes, 1993, p. 352). A four dimensional matrix of this nature pushes beyond the graphic capabilities developed here.

It has been suggested that there are dangers in developing an overly mechanistic approach to imposing formal structures associated with these complex structures, and that the international firm in many cases has been moving towards developing more flexible systems of managing interdependencies between units (Bartlett, 1986). The firm in some cases operates more like an integrated network of cooperative relationships (Bartlett, 1986, p. 381; Dunning, 1993, p. 220) in which connections may follow guide lines of complementary and synergistic relations as in Fig. 12.9. The network organization has become the subject of much recent research[13] and introduces major new issues of management and organization. For our purposes here, it is sufficient to note that this reinforces the point that there is not necessarily just one set of templates that can be drawn upon to deal with issues of organizational design. The basic problem tends to be the same in all cases however; how to balance the trade-offs involved in facilitating some interdependencies while potentially impeding others. Bartlett also emphasizes (1993, p. 369) the importance of company heritage and history in constraining what is possible or desirable in organizational design terms. This is an important point which suggests that organizational structure may be path dependent. What looks like a logical solution seen from the perspective of interdependencies may turn out to be problematic given a particular company's style and traditions.

Finally, it can be noted that the introduction of the notion of resource links across businesses in the analysis here has fundamentally changed the way the organizational design problem is looked at compared to transaction cost economics. The design problem in transaction cost economics revolves around the organization of *businesses*, whether it is the small specialized firm adopting a U-form structure, or the conglomerate adopting an M-form structure. In the analysis here the fundamental question revolves around organization of *links*. The typical large firm has to manage a complex web of interactions and has to work out which decomposition will do least harm to these interactions. As we have seen, organizational design is facilitated if there is some coherent pattern of linkages that allows hierarchical decomposition to proceed in an orderly and consistent fashion. However, organizational solution will typically involve structures which do not look like the ideal types of the U-form and the M-form. The truly general case involves hybrid solutions to complex patterns of linkages and the pure U-form and M-form ideal types are likely to be very much unusual cases, even for coherent strategies exhibiting strong patterns of the type analysed in Chapter 7. This is a contrary view to Hay and Morris's conclusion (1991, p. 309) that 'for general analysis the distinction between U-form and M-form is adequate'. If economic analysis simply concerns itself with the special cases of the U-form and the M-form, then it effectively excludes itself from a number of core issues influencing the efficiency of organizations.

12.5. Conclusions

It has been suggested here that there are two basic kinds of interaction between resources in the firm: interactions based on similarity in resources which can generate economies of scope or synergy, and interactions based on complementarity where different resources in combination contribute to the pursuit of some economic activity. A particular resource or resource bundle may interact with a number of other resources or resource bundles within the firm, and it is this multiplicity of interactions that creates the basic problem for organizational design. As the organization grows, decomposition of the organizational task into sub-tasks becomes necessary for the management of the increasingly complex operations of the firm. However, any particular decomposition will tend to facilitate some interactions between resources (by grouping them together), and impede the ability of other resources to interact (by separating them into different units). The organizational design problem is to handle this trade-off as sensitively as possible by ensuring that priority is given to locating together richly interacting resources. The analysis assumed that significant technological and/or marketing linkages would typically be associated with stronger interactions than complementary relations, and this provided the basis for the subsequent analysis of strategy/hierarchy relationships. The usual corporate strategy involves complex trade-offs even for the best fitting organizational design. Mapping the pattern of linkages in the firm appears to be helpful in understanding the efficiency implications of alternative organizational designs. The analysis helps to show that there is a fundamental unity underlying a large variety of hierarchical solutions in their adherence to simple, shared design principles.

NOTES

1. There is a whole line of research in the organizational field concerned with the problems of integrating the diverse activities of organizations. See in particular Thompson (1967) and Lawrence and Lorsch (1967). See Mintzberg (1979) and Child (1984) for good surveys of this literature and its findings.
2. For an interesting and little known early study that also interprets Chandler's work in terms of the efficiency implications of U-form and M-form structures, see Ansoff and Brandenburg (1971, *a* and *b*). Ansoff and Brandenburg are more circumspect regarding the supposed efficiency advantages provided by the M-form over the U-form, and their analysis of efficiency considerations in terms of trade-offs is close to the spirit in which our analysis is developed.
3. See Cable (1988) for a survey of empirical tests of the M-form hypothesis.
4. See also Kay 1992*a*.
5. Corresponding distinctions in terms of similarity/complementarity in relationships have been made by researchers into network behaviour (e.g. see Ibarra, 1992, pp. 180–1).
6. For example, Mintzberg (1979, pp. 380–430), and Johnson and Scholes (1993, pp. 346–47) analyse possible disadvantages as well as advantages of M-form organization. It is useful to contrast the perspectives of these writers with that of Williamson (1975, 1985).
7. Similar results were found for the UK, Germany and France by Channon (1973), and Dyas and Thanheiser (1976), although the process of large firm diversification had typically not gone as far as in the USA at the time of the studies.
8. For the sake of simplicity, we are skating over some problems that a fuller analysis should attend to. For example, even in the related-constrained strategy the hybrid solution may not mean an entire function is removed to corporate level; if a corporate level marketing department is created, divisions frequently retain some responsibility for product-specific sales and distribution, while corporate R&D may still co-exist with product-specific development work being carried out within divisions. Such splitting of functions means that the hybrid form may involve coordination barriers being created within functions as well as between them.
9. Williamson (1975) characterizes the divisions within the M-form as 'scaled down, specialised U-form structures' (pp. 136–7).
10. In the case of Hewlett Packard, the tiering goes beyond the three levels set out in our example, with groups of divisions themselves forming clusters (e.g. Microwave and Communications Instruments Group and Electronic Measurements Group forming the Instruments cluster.

11. See Bartlett (1986), Bartlett and Ghoshal (1989), and Johnson and Scholes (1993, pp. 349–58) for discussion of the international division as well as other multinational solutions discussed here.
12. See Mintzberg (1979, pp. 168–75), and Johnson and Scholes (1993, pp. 349–51) for a summary of major advantages and disadvantages associated with this form.
13. See particularly Nohria and Eccles (1992), and Thompson, Frances, Levacic and Mitchell (1991).

13.   Conclusions

In this work we have looked at a variety of issues relating to the firm as a non-decomposable system. We hope that this work has provided an improved explanation of the behaviour of some phenomena in the areas of the theory of the firm and industrial organization. It is hoped that some progress has been made in dealing with behaviour which has not been properly dealt with in economics to date. The test is whether it is felt to perform better than alternative approaches, and it is really for others to judge this question. However, the approach here does have the advantage of building up explanations of a variety of strategies and behaviour patterns out of a few simple concepts and rules. It is difficult to see how conventional economics approaches (with their emphasis on methodological individualism and decomposability) could do the same. The resource-based concept of linkage has been central to the analysis of the work, helping to build up maps of corporate strategy and illuminating patterns of firm and sectoral behaviour. We also prefer to use the phrase 'coordination costs' to refer to costs associated with alternative modes of economic organization. This is because the concept of 'transaction costs' has become so strongly associated with Williamson's approach (1975, 1985) to the extent that his approach is labelled 'transaction cost economics'. The concept of transaction costs is so closely tied up with this highly specific approach that we prefer to use a more neutral term.

In this chapter we shall briefly review the book's chapters in section 13.1. Section 13.2 considers the possible relationships between the perspective developed here, and (a) systems theory and (b) evolutionary theory. Some possibilities for future research are explored in section 13.3.

13.1. Review

It may be helpful to review the coverage of the work, and what it is felt it may have achieved. Chapter 2 set the context for subsequent discussion by exploring how alternative approaches to the theory of the firm tended to have a spoke to hub relationship with neoclassical theory. Chapters 3 and 4 were concerned with problems relating to the existence of firms and the establishment of their boundaries. It was argued that transaction cost economics explanations for the existence of firms and the determination of their limits were flawed. In particular, the focus on the transaction as a basic unit of analysis was seen as misplaced, whilst the prominence given to asset specificity leads to the vertical integration problem being regarded as the definitive internalization strategy. Firms tend to internalize resources and bundles of tasks (rather than discrete transactions) and it is the question of replaceability of resources rather than their specialized nature that is an essential feature of explanations of phenomena such as vertical integration. It was also suggested that it could be difficult to make sense of the development of firms in particular cases (such as in the petroleum industry) without recognizing the path dependent nature of corporate evolution. The idea of linkages as double edged swords (that may facilitate exploitation of economies but also generate vulnerability to environmental threats) was developed in Chapter 4. Chapter 4 also introduced another puzzle: how can natural selection arguments be applied to the survival of large firms when almost all of them survive, almost all of the time? The answer suggested was that environments could be classified into three main types: (a) hard selection environments in which the elimination of individuals is an integral aspect of its operation; (b) contingent selection environments in which the survival of the individual depends on the attainment of a satisfactory level of performance; and (c) soft selection environments in which the elimination of individuals is abnormal or even pathological. It was suggested that many large firms operate in soft selection environments with club-like features. The problem then becomes one of accounting for the entrenchment of these firms and it was suggested that diversification could play an important role in some cases. Collectively, Chapters 3 and 4 help to establish the context for the rest of the book. The role of diversification in softening corporate environments is an important theme in Chapters 6 and 7, while soft selection and club behaviour also contribute to explanations of behaviour in later chapters, such as Chapters 5 and 7.

Chapter 6 selected five major UK corporations and mapped the logic of their respective strategies using resource linkages. The resulting maps helped to illuminate form and pattern in the development of corporate strategies. It was suggested that a competencies or capabilities perspective on corporate development which asked 'what are our resources?' better fitted the strategic management problem than ones which asked 'what is our business?' The option of responding to environmental threats by internalizing them is something that recurred in the cases we looked at; it seems that if you cannot beat them, try to join them or buy them. This is consistent with the soft selection arguments of Chapter 3. It also suggests that while Schumpeter's processes of creative destruction may be a good description of hard selection processes at the level of individual businesses, it faces problems if it is extended to the soft selection level of large diversified firms.

Chapter 7 looked at the development of large firms and argued that they tended to grow according to simple rules that helped maintain consistency or balance in terms of the relationship of the component parts to each other, and to the whole. It was argued that firms which evolved according to such coherence principles would adopt one of four basic developmental routes; specialization, related-constrained, related-linked, and the conglomerate. It was suggested that these arguments helped to sort out basic patterns of large firm diversification outlined in Richard Rumelt's doctoral dissertation. Also, soft selection, path dependency, and lock-in arguments helped to explain the stickiness of large firm strategies in Rumelt's work. One interesting issue related to the persistence of conglomerates in spite of arguments that these were inferior forms that would 'disappear' as environments became more hostile, as in a recession. It was argued to the contrary that evolutionary arguments were entirely consistent with the perpetuation of relatively inefficient forms, and that the empirical evidence tended to support this. The whole chapter integrates soft selection and path dependency arguments with coherence principles to provide an approach to analysing broad patterns in the evolution of the large diversified firm.

Chapter 8 looked at one particular path in corporate development—multinational enterprise. This is an area in which there is an abundance of empirical evidence, in contrast to some other areas of industrial organization such as corporate diversification (possibly reflecting the greater insulation of the agenda in the international business area from neoclassical influences). The perspective encouraged by analysis of linkages is that the evolution of a multinational enterprise requires that opportunity of one kind must co-exist with a certain deficiency of opportunity in other respects. For example, technological opportunity is not sufficient to explain multinationalism as long as exporting or domestic diversification can exploit richer linkages. The multinational must be justified in terms of the opportunity cost of alternative options. The perspective developed here is consistent with evidence that multinationals tend to be large, diversified, and knowledge intensive firms. It also helps to explain research evidence which suggests that industrial concentration alone appears not to be a sufficient condition for multinational development, but instead appears to require additional conditions such as R&D intensiveness at the level of the firm. The nature of linkages also helps analysis of varieties of multinational expansion, including technology-based, marketing-based, and conglomerate types. The major contribution this chapter makes is in suggesting how the distinctive issues associated with multinational expansion can be analysed using the principles discussed in the earlier chapters.

Chapters 9 and 10 analysed co-operative activity between firms and helps to explain why major collaborative activity such as joint venture tends to involve large diversified firms. Such options were here seen as typically the least efficient alternative considered at the business strategy level, and it required particular circumstances to force firms to consider them as a last resort. It is difficult to see how such explanations can be developed in the absence of an analysis of linkages, since it is the evolution of the firm from simple atom to complex molecule that stimulates collaborative activity in this perspective. By way of contrast, conventional economics explanations tend to restrict themselves to business level considerations, which makes it difficult or impossible to reconcile the high cost aspects of joint venture activity with the willingness of firms to adopt them voluntarily in certain circumstances. The approach here also helps to explain why collaborative activity has proliferated in recent years; collaborative activity is not just a substitute for (current) merger activity, it can be triggered by (past) merger activity. Conditions which were consistent with the involvement of small firms in collaborative activity were identified, and an analysis of links used to help to suggest that we would expect to find small firm involvement in cases where they had multiple partners who were themselves large and diversified. The biotech-based pharmaceutical industry exhibited behaviour which was consistent with these expectations. A feature of the analysis here is that it began to trace clustering effects at collaboration and firm level; collaborative agreements appear to cluster between partners, whilst partners themselves appear to cluster and form clubs. The prior analysis of firms as complex systems was seen as essential in trying to discern both logic and pattern in such clustering.

Chapters 11 and 12 shifted the focus from strategy to structure. Chapter 11 explored the relationship between strategy and structure and showed how nesting of linkages allowed the firm to deal with complex decisions. Nesting led to new linkages and problems appearing whether we moved up or down the corporate hierarchy. Contrary to the received wisdom, lower levels in the firm typically deal with higher orders of complexity than higher levels. There is generally a novelty/complexity trade-off in which routine and repetition associated with lower level situations allow decision-makers at those levels to handle greater degrees of complexity than that associated with strategic management levels. Whilst Chapter 11 was concerned with the layering of decision-making in the firm, Chapter 12 developed the analysis of linkages to show how it might be useful in looking at the relationship between strategy and structure. Using just two basic types of resource relationship (synergy and complementarity) and a simple rule (synergy dominates complementarity) the logic of a wide variety of organizational structures was explored. Mapping the linkages associated with strategies helped us to investigate the opportunity cost of alternative structures for the respective strategies. This allowed the integration of the study of strategy and structure in our analysis.

13.2. System, Pattern, and Evolution

The framework developed here owes its greatest debt to perspectives developed outside economics. If there is a concept that defines the present work, it is the concept of *system*. A basic definition of this concept is 'a set of inter-related entities, of which no subset is unrelated to any other subset' (Kramer and Smit, 1977, p. 14). System contrasts with the concept of an aggregate in which parts are simply added together (Kramer and Smit, 1977, p. 13). At first sight this definition of system may not seem to add much to economics. As we noted in Chapter 1, we already talk in economics about the economics 'system', and indeed general equilibrium is concerned with the interdependency of markets: 'for a complete and precise solution of the partial problems of the economic system, it is inevitable that one must consider the system as a whole' (Cournot, quoted in Blaug, 1978, p. 603). In this respect we have returned full circle to the problems of ambiguity and mental set with which we started the book. However, when economists have explicitly drawn on systems thinking as in Vining's (1949) argument that the whole is greater than the sum of its parts,[1] a typical response by mainstream economists has been to dismiss such holistic arguments as unscientific and even characterized by 'mysticism' (e.g. Arrow, 1968). Faced with the Scylla of lack of originality and the Charybdis of mysticism, it is perhaps not surprising that explicitly systems-based theorizing has failed to catch on in economics.[2] The problem is also exacerbated by a tendency for writers to have inconsistent interpretations of what constitutes the systems approach in many cases.

The essential point is that concepts of relations at a point in time (or synchronic relations; Levi-Strauss, 1963) are normal and widely accepted ways of describing phenomena, yet are alien to the traditional reductionist perspective of the economics discipline. Again, as long as neoclassical theory provides acceptable explanations of economic behaviour, this simple view of the world is to the credit of neoclassical theory. All that is being hoped for at this point is that it is acknowledged that economic behaviour in some contexts may be better understood by recognizing the existence of relations at a point in time. Even if this appears a reasonable plea in the light of the previous discussion, it is not something which may be easily achieved. When economists like Williamson (1975), Jenson and Meckling (1986) and Milgrom and Roberts (1992) look at hierarchy, they tend to analyse it as characterized by contractual relations between individuals or individual units, and internal markets such as internal labour markets, internal capital markets and internal intermediate product markets. This encourages an individualistic, reductionist perspective in which intra-firm relations between elements tend to be analysed in causal terms, just as in the traffic signals example discussed in Chapter 1. That is, economists tend not to leave their methodological tool kit at the door of the firm when they step inside, but prefer to take it with them. It is not so much the approach that varies as the context.

The approach here relies heavily on the existence of relations between elements at a point in time. In view of the discussion above, we might expect that analogies could be drawn between complex molecules in chemistry and the complex firms of our analysis.[3] However, such comparisons should not be pushed too far; economic problems in practice do not resemble chemical problems any more than systems relations in architecture resemble systems relations in anthropology or anatomy. What these approaches do—or should—have in common is a concern with such concepts as structure, pattern, form, and organization. Shaking off the reductionist, aggregative perspective of neoclassical theory is a precondition for the perception of systems relations. It is hoped that the present work has demonstrated how a systems perspective might be usefully applied to analysis of resource allocation, by and between firms.

Is the approach developed here an evolutionary one? The major focus has been in terms of developing a resource-based approach that can be integrated into a systems perspective. However, the analysis has benefited considerably from the work of evolutionary theorists, and while it is not claimed to present an evolutionary theory as such, it does benefit from the incorporation of evolutionary elements. Nelson (1995) argues that an evolutionary theory should involve: (a) a variable or a system changing over time and a search for understanding of the dynamics behind the change; (b) the variable or system in question being subject to somewhat random variations or perturbations, with selection mechanisms acting on the variation; (c) strong inertial tendencies preserving what has survived in the selection process; (d) possibly also forces providing for variation, 'grist for the selection mill' (Nelson, 1995, p. 54). Features of the present analysis which reflect such considerations include: the progressive unfolding of strategy, lock-in of strategies, the role of environmental 'surprises', and the internalization of creative destruction. However, our systems do operate in a soft selection environment which is distinctive from the usual selection mechanisms associated with evolutionary theories. This affords discretion over strategy and structure design possibilities, and in particular raises the possibility that the firm can pursue consistent patterns in its strategic development. Also, the approach here does not have the degree of sophistication and detail concerning decision rules to be found in Nelson and Winter (1982). All that is expected of the decision-makers is that their strategies should conform to certain simple principles, and it was the implications of the associated patterns that were generated in the respective cases that was the subject of analysis.

If the analysis has some legitimacy as an evolutionary account of firm behaviour, it lies in its analysis of the evolution of complex systems from simple beginnings. One of the central ideas of the book (especially Chapters 9 and 10) is that past strategies or modes of organization may constitute the preconditions or triggers that stimulate the development of new strategies or modes of organization. By making linkages explicit, the relationship between these triggers and the development of new solutions can be analysed. This was demonstrated most powerfully in the analysis of joint ventures, alliances and networks. Unless the patterns of corporate evolution preceding these stages are recognized and identified, there is no framework around which to explain the evolution of patterns of cooperative agreements. The analysis here attempted to make sense of the evolution of firms and sectors as they moved to stages associated with increasingly complex solutions in a path dependent fashion. A satisfactory feature of the explanations provided in this context is that the triggers are endogenous to the phenomena under discussion, and there is no need to invoke some *Deus ex machina* such as increased complexity or uncertainty to explain the evolution of cooperative agreements, alliances, and networks in recent years.

13.3. Possibilities for Future Research

There are a number of areas of research signalled by the work. The notion of resource replaceability (Chapter 3) appears to be a very promising basis for analysing the incidence and form of vertical integration, and it offers routes which invite further analysis and development. Also, it would be interesting to explore further the argument that environments can be categorized in terms of different selection criteria and see to what extent the distinction does go along with different behavioural characteristics. We have also only sketched the different nature of the environments and there will be questions of interactions between different levels, for example the (soft selection?) environment at firm level and the (contingent selection?) environment that individual managers face. Also, there appears to be no reason why the mapping of linkages in Chapter 6 could not be of wider assistance in helping analysis of corporate strategies in general. It could be particularly useful in building up pictures of corporate strategies of firms in particular sectors for comparative purposes. For example, mapping the corporate strategies of the major players in the post-war aero-engine business (United Technologies, General Electric, and Rolls Royce) would reveal striking scale and linkage differences between these rivals; mapping these differences might help to add perspective to the potential interplay between corporate strategy and the aero-engine business strategy in the respective firms. In the course of the work we have also found it convenient to distinguish between weak and strong patterns of linkages. Weak patterns exist where linkages may vary though in a consistent way (as when firms seek to exploit richer linkages first), whilst strong patterns exist where linkages behave in a consistent fashion over the course of the strategy (as in the case of the single-linked related-constrained strategy). The two types of pattern are not necessarily inconsistent with each other; for example a firm may exhibit a related-constrained strategy (and strong pattern) at corporate level, while instructing its constituent groups or divisions to pursue synergy-rich expansion strategies first (and so generate weak patterns of linkages within groups or divisions). The analysis of Chapters 11 and 12 showed how hierarchy could enable the firm to cluster resources according to different rules at different levels, and it is entirely possible for the firm to simultaneously pursue weak pattern/strong pattern strategies at different levels also. At the same time, Chapter 7 argued that strategies displaying strong pattern (or coherence) were likely to represent ideal types rather than realizable outcomes for most firms. This raises the possibility that firms may face a conflict between pursuing the ideal of strong pattern and settling for weak pattern in some cases. The existence of such tensions (or indeed the dominance of one or other types of pattern seeking behaviour) represents a line that future research could pursue.

The approach could also contribute to historical analysis of the evolution of individual corporate strategies, and indeed whole sectors. Mapping the evolution of corporate strategy over a period of some years should help to give a better understanding of the role of capabilities in maintaining the firm. As far as the large diversified firm is concerned, soft selection means that obsolescence of some of its capabilities can be absorbed and neutralized. However, what form does this absorption take in particular circumstances? Does the firm send repair teams to upgrade and replace worn out capabilities and still remain in the business or businesses to which they contribute? Is the threatened business jettisoned along with the capabilities? Does the internalization of creative destruction discussed in Chapter 4 mean that the fierce gales of Schumpeterian competition are replaced by the calmer breezes of technological upgrading? These are all possibilities and we would expect the answer to vary depending on time and context. However, the analysis of Chapter 6 suggests that some firms, at least some of the time, may be able to manage the process of transforming capabilities fairly smoothly (e.g. Cadbury Schweppes); other firms, at least some of the time, may find that more radical reshaping of the boundaries of the firm is forced on them by environmental developments (e.g. Thorn EMI, Ladbroke). Also, the approach is designed to deal with the particular problems facing large firms and it would be interesting to explore what modifications may be required to apply it to small and medium sized firms.

One lesson that was learnt during the mapping exercise of Chapter 6 is that there appeared to be a trade-off between the level of strategy and the detail with which linkages could be modelled. For example, if it is wished to analyse linkages between two businesses, then analysis can handle a great deal of detail in the analysis of linkages. On the other hand, if we wish to look at linkages at the level of corporate strategy, it helps if linkages are restricted to broad brush categories. The later discussion in Chapter 11 regarding the relationship between complexity and hierarchy suggests that this trade-off between detail and breadth is paralleled in the decision-making agenda associated with different levels in the firm. Thus, while some compromises had to be made to accommodate the level of detail that the mapping could handle, the reduction in detail at least appears to track what actually happens in reality. Nevertheless, it may be that it is possible to identify linkages in rather more detail than is generally the case here; for example, Prahalad and Hamel (1990) analyse the strategy of Canon as basically built around three technological linkages in precision mechanics, fine optics, and microelectronics. Some of Canon's products draw on all three linkages, some draw on two and some only on one. However, these linkages both open up and help define areas of opportunity for Canon, and in turn help to determine how the boundaries of the firm are drawn. The approach developed here should in principle be adaptable to such fine-tuned levels of analysis, and the analysis in Chapter 6 could probably be pushed further in this respect.

One of the implications of Chapters 7, 8, 9, and 10 considered together is that collectively they portray a picture of firms and sectors evolving through various stages and following alternative paths. One path based on Chapters 9 and 10 could be characterized in terms of stages of (1) atomism, (2) specialization (economies of scale), (3) simple diversification (related-constrained), (4) complex diversification (related-linked), (5) collaboration (between business units), (6) partnership (between firms), (7) networks or clubs (involving multiple firms). Another path based on Chapter 7 would split off at an early stage and trace the evolution of conglomerates. A fuller elaboration would combine Chapters 7, 8, 9, and 10, and observe the evolution of multinationals after domestic opportunities for diversification have been saturated, and then the evolution of different patterns of international strategic alliance. It would be interesting to see the extent to which sectors adhere to the progression of stages as suggested in Chapters 7, 9, and 10: do the stages tend to follow the order predicted here? Are there reversals of stage order or emphasis? Is there skipping of stages?

In each case, analysis of linkages would provide a basis for relating strategy to structure, or hierarchy. We would expect to find evidence of path dependency here; if a firm is moving on to a new stage of strategy development, it might find that the hierarchical suit inherited from an earlier stage fits less well in later stages. Casual evidence of this included the tendency for the U-form structure to outlive its sell-by date in the early days of the M-form innovation (Chandler, 1962), and the bolt-on nature of many international division extensions to the basic M-form structure in emerging multinationals. With this caveat in mind, analysing patterns of complementary and synergistic relations between corporate activities may contribute to the analysis of the evolution of hierarchy. It offers a simple and coherent basis for analysing the relation between strategy and structure at different stages of strategy development. Once the strategy of the firm has been mapped, certain organizational solutions may appear more attractive (efficient) than others. Patterns of linkage not only trace the logic of strategy, they mark out the guidelines for structure. Analysis of linkages provides the basis through which the study of strategy and structure can be more fully integrated. It was also noted in Chapter 3 that disciplinary influences often led to economists and organization theorists focusing on different aspects of hierarchy; analysis of linkages may help to provide a vehicle that helps to connect economics-oriented approaches with the rich research tradition in organization theory.

The analysis of Chapter 7 raises questions of why firms tend to adopt one diversification route rather than another. For example, is the conglomerate route initially triggered by limited diversification opportunities in the early stages of corporate growth, and then sustained by coherence, path dependency and soft selection principles? Or was the initial stimulus the mood of the capital market at a critical point in corporate development? Chapter 8 also suggests that interactions between different kinds of know-how (e.g. technical, marketing) may be important in influencing patterns of multinational activity, and this is a possibility that could be explored further.

Chapter 9 suggests that major collaborative activity such as joint venture tends to involve large diversified firms, and to the extent that smaller firms are involved in collaborative activity, they tend to have multiple partners who are themselves large diversified firms. The evidence so far tends to be consistent with this, and it suggests further lines of investigation; for example, it would be useful to investigate more fully what patterns of large and small firm involvement in major collaborative activity actually obtains in particular sectors. One issue which has not been really well explored in the literature is that the umbrella term of co-operative agreements can cover a multitude of situations (ranging from casual know-how trading to full blown joint ventures) and that these may have very different implications for coordination costs in the respective cases. It has already been suggested that differences between alternative forms of arrangement may influence whether and how they are coordinated, and further research to establish the implications of the nature and characteristics of different forms of arrangements in terms of their associated coordination costs would be worth pursuing.

A interesting question suggested by Chapter 10 is, how stable are the different clusters identified at various levels likely to be in practice? The analysis here suggests that there is likely to be interaction between business (collaborative), corporate (partnership or alliance) and inter-firm (network or club) levels. To what extent do established relations at one level tend to stabilize relations at other levels (e.g. do firms prefer to join clubs that have existing partners as members? Do firms prefer to select partners that are associated with the same club?). Are higher levels more stable than lower levels? To what extent do path dependency issues favour stability of relations as opposed to flexibility? There are clearly a number of lines that may be pursued here.

The analysis of hierarchy in Chapters 11 and 12 provides a simple basis for organizational design based on the analysis of linkages from the previous chapters, and it appears consistent with many observed solutions in practice. Two issues in particular invite further consideration. It was argued that in all but a few special cases, organizational design involves trade-offs. We have suggested some ways organizations may respond to these trade-offs, but the organizational literature identifies even more sophisticated solutions than the ones suggested here (e.g. see Mintzberg, 1979). This literature is likely to continue to provide considerable benefits for analysis of the type developed here, particularly in signalling alternative solutions for dealing with particular trade-offs. The second issue is, how important is path dependency in organizational design? Judging from the willingness and enthusiasm with which many firms have embraced reorganization, it does seem to be easier for firms to change their structure than their strategy. At the same time, complete transformation (say from M-form to matrix) may not be easy to achieve, especially given that individuals in the firm are likely to be used to established routines and relationships. Organizational structure is unlikely to be easily adopted and discarded, instead such processes of organizational change may be characterized by significant costs.

13.4. Last Words

At the beginning of the work, it was stated that it was seen as a contribution following in a systems theory tradition. Not too much has been made of this point in the body of the work, the preference being instead to concentrate on the issues raised in each topic area. However, a systems approach it is; the typical firm is seen as a nondecomposable system in which the whole is not the simple aggregation of the component parts. It has to be said that this perspective does pose problems given the dominance of methodological individualism in economics, with a major disadvantage being problems of communicating with other economists. An advantage is that it is hoped that it does open up new and useful ways of looking at questions of resource allocation within and between firms. For better or worse, the present work is still economics based, with themes such as rationality, value, efficiency, and opportunity cost running through the various topics. The difference here is that the subjects of decision are usually complex systems in their own right, rather than individual elements or units.

The question at the end is how we look at the world. As long as economics reduces complex phenomena to their constituent components, then non-conglomerate diversification will continue to be neglected, the relationship of multinational enterprise to alternative strategies will be obscured, co-operative behaviour between firms will be generally misinterpreted in terms of efficiency considerations at product-market level, and hierarchy will be misrepresented as a contractual arrangement involving internal markets. However, if there is a disposition to look for form and pattern in the strategy and the structure of the firm, then it becomes easier to analyse certain phenomena. It is also possible to build up pictures of how firms' strategies evolve, with complex varieties of diversification, multinational enterprise, and co-operative behaviour all tending to develop from simple specialized beginnings and interact with each other. The outcomes of previous stages of firm growth may serve as the triggers for the next stage; clubs or networks of firms do not suddenly manifest themselves out of thin air, but may be the consequence of history and the earlier build-up of partnerships at firm level, which in turn is likely to have emerged from deepening collaboration at business level, which in turn may have been stimulated by previous diversification precluding further merger—and so on. Break up these topics into the separate issues, and the integrated interdependent nature of the firm's strategic agenda is lost. Focus instead on the nature of the firm and its constituent linkages, and the possibilities of developing coherent explanations are improved accordingly. Economics has traditionally excelled in the sophistication with which it has provided answers to questions. However, how well we explain economic phenomena depends not just on how well we phrase our answers, but on how well we phrase our questions.

NOTES

1. This is a common way to describe behaviour in systems approaches, (e.g. see Kramer and Smit, 1977, p. 3).
2. For a work that looks at systems theorizing in economics, see Hodgson (1988).
3. See Hodgson (1993*a*) for an excellent review of the use of scientific analogies in economics.

REFERENCES

Alchian A. A. (1950) 'Uncertainty, evolution and economic theory', *Journal of Political Economy*, 58, 211–22.

Alchian, A. A. and Woodward, S. (1987) 'Reflections on the theory of the firm', *Journal of Institutional and Theoretical Economics*, 143, 110–36.

Aliber, R. Z. (1970) 'A theory of direct investment', in C. P. Kindleberger (ed.) *The International Corporation*, Cambridge, Mass., MIT Press, pp. 17–34.

Amin, A. (1993) 'The globalisation of the economy: an erosion of regional networks?' in G. Grabher (ed. 1993*b*) pp. 278–95.

Anderson, E. and Schmittlein, D. (1984) 'Integration of the sales force: an empirical examination', *Rand Journal of Economics*, 15, 385–95.

Anslinger, P. L. and Copeland, T. E. (1996) 'Growth through acquisitions: a fresh look', *Harvard Business Review*, 74 (1), pp. 126–35.

Ansoff, H. I. (1968) *Corporate Strategy*, London, Penguin.

Ansoff, H. I. (1987) *Corporate Strategy*, 2nd edn. London, Penguin.

Ansoff, H. I. and Brandenburg, R. G. (1971*a*) 'A language for organization design, part I', *Management Science*, 17, B:705–16.

Ansoff, H. I. and Brandenburg, R. G. (1971*b*) 'A language for organization design: part II', *Management Science*, 17, B:717–31.

Armour, H. O. and Teece, D. J. (1978) 'Organizational structure and economic performance; a test of the multidivisional hypothesis', *Bell Journal of Economics*, 9, 106–22.

Arrow, K. (1962) 'Economic welfare and the allocation of resources for invention', in *The Rate and Direction of Inventive Activity: Economic and Social Factors*, National Bureau of Economic Research, Princeton University Press, pp. 609–26.

Arrow, K. (1968) 'Mathematical models in the social sciences', in M. Brodbeck (ed.) *Readings in the Philosophy of the Social Sciences*, New York, Macmillan, pp. 635–67.

Arrow, K. (1969) 'Classificatory notes on the production and distribution of technological knowledge', *American Economic Review*, 59, 29–35.

Arthur, B. (1989) 'Competing technologies, increasing returns and lock-in by historical events', *Economic Journal*, 99, 116–31.

Axelsson, B. and Easton, G. (1992) *Industrial Networks: A New View of Reality*, London, Routledge.

Badaracco, J. L. Jr (1991) *The Knowledge Link: How Firms Compete through Strategic Alliances*, Boston, Harvard Business School.

Barley, S. R., Freeman, J., and Hybels, R. C. (1992) 'Strategic alliances in commercial biotechnology', in N. Nohria and R. Eccles (eds.) (1992) pp. 311–47.

Bartlett, C. (1986) 'Building and managing the transnational: the new organizational challenge', in M. E. Porter (ed.) *Competition in Global Industries*, Cambridge, Mass., Harvard University Press.

Bartlett, C. and Ghoshal, S. (1989) *Managing across Borders: the Transnational Corporation*, Cambridge, Mass., Harvard Business School.

Baumol, W. J. (1959) *Business Behavior, Value and Growth*, New York, Macmillan.

Baumol, W. J. (1962) 'On the theory of the expansion of the firm', *American Economic Review*, 52, 1078–87.

Beath, J., Katsoulacos,Y., and Ulph, D. (1994) 'Strategic R&D and innovation', in J. Cable (ed.) *Current Issues in Industrial Economics*, Basingstoke, Macmillan.

Berg, S. V. and Friedman, P. (1978) 'Joint ventures in American industry: an overview', *Mergers and Acquisitions*, Summer, 28–41.

Berg, S. V. and Hoekman, J. M. (1988) 'Entrepreneurship over the product life cycle: joint venture strategies in the Netherlands', in F. J. Contractor and P. Lorange (1988*b*) pp. 145–67.

Berg, S. V.. Duncan, J.. and Friedman P. (1982) *Joint Venture Strategies and Corporate Innovation*, Cambridge, Mass., Oelgeschlager, Gunn and Hain.

Bergsten, C. F., Horst, T., and Moran, T. H. (1978) *American Multinationals and American Interests*, Washington D.C., Brookings.

Berle A. A. and Means G. C. (1932) *The Modern Corporation and Private Property*, New York, Commerce Clearing House.

Blaug, M. (1978) *Economic Theory in Retrospect*, 3rd edn. Cambridge, Cambridge University Press.

Blaug, M. (1992) *The Methodology of Economics: or How Economists Explain*, 2nd edn. Cambridge, Cambridge University Press.

Bovee, C. L. and Arens, W. F. (1982) *Advertising*, Homewood, Irwin.

Bower, G. H. and Springston, F. (1970) 'Pauses as recoding points in letter series', *Journal of Experimental Psychology*, 83, 421–30.

Boyle, S. E. (1968) 'An estimate of the number and size distribution of domestic joint subsidiaries', *Antitrust Law and Economic Review*, Spring, 81–92.

Bradshaw, J. L. and Nettleton, N. E. (1981) 'The nature of hemispheric specialisation in man', *Behavior and Brain Sciences*, 4, 51–91.

Buckley, P. J. and Casson, M. (1976) *The Future of the Multinational Enterprise*, London, Holmes and Meier.

Buckley, P. and Casson, M. (1988), 'A theory of cooperation in international business', in F. Contractor and P. Lorange (eds.) (1988*b*), pp. 31–53.

Buckley, P. J. and Casson, M. (1991) *The Future of the Multinational Enterprise*, 2nd edn. London, Macmillan.

Burgers, W. P., Hill, C. W. L., and Kim, W. C. (1993) 'A theory of global strategic alliances: the case of the global auto industry', *Strategic Management Journal*, 14, 419–32.

Burt, R. S. (1992) 'The social structure of competition', in R. Nohria and R. Eccles (eds.) (1992), pp. 37–91.

Cable, J. R. (1988) 'Organisation form and economic performance', in R. S. Thompson and M. Wright (eds.) (1988) pp. 12–37.

Cantner, U. and Hanusch, H. (1994) 'Schumpeter, Joseph Alois', in Hodgson, G. M., Samuels, W. J., and Tool, M. R. (eds.) (1994) pp. 273–8.

Casson, M. (1987) *The Firm and the Market: Studies on Multinational Enterprise and the Scope of the Firm*, Oxford, Blackwell.

Caves, R. E. (1982) *Multinational Enterprise and Economic Analysis*, Cambridge, Cambridge University Press.

Caves, R. E. and Bradburd, R. M. (1988) 'The empirical determinants of vertical integration', *Journal of Economic Behavior and Organization*, 9, 265–79.

Chamberlin, E. H. (1933) *The Theory of Monopolistic Competition*, Cambridge, Mass., Harvard University Press.

Chandler, A. D. (1962) *Strategy and Structure*, Cambridge, Mass., MIT Press.

Chandler, A. D. (1977) *The Visible Hand: the Managerial Revolution in American Business*, Cambridge, Harvard University Press.

Chandler, A. D. (1990) *Scale and Scope: the Dynamics of Industrial Capitalism*, Cambridge, Mass., Harvard University Press.

Channon, D. F. (1973) *The Strategy and Structure of British Enterprise*, London, Macmillan.

Channon, D. F. and Jalland, M. (1979) *Multinational Strategic Planning*, London, Macmillan.

Child, J. (1984) *Organization: A Guide to Problems and Practice*, 2nd edn, London, Harper Row.

Clausewitz, C. V. (1968) *On War* (ed. A. Rapoport), London, Penguin.

Clegg, J. (1987) *Multinational Enterprise and World Competition*, London, Macmillan.

Coase, R. H. (1937) 'The nature of the firm', *Economica*, 4, 386–405.

Coase, R. H. (1984) 'The new institutional economics', *Journal of Institutional and Theoretical Economics*, 140, 229–31.

Coase, R. H. (1988a) 'The nature of the firm: meaning', *Journal of Law, Economics, and Organization*, 4, 19–32.

Coase, R. H. (1988b) 'The nature of the firm: influence', *Journal of Law, Economics, and Organization*, 4, 33–47.

Coase, R. H. (1993) 'Coase on Posner on Coase', *Journal of Institutional and Theoretical Economics*, 149, 96–8.

Cohen, W. M. and Levin, R. C. (1989) 'Empirical studies of innovation and market structure', in R. Schmalensee and R. D. Willig (eds.) *Handbook of Industrial Organization*, Amsterdam, North Holland, 1059–107.

Cohen, M. D., March, J. G., and Olsen J. P. (1972) 'A garbage can model of organizational choice', *Administrative Science Quarterly*, 17, 1–25.

Collis, D. J. (1996) 'Related corporate portfolios', in M. Goold and K. S. Luchs (eds.), *Managing the Multibusiness Company: Strategic Issues for Diversified Groups*, London, Routledge, pp. 122–42.

Commission of the European Communities (1988) *The European Community and cooperation among small and medium-sized enterprises* (*European File*), Luxembourg, Commission of the European Communities.

Conrath, D. W. (1973) 'Communications environment and its relationship to organisational structure', *Management Science*, 20, 586–62.

Contractor, F. J. and Lorange, P. (1988a) 'Why should firms cooperate? The strategy and economics basis for cooperative ventures', in F. J. Contractor and P. Lorange (eds.) (1988b), pp. 3–28.

Contractor, F. J. and Lorange, P. (eds.) (1988b) *Cooperative Strategies in International Business: Joint Ventures and Technology Partnerships between Firms*, Lexington, D. C. Heath.

Coyne, J. and Wright, M. (1985) 'An introduction to divestment: the conceptual issues', in J. Coyne and M. Wright (eds.) *Divestment and Strategic Change*, Oxford, Philip Alan, pp. 1–26.

Cyert, R. M. and March, J. G. (1963) *A Behavioral Theory of the Firm*, New Jersey, Prentice Hall.

Dasgupta, P. (1986) 'The theory of technological competition', in K. Binmore and P. Dasgupta (eds.) *Economic Organizations as Games*, Oxford, Blackwell, pp. 139–64.

Dasgupta, P. and David, P. A. (1994) 'Towards a new economics of science', *Research Policy*, 23, 487–521.

David, F. R. (1991) *Concepts of Strategic Management*, 3rd edn. New York, Macmillan.

David, P. A. (1985) 'Clio and the economics of QWERTY', *American Economic Review*, Pap. and Proc. 75, 332–7.

David, P. A. (1992) 'Heroes, herds and hysteresis in technological history: Thomas Edison and the "battle of the systems" reconsidered', *Industrial and Corporate Change*, 1, 129–80.

Davidson, W. H. and McFetridge, D. G. (1985) 'Key characteristics in the choice of international technology transfer mode', *Journal of International Business Studies*, 16, 5–21.

Day, R. H. (1967) 'Profits, learning and the convergence of satisficing to marginalism', *Quarterly Journal of Economics*, 81, 302–11.

Delis, D. C., Robertson, L. C., and Efron, R. (1986) 'Hemispheric specialization of memory for visual hierarchical stimuli', *Neuropsychologia*, 24, 205–14.

Demsetz, H. (1969) 'Information and efficiency: another viewpoint', *Journal of Law and Economics*, 12, 1–22.

Demsetz, H. (1988) 'The theory of the firm revisited', *Journal of Law, Economics and Organization*, 4, 141–61.

Dietrich, M. (1991) 'Firms, markets and transaction cost economics', *Scottish Journal of Political Economy*, 38, 41–57.

Dietrich, M. (1994) *Transaction Cost Economics and Beyond: Towards a New Economics of the Firm*, London, Routledge.

Dodgson, M. (1993) *Technological Collaboration in Industry: Strategy, Policy, and Internationalization in Innovation*, Routledge, London.

Dosi, G., Gianetti, R., and Toninelli, P. A. (eds.) (1992) *Technology and Enterprise in an Historical Perspective*, Oxford, Clarendon.

Dosi, G., Teece, D. J., and Winter, S. (1992), 'Toward a theory of corporate coherence: preliminary remarks', in G. Dosi, R. Gianetti, and P. A. Toninelli (eds.) (1992) pp. 185–211.

Drucker, P. (1974) *Management: Tasks, Responsibilities, and Practices*, New York, Harper and Row.

Dunning, J. H. (1991) 'The eclectic paradigm of international production: a personal perspective', in C. N. Pitelis and R. Sugden (eds.) (1991) pp. 116–36.

Dunning, J. H. (1993) *Multinational Enterprises and the Global Economy*, Wokingham, Addison-Wesley.

Dyas, G. P. and Thanheiser, H. T. (1976) *The Emerging European Enterprise: Strategy and Structure in French and German Industries*, London, Macmillan.

Earl, P. E. (1984) *The Corporate Imagination: How Big Companies Make Mistakes*, Brighton, Wheatsheaf.

Earl, P. E. (1990) 'Economics and psychology: a survey', *Economic Journal*, 100, 718–55.

Egan, D. E. and Schwartz, B. J. (1979) 'Chunking in recall of symbolic diagrams', *Memory and Cognition*, 7, 149–58.

Egelhoff, W. G. (1988) 'Strategy and structure in multinational corporations: a revision of the Stopford and Wells model', *Strategic Management Journal*, 9, 1–14.

Eggertsson, T. (1990) *Economic Behavior and Institutions*, Cambridge, Cambridge University Press.

Ferguson, P. R., Ferguson, G. J., and Rothschild, R. (1993) *Business Economics*, London, Macmillan.

Fligstein, N. (1990) *The Transformation of Corporate Control*, Cambridge, Mass., Harvard University Press.

Flood, R. L. (1987) 'Complexity: a definition by way of a conceptual framework', *Systems Research*, 4, 177–85.

Fourie, F. C. v. N. (1993) 'In the beginning there were markets', in C. Pitelis (ed.) (1993), pp. 41–65.

Freeman, C. (1994) 'The economics of technical change', *Cambridge Journal of Economics*, 18, 463–514.

Freeman, C. (1995) 'The "national system of innovation" in historical perspective', *Cambridge Journal of Economics*, 19, 5–24.

Freeman, J. and Barley, S. R. (1990) 'The strategic analysis of inter-organizational relations in biotechnology', in R. Loveridge and M. Pitt (eds.) (1990) *The Strategic Management of Technological Innovation*, New York, Wiley, pp. 127–56.

Friedman, M. (1953) 'The methodology of positive economics', in M. Friedman, *Essays in Positive Economics*, Chicago, Chicago University Press, 3–43.

Fukuyama, F. (1995) *Trust: the Social Virtues and the Creation of Prosperity*, London, Hamish Hamilton.

Galbraith, C. S. and Kay, N. M. (1986) 'Towards a theory of multinational enterprise', *Journal of Economic Behavior and Organization*, 7, 3–19.

Galbraith, J. K. (1952) *American Capitalism: the Concept of Countervailing Power*, Boston, Houghton Mifflin.

Galbraith, J. K. (1967) *The New Industrial State*, Boston, Houghton Mifflin.

Gomes-Casseres, B. (1988) 'Joint venture cycles: the evolution of ownership strategies of U.S. MNEs, 1945–75', in F. J. Contractor and P. Lorange (1988*b*), pp. 112–28.

Gomes-Casseres, B. (1994) 'Group versus group: how alliance networks compete', *Harvard Business Review*, 72 (4), pp. 62–74.

Goreski, P. K. (1974) 'The measurement of enterprise diversification', *Review of Economics and Statistics*, 56, 399–401.

Gort, M. (1962) *Diversification and Integration in American Industry*, Princeton, Princeton University Press.

Gould, S. J. (1977) *Ever Since Darwin: Reflections in Natural History*, New York, London.

Gould, S. J. (1980) *The Panda's Thumb: More Reflections in Natural History*, New York, Norton.

Gould, S. J. (1989) *Wonderful Life: the Burgess Shale and the Nature of History*, New York: Norton.

Gould, S. J. (1993) *Eight Little Piggies: Reflections in Natural History*, New York, Norton.

Grabher, G. (1993*a*) 'The weakness of strong ties: the lock-in of regional development in the Ruhr area', in G. Grabher (ed.) (1993*b*), pp. 256–7.

Grabher, G. (ed.) (1993*b*) *The Embedded Firm: On the Socioeconomics of Industrial Networks*, London, Routledge.

Granovetter, M. S. (1973) 'The strength of weak ties', *American Journal Of Sociology*, 78, 1360–80.

Grossman, S. J. and Hart, O. D. (1980) 'Takeover bids, the free-rider problem and the theory of the corporation', *Bell Journal of Economics*, 11, 42–64.

Grossman, S. J. and Hart, O. (1986) 'The costs and benefits of ownership: a theory of vertical and lateral integration', *Journal of Political Economy*, 94, 691–719.

Group of Thirty (1984) *Foreign Direct Investment 1973–1987*, NY, Group of Thirty.

Habib, M. M. and Victor, B. (1991) 'Strategy, structure, and performance of U.S. manufacturing and service MNCs: a comparative analysis', *Strategic Management Journal*, 12, 589–606.

Hagedoorn, J. (1993*a*) 'Strategic technology alliances and modes of cooperation in high-technology industries', in G. Grabher (ed.) (1993*b*) pp. 116–37.

Hagedoorn J. (1993*b*) 'Understanding the rationale of strategic technology partnering: interorganizational modes of cooperation and sectoral differences', *Strategic Management Journal*, 14, 371–85.

Hagedoorn, J. (1995) 'A note on international market leaders and networks of strategic technology partnering', *Strategic Management Journal*, 16, 241–50.

Hagedoorn J. and Schakenraad, J. (1990) 'Inter-firm partnerships and co-operative strategies in core technologies', in C. Freeman and L. Soete (eds.) (1990) *New Explorations in the Economics of Technical Change*, London, Pinter, pp. 4–37.

Hagedoorn J. and Schakenraad J. (1991) *The Role of Interfirm Cooperation Agreements in the Globalisation of Economy and Technology*, Brussels, Commission of the European Communities.

Hakansson, H. and Johanson, J. (1988) 'Formal and informal cooperation strategies in international industrial networks', in F. J. Contractor and P. Lorange (1988*b*), pp. 369–79.

Hannan M. T. and Freeman, J. (1977) 'The population ecology of organisations', *American Journal of Sociology*, 82, 929–64.

Hannan M. T. and Freeman, J. (1989) *Organisational Ecology*, Cambridge Mass., Harvard University Press.

Hanson, N. R. (1961) *Patterns of Discovery*, London, Cambridge University Press.

Harrigan, K. R. (1987) 'Joint ventures: a mechanism for creating strategic change', in A. Pettigrew (ed.) (1987), pp. 195–230.

Harrigan, K. R. (1988*a*) *Strategies for Joint Ventures*, Lexington, D. C. Heath.

Harrigan, K. R. (1988*b*) 'Strategic alliances and partner asymmetries', in F. J. Contractor and P. Lorange (1988*b*), pp. 205–26.

Hart, O. (1988) 'Incomplete contracts and the theory of the firm', *Journal of Law, Economics and Organization*, 4, 119–39.

Hart, O. (1995) *Firms, Contracts, and Financial Structure*, Oxford, Oxford University Press.

Hart, O. and Holmstrom, B. (1987) 'The theory of contracts', in T. Bewley (ed.), *Advances in Economic Theory; Fifth World Congress*, Cambridge, Cambridge University Press.

Hay, D. A. and Morris, D. J. (1991) *Industrial Economics and Organization: Theory and Evidence*, 2nd edn. Oxford, Oxford University Press.

Hennart, J.-F. (1982) *A Theory of Multinational Enterprise*, Ann Arbor, University of Michigan Press.

Hennart, J.-F. (1988*a*) 'A transactions cost theory of equity joint ventures', *Strategic Management Journal*, 9, 361–74.

Hennart, J.-F. (1988*b*) 'Upstream vertical integration in the aluminium and tin industries: a comparative study of the choice between market and intrafirm coordination', *Journal of Economic Behavior and Organization*, 9, 281–99.

Hennart, J.-F. (1991) 'The transaction cost theory of the multinational enterprise', in C. N. Pitelis and R. Sugden (eds.), pp. 81–116.

Hergert, M. and Morris, D. (1988) 'Trends in international collaborative agreements', in F. J. Contractor and P. Lorange (1988*b*), pp. 99–109.

Hirtle, S. C. and Jonides, J. (1985) 'Evidence of hierarchies in cognitive maps', *Memory and Cognition*, 13, 208–17.

Hodgson, G. M. (1988) *Economics and Institutions: A Manifesto for a Modern Institutional Economics*, Cambridge, Polity Press.

Hodgson, G. M. (1993*a*) *Economics and Evolution: Bringing Life Back into Economics*, Cambridge, Polity Press.

Hodgson, G. M. (1993*b*) 'Transaction costs and the evolution of the firm', in C. Pitelis (ed.) (1993), pp. 77–100.

Hodgson, G. M., Samuels, W. J., and Tool, M. R. (eds.) (1994) *The Elgar Companion to Institutional and Evolutionary Economics, L–Z*, Aldershot, Elgar.

Hofstadter, D. R. (1980) *Godel, Escher, Bach: An Eternal Golden Braid*, New York, Vintage.

Holmstrom, B. and Milgrom, P. (1994) 'The firm as an incentive system', *American Economic Review*, 84, 972–91.

Holmstrom, B. R. and Tirole, J. (1989) 'The theory of the firm', in R. Schmalensee and R. D. Willig (eds.) *Handbook of Industrial Organization*, vol. 1, Amsterdam, North Holland, 61–133.

Hoskisson, R. E., Hitt, M. A., Johnson, R. A., and Moesel, D. S. (1991) 'Construct validity of objective (SIC-based) categorical measures of diversification strategy'. Paper presented at the National Academy of Management meetings, Miami, Florida.

Hoskisson, R. E. and Johnson, R. A. (1992) 'Corporate restructuring and strategic change: the effect on diversification strategy and R&D intensity', *Strategic Management Journal*. 13, 625–34.

Ibarra, H. (1992) 'Structural alignments, individual strategies, and managerial action: elements toward a network theory of getting things done', in N. Nohria and R. Eccles (eds.) (1992), pp. 165–88.

Ijiri, Y. and Simon, H. A. (1964) 'Business firm growth and size', *American Economic Review*, 54, 77–89.

Ijiri, Y. and Simon, H. A. (1967) 'A model of business firm growth', *Econometrica*, 35, 348–55.

Jacobs, L. (1939) *The Rise of the American Film Industry: a Critical History*, New York, Harcourt and Brace.

Jaques, E. (1990) 'In praise of hierarchy', *Harvard Business Review*, Jan–Feb, pp. 127–33.

Jarillo, J. C. (1988) 'On strategic networks', *Strategic Management Journal*, 9, 31–41.

Jensen, M. and Meckling, W. (1986) 'Theory of the firm: managerial behavior, agency costs and ownership structure', in L. Putterman (ed.) *The Economic Nature of the Firm: a Reader*, Cambridge, Cambridge University Press, pp. 209–29.

John, G. and Weitz, B. A. (1988) 'Forward integration into distribution: an empirical test of transaction cost analysis', *Journal of Law, Economics and Organization*, 4, 337–55.

Johnson, G. and Scholes, K. (1993) *Exploring Corporate Strategy*, 3rd edn. Hemel Hempstead, Prentice Hall.

Joskow, P. L. (1985) 'Vertical integration and long-term contracts: the case of coal-burning electric generating plants', *Journal of Law, Economics and Organization*, 1, 33–80.

Joskow, P. L. (1987) 'Contract duration and relationship-specific investments: empirical evidence from the coal markets', *American Economic Review*, 77, 168–85.

Joskow, P. L. (1988) 'Asset specificity and the structure of vertical relationships: empirical evidence', *Journal of Law, Economics, and Organization*, 4, 95–118.

Jovanovic, B. (1993) 'The diversification of production', *Brookings Papers on Economic Activity: Microeconomics (1)*, 197–247.

Kaldor, N. (1934) 'The equilibrium of the firm', *Economic Journal*, 44, 60–76.

Kamien, M. and Schwartz, N. L. (1982) *Market Structure and Innovation*, Cambridge, Cambridge University Press.

Kay, J. (1993) *Foundations of Corporate Success*, Oxford, Oxford University Press.

Kay, J. and Silberston, A. (1995) 'Corporate governance', *National Institute Economic Review*, no. 153, 84–97.

Kay, N. M. (1979) *The Innovating Firm: a Behavioural Theory of Corporate R&D*, London, Macmillan; New York, St. Martins Press.

—— (1982) *The Evolving Firm: Strategy and Structure in Industrial Organisation*, London, Macmillan.

—— (1983) 'Multinational enterprise: a review article', *Scottish Journal of Political Economy*, 30, 394–12.

—— (1984) *The Emergent Firm: Knowledge, Ignorance and Surprise in Economic Organisation*, London, Macmillan.

—— (1991) 'Multinational enterprise as strategic choice: some transaction cost perspectives', in C. N. Pitelis and R. Sugden (eds.) (1991) pp. 137–54.

—— (1992*a*) 'Markets, false hierarchies, and the evolution of the modern corporation', *Journal of Economic Behavior and Organization*, 17, 315–33.

—— (1992*b*) 'Collaborative strategies of firms: theory and evidence', in A. Del Monte (ed.) *Recent Developments in the Theory of Industrial Organisation*, London, Macmillan, pp. 201–31.

—— (1993) 'Markets, false hierarchies and the role of asset specificity', in C. Pitelis (ed.) (1993), pp. 242–61.

—— (1995*a*) 'Alchian and "the Alchian thesis" ', *Journal of Economic Methodology*, 2, 281–6.

—— (1995*b*) 'Harmony, mood and turbulence in corporate evolution', *Competition and Change*, 1, 1–27.

—— (forthcoming) 'The economics of trust', *International Journal of the Economics of Business*.

—— Robe, J.-P., and Zagnoli, P. (1987) 'An approach to the analysis of joint ventures', Florence, European University Institute.

Killing, J. P. (1983) *Strategies for Joint Venture Success*, London, Croom Helm.

Kindleberger, C. P. (1969) *American Business Abroad*, New Haven, Yale University Press.

Klein, B. (1980) 'Transaction cost determinants of "unfair" contractual arrangements', *American Economic Review, Papers and Proceedings*, 70, 356–62.

Klein, B., Crawford, R., and Alchian, A. A. (1978) 'Vertical integration, appropriable rents, and the competitive contracting process', *Journal of Law and Economics*, 21, 297–326.

Knickerbocker, F. T. (1973) *Oligopolistic Reaction and the Multinational Enterprise*, Boston, Harvard University Press.

Koffka, K. A. (1935) *Principles of Gestalt Psychology*, New York, Harcourt Brace.

Kogut, B. (1988) 'A study of the life cycle of joint ventures', in F. J. Contractor and P. Lorange (1988*b*), pp. 169–85.

Kogut, B., Shan, W., and Walker, G. (1992) 'The make-or-cooperate decision in the context of an industry network', in N. Nohria and R. Eccles (eds.) (1992), pp. 348–65.

Kogut, B., Shan, W., and Walker, G. (1993) 'Knowledge in the network and the network as knowledge', in G. Grabher (ed.) (1993*b*), pp. 68–94.

Kramer, N. J. T. A. and Smit, J. de (1977) *Systems Thinking: Concepts and Notions*, Leiden, Martinus Nijhoff.

Kreps, D. M. (1990) *Game Theory and Economic Modelling*, Oxford, Oxford University Press.

Langlois, R. N. (ed.) (1986*a*) *Economics as a Process: Essays in the New Institutional Economics*, Cambridge, Cambridge University Press.

Langlois, R. N. (1986*b*) 'The new institutional economics: an introductory essay', in R. N. Langlois (ed.) (1986*a*) pp. 1–25.

Langlois, R. N. (1986*c*) 'Rationality, institutions and explanation', in R. Langlois (ed.) (1986*a*) pp. 225–55.

Langlois, R. N. and Robertson, P. L. (1995) *Firms, Markets and Economic Change*, London, Routledge.

Latsis, S. J. (1972) 'Situational determinism in economics', *British Journal for the Philosophy of Science*, 23, 207–45.

Lawrence, P. R. and Lorsch, J. W. (1967) *Organization and Environment: Managing Differentiation and Integration*, Boston, Harvard Business School.

Lazarson, M. (1993) 'Factory or putting out? Knitting networks in Modena', in G. Grabher (ed.) (1993*b*), pp. 203–26.

Lecraw, D. J. (1983) 'Performance of transnational corporations in less developed countries', *Journal of International Business Studies*, 14, 15–33.

Levi-Strauss, C. (1963) *Structural Anthropology*, London, Penguin.

Lewis, J. D. (1990) *Partnerships for Profit: Structuring and Managing Strategic Alliances*, New York, Free Press.

Lewis, R. and Pendrill, D. (1994) *Advanced Financial Accounting*, 4th edn. London, Pitman.

Lichtenberg, F. R. (1992) 'Industrial de-diversification and its consequences for productivity', *Journal of Economic Behavior and Organization*, 18, 427–38.

Lippman, S. A. and Rumelt, R. P. (1982) 'Uncertain imitability: an analysis of interfirm differences in efficiency under competition', *Bell Journal of Economics*, 13, 418–38.

Loasby, B. J. (1967) 'Long-range formal planning in perspective', *Journal of Management Studies*, 4, 300–8.

Loasby, B. J. (1976) *Choice, Complexity and Ignorance*, Cambridge, Cambridge University Press.

Lorange, P. and Roos, J. (1993) *Strategic Alliances: Formation, Implementation and Evolution*, Cambridge, Mass., Blackwell.

Machlup, F. (1967) 'Theories of the firm: marginalist, behavioural, managerial', *American Economic Review*, 57, 1–33.

Madhok, A. (1995) 'Revisiting multinational firms' tolerance for joint ventures: a trust based approach', *Journal of International Business Studies*, 26, 117–37.

Mahoney, J. T. and Pandian, J. R. (1992) 'The resource-based view within the conversation of strategic management', *Strategic Management Journal*, 13, 363–80.

Malerba, F. and Orsenigo, L. (1993) 'Technological regimes and firm behavior', *Industrial and Corporate Change*, 2, 45–71.

Malerba, F. and Orsenigo, L. (1995) 'Schumpeterian patterns of innovation', *Cambridge Journal of Economics*, 19, 47–65.

Mansfield, E., Romeo, A., and Wagner, S. (1979) 'Foreign trade and U.S. research and development', *Review of Economics and Statistics*, 61, 49–57.

Mansfield, E., Schwartz M., and Wagner, S. (1981) 'Imitation costs and patents: an empirical study', *Economic Journal*, 91, 907–18.

March, J. G. and Olsen, J. P. (1976*a*) 'Attention and the ambiguity of self-interest', in J. G. March and J. P. Olsen (1976*b*) pp. 38–53.

March, J. G. and Olsen, J. P. (1976*b*) *Ambiguity and Choice in Organizations*, Bergen, Universitsforlaget.

March, J. G. and Simon, H. A. (1958) *Organizations*, N.Y., Wiley.

Markides, C. (1993) Corporate refocusing, *Business Strategy Review* 4, 1–15.

Marks, L. E. and Miller, G. A. (1964) 'The role of semantic and syntactic constraints on the memorization of English sentences', *Journal of Verbal Learning and Verbal Behavior*, 3, 1–5.

Marris, R. (1964) *The Economic Theory of Managerial Capitalism*, London, Macmillan.

Marx, K. (1976) *Capital: a Critique of Political Economy*, vol. 1, London, Penguin.

Masten, S. E. (1984) 'The organization of production: evidence from the aerospace industry', *Journal of Law and Economics*, 27, 403–18.

Masten, S. E., Meehan, J. W. Jr., and Snyder, E. A. (1991) 'The costs of organization', *Journal of Law, Economics and Organization*, 7, 1–25.

Matlin, M. E. (1994) *Cognition*, 3rd edn. Fort Worth, Harcourt Brace.

Measday, W. S. (1982) 'The petroleum industry', in W. Adams (ed.) *The Structure of American Industry*, New York, Macmillan, pp. 36–72.

Melin, L. (1992) 'Internationalization as a strategy process', *Strategic Management Journal*, 13, 99–118.

Metcalfe, J. S. (1995) 'Technology systems and technology policy in an evolutionary framework', *Cambridge Journal of Economics*, 19, 25–46.

Milgrom, P. and Roberts, P. (1992) *Economics, Organization and Management*, New Jersey, Prentice-Hall.

Miller, A. and Dess, G. M. (1996) *Strategic Management*, International/second edition, New York, McGraw-Hill.

Miller, G. A. (1956) 'The magical number seven, plus or minus two: some limits on our capacity for processing information', *Psychological Review*, 63, pp. 81–97.

Mintzberg, H. (1979) *The Structuring of Organizations: a Synthesis of the Research*, Englewood Cliffs, Prentice-Hall.

Mintzberg, H. (1991) 'Five P's for strategy', in H. Mintzberg and J. B. Quinn (eds) (1991*a*).

Mintzberg, H. and Quinn, J. B. (eds.) (1991*a*) *The Strategy Process: Concepts, Contexts, Cases*, 2nd edn. New Jersey, Prentice-Hall.

Mintzberg, H. and Quinn J. B. (1991*b*) 'The Hewlett Packard company', in H. Mintzberg and J. B. Quinn (eds.) (1991*a*) pp. 457–80.

Mirabelle, L. (ed.) (1990) *International Directory of Company Histories*, vol. 2, Chicago. St. James Press.

Moar, I. and Bower, G. H. (1983) 'Inconsistency in spatial knowledge', *Memory and Cognition*, 11, 107–13.

Monteverde, K. and Teece, D. (1982) 'Supplier switching cost and vertical integration in the automobile industry', *Bell Journal of Economics*, 13, 206–13.

Montgomery, C. A. (1994) 'Corporate diversification', *Journal of Economic Perspectives*, 8, 163–78.

Montgomery, C. A. and Thomas, A. R. (1988) 'Divestment: motives and gains', *Strategic Management Journal*, 9, 93–7.

Mowery, D. C. (1983) 'The relationship between intrafirm and contractual forms of industrial research in American manufacturing, 1900–1940', *Explorations in Economic History*, 20, 351–74.

Mueller, D. C. (1969) 'A theory of conglomerate mergers', *Quarterly Journal of Economics*, 83, 643–59.

Mytelka, L. (1991) 'Crisis, technological change and the strategic alliance', in L. Mytelka (ed.) *Strategic Partnerships: States, Firms and International Competition*, London, Pinter.

Navin, T. R. (1970) 'The 500 largest American industrials in 1917', *Business History Review*, 44, 360–86.

Navon, D. (1977) 'Forest before trees: the precedence of global features in visual perception', *Cognitive Psychology*, 9, 353–83.

Navon, D. (1981) 'Do attention and decision follow perception? Comment on Miller', *Journal of Experimental Psychology: Human Perception and Performance*, 7, 1175–82.

Nelson, R. R. (1959) 'The simple economics of basic scientific research', *Journal of Political Economy*, 67, 297–306.

Nelson, R. R. (1991) 'Why do firms differ and how does it matter?' *Strategic Management Journal*, 12, 61–74.

Nelson, R. R. (1995) 'Recent evolutionary theorizing about economic change', *Journal of Economic Literature*, 33, 48–90.

Nelson, R. R. and Winter, S. G. (1982) *An Evolutionary Theory of Economic Change*, Cambridge, Mass., Harvard University Press.

Nerlove, M. and Arrow, K. J. (1962) 'Optimal advertising policy under dynamic conditions', *Economica*, 29, 129–42.

Nickell, S. J. (1995) *The Performance of Companies: the Relationship between the External Environment, Management Strategies and Corporate Performance*, Oxford, Blackwell.

Nohria, N. (1992) 'Information and search in the creation of new business ventures: the case of the 128 Venture Group', in N. Nohria and R. Eccles (eds.) (1992) pp. 240–61.

Nohria, N. and Eccles, R. (eds.) (1992) *Networks and Organizations*, Boston, Mass., Harvard University Press.

North, D. (1990) *Institutions, Institutional Change and Economic Performance*, Cambridge, Cambridge University Press.

Nystrom, P. C. and Starbuck, W. (eds.) (1981) *Handbook of Organisational Design*, New York, Oxford University Press.

Ollinger, M. (1994) 'The limits to growth of the multidivisional firm: a case study of the U.S. oil industry from 1930–90', *Strategic Management Journal*, 15, 503–20.

Patel, P. (1995) 'Localised production of technology for global markets', *Cambridge Journal of Economics*, 19, 141–53.

Pavitt, K. (1984) 'Sectoral patterns of technical change; towards a taxonomy and a theory', *Research Policy*, 13, 343–73.

Pavitt, K. (1987) 'Commentary on chapter 3', in A. Pettigrew (ed.) (1987) pp. 123–7.

Pavitt, K. (1992) 'Some foundations for a theory of the large innovating firm', in G. Dosi, R. Gianetti, and P. A. Toninelli (eds.) (1992) pp. 212–28.

Pavitt, K., Robson, M., and Townsend, J. (1989) 'Technological accumulation, diversification and organisation in UK companies, 1945–83', *Management Science*, 35, pp. 81–99.

Pearce, R. D. (1993) *The Growth and Evolution of Multinational Enterprise: Patterns of Geographical and Industrial Diversification*, Aldershot, Edward Elgar.

Penrose, E. T. (1959) *The Theory of the Growth of the Firm*, Oxford, Blackwell.

Perrow, C. (1992) 'Small firm networks', in N. Nohria and R. Eccles (eds.) (1992), pp. 445–70.

Peteraf, M. A. (1993) 'The cornerstones of competitive advantage: a resource-based view', *Strategic Management Journal*, 14, 179–91.

Pettigrew, A. (ed.) (1987) *The Management of Strategic Change*, Oxford, Blackwell.

Pettigrew, A. and Whipp, R. (1991) *Managing Change for Competitive Success*, Oxford, Blackwell.

Pfeffer, J. and Salancik, G. R. (1978) *The External Control of Organizations: a Resource Dependence Perspective*, New York, Harper and Row.

Piore, M. J. and Sabel, C. F. (1984) *The Second Industrial Divide: Possibilities for Prosperity*, New York, Basic Books.

Pisano, G. P. (1990) 'The R&D boundaries of the firm; an empirical analysis', *Administrative Science Quarterly*, 35, 153–76.

Pitelis, C. N. (ed.) (1993), *Transaction Costs, Markets and Hierarchies*, Oxford, Blackwell.

Pitelis, C. N. and Sugden, R. (eds.) (1991) *The Nature of the Transnational Firm*, London, Routledge.

Polanyi, M. (1958) *Personal Knowledge*, Chicago, University of Chicago Press.

Polanyi, M. (1967) *The Tacit Dimension*, London, Routledge and Kegan Paul.

Porter, M. (1980) *Competitive Strategy: Techniques for Analyzing Industries and Competitors*, New York, Free Press.

Porter, M. (1985) *Competitive Advantage: Creating and Sustaining Superior Performance*, New York, Free Press.

Porter, M. (1987) 'From competitive advantage to competitive strategy', *Harvard Business Review*, May/June, 43–59.

Porter, M. (1990) *The Competitive Advantage of Nations*, London, Macmillan.

Porter, M. (1991) 'Towards a dynamic theory of strategy', *Strategic Management Journal*, 12, 95–117.

Porter, M. and Fuller, M. B. (1986) 'Coalitions and global strategy', in M. Porter (ed.) *Competition in Global Industries*, Boston, Harvard Business School, pp. 315–43.

Posner, R. A. (1993) 'The new institutional economics meets law and economics', *Journal of Institutional and Theoretical Economics*, 149, 73–87.

Postrel, S. (1991) 'Burning your britches behind you; can policy scholars bank on game theory?' *Strategic Management Journal*, 12, 153–5.

Powell, W. W. and Brantley, P. (1992) 'Competitive cooperation in biotechnology: learning through networks?' in N. Nohria and R. Eccles (eds.) (1992) pp. 366–94.

Prahalad, C. K. and Bettis, R. A. (1986) 'The dominant logic: a new linkage between diversity and performance', *Strategic Management Journal*, 7, 485–501.

Prahalad, C. K. and Hamel, G. (1990) 'The core competence of the corporation', *Harvard Business Review*, May–June, pp. 79–91.

Putterman, L. (1986) 'The economic nature of the firm: overview', in L. Putterman (ed.) *The Economic Nature of the Firm: a Reader*, Cambridge University Press, Cambridge, pp. 1–29.

Ramanujam, V. and Varadarajan, P. (1989) 'Research on corporate diversification: a synthesis', *Strategic Management Journal*, 10, 523–51.

Rasmussen, E. (1989) *Games and Information: an Introduction to Game Theory*, London, Blackwell.

Reed, R. (1991) 'Bimodality in diversification: an efficiency and effectiveness rationale', *Managerial and Decision Economics*, 12, 57–66.

Reed, R. and Sharp, J. A. (1987) 'Confirmation of the specialization ratio', *Applied Economics*, 19, 393–405.

Richardson, G. B. (1972) 'The organisation of industry', *Economic Journal*, 82, 833–96.

Ring, P. S. and Van de Ven, A. H. (1992) 'Structuring cooperative relationships between organizations', *Strategic Management Journal*, 13, 483–98.

Riordan, M. H. and Williamson, O. E. (1985) 'Asset specificity and economic organization', *International Journal of Industrial Organization*, 3, 365–78.

Robertson, D. H. (1930) *Control of Industry*, London, Nisbet.

Robertson, L. C. and Lamb, M. R. (1991) 'Neuropsychological contributions to theories of part/whole organization', *Cognitive Psychology*, 23, 299–330.

Robinson, J. (1933) *The Economics of Imperfect Competition*, London, Macmillan.

Rowlinson, M. (1995) 'Strategy, structure and culture: Cadbury, divisionalization and merger in the 1960s', *Journal of Management Studies*, 32, 121–40.

Rugman, A. M. (1981) *Inside the Multinationals: the Economics of Internal Markets*, London, Croom Helm.

Rumelt, R. P. (1986) *Strategy, Structure and Economic Performance*, 2nd edn. Boston, Harvard Business School.

Rumelt, R. P. (1990) 'Discussion comments at conference', *Fundamental Issues in Strategy: A Research Agenda for the 1990's*, Napa.

Rutherford, M. (1994) *Institutions in Economics: the Old and the New Institutionalism*, Cambridge, Cambridge University Press.

Samuels, W. J. (1995) 'The present state of institutional economics', *Cambridge Journal of Economics*, 19, 569–90.

Samuelson, P. A. (1976) *Economics*, 10th edn. Tokyo, McGraw-Hill Kogakusha.

Samuelson, P. A. and Nordhaus, W. D. (1985) *Economics*, 12th edn. New York, McGraw-Hill.

Scherer, F. M. (1992) *International High Technology Competition*, Cambridge, Harvard University Press.

Scherer, F. M. and Ross, D. (1990) *Industrial Market Structure and Economic Performance*, 3rd edn. Boston, Houghton Mifflin.

Schiano, D. J. and Tversky, B. (1992) 'Structure and strategy in encoding simplified graphs', *Memory and Cognition*, 20, 12–20.

Schumpeter, J. A. (1942) *Capitalism, Socialism and Democracy*, New York, Harper and Row.

Schumpeter, J. A. (1954) *Capitalism, Socialism and Democracy*, 4th edn. London, Unwin.

Shelanski, H. A. and Klein, P. G. (1995) 'Empirical research in transaction cost economics: a review and assessment', *Journal of Law, Economics and Organization*, 11, 335–61.

Simon, H. A. (1955) 'A behavioral model of rational choice', *Quarterly Journal of Economics*, 69, 99–118.

Simon, H. A. (1957) *Models of Man*, New York, Wiley.

Simon, H. A. (1981) *The Sciences of the Artificial*, 2nd edn. Cambridge, MIT Press.

Simon, H. A. and Bonini, C. P. (1958) 'The size distribution of business firms', *American Economic Review*, 48, 607–17.

Simon, J. L., Mokhtari, M., and Simon, D. H. (1996) 'Are mergers beneficial or detrimental? Evidence from advertising agencies', *International Journal of the Economics of Business*, 3, 69–82.

Skinner, B. F. (1969) *Contingencies of Reinforcement*, N.Y., Appleton-Century-Crofts.

Smith, A. (1976) *An Inquiry into the Nature and Causes of the Wealth of Nations* (2 vols; originally published 1776) ed. R. H. Campbell and A. S. Skinner, London, Methuen.

Sraffa, P. (1926) 'The laws of returns under competitive conditions', *Economic Journal*, 36, 535–50.

Steer, P. and Cable, J. (1978) 'Internal organisation and profit; an empirical analysis of large UK companies', *Journal of Industrial Economics*, 27, 13–30.

Stevens, A. and Coupe, P. (1978) 'Distortions in judged spatial relations', *Cognitive Psychology*, 10, 422–37.

Stiglitz, J. E. (1985) 'Credit markets and the control of capital', *Journal of Money, Credit and Banking*, 17, 133–52.

Stopford, J. M. and Wells, L. T. Jr. (1972) *Managing the Multinational Enterprise*, New York, Basic Books.

Stuckey, J. (1983) *Vertical Integration and Joint Ventures in the Aluminium Industry*, Cambridge, Mass., Harvard University Press.

Teece, D. J. (1980) 'Economies of scope and the scope of the enterprise', *Journal of Economic Behavior and Organization*, 1, 223–47.

Teece, D. J. (1982) 'Towards an economic theory of the multiproduct firm', *Journal of Economic Behavior and Organization*, 3, 39–63.

Teece, D. J. (1986a), 'Profiting from technological innovation', *Research Policy*, 15, 286–305.

—— (1986b) 'Transaction cost economics and the multinational enterprise: an assessment', *Journal of Economic Behavior and Organization*, 7, 21–45.

—— (1987a) 'Profiting from technological innovation: implications for integration, collaboration, licensing, and public policy', in D. J. Teece (ed.) (1987b), 185–219.

—— (ed.) (1987b) *The Competitive Challenge: Strategies for Industrial Innovation and Renewal*, New York, Harper and Row.

Thompson, G., Frances, F., Levacic, R., and Mitchell, J. (eds.) (1991) *Markets, Hierarchies and Networks*, London, Sage.

Thompson, J. D. (1967) *Organizations in Action*, New York, McGraw-Hill.

Thompson, R. S. (1981) 'Internal organisation and profit; a note', *Journal of Industrial Economics*, 30, 201–11.

—— (1988) 'Agency costs of internal organisation', in R. S. Thompson and M. Wright (eds.) (1988); pp. 65–85.

—— and Wright M. (eds.) (1988) *Internal Organisation, Efficiency and Profit*, Oxford, Philip Allan.

Tirole, J. (1988) *The Theory of Industrial Organization*, Cambridge, Mass., MIT Press.

Tushman, M. L. and Anderson, P. (1986) 'Technological discontinuities and organizational environments', *Administrative Science Quarterly*, 31, 439–65.

Tversky, B. (1981) 'Distortions in memory for maps', *Cognitive Psychology*, 13, 407–33.

—— and Schiano, D. J. (1989) 'Perceptual and conceptual factors in distortions in memory for graphs and maps', *Journal of Experimental Psychology: General*, 118, 387–98.

Ullman, A. (1994) 'The Swatch', in R. De Wit and R. Meyer (eds.) *Strategy: Process, Content, Context*, Minneapolis/St. Paul, West Publishing, 619–34.

Veblen, T. (1925) *The Theory of the Leisure Class: An Economic Theory of Institutions*, London, Allen and Unwin.

Vernon, R. (1966) 'International investment and international trade in the product cycle', *Quarterly Journal of Economics*, 80, 190–207.

Vining, R. (1949) 'Koopmans on the choice of variables to be studied and of methods of measurement', *Review of Economics and Statistics*, 31, 77–86.

Von Hippel, E. (1987) 'Cooperation between rivals: informal know-how trading', *Research Policy*, 16, 291–302.

—— (1988) *The Sources of Innovation*, Oxford, Oxford University Press.

Walker, G. and Poppo, L. (1991) 'Profit centers, single-source suppliers and transaction costs', *Administrative Science Quarterly*, 36, 66–87.

—— and Weber, D. (1984) 'A transaction cost approach to make-or-buy decisions', *Administrative Science Quarterly*, 29, 373–91.

Watkins, R. E. (1977) 'Transport of crude oil, gas and products by pipeline', in *Our Industry, Petroleum*, London, British Petroleum, 179–96.

Watson, B. F. (1924) *Behaviorism*, Chicago, University of Chicago Press.

Williams, J. R., Paez, B. L., and Sanders, L. (1988) 'Conglomerates revisited', *Strategic Management Journal*, 9, 403–14.

Williamson, J. (1966) 'Profit, growth and sales maximisation', *Economica*, 33, 1–16.

Williamson, O. E. (1964) *The Economics of Discretionary Behavior: Managerial Objectives in a Theory of the Firm*, New Jersey, Prentice-Hall.

—— (1967) 'Hierarchical control and optimum firm size', *Journal of Political Economy*, 75, 123–38.

—— (1975) *Markets and Hierarchies: Analysis and Antitrust Implications*, New York, Free Press.

—— (1985) *The Economic Institutions of Capitalism: Firms, Markets, Relational Contracting*, New York, Free Press.

—— (1986) *Economic Organization: Firms, Markets and Policy Control*, Brighton, Harvester Wheatsheaf.

—— (1990) 'A comparison of alternative approaches to economic organization', *Journal of Institutional and Theoretical Economics*, 146, 61–71.

—— (1993*a*) 'The evolving science of organization', *Journal of Institutional and Theoretical Economics*, 149, 36–63.

—— (1993*b*) 'Transaction cost economics meets Posnerian law and economics', *Journal of Institutional and Theoretical Economics*, 149, 99–118.

Winter, S. G. (1982) 'An essay on the theory of production', in S. H. Hymans (ed.) *Economics and the World Around It*, Ann Arbor, University of Michigan Press, pp. 55–91.

—— (1987) 'Knowledge and competence as strategic assets', in D. J. Teece (ed.) (1987) pp. 159–84.

—— (1988) 'On Coase, competence and the corporation', *Journal of Law, Economics, and Organization*, 4, 163–80.

Wright, M., Chiplin, B., and Thompson, S. (1993) 'The market for corporate control', in M. Bishop and J. Kay (eds.) *European Mergers and Merger Policy*, Oxford, Oxford University Press.

Wrigley, L. (1970) 'Divisional autonomy and diversification', Boston, Harvard Business School, unpublished doctoral dissertation.

You, J.-I. (1995) 'Small firms in economic theory', *Cambridge Journal of Economics*, 19, 441–62.

Young, S., Hamill, J., Wheeler, C., and Davies, J. R. (1989) *International Market Entry and Development*, Hemel Hempstead, Harvester Wheatsheaf.

Zaheer, A. and Venkatraman, N. (1995) 'Relational governance as an interorganizational strategy: an empirical test of the role of trust in economic exchange', *Strategic Management Journal*, 16, 373–92.

INDEX OF NAMES

Index compiled by Frank Pert

SUBJECT INDEX

Index compiled by Frank Pert